The Unconquerable World

The
Unconquerable
WORLD

POWER, NONVIOLENCE, AND
THE WILL OF THE PEOPLE

JONATHAN SCHELL

METROPOLITAN BOOKS
Henry Holt and Company | New York

Metropolitan Books
Henry Holt and Company, LLC
Publishers since 1866
115 West 18th Street
New York, New York 10011

Metropolitan Books™ is a registered
trademark of Henry Holt and Company, LLC.

Library of Congress Cataloging-in-Publication Data

Schell, Jonathan, 1943–
    The unconquerable world : power, nonviolence, and the will of the people /
Jonathan Schell.—1st ed.
        p.   cm.
    Includes bibliographical references and index.
    ISBN 0-8050-4456-6
    1. Nonviolence.   2. War.   3. Social change.   I. Title.
HM1281 .S34 2003
303.6'1—dc21   2002191235

First Edition 2003

Designed by Kelly S. Too

Printed in the United States of America

1   3   5   7   9   10   8   6   4   2

*I dedicate this book
to the memory of my
mother, fighter for peace.*

Liberty, when men act in bodies, is power.

—EDMUND BURKE

Reflections on the Revolution in France

Contents

The Unconquerable World

The Towers and the Wall

"Of Arms, and the man I sing." So wrote Virgil, celebrator of the imperial Rome of his patron Caesar Augustus, in the opening lines of *The Aeneid,* as rendered in the seventeenth century by Dryden and memorized by generations of English schoolboys, who were soon sent out to rule an empire even more far-flung than Rome's. "The man": a patriot, bound to fight, and perhaps to die, for his country and all that it possessed and stood for. "Arms": the means whereby the man could vindicate his honor and defend his country or aggrandize its power and interests. The fighting man took life but also was ready to lay down his own, thereby bowing, in the mayhem of war, to a kind of rudimentary justice. Four centuries before Virgil, the Athenian statesman Pericles, much admired in both imperial Rome and imperial England, eulogized him in his funeral oration for the soldiers of Athens who had died at Marathon. "As for success or failure," Pericles said, "they left that in the doubtful hands of Hope, and when the reality of battle was before their faces, they put their trust in their own selves . . . and, in a small moment of time, the climax of their lives, a culmination of glory, not of fear, would be swept away from us." And so they would be accorded "praises that never grow old, the most splendid of sepulchres—not the sepulchre in which their bodies are laid, but where their glory remains eternal in men's minds, always there on the right occasion to stir others to speech or to action." On these foundations was reared a system—a system, at its best, of standing up for principle with force, right with might; at its worst, of plunder, exploitation, and massacre—that was to last from Pericles' time down to ours.

Yet alongside the martial tradition another, contrary one was born. At almost the very moment that Virgil was writing his lines, Jesus, the New Testament says, was speaking the even better-known words, "Put up thy sword. For they that live by the sword shall die by the sword." Following in the tradition of some of the Old Testament prophets, he sang of the man without arms. The sword in question was no symbolic weapon. It was the disciple Simon Peter's sword, and he had just cut off the ear of one Malchus, a servant of the high priest, who had been in the act of arresting Jesus in Jerusalem. It was in the heat and fury of this bloody altercation, not in the quiet of a philosopher's study, that Jesus gave his advice. And these words, too, took root somehow in people's hearts, and lasted down the centuries.

Since then, the two conflicting traditions—one worldly, sanctioning violence, the other spiritual, forbidding it—have coexisted. Each has seemed to express an ineradicable truth. Each has retained its power to inspire in spite of the other. Neither has been discarded in the name of the other. Western civilization has lived according to the rules laid down by Virgil's patron Augustus but has dated its calendar from the birth of Jesus. On the intellectual plane, many attempts to reconcile the two traditions have been made. The most notable was to declare, with St. Augustine—the great conjoiner of Roman and Christian thought of the early fifth century—that each principle applied to a distinct realm of existence. One was the City of God, a spiritual and personal realm, in which Jesus' law of non-violence and love should be followed, the other the fallen City of Man—the public, political realm, in which Caesar's law of force must, however regrettably, hold sway. Echoes of this distinction also sounded down the centuries: in Catholic just-war theory, in Machiavelli's distinction between what is good for one's soul and what is good for the republic, in Montesquieu's distinction between the virtue of the political man and the virtue of the Christian man. There is even a shadow of it in the modern separation of church and state. Certainly, Jesus' counsel was rejected for political affairs, except among a few people, regarded by almost everyone as dreamers or fools, blind to the iron laws that govern the political world.

And who with the slightest acquaintance with history, whether in the Western world or elsewhere, can deny the primal connection between politics and violence? Indeed, what may be the earliest historical document discovered so far, the so-called Scorpion Tableau, carved in stone some 5,250 years ago in Egypt and unearthed by archaeologists in 1995, seems to depict a scene of victory in battle. It shows a man with an upraised mace standing over a bound captive. The captor, the discoverers of the document believe, is one King Scorpion, the first unifier of ancient Egypt, and the captive is a king he has defeated and is leading to public execution.

Yet history has not left the character of violence unchanged. The bloody record of the twentieth century, which seemed to confirm as never before the strength of the tie between politics and violence, also showed that violence did not stay everlastingly the same. It was capable of fantastic mutation and expansion. If an evil god had turned human society into an infernal laboratory to explore the utmost extremes of violence, short only of human extinction, he could scarcely have improved upon the history of the twentieth century. Totalitarian rule and total war each in its own way carried violence to its limits—reaching what we can call total violence, as distinct from the technically restricted violence of earlier times. Violence was old, but total violence—violence that, as in nuclear conflict, can kill without limit, reaching no decision, no point of return—was new. Rule, when it resorted to total violence, turned out no longer to be rule, for rule is domination over living human beings, and the totalitarian regimes, in their most ferocious epochs, became factories of corpses. And war, when it laid hold of its ever more powerful instruments of destruction, was no longer war but annihilation, and annihilation was as unlike war as it was unlike peace. The means of annihilation paradoxically put their possessors in a predicament that was better described by the precepts of Jesus than by those of Augustus. Through the creation of the nuclear arsenals of the Cold War and their doctrinal accoutrement the strategy of nuclear deterrence, it became literally true that the users of the sword would die by the sword. (Nuclear rivals have been likened to scorpions in a bottle, creating the possibility that history's last document as well as its first will refer to the doings of scorpions.) The increase in available force, rooted in, among other things, fundamental scientific discoveries of the twentieth century, is not a change in attitude or beliefs but an irrevocable change in the world, at least as durable as any state or empire. It has called into question the age-old reliance of politics on violent means. The iron laws of the world have become different laws, and those who wish to live and act in the world as it really is must think and act differently.

The people of the twentieth century were, of course, dismayed by the unprecedented violence visited upon them and tried to find ways to escape it. Twice in the first half of the century the world went to war. Twice in the aftermath the victors attempted to uproot the system of war and replace it with a system of law—with the League of Nations in 1919 and the United Nations in 1945. And twice they failed. In the latter half of the century, a third global struggle was waged—not a hot war this time but the cold one—and on November 9, 1989, the day the Berlin Wall was breached by joyful East Berliners, it ended. In many respects, the opportunity to found an enduring peace appeared more favorable than ever before. No defeated power awaited the hour of vengeance, as defeated Germany had after its humiliation by the onerous terms of the Versailles treaty at the end the First World War. No ideological division threatened to divide the camp of the victors, as the antagonism between Soviet communism and liberal democracy had at the end of the Second World War. This time, however, no great effort was made to secure the peace. The victorious powers turned their minds to economic and other matters. A conviction seemed to settle in that the horrors of the twentieth century had ended of their own accord. Mere opportunity was mistaken for accomplishment, and nothing was done.

It is difficult to assign a cause to neglect, and perhaps it would be a mistake to spend much effort trying. Why, at the beginning of the twentieth century, did Europe blind itself to the approach of the First World War? Why, after that war, did the United States withdraw into isolation, condemning itself to fight again in the Second World War? The insouciance of the 1990s is equally hard to explain. Perhaps the victors of the Cold War wanted a vacation from its chronic apocalyptic anxieties, and so turned their attention to more agreeable matters—above all, to the getting and spending of the era of economic globalization. Perhaps they believed that the welcome reduction of the threat of nuclear war that the end of the Cold War brought had removed all nuclear peril. Or perhaps the United States, where a sort of complacent triumphalism developed, was simply too pleased with the status quo to imagine that it could be upset.

Whatever the reason, the spell was broken, of course, on September 11, 2001. The slumbering dragon of total violence had only twitched its tail; and yet with that one stroke the United States was brutally startled out of its sleep. This crime, in which, out of a clear blue sky one sparkling fall morning, the most imposing buildings in New York and Washington were attacked and struck down, leaving thousands dead, drove home a truth that the world should never have forgotten but did: that in our age of weapons of mass destruction all buildings, all cities, all nations, all people can likewise be reduced to ash in an instant.

And yet the awakening was selective. Even as the underlying dangers of the time were brought to shocking life, the equally remarkable and equally neglected opportunities to create a lasting peace that had appeared with the end of the Cold War were pushed into still deeper obscurity. The United States, facing the threat of further attack from a global, stateless terrorist network, launched its war on terrorism. Then it embarked on a full-scale revolution in its foreign policy that, while taking September 11 as its touchstone, adopted goals and means that extended far beyond the war on terror. The policy's foundation was an assertion of absolute, enduring American military supremacy over all other countries in the world, and its announced methods were the overthrow of governments ("regime change") in preemptive, or preventive attacks. Almost immediately, other nations, as if taking their cue from the United States, also went to war or the brink of war. Palestinians stepped up their campaign of suicide bombings against Israel, and Israel responded with military incursions against the Palestinian Authority in the West Bank and Gaza. Russia intensified its war against "terrorism" in Chechnya. Nuclear-armed India embarked on its confrontation with nuclear-armed Pakistan after the parliament in New Delhi was attacked by terrorists whom India linked to Pakistan, and the danger of nuclear war became a permanent feature of life in South Asia. The optimism and hope of the immediate post–Cold War years gave way to war fever and war. The burning towers of 2001 eclipsed the broken wall of 1989.

What never occurred, as complacency gave way to sudden alarm, was a considered stocktaking of both the perils and the opportunities of the new era. In these pages, I will try to look past history's feints and tricks of timing and, in a view that encompasses both the wall and the towers, pose afresh the issue of war and peace, of annihilation and survival. The terrible violence of the twentieth century, I will argue, holds a lesson for the twenty-first. It is that in a steadily and irreversibly widening sphere, violence, always a mark of human failure and a bringer of sorrow, has now also become dysfunctional as a political instrument. Increasingly, it destroys the ends for which it is employed, killing the user as well as his victim. It has become the path to hell on earth and the end of the earth. This is the lesson of the Somme and Verdun, of Auschwitz and Bergen-Belsen, of Vorkuta and Kolyma; and it is the lesson, beyond a shadow of a doubt, of Hiroshima and Nagasaki.

As the British scholar and political thinker Isaiah Berlin has rightly observed, no revolution in the twentieth century had a formative influence comparable to that of the French revolution on the nineteenth. It was not in fact a revolution but a war—the First World War—that played this decisive role, setting in motion a spiral of violence whose effects are still felt today. The century's first decade, like its last, was a period of economic growth, globalization, spreading liberalism, and peace. At a stroke, the First World War reversed all four tendencies, ushering in an era of depression, contraction of global trade, dictatorship, and war. In August 1914 there were two hundred divisions prepared to go to battle in Europe. When war broke out, "The submerged warrior society . . . sprung armed through the surface of the peaceful landscape," as the historian of war John Keegan has put it. In a sense, that warrior society never returned to its barracks. In defeated Germany and Russia, the suffering, humiliation, and incalculable social disorganization caused by the war created conditions that made possible the rise to power of mass totalitarian parties in the two countries. The seventy-five-year Bolshevik terror—which Solzhenitsyn called the Red Wheel—rolled out of the trenches of the First World War, as did its jagged counterpart the Nazi swastika, and the aggression and antagonism of these regimes led straight to the Second World War. For the next three decades, every effort to restore peace and sanity seemed doomed to failure in advance. In the words of the twentieth-century political thinker

Hannah Arendt, "Nothing which was being done, no matter how stupid, no matter how many people knew and foretold the consequences, could be undone or prevented. Every event had the finality of a last judgment, a judgment that was passed neither by God nor by the devil, but looked rather like the expression of some unredeemably stupid fatality."

As the new century begins, no question is more important than whether the world has now embarked on a similar cycle of violence, condemning the twenty-first century to repeat, or even outdo, the bloodshed of the twentieth. The elements of the danger are obvious. They are not, as before, the massed conventional armies and systematized hatreds of rival great powers. They are the persistence and steady spread of nuclear weapons and other weapons of mass destruction, the unappeased demons of national, ethnic, religious, and class fury, and, I believe, the danger that the world's greatest power, the United States, responding disproportionately and unwisely to these realities, will pursue the Augustan path of force and empire. These elements could, at some unforseeable point of intersection, bring an explosion, some nuclear 1914 or anthrax 1914, that would send history off the rails as irremediably as the guns of August did almost a hundred years ago. The use of just a few dozen of the world's thirty thousand or so nuclear weapons, let us recall, could kill more people in a single unthinkable afternoon than the two world wars put together. These dark prospects require that we step back from the emergencies of the moment and ask whether there is another path to follow.

I contend that, notwithstanding the shock of September 11 and the need to take forceful measures to meet the threat of global terrorism, such a path has opened up, and remains open. For in twentieth-century history another, complementary lesson, less conspicuous than the first but just as important, has been emerging. It is that forms of nonviolent action can serve effectively in the place of violence at every level of political affairs. This is the promise of Mohandas K. Gandhi's resistance to the British Empire in

India, of Martin Luther King, Jr.'s civil-rights movement in the United States, of the nonviolent movements in Eastern Europe and in Russia that brought down the Soviet Union, and of the global success of democracy in its long contest with the totalitarian challenge. It is even one of the unexpected lessons of the nuclear strategies of the Cold War. The century of total violence was, however discreetly, also a century of nonviolent action. Its success often surprised those who used it and always surprised those against whom it was used. Some of its forms, such as Gandhi's satyagraha and the social movements that pushed the Soviet Union into its grave, were radically new; others, such as the revival of liberal democracy in the century's last decades, were a fulfillment of developments whose roots went back hundreds, even thousands, of years.

The appearance of these forms did not herald the Second Coming. They did not float down from the City of God but were born in strife on the streets of the City of Man. They sprang up in revolution, in civil life, and even in the midst of war. They were as real and as consequential in history as the new forms of violence to which they were a response. They were mainly a product of action, as often stumbled upon as consciously invented, although political imagination of the highest order was also at work. In the mountainous slag heaps of twentieth-century history, they are the flecks of gold that the twenty-first century must sift out and put to use.

As I wrote these pages, I often paused to ask myself whether I had become a pacifist. Although my debt to pacifist thinkers and activists was large, I had to answer that I had not. As soon as I pictured myself a pacifist, my mind would teem with situations, both historical and imaginary, in which it was clear that I would support the use of force or myself use it. The difficulty with the creed for me was not the root of the word, *pax*, but its suffix, *ist*—suggesting that one rule was applicable to all imaginable situations. The emphasis of the word was at any rate wrong for this book. For it was not so much the horrors of twentieth-century violence, immense as they were, that I was seeking to describe as the birth, fostered by historical events, of an alternative—of what William James called "the moral equivalent of war." The path of relying on violence as the answer to violence lies open, and the world has seemed, in a wrong turn of epic proportions, to start down it, as it did in August of 1914. But there is another way.

Then shall the world, at long last, say its farewell to arms? That unrealized vision, I know, is as old as arms themselves. Is it necessary to add that today, too, the obstacles are mountainous; that the temptations of violence, including the longing for revenge, power, or loot—or, for that matter, visions of heaven on earth or of mere safety—still grip the imagination; that the quandaries facing the peacemakers confound the best minds; that as old forms of violence exit the historical scene new ones enter; that in many parts of the world growing scarcity and ecological ruin add new desperation to the ancient war of all against all; that one day's progress unravels the next day; that while in some places nonviolence advances, in others barbarism, including genocide, is unleashed with new vigor and ferocity; that both terror and counterterror are escalating; that the callousness of the rich incites the fury of the poor; that the dream of dominion has fresh allure in the counsels of the powerful; and that hardly a single step toward peace takes place without almost superhuman tenacity and sacrifice, including the supreme sacrifice, made by such heroes as Gandhi, King, Jan Palach, Anwar Sadat, and Yitzhak Rabin, to mention just a few? In downtown Grozny, the Congo jungles, Sierra Leone, Kashmir, Jenin, or Jerusalem, it is difficult to make out, even in the distance, the outlines of a world at peace. I shall contend, nevertheless, that quiet but deep changes, both in the world's grand architecture and in its molecular processes, have expanded the boundaries of the possible. Arms and man have both changed in ways that, even as they imperil the world as never before, have created a chance for peace that is greater than ever before. To describe those changes is the business of this book.

PART ONE

Violence

1

The Rise and Fall of the War System

Some of the most important changes for the future of war have come from within war itself. Those who have planned, equipped, and fought wars have done more to alter the character of war than those who have opposed it. In the modern age, war has in fact undergone a metamorphosis so thorough that its existence has been called into question. This metamorphosis has proceeded in two distinct arenas: the traditional one of conventional war and the new one of people's war. The transformation of conventional war, propelled above all by the scientific revolution of modern times, led finally to the invention of nuclear weapons and the gruesome riddles of nuclear deterrence, whereby great-power war was immobilized, and the immense arsenals were deployed, according to the strategists, mostly to prevent their own use. At the same time, the advent of people's war was paradoxically fore-shadowing the forms of peaceful resistance that proved so success-ful against dictatorial regimes of both the right and the left in the final decades of the twentieth century. At no stage in either jour-ney did the warriors involved in either transformation cultivate principles of nonviolence; on the contrary, they often were bent on using violence to the hilt. Nevertheless, nonviolence of a sort was the destination at which each journey wound up.

Clausewitz on War

In trying to understand the changes that have overtaken war in modern times, it's useful to begin with the eighteenth-century Prussian general and philosopher of war Carl von Clausewitz, who was born in 1780 and died in 1831. He lived and fought and wrote during one of the most important turning points in the history of war. For most of the eighteenth century, war had been largely the business of kings and aristocrats and whatever commoners they could hire or force into their service. Battles usually involved tens of thousands, not hundreds of thousands, of men on each side. The ends of war were often modest, and military strategy often consisted as much of maneuvers as of combat.

With the success of the French Revolution and the rise a decade later of Napoleon Bonaparte, a new force—the energy of an entire population fired with patriotic zeal—was poured onto the battlefield. As an officer in the Prussian service, Clausewitz experienced the effects of the change at first hand, and never more painfully than at the battle of Jena, in 1806, when Napoleon led his forces to a decisive victory over the numerically superior but antiquated and ill-led Prussian force. The French completed the conquest of Prussia in six weeks, and forced her to accept a 50 percent reduction of her territory in the Treaty of Tilsit, in 1807.

Clausewitz's experience turned him into one of the leaders of Prussian military reform. It also propelled him into a lifetime of reflection on the nature of war in general and the reasons for Napoleon's victories in particular. His magnum opus, On War, which many have called the greatest formal analysis of war ever made, was neither published nor even completed in his lifetime. His description of war does not fit war as we know it today. But precisely because he defined the war of his time and of times past more carefully and exactly than anyone had done before or has since, he provided us with a benchmark against which we can measure the revolutionary changes that it is the business of this inquiry to understand. It is exactly the dated aspects of his analysis that make it most interesting.

Three basic concepts define the structure of war as Clausewitz understood it. The first is his concept of "ideal war." By "ideal," Clausewitz did not mean ideally good, as when we speak of the ideal society; he meant what is perfect of its kind, as when we speak of an ideal specimen. He believed that war possesses a singular nature and, once the decision to draw the sword has been taken, develops according to a "logic" peculiar to itself. When this development is allowed to proceed unfettered, ideal war—war without constraint, fought to the death—is the result. If two armies are supplied with all their needs (munitions, logistics, manpower, a clear field of operation) but otherwise battle in a vacuum, like gladiators in a stadium, they will fight an ideal war.

Clausewitz recognized, however, that in actuality war is rarely supplied with all the materials it ideally needs and is never fought in a vacuum. Constraints are always present. For one thing, the plans and operations of armies are impeded by innumerable practical obstacles, all of which Clausewitz subsumes under the heading of "friction." Owing to friction, Clausewitz added to ideal war a second concept, that of "real war." Real war differs from ideal war in the way that a real vase, because it is chipped or slightly misshapen, differs from an ideal vase. A greater constraint than friction on ideal war is politics. Politics, in Clausewitz's view, is not something that unfortunately gets in the way of war; it is, or should be, in command of the entire operation. For war, Clausewitz believes, should be completely subordinate to the goals of the state that wages it. The supremacy of political goals over military goals is the third of his basic concepts. "War"—to give one variant of his most famous saying—"is a true political instrument, a continuation of political intercourse, carried on with other means." Clausewitz's writings sometimes seem to reflect a disappointment that ideal war is spoiled by friction, but he does not regret that war is held in check by politics. On the contrary, he regarded war that has broken free of political guidance as "something pointless and devoid of sense."

The Logic of War

The formulations that Clausewitz gave for the operations of ideal war may at first seem obvious, but when he has placed them in the wider context of politics, any appearance of self-evidence vanishes. On the first page of *On War,* Clausewitz wrote, "Countless duels go to make up war, but a picture of it as a whole can be formed by imagining a pair of wrestlers. Each tries through physical force to compel the other to do his will; his *immediate* aim is to *throw* his opponent in order to make him incapable of further resistance."

From this definition, a basic rule followed: Both sides must exert themselves to the utmost: "War is an act of force, and there is no logical limit to the application of that force. Each side, therefore, compels its opponent to follow suit; a reciprocal action is started which must lead, in theory, to extremes." There is nothing abstract or metaphysical about this logic. It is the logic of any contest of strength in which the last one standing is the winner: "The fact that slaughter is a horrifying spectacle must make us take war more seriously, but not provide an excuse for gradually blunting our swords in the name of humanity. Sooner or later someone will come along with a sharp sword and hack off our arms." Attempts in principle to avoid the extremes "always lead to logical absurdity."

The reciprocal action pressing the two sides to the extremes of available force is the logic that drives war to assume its ideal nature, which Clausewitz also calls "absolute war." Ideal war and absolute war are the same. So are real war and limited war—except in those few cases in which the demands of politics and the absence of crippling friction permit war to run to its extremes. Then the real approaches the ideal and the absolute.

It's important to understand, however, that even though each side is driven to employ its strength to the limit, weakness is an indispensable element of war *as a system*. The importance of weakness for war is usually overlooked. Yet without it war could never decide anything, for no one could ever be rendered powerless. "All war," Clausewitz wrote, "presupposes human weakness and seeks to exploit it." Defeat—in which the strength of one side buckles and gives way—is the pivot of war. The victor only goes on doing what he had wanted to do and planned to do in the first place. It's on the losing side that the crisis, the reversal of fortune, the shattering of expectations, and the collapse of all plans, takes place. That is why "the loser's scale falls much further below the original line of equilibrium than the winner's side rises above it."

What Is Defeat?

The weakness, or "powerlessness," that precipitated defeat was not a simple thing. How could the victor know when defeat had occurred? Was it when the foe's armed forces fled the field of battle? When their capital was occupied? Clausewitz's definitions of war contain an ambiguity. In the metaphor of the wrestling match, the victor renders his opponent "incapable of further resistance." If we picture this—let's call it physical defeat—we see the opponent lying flat on the ground, incapacitated or dead. But Clausewitz calls this merely the immediate aim of war. The victor's larger—and crucially different—goal is to make the enemy "do his will." The distinction between the two becomes clearer in another passage: "The battle . . . is not merely reciprocal slaughter, and its effect is more a killing of the enemy's courage than of the enemy's soldiers," for "loss of moral force is the chief cause of the decision." Following Clausewitz's cue, let us call this moral defeat.

In physical defeat, scenes of which are familiar from heroic paintings, we see slain soldiers carpeting the battlefield, perhaps with the victorious general and a few of his aides surveying them on horseback. But in the second (less often painted) picture of moral defeat, we see the former enemies up and about, busily doing what the victor has commanded—for example, paying tribute, handing over a portion of the harvest, paying a tax, or even worshiping the victor's god. In this scene, the battle is long over. The victor or his proconsul has taken up residency in the capital of the defeated nation. He issues an order. Do the defeated people obey? Do they "do his will"? Perhaps he thought he had won the victory when the enemy forces dissolved; but now it turns out, according to Clausewitz, that the decision made by civilians far from the field of battle will determine whether he really was victorious after all. For the war "cannot be considered to have ended so long as the enemy's *will* has not been broken: in other words, so long as the enemy government and its allies have not been driven to ask for peace, or the population made to submit."

Even the early nineteenth century offered examples of generals who believed a foe had been defeated only to find that he went on fighting, and sometimes prevailed. Clausewitz cites Napoleon's invasion of Russia in 1812. Napoleon won every battle on his march to Moscow. The Russian forces retreated steadily, until he finally occupied the city, which then burned in a great fire. (It has never been determined whether it was started deliberately by the population or was accidental.) Weren't the Russians beaten? In fact, as all readers of Tolstoy's *War and Peace* know, the will of Russia was intact. It was Napoleon who was on his way to ruin.

The Great Democratic Revolution

The reciprocal action of the duel pushes it toward the extremes, toward absolute war. *Friction* clogs the gears, slows things down, perhaps brings them to a halt. Fear is a potent form of friction, as are exhaustion, faulty intelligence, and chance events so various that no category can easily encompass them. Weather is a good example of friction in war: "Rain can prevent a battalion from arriving, make another late by keeping it not three but eight hours on the march, ruin a cavalry charge by bogging horses down in the mud."

These are mundane matters, seemingly unsuitable for philosophical reflection, yet friction—this "resisting medium," in which war takes place—does have a grander aspect. Clausewitz is acutely conscious that different historical periods impose extremely different degrees of friction on war. He firmly believes that his picture of ideal war describes a potentiality that is timeless, but he is aware that it can be realized only in certain periods. In some periods, conditions are like molasses, in which war can scarcely get started and, if it does, remains a sorry, sluggish business.

When Clausewitz surveyed the history of war, he found his own period all but unique. Rarely, if ever, he believed, had war come so close to realizing its ideal form. The underlying reason was the French Revolution, which began in 1789, when Clausewitz was a boy. In 1793, when France sent immense conscripted armies into the field, he wrote, "a force appeared that beggared all imagination. Suddenly, war again became the business of the people—a people of thirty million, all of whom considered themselves to be citizens. . . . Nothing now impeded the vigor with which war could be waged." Not since the days of ancient Rome, he believed, had the ideal face of war shown itself more clearly. In the intervening centuries, war had for the most part been a crippled, faltering affair, dragging itself along "slowly, like a faint

and starving man." In the preceding century, monarchical governments, cut off from popular support, had fought war in a formal,
gentlemanly style. "Their means of waging war came to consist of
the money in their coffers and of such idle vagabonds as they
could lay their hands on." War thereby had been deprived of its
"most dangerous" innate characteristic, the "tendency toward the
extreme" dictated by its inner logic.

The larger force that swept aside these cobwebs of restraint was
what the French political writer Alexis de Tocqueville, in 1835,
called "the great democratic revolution" that "is going on amongst
us." Because this democratic revolution touches the story of both
war and nonviolence at every point, it requires discussion here.
The revolution embraced not only the political upheavals that,
beginning in the late eighteenth century, brought democratic governments to power, first in the United States and France and later
in other parts of the world, but also the much deeper and broader
democratization of the public world associated with a steady
increase in the participation by masses of people in every phase
of public life. This was the revolution that the early-nineteenth-
century French novelist and political thinker Benjamin Constant
envisioned as "mankind, emerging from an impenetrable cloud
that obscures its birth, advancing toward equality over the debris
of all sorts of institutions"; that the English historian Thomas Carlyle around the same time called "the new omnipotent Unknown
of Democracy"; that in 1932 the Spanish philosopher Ortega y
Gasset balefully assessed in *The Revolt of the Masses,* asserting
that "one fact [of] the utmost importance in the public life in
Europe" is "the accession of the masses to complete social power."

Those masses arrived by innumerable paths and in innumerable
roles—as climbers in all the old hierarchies of privilege, as crowds
on the barricades, as soldiers in conscripted armies, as guerrillas in
jungles and deserts, as citizens in town meetings, as trade unionists
on strike, as patriotic cheering sections for imperial conquests, as
outraged native populations protesting those same conquests, as

the ghostly bearers of "public opinion" in opinion polls, and, most recently, as women leaving the confines of the home, to take their places in the worlds of work and politics, or as homosexual men and women asserting their human dignity and demanding equality with heterosexuals. Everywhere these masses came, they brought a new, popular energy, a new power, destined to transform politics, war, and the relationship between the two.

What were the causes of this democratic revolution? Almost anything you cared to mention, according to its most profound expositor, Tocqueville. "The various occurrences of national existence have everywhere turned to the advantage of democracy," he wrote; "all men have aided it by their exertions: those who have intentionally labored in its cause and those who have served it unwittingly; those who have fought for it and those who have declared themselves its opponents, have all been driven along in the same track, have all labored to one end, some ignorantly and some unwillingly; all have been blind instruments in the hands of God." Even the achievements of democracy's enemies helped it, by "throwing into relief that natural greatness of man," which was perhaps the true source of the new energy. So deep-seated was the democratic principle of equality, Tocqueville thought, that its gradual development should be regarded as "a providential fact."

The French Revolution was the channel through which the stream of the democratic revolution first flowed onto the battlefields of Europe. In the words of the nineteenth-century French historian Adolphe Thiers, "The revolution, by setting the public mind in motion, prepared the epoch of great military achievements." In 1793, when the French Revolutionary Convention ordered the mass recruitment of citizens known to history as the *levée en masse,* its decree was the definitive announcement of society's unprecedented militarization. "From this moment on, until the enemies have been chased from the territory of the Republic," the convention ordained, "all Frenchmen are in permanent requisition for the service of the armies. The young men will go to combat; married men will forge weapons and transport food; women will make tents and uniforms and will serve in the hospitals; children will make bandages from old linen; old men will present themselves at public places to excite the courage of the warriors, to preach hatred of kings and the unity of the Republic." But it was Napoleon, the Corsican corporal who had himself been crowned emperor of France, who first made full use of the modern democratic army. It was under him that war, as Clausewitz put it, "took on an entirely different character, or rather closely approached its true character, its absolute perfection." Finally, "War, untrammeled by any conventional restraints, had broken loose in all its elemental fury."

War as the Final Arbiter

Friction, in Clausewitz's scheme, was an impediment to the logic of absolute war only *in fact*. The supremacy of politics over war was an impediment *in principle*. The first was an obstacle to war, like another foe in the field, the second a guiding rule that, in his view, must shape strategy from start to finish. Clausewitz has often been scolded as the intellectual founding father of absolute war, and has even been held responsible for the militarism in Germany that did so much to bring on the two world wars of the twentieth century. Nothing, as Clausewitz's biographer Peter Paret has pointed out, could be further from the truth. Having set forth his concept of ideal war, Clausewitz went on to argue with rigor and passion that the operations of war must be thoroughly subordinated to political ends. What is more, he fully understood that his two prescriptions for action—that, on the one hand, the logic of war required that it must be fought to the limit of one's strength and that, on the other, political considerations must limit and constrain war—were in conflict across the board. A lesser thinker might have expounded just one of these rules, but Clausewitz embraces both, and his attempt to reconcile them, though perhaps unavailing, forms one of the richest and most invaluable parts of his work. The following passage gives the context of his renowned saying, already quoted, concerning politics and war:

> It is, of course, well-known that the only source of war is politics— the intercourse of government and peoples; but it is apt to be assumed that war suspends that intercourse and replaces it by a wholly different condition, ruled by no law but its own.
>
> We maintain, on the contrary, that war is simply a continuation of political intercourse, with the addition of other means. . . . How could it be otherwise? Do political relations between peoples and between their governments stop when diplomatic notes are no longer exchanged?

In holding that war must be subordinate to politics, Clausewitz placed himself in the mainstream of the Western political tradition. Since Pericles praised the Athenian soldiers for their defense of their city and its way of life, war has been considered the ultima ratio—the final arbiter—in international affairs. In this tradition, war was seen not as an end in itself but as a servant of the polis— necessary for both its defense and its aggressive purposes. Whatever the costs of war or the wisdom or unwisdom of its goals, it was a political instrument of unquestionable worth. With war, empires were created, enlarged to the edges of the known world, or broken up; countries founded or extinguished; trade protected or cut off; plunder seized; tribute exacted; enemies punished; religions propagated or suppressed; balances of power preserved or upset. We shall never understand war until, even as we face its horror, we acknowledge, with Clausewitz and so many others, how great its usefulness and appeal as an arbiter has been. If we ask, "Arbiter of what?" the response is: Of those political disputes that could not be resolved peacefully. If we ask "Why final?" the tradition answers: Force should be introduced only after peaceful means have been exhausted. Arbitration by force is final, in the last analysis, because death is final, because the dead on the battlefield cannot pick themselves up to fight.

If the saying that war is the continuation of politics by other means assigned to war the last word in disputes, it also fixed limits on war by subordinating it to political goals. "Is war not just another expression of [a government's] thoughts?" Clausewitz asked. "Its grammar, indeed, may be its own, but not its logic." Yet this assertion apparently contradicted his claim that war did have a logic of its own—the logic that drove it to become absolute war. War thus appeared to be in the grip of two contending logics: one proceeding from war itself, the other from politics. If the politicians fixed upon "absolute" political ends (for example, the full conquest of an enemy's territory), then military and political policy might move smoothly in tandem. Clausewitz had lived through such a time—Napoleon's rise and fall. But in most periods, he knew, the logic of politics had worked against the absolutizing logic of war. Usually, the war aims fixed on by statesmen were not large enough to justify the extraordinary efforts and sacrifices required by absolute war. If in those circumstances the politicians let the logic of war take over, then "all proportion between action and political demands would be lost: means would cease to be commensurate with ends, and in most cases a policy of maximum exertion would fail because of domestic problems it would raise"— or, worse, the military tail would begin to wag the political dog. "Were [war] a complete, untrammeled, absolute manifestation of violence . . . war would of its own independent will usurp the place of policy the moment policy had brought it into being; it would then drive policy out of office and rule by the laws of its own nature." Clausewitz has been called a militarist, but rarely has a clearer warning against militarism been sounded by a military man.

The necessary remedy was to make certain that the restraining hand of policy overruled the logic of war, even though this might convert "the terrible battle-sword that a man needs both hands and his entire strength to wield, and with which he strikes home once and no more, into a light, handy rapier—sometimes just a foil for the exchange of thrusts, feints and parries." If we can hear a note of regret at this diminution of war, that only underscores the strength of Clausewitz's resolve to place politics in command.

Clausewitz was the first analyst to clearly identify the two logics that contended for the direction of war. The logic born out of war itself was not some Platonic form, floating above events; it was a dynamic principle, a compulsion, located in the activity of war itself. War was like the biblical mustard seed. You might choose not to plant that seed, but if you did, and nourished it properly, you should expect a mustard plant, not a lily. War had a life of its own, which, if not checked or limited (and the democratic revolution, by firing entire peoples with martial enthusiasm, removed limits previously in place), would dominate events. But since political logic, more often than not, defined aims that were less than absolute, it usually worked against the logic of war, reducing it to the level of modest, restrained real war—the thing encountered in most of history.

Clausewitz's account, however, contained an inconsistency. If politicians, unable to get the results they wanted by peaceful means, turned to soldiers to get them by force of arms, but then restrained those soldiers from running to the extremes at which decisions by arms occurred, how was war to be of any use to politics? Let us suppose, for example, that the politicians had in mind a limited military campaign to seize an island of only modest importance, and the enemy stalemated the attack with equal force. No extreme would have been reached, no one would have been rendered "powerless," no decision would have been rendered. What to do next? Give up? But then why make the attempt in the first place? Escalate? But then the vital "proportion" between the political goal and the military means that were used to attain it would be lost.

Napoleonic war, which extended the extremes at which the

decision by arms was reached, only made this conflict more acute. Clausewitz saw the problem plainly. The growing mismatch between political logic and military logic, he wrote, "poses an obvious problem for any theory of war that aims at being thoroughly scientific." By asserting the primacy of politics, he believed, the restraint needed to fight for small objectives could still be achieved. "The natural solution soon emerges," he explained: mastered by political calculation, "the art of war will shrivel into prudence, and its main concern will be to make sure the delicate balance is not suddenly upset in the enemy's favor, and the half-hearted war does not become a real war after all." Once this process is understood, "no conflict need arise any longer between political and military interests."

With the advantage of almost two centuries of hindsight, we can see that Clausewitz was mistaken. The gap between the two logics was in fact about to widen steadily. Indeed, what some historians are calling the "long nineteenth century" in Europe—lasting from Napoleon's defeat in 1815 to the outbreak of the First World War in 1914—can be seen as a protracted, ultimately unsuccessful effort to reconcile the two logics. With the outbreak of the First World War, the logic of war triumphed over the logic of politics, engulfing the world in a series of violent catastrophes that were to dominate the rest of the twentieth century.

Clausewitz's main misjudgment was to regard Napoleonic war as absolute war. The term "absolute," borrowed from philosophy and theology, clearly suggested a culmination, with no further developments to be expected. But we know now that Napoleonic war was in fact only an early stage of a lengthy development that would steadily expand the extremes of which war was capable. War should be a mere "instrument," Clausewitz had said. But the instrument was about to come alive in the hands of its user, and embark on a process of nonstop development that in the next century and a half would produce a revolution not only in war but in the relationship of war to its would-be employer and master, politics. It was not, indeed, until the invention of nuclear weapons that any true absolute—the unquestionable power of each side to annihilate the other—was reached. At that point, strange to say, war ceased, strictly speaking, to exist among the greatest powers. True absolute war, it turned out, was not war at all but some new thing, for which no one really had a good name.

The War System

The transformation of war that lay ahead took place in the context of the European conquest of most of the globe. When, as in Clausewitz's Europe, a number of armed states contend in a single geographical arena, sometimes making war, sometimes peace, sometimes making alliances, sometimes breaking or switching them, we can speak not merely of war but of a war system—or, when the arena is the whole world, of a global war system. In a war system, the logic of war is extended to the entire system, now pushing far-flung alliances toward the extremes at which decisions by arms are rendered. Military necessity then becomes such a powerful force that the formation of alliances may override all ideological or political considerations.

As in a game, the action in a war system may be complex, but the underlying strategies available to the players are simple and well known. All were discovered by the ancient Greek city-states. The most aggressive is the strategy of universal empire, and in the West ancient Rome was the first and last to succeed in it. The most common strategy historically has been the defensive one of seeking to maintain a balance of power, whereby one or more nations or an alliance of nations tries to hold any hegemonist at bay, as England did in Europe in the face of the rising power of France in the seventeenth, eighteenth, and nineteenth centuries. An alternative to both is collective security—rarely, if ever, successful—in which a league of nations agrees to keep peace among themselves by pooling their collective force to constrain any aggressor.

It would be wrong, however, if, by referring to a war system, we seemed to suggest that it was designed by somebody. It was not. Lack of a designer, however, does not mean lack of design. There are unintended systems as well as intended ones. The street grid of New York City and the constitutional system of the United States are intentional systems. Evolution and the market economy are unintended ones—systems that had no designer (though the market system soon had many powerful champions). In both, certain patterns and rules developed of their own accord, out of conditions that were provided largely or completely without planning.

The war system is such a system. When the curtain of recorded history goes up, a plurality of states are simply there, bristling with arms and ready to fight. To suggest that the war system was an intentional system would be to falsify and simplify the dilemma of war by seeming to suggest that it was the product of some "masters of war" to whom humanity could appeal to unmake their work.

Systems may also be either static—governed by rules that do not change—or dynamic, thus subject to development. The solar system is a static system. The planets will wheel around the sun without change until the system expires. Evolution and the market economy, by contrast, are dynamic systems. More specifically, they are dynamic systems of the adapt-or-die variety. An adapt-or-die system is one in which competitors can, by adapting themselves with particular skill to a changing environment, put themselves in a position to drive their rivals out of existence. The war system is a system of this kind. Adapt-or-die systems must be supplied with some reliable source of innovation—of new, advantageous possibilities *to which* the actors can strive to be the first to adapt. In the evolutionary system, one source of innovation is the random mutation of genes. In the market system, the chief source of change is technical innovation, which provides a ceaseless supply of new inventions that producers can exploit to make better or cheaper products.

For most of the history of war, few innovations were available. Combat was chiefly hand to hand, and the instruments of war—the sword, the spear, the bow and arrow, the chariot, the horse, the battering ram, the trireme, the fortification—were widely available and slow to evolve. Nations could rarely achieve a sudden, decisive advantage through an improvement in weapons or technique. (Briefly, the longbow conferred such an advantage.) In the modern period, however, the pace of innovation picked up abruptly, and the adapt-or-die character of the war system became all-important.

The Vortex of Power

It was an adaptive innovation—the mobilization of citizens by democratic revolutions—that prompted Clausewitz to announce prematurely that the era of absolute war had arrived. In the modern age, however, the democratic revolution was only one of four distinct great forces that poured newly created energy into the war system. The other three were the scientific revolution; the industrial revolution, whose mass-produced goods began to be incorporated into military armories in the mid-nineteenth century; and imperialism, which dragged the rest of the globe into the European war system. "The Great Powers were, as their name implies, organizations for power, that is, in the last resort for war," the historian A. J. P. Taylor has written. "They might have other objects—the welfare of their inhabitants or the grandeur of their rulers. But the basic tenet for them as Great Powers was their ability to wage war." Defining power this way was hardly new. What was new was the availability of the new forces of the modern age for military purposes. It was the dependence of military power on all four of its new sources of strength that turned the war system into a fast-paced, world-spanning, inescapable, adapt-or-die system, from whose ever-increasing pressure virtually no social enter-prise—and certainly no nation—was exempt.

These forces did a great deal more than transform war. They were the constitutive elements in the rise of what some have called the modern world system and others have called the Western world system, as it led to Western domination of the globe. In the late nineteenth and early twentieth centuries, this system, implac-able and merciless, compelled all "backward" nations to reform on pain of death—in short, to adapt to the modern Western system or die as independent countries. And which country was not, at some historical moment or other, "backward" and forced to play catch-up with some feared "advanced" nation? In the early mod-ern age, only England—the first nation to avail itself of the mod-ern financial, industrial, and scientific resources for war—escaped this role, with its burden of humiliation, *ressentiment,* and well-justified fear of subjugation. (Joseph Stalin, who explained many of his most ruthless measures as attempts to catch up with the capitalist West, said, "She [Russia] was beaten [in the First World War] because of her backwardness, because of her military, cul-tural, political, industrial, and agricultural backwardness. . . . Do you want our socialist fatherland to be beaten and to lose its inde-pendence? If you do not want that, then you must in the short-est possible time abolish its backwardness and develop a really Bolshevik pace in the establishment of its socialist economy.") Bolshevization, in the minds of its practitioners, was emergency modernization.

Military power, indeed, can be seen as a sort of clearinghouse in which the new forces of the modern age were assembled, brought into relation, and thrown into the contests in which the life or death of nations and empires was determined. We might say that in relation to this modern military exchange-market, each force brought forth both a benefit proper to it, analogous to what the economists call a "use-value," and a secondary, military benefit, analogous to what the economists call an "exchange-value." Use-value is the value a thing has directly for life. (The use-value of a glass of water is to slake a person's thirst, the use-value of a diamond is to be displayed.) Exchange-value is the price the thing will get when it is sold or bartered. So also in the modern world system, the fruits of democracy, science, industry, and imperialism had both a kind of direct use-value and a kind of exchange-value in the burgeoning market of military power. The democratic revolution brought the Rights of Man *and* millions of willing recruits for war; the scientific revolution offered pure knowledge *and* better artillery and explosives; the industrial revolutions created consumer goods *and* provided more matériel for larger and longer wars; imperial possession won trade and spoils *and* strategic global position.

Many writers have pointed out that through the process of "commodification" the free market possesses a remarkable capacity to draw ever-widening spheres of life into its orbit. The exchange market of modern military power had an even greater capacity to subordinate other realms of endeavor to its purposes, for, in that market, not just commodities but the democratic loyalty of citizens, the knowledge of scientists, the material wealth of industry, and the territories of empire were traded in for the common coin of military power—power that, in turn, could be used to gain more fervent loyalty, more material wealth, more territory, and so forth.

Pursuit of Knowledge, Pursuit of Power

The scientific revolution, as many observers have said, has changed the conditions of human life more radically than any other single, sustained force in history. The first round of the technical transformation of war of modern times—the gunpowder revolution—had already occurred by Clausewitz's time. Its effects had been felt in the entire organization of the modern state, having been no small factor in the rise of the absolute monarchs of continental

Europe. In the succinct formulation of the sociologist Charles Tilly, "War made the state and the state made war." A technical and economic rivalry among states was triggered, dictating, in an early demonstration of the modern adapt-or-die process, that the smaller states, like small firms in a cutthroat market, "must increase in size or go bankrupt." The cannon-bearing sailing ship, in its turn, laid the basis for the armed seafaring expeditions of the sixteenth and seventeenth centuries.

Fundamental characteristics of modern science—its grant of power, its irrevocability, its mobility, and its unpredictability—have been of immense importance for the development of war. In 1608, Francis Bacon, the first great philosopher of modern science, made the essential point regarding irrevocability. "The benefits of [scientific] discoveries may extend to the whole race of men, civil benefits only to a few particular places; the latter last not beyond a few ages, the former through all time." When analysts of the nuclear question rightly point out that nuclear weapons cannot be disinvented, they are describing a characteristic of all scientific invention. Scientific findings are mobile for the same reason that they are unrepealable—once made, they sooner or later can be repeated by any competent person in the world. Knowledge is by its nature ambulatory. And because science is a process of discovery, its findings—no less than its social applications—are unpredictable. A scientist's investigations are directed by hypotheses, which are in turn directed by theories, both of which enable scientists to make reasonable guesses regarding what they may find in any particular investigation. But they are in the dark when it comes to guessing what other scientists years in the future, guided by still undreamed-of hypotheses and theories, will discover. They are as unable to predict what science will bring to light fifty years ahead as Columbus was to predict what he would discover when he sailed west across the Atlantic.

These characteristics of science—each a positive feature in the context of science's own remarkable progress—are responsible in no small measure for the tyrannous, lethal pressure that the modern war system has placed on nations. They have left society quadruply helpless. Because science was power, nations felt unable to forgo the most destructive inventions; because science was irrevocable, they were unable to rid themselves of any invention once acquired; because science was unpredictable, they were helpless to know what inventions they would be handed next by scientists, and so to foresee the direction in which science was dragging them. On the bridge of the great ship of basic science, where, as Bacon put it, pure scientists were enjoying "contemplation of things as they are, without superstition or imposture, error or confusion," all was peaceful, calm, and orderly, but in the ship's mighty wake every other vessel, especially every military vessel, was buffeted by the currents or sucked under the waves.

The resemblances between the scientific and the democratic revolutions are striking. If ours has been an age of fantastic growth of human powers, then science and democracy have been the two deepest wellsprings of it. Both have been sleepless dynamos of historical change, spilling fresh energy decade after decade into the modern world. Both revolutions seemed to most observers in the eighteenth and nineteenth centuries to be agencies of continuous, cumulative human betterment. Both have been global and have tended to produce uniformity—eroding not only tradition but all local particularity. Both have proved, to use Tocqueville's word, "irresistible" and (so far, at least) irreversible. Both have transformed and continue to transform the world, including war, in ways unanticipated by the actors involved. Both have proffered gifts of previously undreamed-of human power yet have left nations unable to reject these gifts (new destructive inventions, new recruits for armies) if they so wished. Hasn't this powerlessness of humankind *not* to accept windfalls of unimagined power been a defining feature of the modern period?

From the Rights of Man to the Levée en Masse

In the nineteenth century, a pattern emerged in which the benefits proper to each of the new forces of the modern age yielded to exigencies of military need. The promise of both the American and the French revolutions was democracy itself—liberty, fraternity, equality, the Rights of Man. But the American revolutionaries found themselves instantly at war, and the French Revolution, as Clausewitz noted, was immediately militarized. No sooner had the Frenchman become a citizen than he rushed off to the front. The revolutionary zeal for war was memorably articulated by the leader of the dominant Gironde faction in the French Assembly, Jacques-Pierre Brissot, who proclaimed, "We cannot rest till Europe, and all Europe, is ablaze."

In one respect, as it turned out, the Girondins fatally miscalculated, for the emergency of war created ideal conditions for the rise of the Jacobin terror, in which many of them perished. But in another respect, the Girondins had prophesied truly, for after initial reverses the French revolutionary armies embarked on a series of smashing triumphs over neighboring monarchies that was not reversed until Waterloo, in 1815. "Here begins modern war," the nineteenth-century French historian Jules Michelet wrote. "Tacticians could never have invented such tactics. No calculation was involved."

Whereas the French had started with democracy and only then discovered the power of mass armies, the Prussians began with mass armies—French ones, invading their country—and only then discovered the need for popular reforms. Democracy always and everywhere involves the participation of the people; but whereas in France democracy initially meant the elevation of the French people over aristocrats and kings, in Germany it meant, from the start, recruitment of the people to fight other peoples, including, above all, the detested French conquerors (who were indeed defeated by the Germans in 1871). These effects of the democratic revolution deepened and were systematized throughout the nineteenth century, as states, in the wake of the French revolutionaries' *levée en masse*, mastered the techniques of conscription and mass propaganda. During the nineteenth century, Europe as a whole witnessed a slow evolution from "liberal nationalism," which pitted the common people ("the nation") of each country against its own monarchs and privileged classes, toward an increasingly militaristic, right-wing nationalism, which pitted all classes of the nation, plebeian and privileged alike, against other nations. Nationalism (a word that doesn't come into wide use until the end of the nineteenth century) was the militarization of democracy.

From Laissez-Faire to the Military Revolution

A parallel process of militarization occurred in the evolution of the industrial revolution. In Clausewitz's day, the effects of industrialization had yet to make themselves fully felt in war. The early champions of the free market, most of them British, had in fact looked to industry mainly to create the wealth of nations, as the title of Adam Smith's classic book had it, not the *power* of nations, which had been the preoccupation of their mercantilist predecessors. The advocates of laissez-faire declared the independence of economics from state power. (The eventual coining of the word "economics," identifying a distinct realm of human activity subject to its own laws, was one sign of their faith in that independence.) The market worked best, the worldly philosophers of the late eighteenth century believed, when the government kept its hands off it. Classical economics, in fact, "had no place for the nation, or any collectivity larger than the firm."

Smith's successors proceeded even further in this line of thinking. In the early nineteenth century, the most prominent champions of the market, including the British champions of laissez-faire Richard Cobden and John Bright, contended that free trade, by breaking down or ignoring national boundaries, naturally tended to foster world peace. The market, they ardently believed, was a solvent of national units and a pacifier of national conflicts. "I see in the Free Trade principle," Richard Cobden said in a speech in 1846, "that which shall act on the moral world as the principle of gravitation in the universe, drawing men together, thrusting aside the antagonism of race, and creed, and language, and uniting us in the bonds of eternal peace." In the United States, Ralph Waldo Emerson declared that "trade was the principle of Liberty; that trade planted America and destroyed Feudalism; that it makes peace and keeps peace; and it will abolish slavery." An unbroken thread of faith in free trade as an abettor of peace runs through the entire tradition of liberal internationalism, surviving many disappointments and continuing, if in attenuated form, to this day.

Yet soon a different relationship of markets to war emerged. Just as the nations of Europe could scarcely help noticing, in the wake of the French Revolution, that the mobilization of masses of people had hugely strengthened armies, so as the nineteenth century progressed they observed that the industrial revolution was doing the same. The military advantages of industrialism were put on convincing display in the American Civil War. Railroads and the mass manufacture of weapons played an important part in both its immense destructiveness and the ultimate victory of the North. In 1871, the Prussian victory over France drove the lesson home in Europe. If in the Napoleonic wars France had taught Prussia the value of patriotic masses, now Prussia's taught France—and all Europe—the value of industrialization and organizational skill. The Prussian victory was due in part to what came to be called the Prussian military revolution, in which the resources of industry, technology, and even education were exploited as never before for military purposes. This superiority of machine over man in war was sealed in the slaughter of the First World War, in which artillery and the machine gun—the emblems par excellence of the mechanization of war—laid waste to so many millions of young men. For the rest of the history of war, the strength of industrial economies and military power would be closely linked.

Imperialism's gift to the modern war system was access to nearly every inch of the earth for the military operations of the imperial powers. In the late nineteenth century, economic motives for empire steadily yielded to geopolitical ones. The importance of territory for war had always been recognized. It was not, however, until the forced opening of China and Japan in the mid-nineteenth century and the ensuing "scramble" for Africa and other imperial possessions that the whole earth became an indivisible military theater whose center was Europe. Between 1870 and 1900, European nations seized control of some ten million square miles of territory, on which a hundred and fifty million people lived. Only then was it possible to regard military initiatives in Siam, Natal, or Peking as moves on the chessboard of a truly global war system. The nineteenth-century English historian Frederic Seebohm famously commented that the British Empire was "acquired in a fit of absence of mind," but by the 1880s, absence of mind was at an end, replaced by jingoistic pride and ceaseless global military strategizing. In *Africa and the Victorians,* the scholars Ronald Robinson and John Gallagher have chronicled the change. The early Victorians, faithful to their laissez-faire principles, were content to let private interests take the lead in empire-building. The British government abjured direct rule, believing that the spread of commerce would itself lead "civilization with one hand, and peace with the other, to render mankind happier, wiser, better," in the words of Britain's foreign secretary, Lord Palmerston, in 1842. Even his gunboat diplomacy was aimed only at "opening" countries to trade, not ruling them. As late as 1890, the prime minister, Lord Salisbury, opposing direct British rule of Egypt, said, somewhat facetiously, "The only form of control we have is what is called moral influence, which in practice is a combination of nonsense, objurgation, and worry." He added, "In this, we are supreme."

However, events did not proceed as the liberal dabblers in

empire expected—neither in Asia nor in Africa nor in the Ottoman Empire. The economic arrangements forced upon those lands
did not strengthen and liberalize their governments but undermined them and drove them, one after another, toward collapse.
The Egyptian government, for example, accepted loans from
Europe, spent the funds on large but unproductive public projects,
and, when these failed, sought to keep up payments on the loans
by raising taxes on the poor, who grew discontented and rebellious. The imperial powers then were faced with what seemed a
drastic choice: between withdrawing entirely and imposing direct
rule. They chose direct rule.

By the turn of the century, most of the territories of the globe
had been incorporated by imperialism into the European vortex.
Any move anywhere—in the heart of Africa, in the Bay of Bengal,
in the Strait of Tsushima—by any of the great powers now seemed
to the others likely to upset a global balance of power and to
require a countermove. The conservative British politician Lord
Curzon spoke for his whole generation of statesmen when, after a
long journey to the Middle East in 1890, he wrote, "Turkestan,
Afghanistan, Transcaspia, Persia—to many these names breathe
only a sense of utter remoteness or a memory of strange vicissi-
tudes and of moribund romance. To me, I confess, they are the
pieces on a chessboard upon which is being played out a game for
the dominion of the world." Lord Haldane, describing his participation in the unsuccessful Anglo-German negotiations on naval
reductions of 1912, said, "I thought, from my study of the German General Staff, that once the German war party had got into
the saddle, it would be war not merely for the overthrow of France
or Russia but for the domination of the world." From that time
on, fear that one power or another would take control of the
planet became the nightmare of statesmen and peoples. It was a
dread inherent in the logic of war once the war system had drawn
all nations into its sphere.

The Triumph of the Logic of War

As the nineteenth century came to a close, the European war system, nourished by science, democracy, industry, and imperial conquest, was swollen with powers hardly dreamed of at the century's beginning. If, elaborating on Clausewitz, we liken war to a race that must be run to its finish before the prizes of victory and defeat can be handed out, then we might say that what had been a hundred-yard dash in Napoleon's time had become a potential marathon. Then, states might have had to sacrifice tens of thousands of men before the race was won; now the price would be the blood of millions. Then, Europe was chiefly involved; now the struggle would involve every continent. Then, soldiers marched to battle with muskets on their shoulders; now they would arrive by train with machine guns. The gap between the often modest political objectives of international diplomacy and the military means necessary to secure or defend them had widened into an abyss. And yet, because the war system was now global, tiny events in out-of-the-way places, in themselves without significance to the great powers, were vested with apocalyptic importance. Europe was at peace, but the logic of war had eclipsed the logic of politics.

Two diplomatic-military events—one in the colonial world, another in the heart of Europe—can illustrate the depth of the abyss with particular clarity. One is the Fashoda crisis of 1898, which brought France and England to the brink of war over minuscule claims in what is now southern Sudan. England, in full control of Egypt, did not yet rule its neighbor Sudan, which a few years earlier had been taken over by a radical Islamic movement, whose leader was called the Khalifah. The French, embittered by their exclusion from Egypt when England had occupied it in 1882, concocted a far-fetched scheme to turn the tables against England. An expedition of a hundred and fifty Senegalese and eleven Frenchmen under the leadership of Captain Jean-Baptiste

Marchand was dispatched on a thousand-mile overland expedition from West Africa to seize a small Sudanese town called Fashoda—a godforsaken place of "blazing heat, solvent humidity, elephant grass, and enveloping mud (when the rain began in May) and horizon-to-horizon mosquitoes."

Meanwhile, England dispatched an army of thirty thousand men under Lord Kitchener to destroy the Islamic forces in Sudan. For two years, he marched his army south along the Nile, accompanied by gunboats on the river, until, on August 31, 1898, he encountered the Khalifah and his forces at Omdurman and annihilated them. On September 19, he reached Fashoda. Marchand had arrived two months earlier with his small band of fellow explorers and claimed the town for France.

The two men met and had a cordial conversation. Yet for the next few weeks Britain and France stood at the edge of war over a fetid swampland, which neither country valued. The verdict of political logic regarding Fashoda was clear: it was worthless. But the logic of the military chessboard led to an opposite evaluation. Because Fashoda, like Egypt, supposedly sat astride England's "road to India," and since India was the heart of the British Empire, Fashoda must be defended at all costs. The disparity between the puniness of the prize and the immensity of the war being risked in Europe disturbed even the most pugnacious imperialists. Queen Victoria, ordinarily a hard-liner in imperial matters, remarked to Prime Minister Salisbury that "a war for so miserable and small an object is what I could hardly consent to." Yet at the height of the crisis war orders were sent to the English fleet in the Mediterranean. France, lacking comparable naval forces in the region, and holding a position at Fashoda that was, in Kitchener's words by telegraph to London, "as impossible as it is absurd," backed down. The crisis, which bore a close resemblance to others of the period—in Morocco, in Siam, in China—was one of many clear but unheeded warnings that confrontations in out-of-the-way places could push the world toward a pointless, global catastrophe.

The event in Europe that illustrated the same widening abyss between military and political logic was the negotiation, four years earlier, of the Franco-Russian alliance, forged to counter the growing power of Germany, which was allied with Austria and Italy. The treaty's aims, as the American diplomat and scholar George Kennan observes in his book *The Fateful Alliance*, were solely to win a war with Germany, and the treaty made no mention of any political object of the fighting. Instead, its provisions simply stated that if either power were attacked, no matter what the reason, the other would come to its aid by launching all-out war.

The framers of the treaty seem to have learned everything that Clausewitz had to say about the requirements of absolute war but nothing of what he said about the need to subordinate war to the goals of policy. In a state paper that laid the foundation for the treaty, Russian adjutant general Nikolai Obruchev observed, "Once we have been drawn into a war, we cannot conduct that war otherwise than with all our forces, and against all our neighbors. In the face of the readiness of entire peoples to go to war, no other sort of war can be envisaged than the most decisive sort." Not only must the war be total but it must be instantaneous. "The term 'mobilization' must now signify the inauguration of military operations themselves," Obruchev wrote. Therefore, once war had begun, "further diplomatic hesitation is impermissible." Would the diplomats and the statesmen at least have an opportunity to decide on political goals for the war *before* embarking on it? Not according to Obruchev. War against "all neighbors" meant that even partial mobilization by any member of the opposing alliance would have to be met with an immediate, full-scale attack on the entire alliance, for "it is hard to conceive that any war beginning on the continent could be limited to an isolated struggle between any two states."

The politicians undertaking the agreement apparently did not see a need to specify any war aims. The Russian foreign minister, Nikolai Giers, asked Czar Alexander III what the purpose of victory over Germany would be, and the Czar answered, "What we would gain would be that Germany, as such, would disappear." And when General Raoul Mouton de Boisdeffre, the principal architect of the treaty on the French side, was asked what France's intentions regarding Germany would be after a victory, he replied, "Let us begin by beating them; after that it will be easy." Regarding the war's aim, Kennan concluded, "There is no evidence, in fact, that it had ever been discussed between the two governments."

In the Fashoda crisis and the Franco-Russian treaty, we catch two glimpses of a world in which, though peace still reigned, military victory had become an end in itself. The logic of politics had not been merely challenged by the logic of war, it had been shut out completely. The war that now threatened had become the senseless thing that Clausewitz had once feared: "a complete, untrammeled, absolute manifestation of violence" that would "drive policy out of office and rule by the laws of its own nature."

The causes of war now arose not so much from political differences as from the structure of the war system itself—from each country's fear that, if war broke out, some small advantage won by a speedier or better-prepared rival would tip the scales of victory and defeat. When war did come in 1914, it fit this description exactly. It exhibited the grotesque disproportion foreshadowed by the Fashoda crisis and the Franco-Russian treaty. The immediate cause of war—the political fortunes of the small state of Serbia in southeastern Europe—was of negligible intrinsic importance to the great powers, but once the full machinery of the global system was mobilized for battle, the slaughter proved unstoppable until a true Clausewitzian victory had been won by the Allied forces. Nations that had no direct stake in the fortunes of Serbia—England, for example—suffered millions of casualties. As the war historian John Keegan has observed, "The war's political objects—difficult enough to define in the first place—were forgotten. . . . Politics played no part in the conduct of the First World War worth mentioning."

The statesmen of 1914 were notoriously unaware how bloody and protracted total war would be. Most believed that the fighting would last only a few months. One reason was that they saw at least three of the four great modern forces that had fed the war machine—science, democracy, and industry—chiefly as motors of human progress. They identified these forces with the advance of civilization, not its downfall. Even imperialism, in such bad repute later, was touted then as an advance guard of the "three Cs": civilization, Christianity, and commerce.

Among military men, however, the idea that war in Europe could only be total was widespread. In France, Marshal Foch, soon to command the French forces, was saying, "You must henceforth go to the limits to find the aim of war. Since the vanquished party now never yields before it has been deprived of all means of reply, what you have to aim at is the destruction of those very means of reply." From a Clausewitzian point of view, such a statement, which left political goals out of military calculations, was folly. But was it in fact baseless? The advocates of total war, who were ready to unleash war over a Fashoda and did so over Serbia, have often been blamed. Several generations of historians have accused them of losing a sense of proportion—"of forgetting that force should be used in amounts commensurate to the purpose at hand, no more, no less," in Kennan's words. Given the pressures of the adapt-or-die war system, however, was it realistic to expect nations to exercise restraint?

Attempts to reach disarmament agreements, such as the Anglo-German naval discussions of 1912, almost invariably failed; and unilateral restraints were as unthinkable for patriotic publics as they were for governments. Which country, in the name of preserving a peace that might shortly break down, dared to be the one to stop its armies short of a Fashoda or a Sarajevo and let the enemy plant his flag there first, or rest content with a smaller naval gun, or fix a slower timetable for mobilization, or reject an alliance with another power in the face of mortal peril from a third and fourth? And when war did come, was it possible *then,* in the midst of unprecedented slaughter, to *reintroduce* political calculations, and bring the fighting under control? Once the tremendous twentieth-century war machines had been assembled and hurled at one another, was it likely, or even conceivable, that they could be used in a refined, controlled manner—like Clausewitz's handy rapier—to adjudicate such modest, or even trifling, issues as the future of this or that African swamp or Balkan backwater? History famously discloses no alternatives, but the military history of the entire twentieth century strongly suggests that, whatever theorists might have recommended, the modern war machines, once built, had to be used to the full or left unused. Since 1870, no great powers have fought "limited" wars directly against one another (although many have fought small powers). They have fought total war or they have not fought at all.

The Collapse of Weakness

The First World War was a watershed not only for war but for the civilization that produced it. Europe, without quite knowing what it was doing, had for more than a century been pouring the awesome energies of modernity into the war system, and the result was the catastrophe of 1914. Now the influence between war and society started to run in the opposite direction, shaping the domestic life of nations, above all in ravaged Russia and Germany, which, in the wake of defeat and anarchy, soon gave birth to the Bolshevik and Nazi regimes. Meanwhile, the technology of war kept improving. By 1918, the democratic revolution—which had galvanized people, fueled the conscription of millions of young men into the armies, and propelled them to the front to die—had contributed all it had to offer to the war system. Mutinies in the French and Russian armies in the last years of the war had even suggested a limit to popular endurance for patriotic gore. The art of harnessing industry to war had been mastered. Imperialism likewise had reached its high tide. Science and industry, however, had much yet to give. The decades ahead would witness the development of tanks, more powerful explosives, and air forces, including long-range bombers, rockets, radar, and aircraft carriers, to name just a few of technology's new contributions to war. After the First World War, the biologist J. B. S. Haldane recollected his wartime experience with artillery and poison gas this way:

> Through a blur of dust and fumes there appear, quite suddenly, great black and yellow masses of smoke which seem to be tearing up the surface of the earth and disintegrating the works of man with an almost visible hatred. These form the chief parts of the picture, but somewhere in the middle distance one can see a few irrelevant-looking human figures, and soon there are fewer. It is hard to believe that these are the protagonists in the battle. One would rather choose those huge substantive oily black masses which are much more conspicuous, and suppose that the men are in reality their servants, and playing an inglorious, subordinate and fatal part in the combat. It is possible, after all, that this view is correct.

In *Weapons and Hope,* the physicist Freeman Dyson comments that observations such as this, which he absorbed as a child, led him and many of his friends in the interwar years to regard technology as "a malevolent monster broken loose from human control." Technology, however, had no will of its own, and to think that it did people had to hide from themselves the human wills that were in fact propelling it. We know who they were—the scientists who developed the technology and the statesmen and generals who ordered its use. And yet in a sense Haldane and Dyson were right, because these people lacked the discretion, except at terrible risk to their nations, to forgo the new inventions of war. They were as thoroughly trapped on the treadmill of the modern adapt-or-die war system as the soldiers in the trenches.

All the new inventions were used to the full in the Second World War, in which an estimated seventy million human beings were killed. But it was the last time. Even as the war was being fought, an instrument that would make such wars forever impossible was being prepared in the desert of New Mexico. Never has a single technical invention had a more sudden or profound effect on an entrenched human institution than nuclear weapons have had on war. For war was a paradoxical freak of evolution: a creature that depended for its survival on that unsung virtue of arms, their weakness—without which war's critical event, its gift to politics, defeat, could not occur. But human weakness, in the twentieth century, proved a dwindling asset. Like clean air, rain forests, stratospheric ozone, and passenger pigeons, it was being steadily depleted by technical progress. In July of 1945, it ran out. The logic of total war had carried its practitioners to the brink of a destination, the far side of human existence, to which the logic of politics could never follow. For politics was a human activity, and in the post-nuclear landscape there might be no human beings. The bomb revealed that total war was not an everlasting but a historical phenomenon. It had gone the way of the tyrannosaurus rex and the saber-toothed tiger, a casualty not of natural but scientific evolution, whose new powers, as always, the war system could not refuse. Its day was done.

2

"Nuclear War"

The atomic bomb that destroyed Hiroshima reverberated in every domain of human existence. It placed the human species at risk of extinction by its own hand. It signaled a reversal in the balance of power between humankind and nature, placing nature in jeopardy from human depradation. It threw into doubt the moral faith on which all civilization must be based—that the collective efforts of human beings will make life better than it otherwise would have been. But in our present context its most important consequence was that it rendered the global war system unworkable beyond any hope of repair. The new state of affairs was recognized by a succession of leaders of the nuclear powers. As early as 1952, President Harry Truman said, in his farewell broadcast to the nation, "Starting an atomic war is totally unthinkable for rational men." At the height of the Cuban missile crisis, the chairman of the Communist Party of the Soviet Union, Nikita S. Khrushchev, acknowledged in a letter to President John F. Kennedy that only "lunatics or suicides, who themselves want to perish and to destroy the whole world before they die," would start a nuclear war. The clearinghouse of the adapt-or-die war system, where the powers of the modern age were cashed in for the universal currency of military power, was abruptly closed for business at the global level. The vast set-piece battles that had long been history's favorite grand decision-making device sank into the past. (Where they did occur—between Iran and Iraq in the 1980s, or between Ethiopia and Eritrea in the nineties—they seemed anachronistic, as "backward" as the countries that were waging them.) Industrialists might still offer their products, scientists their inventions, and citizens their patriotic zeal, but now their contributions could only increase overkill—"strengthen our deterrent," or some such. The critical link between military power and political power, which Clausewitz had struggled to preserve, was severed at the highest level of international operations.

The most obvious solution to the new predicament was to abolish nuclear weapons, or even to liquidate the entire disabled war system. And in fact abolition was proposed by President Truman's representative to the United Nations, Bernard Baruch, in June of 1946. He asked the world to join with the United States in placing all nuclear facilities under international inspection and control and restricting their use to peaceful purposes. The Soviet Union rejected the proposal, and put forward one of its own, which the United States in turn rejected. Liquidation of the whole war system was attempted with the foundation of the United Nations. The U.N.'s central mechanism for peacekeeping was to be a system of collective security enforced by the powers that had just won the Second World War, all of whom were given permanent memberships on the Security Council and a right to veto its decisions. The operations of the council were soon spoiled for these purposes by the onset of the Cold War, which rendered collective decision making in the council impossible. In 1949, the Soviet Union detonated its first atomic bomb.

The great powers of the Cold War now had to decide how to conduct their business in a world that was *not* going to replace the rule of force with the rule of law but instead *was* going to equip itself with nuclear arsenals. Their dilemma was that they could neither use the most powerful instruments of force now at their disposal nor get rid of them. The bomb had ruined war by transforming it into mutual annihilation. Now the most important question was whether humankind would live or die; but the military paralysis of the great powers also raised the separate question of how, in war's absence, international conflicts would be resolved. What would be the final arbiter now?

Never had war "arbitrated" the destinies of nations more sweepingly than in the first half of the twentieth century. The First World War had undone the three imperial dynasties of continental Europe, swept a multitude of national governments from power, and sharpened the appetite for self-determination in colonies around the world. The Second World War had given Hitler the mastery of Europe, then taken it back; subjected the peoples of Asia to Japanese rule and then released them; drawn the Soviet Union deep into Europe; drained the power of England even in victory, giving the coup de grâce to its global empire; and raised up the United States to global preeminence. And now the question had become how, if global war could no longer be fought, conflict in the global order would proceed. People who wanted to make things happen would have to search for other means; but what were they to be? Through what riverbeds would the streams of historical change flow, now that this ancient one was blocked? What were to be the instruments of power?

For human strife had not dried up in deference to the energy released from the atom. On the contrary, a classic global confrontation between two blocs inspired by hostile ideologies was taking shape. At the same time, anticolonial movements were in full flood around the world, and often intersected with the Cold War struggle. Sometimes, regional antagonists dragged the superpowers into their conflicts, and sometimes the superpowers, thwarted by nuclear terror from pursuing their military ambitions directly, deflected them into proxy regional struggles, which, now vested with apocalyptic significance, often escalated back up the military ladder to "the brink," threatening nuclear war. Hanging over the scene was the old fear that one of two great powers, if left unchecked, would dominate the world.

Nuclear strategy had little if anything to offer to the resolution of the burning political issues of the time. At best, the leaders of the day increasingly realized, nuclear arsenals could freeze a global stalemate in place. Even this goal, however, was hard to achieve. Preserving the status quo, after all, is not a modest goal for statesmanship. For almost half a century, for example, it was the primary mission of the Concert of Europe, established following the Congress of Vienna in the wake of Napoleon's defeat, and it has generally been the broad goal of balance-of-power policies wherever these have been practiced. Under the dominant strategic doctrine of the new age, nuclear deterrence, force thus still did in a sense "arbitrate," and on a global scale. That arbitration, however, could deliver only one monotonous verdict: no one can move a muscle, everything must remain as it is.

The question that remained was how nuclear weapons could achieve even this limited goal when they could not be used. A solution was attempted by turning the war system into a system of pure nuclear terror, to which the name "balance of terror" was soon attached. Terror had been employed for political ends from the time of King Scorpion on, and never more lavishly than during the first half of the twentieth century—a period that witnessed the rise of totalitarianism, which used terror as a mainstay of rule, and also the rise of "strategic bombing," whose explicit aim was not to destroy military targets but to break civilian morale. The destruction of Hiroshima was in fact the culmination of a series of destructions of cities by firebombing, in both Germany and Japan.

The nuclear terror of the Cold War nevertheless was categorically different from all previous terror. As a tactic in war, terror is the use of force against some people to intimidate others. A classic example was the Nazi practice in occupied countries of announcing their intention to execute ten or more political prisoners in their jails for every German soldier killed by resistance fighters. Nuclear terror, by contrast, is the paradoxical attempt to produce terror on a mass scale without actually using force—an idea embodied in nuclear deterrence. Under this strategy, military force was handed a role—to prevent its own use—that it had never previously played in the same way before.

The doctrine, which took shape in the 1950s, became the declared policy of the United States in the 1960s, then won a partial, grudging acceptance by the Soviet Union, and went on to become the basis for the first nuclear-arms-control negotiations. According to its central tenet, each side would be stopped from attacking the other by the knowledge that it would be annihilated in return. Historically, military forces had been employed as often to deter war as to fight it. Military leaders had long been fond of the old Roman saying "If you seek peace, prepare for war." But that proposition had in fact been a mere corollary of another, which was too obvious for aphoristic expression: If you seek to fight and win wars, prepare for war. It was this second proposition that the bomb nullified. Seeking war made no sense when war to the finish meant annihilation for all involved. A new proposition, appropriate to the nuclear age, was articulated as early as 1946 by, among others, the American military analyst Bernard Brodie. He wrote, "Thus far the chief purpose of a military establishment has been to win wars. From now on its chief purpose must be to avert them. It can have no other useful purpose." The same argument was put forward by Winston Churchill, when he made his famed remark "It may be that we shall by a process of sublime irony have reached a stage in this story where safety will be the sturdy child of terror, and survival the twin brother of annihilation." Even though the system of nuclear terror was no longer a war system, it was still, let us stress, a system based on force; that is, force had not been exchanged for obedience to law, or for any form of willing cooperation. It was the way in which force was to be exploited that had changed.

If in the new system the *unleashed* force was no longer the final arbiter, we need to ask, then what, exactly, was? The answer was that there occurred a sweeping displacement of military conflicts from theaters of actual combat to a theater of appearances. The battles that *could not* be fought physically were to be fought out instead on psychological terrain. To borrow Clausewitz's concepts again, it was as if the policy makers wanted to achieve their opponents' moral defeat without passing through the stage of physical defeat. Clausewitz had written that "the destruction of the enemy's force underlies all military actions; all plans are ultimately based on it, resting on it like an arch on its abutment." He added, "The decision by arms is for all major and minor operations in war what cash payment is in commerce. Regardless how complex the relationship between the two parties, regardless how rarely settlements actually occur, they can never be entirely absent." But trying to preserve credit—or, in that much-used term of the nuclear age, "credibility"—without ever having to make the cash payment (engaging in nuclear war) was exactly the feat that the superpowers were attempting.

Nuclear credibility—the appearance of a readiness to use nuclear weapons when the chips were down—was a compound of several elements. One was obviously possession of a nuclear arsenal. A second was the readiness to use it. But these were entirely useless without an essential, if strangely intangible, third element, the *appearance* of having the first two. Creating this appearance was therefore *the* essential requirement of nuclear policy. Even with an arsenal in hand, however, creating the desired appearance was no simple matter, considering the suicidal consequences of performing the terrible deed; and a central—almost an obsessive—preoccupation of the Cold War leaders was with making people believe that they possessed the doubtful will to carry out their nuclear threats.

Such demonstrations were necessarily racked with contradictions, all of which were variations on a theme: under no circumstances could the act that gave the deterrent threat its effectiveness—namely, the actual launching of a nuclear attack—make any sense. The operational puzzle was what to do "if deterrence failed." It was a question without a reasonable answer, for it can never be in the interest of a country to perform an act (fighting a nuclear war) whose prevention is itself the goal of its policy. All of which is only a complicated way of saying that it could never make sense for the two rivals to blow themselves off the face of the earth.

In practice, the problem was solved by knowledge on all sides that, whether retaliation was rational or not, it was likely to happen. "The essence of the problem is the difficulty of attaching any rationality whatsoever to the initiation of a chain of events that could well end in the utter devastation of one's own society (even assuming indifference to the fate of the enemy society)," the historian of nuclear strategy Lawrence Freedman has written. "The resulting sense of an enormous bluff is, however, more likely to worry those relying on these threats . . . than those against whom they are directed." He concludes, "The Emperor Deterrence may have no clothes, but he is still Emperor." The mighty sword, curiously, had turned into a mere picture of a mighty sword. Freedman suggested that the Emperor Deterrence had no clothes, but considering the primacy of appearances in nuclear policy, it would perhaps be more appropriate to say that the clothes had no emperor. What this meant in practice can be illustrated by the most perilous episode of the Cold War—the Cuban missile crisis.

A Crisis of Appearances

By the time of the crisis, the peculiar new rules of the nuclear game were in full force, and the progress of the crisis reveals them in operation. On Sunday, October 13, 1962, American U-2 spy aircraft discovered Soviet nuclear-missile sites under construction in Cuba. On Monday, October 22, after a week of secret deliberations, President Kennedy made the fact known in a television address to the American people, and announced that he had imposed a naval quarantine on military goods being sent to Cuba, and was demanding the removal of the missiles. He made clear that the stakes in the crisis were total when he warned that any launch of nuclear weapons from Cuba would be met with "a full retaliatory response upon the Soviet Union," and, in a sentence that summed up the dilemma at the heart of policy in the nuclear age, stated, "We will not prematurely or unnecessarily risk the costs of worldwide nuclear war in which even the fruits of victory would be ashes in our mouth—but neither will we shrink from that risk at any time it must be faced."

Khrushchev's reasons for the deployment were unclear to Kennedy and his advisers. Secretary of Defense Robert McNamara flatly stated to the president that the missiles in Cuba would not materially alter the balance of strategic nuclear power. Most of Kennedy's other advisers agreed. What were Khrushchev's motives, then? Something like a consensus on this matter has subsequently emerged among historians. In the first place, Khrushchev saw the deployment as a means to protect Cuba against a repeat of the kind of attack that the United States had mounted at the Bay of Pigs to overthrow the socialist government of Fidel Castro in 1961, shortly after Kennedy had arrived in office. In the second place, he sought to redress a nuclear imbalance that favored the United States. In the late 1950s and early 1960s, the United States outmatched the Soviet Union in nuclear striking power. In 1960, for example, the United States possessed six thousand nuclear warheads, the Soviet Union three hundred. Of these, only a fraction were mounted on the Soviet Union's mere thirty-five missiles capable of reaching the United States. Khrushchev of course knew this, although during the presidential campaign of 1960 Senator Kennedy had erroneously claimed that it was the

United States that suffered from a "missile gap" with the Soviet Union. For a while the error suited the needs of Khrushchev, who was not only aware of his country's nuclear inferiority but afraid that the Americans would use it to advantage. He adopted a policy of bluster and bluff. In August of 1961, the head of the K.G.B., Aleksandr Shelepin, had proposed to an enthusiastic Khrushchev that the U.S.S.R. launch a campaign of disinformation to persuade the United States that its nuclear forces were more powerful than in fact they were. Khrushchev also threatened intermittently to shut off Western access to Berlin and, if the United States should oppose him, to annihilate its European allies. On one occasion, for example, he noted that six hydrogen bombs would be "quite enough" to destroy the British Isles, and nine would be enough for France. "Why should two hundred million people die for two million Berliners?" he asked.

Once in office, the Kennedy administration discovered, or feigned to discover, that there was no missile gap—or, rather, that there was one and it overwhelmingly favored the United States. In a speech delivered by Undersecretary of Defense Roswell Gilpatric in October of 1961, the administration set forth the facts. "The destructive power which the United States could bring to bear even after a Soviet surprise attack upon our forces," he stated, "would be as great as, perhaps greater than, the total undamaged force which the enemy can threaten to launch against the United States in a first strike." Now Khrushchev's bluff had been publicly called. One of his responses was to detonate the largest hydrogen bomb ever exploded on earth to date or since—a monster that unleashed fifty megatons of explosive power, equivalent to almost four thousand Hiroshima bombs. Another response may have been the decision to place nuclear-armed missiles in Cuba.

Kennedy's national security adviser, McGeorge Bundy, later noted that the administration he served did not believe that its immense nuclear superiority was a source of great political advantage. At the time of the missile crisis, American officials were more impressed, Bundy believed, by the tens of millions of casualties that the Soviet Union *could* cause than by the imbalance in the two countries' nuclear arsenals. Hence they were blind to the danger that Khrushchev, thinking the U.S.S.R. weak, might take reckless action to redress the inequality.

This persuasive account of the origins of the Cuban missile crisis illustrates the novel rules of the game in a nuclear-armed world. Only in the nuclear age could it be considered reckless for a great power to publicly expose the weakness of its adversary. For only in an age in which appearances in military matters take precedence over actualities would an inequality of forces *in fact* appear far more tolerable to the weaker side than an inequality of forces *in appearance*.

The resolution of the crisis teaches the same lesson. Khrushchev, perhaps without quite knowing it, had breached the rules of the game in a nuclear-armed world. He had taken a step that, in his adversary's eyes, threatened fatal damage to its own credibility. And yet reversal of that step would threaten *Soviet* credibility. The logic of credibility, once this situation had arisen, pointed toward war; but war in the nuclear age, as Kennedy and Khrushchev were aware, was senseless.

At the height of the crisis, Khrushchev wrote in his memoirs, he privately asked his generals if they could assure him "that holding fast would not result in the death of five hundred million human beings." He went on to report, "They looked at me as though I was out of my mind or, what was worse, a traitor. The biggest tragedy, as they saw it, was not that our country might be devastated and everything lost, but that the Chinese or the Albanians would accuse us of appeasement or weakness." He was led to wonder, "What good would it have done me in the last hour of my life to know that, though our great nation and the United States were in complete ruin, the national honor of the Soviet Union was intact?" Khrushchev's recollection of his fit of sanity in insane circumstances goes to the heart of the contradiction inherent in the nuclear policies of the Cold War era. On the one side of the nuclear ledger was the need to uphold "national honor," or credibility. This required shows of resolve, even military action. On the other side was the threat to the lives of hundreds of millions of human beings. This required restraint. The main aims that nuclear arsenals were meant to serve—preventing war and pursuing national interests—were now in collision, and one, it seemed, had to be given up.

In a parallel episode, Kennedy at a certain moment took his aide Pierre Salinger outside the room in which the Executive Committee dealing with the crisis was meeting, and asked him whether he thought the people inside realized that if he made a mistake there might be two hundred million dead. It's striking that both leaders felt so alone in their terrible knowledge that they were able to communicate it only in side conversations, or later in their memoirs. Perhaps Kennedy at that moment remembered some advice given him a few months earlier by former secretary of state Dean Acheson regarding the use of nuclear weapons in the Berlin crisis of 1961. Acheson counseled that "the president should himself give that question [whether to use nuclear weapons in a crisis in Europe] the most careful and private consideration, well before the time when the choice might present itself, that he should reach his own clear conclusion in advance as to what he would do, and that he should tell no one at all what that conclusion was." Bundy, who was present, drew the obvious conclusion: that Acheson, "The most ardent and eloquent advocate of energetic action to make nuclear risk credible to Khrushchev, a true believer in fighting hard with strong conventional forces for the freedom of West Berlin, nevertheless believed that at the moment of final choice, the course of 'wisdom and restraint' might be to accept local defeat without the use of nuclear weapons." What is notable about the story is that at the hour of truth the decision not to use nuclear weapons—certainly the most important that any president would ever make—had to be such a deep secret that even the man giving the recommendation to him in a private meeting dared not utter it in plain English. All *public* counsel, all statements of theory and policy, including, most especially, those made by the president, had to support the use of nuclear weapons. To do otherwise would be unilateral disarmament by verbal means. Only the president's private resolve, never to be spoken aloud—frail refuge of sanity, of safety for all humankind!—could counsel restraint. National leaders have often spoken of the loneliness of the decisions they must make. Surely, no decision could ever be lonelier than this.

Later, Kennedy formulated the quandary in which the Cuban missile crisis had placed him no less succinctly than Khrushchev had, and in almost identical terms. He and his advisers were well aware that the Cuban missiles did not change the strategic balance of power significantly. But, Kennedy explained, "it would have politically changed the balance of power. It would have appeared to, and appearances contribute to reality."

How, then, did Kennedy and Khrushchev escape war? The answer, in a word, was *secrecy.* If appearances—of soiled honor, of "weakness," of lost credibility, of lack of resolve, of humiliation in the eyes of Albanians, and so forth—were the problem, then what better solution than to hide the facts that might create those appearances? Khrushchev was the first to resort to this method. He sent two messages to Kennedy—one public, the other private. In the private message—a long, secret, personal letter expressing in vivid terms his horror of nuclear war and his determination to avoid it—he offered a deal in which the Soviet missiles in Cuba would be removed in exchange for a promise by the United States not to invade the island. This was highly acceptable to the United States. However, in his public stance, made known the next day, Khrushchev added a crucial condition—he demanded the removal of American missiles stationed near the Soviet Union in Turkey. While in private Khrushchev could afford to seem "weak," in public he had to appear "tough."

The administration had planned to remove the Turkish missiles soon in any case. Couldn't it simply go ahead with the plan as part of the settlement? The problem was credibility. The actual strategic position of the United States would not be harmed by the removal of the Turkish missiles. However, any public decision for removal under pressure of the Soviet deployment in Cuba would harm U.S. credibility, especially with its NATO allies.

Now it was the United States' turn to take refuge in secret assurances. The president resorted to the ploy of ignoring Khrushchev's tough, public stand while seeking to agree to the more moderate, private one. That was Kennedy's public position—a tough-seeming one, since it yielded no ground on the Turkish missiles. However, like Khrushchev, he also put forward a "weak" private position: he gave in on the Turkish missiles. But he did so only on condition that the concession remain forever secret. Keeping the missiles in Turkey, however useless militarily, had been declared American policy. Invading Cuba had not. Therefore, giving the no-invasion pledge would leave American credibility intact, while removing the missiles would undermine it.

This consideration illuminates an extraordinary action now taken by President Kennedy and a few officials of his administration. Without telling the whole Executive Committee what they were doing, they traded away the Turkish missiles in a back-channel deal. Then they took a vow of silence regarding the secret agreement, demanding and receiving assurances that the Soviets would do the same. We may suspect that the reason was domestic politics, especially when we recall that at a meeting of the Executive Committee McNamara said, "I'll be quite frank: I don't think there *is* a military problem here. . . . This is a domestic political problem." And unquestionably politics was on the minds of the president and his advisers, who feared Republican charges that they were "soft on Communism." But the dictates of high strategy seconded the requirements of domestic politics. In his speech to the nation on October 22, the president had confirmed the crucial geopolitical role of credibility in his thinking when he referred to the placement of the missiles in Cuba as an "unjustified change in the status quo which cannot be accepted by this country if our courage and our commitment are ever to be trusted again by either friend or foe." In a world in which appearances were not an afterthought of policy but its substance, the president and his advisers felt compelled to make their decisions on the basis not of the actual strategic balance but of what it looked like to the world at large.

From beginning to end of the crisis, the president and his advisers never deviated from this iron rule. When the Soviet ambassador, Anatoly Dobrynin, later gave Robert Kennedy a letter expressing his government's agreement to the Turkish missile deal in writing, Kennedy angrily handed it back, saying (according to Kennedy's notes of talking points for the conversation), "Take your letter—Reconsider it & if you feel it is necessary to write letters then we will also write one which you cannot enjoy. Also if you should publish any document indicating a deal then it is off & also if done afterward will further affect the relationship." The Soviets withdrew the letter, and the vow of secrecy was kept on both sides for years afterward.

The ingenuity, if not the propriety, of this bigovernmental conspiracy of silence against the rest of the world is remarkable. At first glance, it might appear that by agreeing to the American demand for secrecy Khrushchev was permitting the United States to preserve its credibility at the expense of his own—no small concession, given the central role that credibility played at all moments in the crisis on both sides. Certainly, Khrushchev was widely perceived by the general public as having backed down without having received much in return. In assessing this question, however, it is important to remember that credibility is an impression made by one party on another. Its value depends on the audience you wish to impress. In the case of the United States that audience included America's allies as well as congressional and public opinion. The record shows that the Kennedy men were particularly worried about the response of NATO to a deal to surrender the Turkish missiles. Secrecy regarding the deal preserved American credibility with its crucial audiences. Khrushchev, who presided over a closed society, on the other hand, needed to maintain his credibility with a much smaller audience: high party members, generals, and the leaders of a few independent-minded communist parties. No congress or public would review his decisions. And no allied government other than the Chinese and Albanian communist parties was in a position to second-guess him. Only his immediate colleagues (who did in fact remove him from power in 1964) were a danger. Khrushchev sent his first, "weak" letter privately but drafted his second, "tough" one in front of the Politburo. With this all-important audience, who knew that Kennedy had yielded on the Turkish missiles, therefore, Khrushchev's credibility might well be preserved. As for the world at large, Khrushchev would have to make do with an American pledge not to invade Cuba.

Two years later, Robert McNamara was asked at a congressional committee hearing, "Are you aware of any agreement, any assurance, by yourself or anyone else in high government office, to Khrushchev that if he would withdraw at the time under the conditions that you showed us, the United States would thereby commit itself to any particular course of action?" McNamara answered, "I am not only unaware of any agreement, it is inconceivable to me that our President would enter in a discussion of any such agreement. Moreover, there were absolutely no undisclosed agreements associated with the withdrawal of the Soviet missiles from Cuba." In calling the decision that the president had actually taken "inconceivable," McNamara kept the administration's vow of secrecy, and gave powerful evidence of the primacy of appearances in the strategies of the nuclear age.

Even if we are critical of this conspiracy of silence, *which included the Soviet government while excluding the American people*, we can still admire the dexterity with which both Khrushchev and

Kennedy extricated themselves from a logic that pushed both of them toward annihilation. Precisely because the most important moves had been made in secret, however, that logic remained unimpaired and in full force throughout the years of the Cold War, though without producing any further crises as severe as the Cuban missile crisis. It's a sobering commentary on the nuclear policy to which the two men were committed that their most statesmanlike decisions were those they had to hide most assiduously from the world.

The shift from the primacy of force to the primacy of appearances was momentous in the history of war. It signified a real, if equivocal, official recognition that the age-old war system had become an anachronism. The true targets of the missiles of the nuclear age have, in the more than half century since Nagasaki, been the minds, not the bodies, of opponents. The true instruments of this warfare have been not actual warheads flying across oceans but the images of those warheads conveyed in public statements and in the media. And the goal of policy, however shot through with contradiction and apocalyptic danger, was to head off war, not to fight it.

The gap between the political ends of foreign policy and the military logic of strategy that had been growing steadily since Clausewitz's time had widened to the point of no return. And if, possibly, the benefits of nuclear deterrence were real, in that a peace that otherwise might have broken down was preserved, so was its unremitting, intolerable cost: that, day by day, it risked the extinction of the human species and involved all the nuclear powers and their peoples in the complicity of actively planning for this supreme crime. But was there some other final arbiter—some method whereby freedom of action would be restored? To answer this question, we need to examine a military development that ran parallel to the nuclear revolution—the rise of people's war.

3

People's War

The ascending spiral of violence in which Clausewitzian war, driven by its own "logical" need to run to extremes, drew the new-born Promethean energies of the modern age, one after another, into its mighty orbit—leading, in a paradoxical culmination, to the terrorized calm of the nuclear stalemate—was one of the two major developments in the metamorphosis of war in the modern age. The second, concurrent development led in an opposite direction: away from the blackboards and computer screens in the superpowers' think tanks, scientific laboratories, and missile ranges, where they pursued ever-more-costly, technically elaborate methods of war, and down into poor, "underdeveloped" peasant villages and remote swamps and jungles, where scientifically unsophisticated people were incubating methods of warfare that, in their own way, were scarcely less "absolute" than the total war of the great powers and, in the long run, were to prove the more successful invention. These were the methods of people's war. If, to anticipate, nuclear weapons, by spoiling the old final arbiter, conventional war, posed the question of how disputes in the international sphere were *now* to be settled, then people's war, though not itself yet the answer the world needed, pointed the way to an answer. For while nuclear weapons were producing stalemate people's war was changing the political map of the earth.

The World Revolt

Like the invention of nuclear weapons, the rise of people's war has a wider context—the centuries-long movement of the peoples of the earth to achieve self-determination. Some rebellions were of colonies in revolt against a mother country, some were of nations with long histories of battling conquerors, and some were of indigenous populations oppressed by imperial overlords. The guiding principle of all of them, however, was to drive out a hated occupier and establish rule by local people—the "self" of the word "self-determination." The freedom to which a movement for self-determination aspired was *sometimes* freedom of the individual; it was *always* freedom of the national, collective self from foreign rule. The period in question is roughly the same as that of the democratic revolution, of which the self-determination movement has been a part.

As its beginning we can plausibly name July 4, 1776, when the American Continental Congress declared to the world that the American people meant to "assume among the powers of the earth the separate and equal station to which the laws of nature and nature's God entitled them." It was also in the American Revolution that a form of people's war, the use of militias, made its first appearance in an anti-imperial cause of modern times. Some years later, one of the signers of the declaration, John Adams, looking toward what would prove a distant future, asked, "When will France, Spain, England and Holland renounce their selfish, contracted, exclusive systems of religion, government, and commerce?" And he answered with a prophecy: "They may depend upon it, their present systems of colonization cannot endure. Colonies universally, ardently breathe for independence. No man who has a soul will ever live in a colony under the present establishments one moment longer than necessity compels him."

Substantial fulfillment of Adams's prophecy came in August of 1991, when the president of Russia, Boris Yeltsin, and the presidents of two other republics of the Soviet Union declared the foundation of the Commonwealth of Independent States and the dissolution of the Soviet Union, the last of the European empires. Between 1776 and that date, all the empires that had existed, whether dynastic, colonial, or both, and all the territorial empires that subsequently arose, including those built on revolutionary foundations, were destroyed. In the former category were the Russian empire of the czars; the Austro-Hungarian Empire of the Hapsburgs; the German empire of the Hohenzollerns; the Ottoman Empire; and the colonial empires of Holland, England, France, Belgium, Spain, and Italy. In the latter category were the Napoleonic empire in the early nineteenth century, the Japanese "Co-Prosperity Sphere" in Asia in the 1930s and forties, Hitler's "thousand-year Reich," and the Soviet empire. (I leave until later the special case of the mainly nonterritorial empire of the United States that arose in the second half of the twentieth century.)

Broadly speaking, the peoples of the earth assumed their "rightful stations" in three waves. The first, which followed soon after the American War of Independence, commenced when the victims of Napoleon's imperial ambitions, including Clausewitz's Prussia, threw off the French yoke, giving birth, in the process, to a fullfledged conservative nationalism that would be replicated in various versions down to our time. It continued until the First World War, when the last of the great European monarchies fell. The example of the nation-states of Europe, in which peoples created states, or else the states created peoples, and in which both were wedded to a precisely defined, jealously defended national territory, became the model for the subsequent waves. Concurrently, the Spanish empire, an early victim of the anticolonial rebellion, was overthrown by the Latin American peoples.

In the second wave, which lasted roughly from 1905, when Japan defeated Russia, until the mid-1970s, when Portugal gave up its empire in Africa, the rest of the peoples of the European colonies and dependencies rose up, in what Leonard Woolf called a "world revolt," to liberate themselves from their Western (and Japanese) masters. Combining imitation with resistance, they adopted whatever they needed of European ideas and techniques to drive the Europeans out. In the nineteenth century, even as the nations of Europe were learning democracy at home, they had been practicing its opposite in the world at large. Their philosophy in the colonies was, on the whole, that of Lord Milner, the English proconsul in Egypt in the 1880s, who wrote in his *England in Egypt* that although, "As a true born Briton, I of course take off my hat to everything that calls itself Franchise, Parliament, Representation of the People, the Voice of the Majority, and all the rest of it," nevertheless, "as an observer of the actual condition of Egyptian society, I cannot shut my eyes to the fact that popular government, as we understand it, is for a longer time than anyone can foresee at present out of the question." Or, as Kipling, describing his vision of imperial rule, wrote approvingly of the English:

> They terribly carpet the earth with dead,
>   and before their cannons cool,
> They walk unarmed by twos and threes,
>   to call the living to school.

As this picture of massacre as a prelude to educational uplift suggests, the imperial policies of the European democracies were founded on a thoroughgoing contradiction. Claiming democracy and national independence, they denied it to the colonial peoples, who unsurprisingly resolved the contradiction in favor of independence.

In the third wave of self-determination, which occurred suddenly, as if the accumulated experience of the anti-imperial movements were now being applied in a hurry, the peoples of Eastern Europe and of the Soviet Union rose up against the Soviet empire, which, like a dynasty of old, departed the stage of history entirely.

The self-determination movement cut across all political dividing lines. No political system, feudal or modern, proved capable of resisting it. Neither monarchies (the Romanovs, the Hapsburgs, the Hohenzollerns, the Ottomans, Spain) nor liberal democracies (England, Holland, the United States) nor military dictatorships (France under Napoleon, Portugal under Salazar and Caetano) nor communist regimes (the Soviet Union; Vietnam, in its Cambodian venture) were able, in the long run, to perpetuate colonial rule. On the other hand, almost every political creed was adequate for winning independence. Liberal democracy (the United States in 1776, Eastern Europe in the 1980s and nineties), communism (China, Vietnam, Cambodia), racism (the Boers of South Africa), militarism (many South American states), theocracy (Iran and Afghanistan in the 1980s), and even monarchy (Germany in the first half of the nineteenth century), have all proved adequate foundations on which to base self-determination.

The methods of the movements were as diverse as their contents. Some resorted to military force (the United States, China, Vietnam, Algeria, to name only four); some were nonviolent (India, the nations of Eastern Europe, with the exceptions of Yugoslavia and Romania). Some arose from "below," after the pattern of the American and French revolutions, and some were led from "above," after the pattern of the foundation, under Bismarck, of modern Germany. Some won success overnight (the republics of the former Soviet Union), others so slowly that the process was almost imperceptible (Canada).

The independence of the countries of the world was not, on the whole, granted willingly but compelled. Even when independence was achieved by mutual agreement—as in India after the Second

World War—it was the result of decades of national struggle. The rulers of empires searched their tool kits of power in vain for the instruments that would bring rebellious colonial populations to heel—a lesson driven home once and for all by the failures of the United States in Vietnam and the Soviet Union in Afghanistan. The movement of resistance and reform in Eastern Europe and the Soviet Union, in the third wave, placed the power of popular resistance on even clearer display. Their victories posed in the sharpest possible form the question that the entire two-century-long movement for self-determination has put before the world: What power has enabled poorly armed or unarmed or entirely nonviolent popular movements to defeat the military forces of the most powerful empires of the past two centuries?

A Transformation of Politics

Although people's war was above all a phenomenon of the twentieth century, it first appeared in Europe during the peninsular war of 1807–14, in which the Spanish people mounted fierce resistance to Napoleonic conquest. (This is the war whose savagery is recorded in the work of Francisco Goya.) As it happens, Clausewitz devoted only one brief section of *On War* to people's war, but in those few pages he recognized the novelty and importance of the new kind of conflict. Guerrilla war per se (the Spanish rebellion gave the world this Spanish word) was not a new phenomenon. In the eighteenth century, it had been called *la petite guerre,* and before that, among other things, Parthian war, after the Parthians of antiquity, who were given to hit-and-run attacks on horseback. The unprecedented element in the early years of the nineteenth century was not guerrilla war but the sustained support given the guerrillas by the civilian population of the nation. Guerrilla bands took control of large areas of the Spanish countryside; waylaid French couriers, forcing them to travel with large armed guards; worked to deny the French supplies; harassed and attacked French troops; and spied on the French for the English. Just as important, they crippled the administration of Joseph Bonaparte by an organized refusal to pay taxes to his regime or otherwise cooperate with it. Soon, Joseph's administrators were going unpaid, his commands unfollowed. The French responded with draconian measures that would become all too familiar over the next two centuries: looting, rape, torture, burning of villages, wholesale executions and reprisals. The rebellion blazed most intensely in the city of Saragossa, where the population fought to "the last wall in the last house." "No supreme command had ordered the city to hold out; there was no supreme command. There was only the instinctive knowledge that a nation cannot keep its identity unless it is prepared to fight for it against all hope." Such was the new form of warfare that flared up in Spain—spontaneous, uncalculating, desperate, savage, unquenchable.

Clausewitz placed the new phenomenon in the wider context of the transformation of war that he was witnessing and analyzing. As examples of the "enormous contribution the heart and temper of a nation can make to the sum total of its politics, war potential, and fighting strength," he listed "the stubborn resistance of the Spaniards," which showed "what can be accomplished by arming a people"; the Russian campaign of 1812, which, by defeating Napoleon, showed that "eventual success does not always decrease in proportion to lost battles, captured capitals, and occupied provinces"; and the Prussian military recovery of 1813, which showed that a "militia can fight as well in foreign countries as at home." The recruitment of Napoleon's revolutionary armies had been Act I in the drama of the democratic revolution's influence on warfare, but now, with the Spanish guerrilla resistance to those armies, there was a second act. Clausewitz observed, "Clearly, the tremendous effects of the French Revolution abroad were caused not so much by new military methods and concepts as by radical changes in policies and administration, by the new character of government, altered conditions of the French people, and the like." He further explains:

> The military art on which the politicians relied was part of a world they thought was real—a branch of current statecraft, a familiar tool that had been in use for many years. But *that* form of war naturally shared in the errors of policy, and therefore could provide no corrective. It is true that war itself has undergone significant changes in character and methods, changes that had brought it closer to its absolute form. But these changes did not come about because the French government freed itself, so to speak, from the harness of policy; they were caused by the new political conditions which the French Revolution created.

In a word, "It follows that the transformation of the art of war resulted from the *transformation of politics.*"

There is no doubt that Clausewitz was right in seeing the French Revolution and the Spanish popular revolt as expressions of a single underlying phenomenon, the democratic revolution of his time. However, with the benefit of our century and a half of hindsight, it's clear that each was also the starting point for one of two long, diverging evolutionary transformations of war that led in different directions. The Prussian mobilization and reform, for example, aimed at raising vast armies of patriotic citizens in imitation of France, and so was a stage in the expansion of the conventional war system that led eventually to the nuclear stalemate of the Cold War. The commanders of conventional war had always wanted more men to fight with; now the "nation in arms" supplied men in unparalleled abundance. The commanders had always sought zealous, brave soldiers; now the recruits, fired by revolutionary and national enthusiasm, brought their inspiration with them.

The relationship of people's war, as practiced in Spain, to conventional war, on the other hand, was entirely different. Whereas the *levée en masse* of the patriotic citizens, like its later Prussian and other derivatives, nourished conventional war, people's war subverted it. In Spain, as in people's war of later times, the side with more men, more and better weapons, more logistical support was regularly bested by a militarily weaker opponent. Such results were completely contrary to the rules that were supposed to govern conventional war. The renowned military writer Henri Jomini, who fought in the French army in Spain, was one of the first to note the change. "No army, however disciplined," he wrote, "can contend successfully against such a system [people's war] applied by a great nation unless it be strong enough to hold all the essential points of the country, cover its communications and at the same time furnish an active force sufficient to defeat the enemy wherever he may present himself." The experience left Jomini with a feeling of awestruck horror: "The spectacle of a spontaneous uprising of a nation is rarely seen; and, though there be in it something grand and noble which commands our admiration the consequences are so terrible that, for the sake of humanity, we ought to hope never to see it." In later years, it would become a commonplace to say that to defeat guerrilla forces a conventional army needed a numerical advantage of ten to one, or even, some said, twenty to one. But how could that be? If superior force, supposedly the final arbiter, was no longer decisive, then what was? Was there, in people's war, an arbiter *beyond* the conventional final arbiter?

In an even more confusing departure from the rules governing conventional war, victory in battles over guerrilla forces did not advance victory in the war as a whole. Clausewitz had firmly stated the seemingly inarguable proposition (and several generations of German and other military leaders were to learn his advice by heart) that "All action is undertaken in the belief that if the ultimate test of arms should actually occur, the outcome would be *favorable.*" Yet a French captain who accompanied Napoleon in

Russia, where his army, in addition to facing the Russian winter, was harassed by guerrilla bands, said, "Every victory is a loss to us"—a saying that the historian of guerrilla war Robert B. Asprey has called "a book of wisdom in a single sentence."

Inasmuch as neither possessing superior forces nor winning battles appeared to be the key to victory in people's war, the race to Clausewitz's "extremes"—to the massing and concentration of ever greater resources of violence characteristic of conventional war—did not take place. The Spanish guerrilla leader Mina, anticipating Mao Zedong by more than a century, said, "When the French pressure gets too hard, I retreat. . . . The French pursue me, and get tired, they leave people behind, and on these I jump." And a Prussian officer serving with the French later penned a lamentation of a kind that was on the lips of many a subsequent soldier sent to fight a guerrilla opponent. "Wherever we arrived, they disappeared," he complained, "whenever we left, they arrived—they were everywhere and nowhere, they had no tangible center which could be attacked." The pitched battle, which was the centerpiece of conventional war, was simply sidestepped in people's war. Rather than seeking to win battles, the people in arms sought mainly to endure. The superior importance in guerrilla campaigns of endurance was summed up by an American who had been in Vietnam, the foreign-service officer Norman B. Hannah, who said, "We ran out of time. This is the tragedy of Vietnam—we were fighting for time rather than space. And time ran out."

The Weapons of Civilization

The expansion of conventional war in the modern age was continuous and smooth. Once mass conscription, light artillery, or tanks were invented by one country, they were available for adoption by every country possessing the necessary technical abilities. The evolution of people's war, by contrast, was fitful. The experience and achievement of one generation often was unknown to the next. Books on people's war written in the nineteenth century went unread in the twentieth. Each imperial power, it seemed, tackled guerrilla resistance to its rule with refreshed ignorance.

During the balance of the nineteenth century, conventional war and the conventional thinking that went with it remained dominant. The center of Europe proved to be stony soil for people's war (although the French fought a rearguard partisan campaign after their defeat by Germany in 1871). By the turn of the century, the big army divisions appeared firmly in charge, and "the days of guerrilla wars seemed to be over," in the words of the historian Walter Laqueur. However, appearances misled. The twentieth century was to witness the fullest flowering of people's war. Colonial resistance to imperialism was its breeding ground.

The confrontation between the modern imperial West and the world's traditional societies presents one of the most extreme disparities in the power of civilizations that has ever existed—a disparity wider by far, for instance, than that between ancient Rome and the peoples she subjugated. When, in 1519, the Spaniard Cortés arrived in Mexico, dreaming of gold; when, in 1620, the first Puritan pilgrims landed in Massachusetts to practice their faith; when, in 1743, the Englishman Robert Clive arrived in India to make his fortune; when, in the early 1840s, English gunboats steamed up the rivers of China to enforce her acceptance of the opium trade; when, in 1853, Commodore Matthew Perry sailed an American fleet into Japanese waters to compel Japan to enter into trade and other relations with the rest of the world; when, throughout the nineteenth century, a swelling stream of merchants, adventurers, missionaries, outcasts, con men, criminals, philanthropists, soldiers, and explorers—in short, the whole gamut of imperial intruders—arrived in the villages of Africa, each of these Westerners was backed by instruments of modern power that most of the native populations were helpless to resist, or even to comprehend. (Incomprehension, at least, was mutual.)

The traditional civilizations of Asia, Africa, the Near East, and

South America were compelled, at gunpoint, to inaugurate full-scale revolutions not just in their politics but also, in most cases, in their economies, their cultures, and their social structures. In Leonard Woolf's words, "in no other period of the world's history has there been such a vast revolution as this conquest of Asia and Africa by Europe in less than 100 years." All felt compelled to Westernize, or modernize (two processes that were all but impossible to distinguish), almost every aspect of their collective lives. A generation of Chinese political reformers and intellectuals, for example, were forced to ask themselves what the sources of Western power were, and what China would have to do to create them. How much of traditional Chinese society and culture could be saved, how much should be thrown out? Could Western technical achievements be grafted onto Eastern social structures? Or were the roots of China's weakness, and of her humiliation at the hands of other powers, deeper still?

Such was the form that the implacable pressure of the adapt-or-die war system took in the colonial world. The pressure on the colonial peoples was of a piece with that felt not so long before by Prussia and Napoleon's other European victims. The difference was that whereas the latter, sharing the achievements of European civilization, were capable of catching up quite rapidly, the former, possessing civilizations largely unrelated to the European, needed more than a century to make their adjustments—if they have yet adjusted. Although the increasing power of the modern West had many roots, its cutting edge, in the East as elsewhere, was military force. Nowhere did A. J. P. Taylor's observation that for the great powers of the nineteenth century power meant the power to make war hold true more obviously than in the imperial theater, where the Great Game was played. And nowhere, in the adapt-or-die system that fastened its grip on the world at this time, was more of the dying going on than in the imperial colonies, in which nations by the dozen, and even whole peoples (for example, the native tribes in the Americas), were being propelled toward the evolutionary scrap heap designated for them in the social Darwinist theory fashionable at the time.

Although imperialism began as often as not with economic exploitation, almost all the confrontations between a traditional society and the West were resolved by a decisive test of arms, in which the power relations of the two sides were brutally clarified. For India, for example, it was the battle of Plassey of 1757; for China, the Opium Wars; for Japan, the mission of Commodore Perry. The sword of the West, honed and tempered in the fires of the modern scientific and social revolutions, sliced with terrifying ease through the Chinese "melon" (as it was called at the turn of the century), through the limbs of the Ottoman "sick man of Europe," through the grass houses of the defenseless villages of Kipling's "lower breeds without the law" in Africa and elsewhere. The story of colonial battles forms a monotonous record of one-sided slaughter, relieved only occasionally by the exceptions (the defeat of an English army by the Afghans in the early 1840s and of Italy by Ethiopia at Adowa in 1896).

The battle of Omdurman waged against the Sudanese forces of the Khalifah in 1898 by Lord Kitchener, on his way to his rendezvous with Marchand at Fashoda, can stand as a representative of all of these battles—the better for having been described firsthand by the talented young war correspondent Winston Churchill.

As Lord Kitchener's army moved up the Nile there stretched behind it those two prime symbols of power in the late nineteenth century, a new-built railroad and a telegraph wire. On the Nile, alongside Kitchener's line of march, proceeded two gunboats, transported, by way of the river, hundreds of miles into the desert. On the day of the battle, young Churchill took up a position on a hill overlooking the scene, and had lunch ("like a meal before the races"). Below him, the British forces had formed a square. Inside the square were Maxim guns; to one side a light-artillery regiment. The two gunboats on the Nile moved within range. The Khalifah's men massed behind a ridge. In midmorning, they appeared on its crest, looking, from where Churchill stood like bushes. He describes what happened next:

> Suddenly the whole black line . . . began to move. It was made of men, not bushes. Behind it other immense masses and lines of men appeared over the crest; and while we watched, amazed by the wonder of the sight, the whole face of the slope became black with swarming savages. Four miles from end to end, and as it seemed in five great divisions, the mighty army advanced swiftly. The whole side of the hill seemed to move. Between the masses horsemen galloped continually; before them many patrols dotted the plain; above them waved hundreds of banners, and the sun, glinting on many thousand hostile spear-points, spread a sparkling cloud.

Churchill confesses to a moment of anxiety. However, he had confidence in "the weapons of science," which he also called "the weapons of civilization." He knew what was waiting for the onrushing Sudanese army: "The ranges were known. It was a matter of machinery." The weapons of civilization opened fire, and

> about twenty shells struck them in the first minute. Some burst high in the air, others exactly in their faces. Others, again, plunged into the sand and, exploding, dashed clouds of red dust, splinters, and bullets amid their ranks. The white banners toppled over in all directions.

For a moment, it seemed that the charging cavalry might reach the English camel corps, but just in time one of the gunboats began to fire its Maxim guns:

> The range was short; the effect tremendous. The terrible machine, floating gracefully on the waters—a beautiful white devil—wreathed itself in smoke. The river slopes of the Kerreri Hills,

crowded with the advancing thousands, sprang up into clouds of dust and splinters of rock.

And the English? Churchill describes a scene more like assembly-line production than war.

They fired steadily and stolidly, without hurry or excitement, for the enemy were far away and the officers careful. Besides, the soldiers were interested in the work and took great pains. But presently the mere physical act became tedious. The tiny figures seen over the slide of the back-sight seemed a little larger, but also fewer at each successive volley. The rifles grew hot—so hot that they had to be changed for those of the reserve companies. . . . Their empty cartridge-cases, tinkling to the ground, formed small but growing heaps beside each man. And all the time out on the plain on the other side bullets were shearing through flesh, smashing and splintering bone; blood spouted from terrible wounds; valiant men were struggling on through a hell of whistling metal, exploding shells, and spurting dust—suffering, despairing, dying.

When it was over, the tally of the dead was thirteen thousand Sudanese and forty-eight Englishmen. The youthful Churchill turned reflective. The Khalifah's military plan had been excellent, he thought. Its only flaw had been the "extraordinary miscalculation of the power of modern weapons." He rejected the thought that the Khalifah's forces were guilty of "mad fanaticism." He had been stirred by the courage of the Sudanese in the face of modern war. "For I hope," he wrote, "that if evil days should come upon our own country, and the last army which a collapsing Empire could interpose between London and the invader were dissolving in rout and ruin, that there would be some—even in these modern days—who would not care to accustom themselves to a new order of things and tamely survive the disaster." Thus did England's future prime minister, as he watched the Khalifah's army fall in the desert of Omdurman, anticipate the battle of Britain—a battle with a better result for the defenders. As he watched the British airmen in their silver planes hold the Nazis across the channel at bay, we may wonder, did he remember the sparkling cloud of the Khalifah's charge almost a half century before?

The lopsided casualty figures were typical of colonial battles. Cortés overthrew the civilization of the Aztecs with five hundred men, ten bronze cannons, and twelve muskets. In the battle of Blood River, in 1838, Boer forces slew three thousand Zulus while losing only three themselves. At the battle of Plassey, Clive, with a force of eight hundred Europeans and two thousand Indians, defeated an army of fifty thousand, with a loss of only twenty-two men. In 1865, in Tashkent, in just one of a series of such battles, a Tatar army of thirty thousand was defeated by a Russian army of two thousand. In 1897, "a Royal Niger Co. force composed of 32 Europeans and 507 African soldiers armed with cannons, Maxim guns, and Snider rifles defeated the 31,000-man army of the Nupe Emirate of Sokoto." In a "battle" that the English invader Young-husband waged against the Tibetans in 1903, six hundred Tibetans were killed without British losses, and then "The remnant simply turned and walked away with bowed heads."

People's war was a means to redress the shocking imbalance revealed by these battles, though not, it is true, the only means. In Japan, the solution was hell-bent imitation of the Western conventional model, including the highly self-conscious importation of the political and social organizations of the West. The Japanese race to adopt Western ways, which the writer Natsumei Soseki likened to an Olympics run by the insane, resulted in Japan's victory over Russia in 1905. Japan had accepted the military system whose rules had been fixed by the West, met a Western country on its own ground, and won. In India, the solution was Gandhi's satyagraha—the nonviolent path to independence from imperial rule, of which we will have more to say later. In China, in Vietnam, and in Algeria, among other places, the solution was people's war.

Politics in Command

Its first practitioners were the people of China. The Chinese revolutionary war of the 1920s through the 1940s was a war for independence (against the Japanese invaders) grafted onto a civil war (between the Communist Party and the Kuomintang government) associated with a worldwide revolutionary movement (the communist movement, presided over by the Soviet-run Comintern) fought within the overall context of a world war (the Second World War). Within this larger framework, however, the specific engine that propelled China toward communist rule was people's war. China was not as weak in relation to Japan as Sudan had been in relation to Lord Kitchener, yet battle after battle demonstrated China's inability to face Japan in conventional war. Mao Zedong, only recently confirmed as the undisputed leader of the Communist Party of China, acknowledged this humiliating fact with complete candor in June of 1938. He stated, "We are still a weak country, and, in striking contrast to the enemy, are inferior in military, economic and political-organizational power." Japan, by contrast, was "a powerful imperialist country which ranks first in military, economic and political-organizational power in the East and counts as one of the five or six outstanding imperialist countries in the world." Unable to compete on the conventional, Clausewitzian field of battle, China would, in a manner of speaking, open up a new field of battle—one on which, Mao believed, China's people themselves could appear in strength.

But how, exactly, could people's war enable a weak and backward people to defeat a modern nation-state equipped with the most technically advanced arms? What advantage did it possess? In a single chorus, the leaders of the Chinese revolution broadcast their answer to the world. It was the very word that Clausewitz had used to explain the surprising power of the Spanish guerrillas in their fight against Napoleon: "politics." Everything—tactics, strategy, recruitment, logistics, intelligence—must be subordinated to politics. Mao never tired of making the point:

> What is the relationship of guerrilla warfare to the people? Without a political goal, guerrilla warfare must fail, as it must if its political objectives do not coincide with the aspirations of the people and their sympathy, co-operation, and assistance cannot be gained.

And the most famous:

> Many people think it impossible for guerrillas to exist for long in the enemy's rear. Such a belief reveals lack of comprehension of the relationship that should exist between the people and the troops. The former may be likened to water and the latter to the fish who inhabit it. How may it be said that these two cannot exist together? It is only undisciplined troops who make the people their enemies and who, like the fish out of its native element, cannot live.

The politics in question were revolutionary politics, which meant winning the support of the population at large. Backed by the people, the communist forces could preserve the high morale of their forces, conceal themselves among the people when necessary, provision themselves in the countryside without incurring resentment, and enjoy an almost bottomless supply of fresh recruits. In the war years, China experienced a double political vacuum. In the first place, the ostensible government, the Kuomintang, had never fully succeeded in unifying the country after the fall of the Qing dynasty, in 1912. The power of the provincial warlords who had moved in to fill the political vacuum left by the dynasty's fall had never been completely broken. In the second place, by 1940 the Japanese invaders in the north of China and in selected areas in the south had pulled down such structures of central authority as existed and replaced them either with military rule or with a variety of puppet administrations. It was into this double vacuum that the Communists, who now enjoyed a secure base area among the peasants in the impoverished northwestern province of Yan'an, moved. In wide areas, and especially behind Japanese lines, "politics" therefore meant the creation from the ground up of civil administration.

In this, the Communist Party excelled. As early as the late 1920s, the Communists had governed "liberated" rural areas of China, and by the late 1930s had fully developed their techniques for educating and indoctrinating entire villages and enlisting them in a web of overlapping groups, associations, and governing units, all of which were finally answerable to the Party. The most enduring and important goal of these organizations was land reform, meaning the redistribution of land from the rich to the poor. In traditional rural China, where the gentry class had been supported largely by rents from its landholdings, the redistribution of farming land meant the destruction of one social class by another.

The Communists' guerrilla campaign against the Japanese, starting in 1937, was both an expression of the Party's political strength and a further source of it. It's no justification of Japanese atrocities, which were on a scale with those of the Nazis in Ukraine and Russia, to point out that when a whole population is enlisted in people's war, then the whole population is exposed to retaliation. The Japanese were the first—but unfortunately not the last—antiguerrilla force to whom it occurred that if the guerrillas were the fish and the people were the water, then one way to fight guerrillas was to drain the water. They engaged in a campaign of annihilation using the "Three-All Method"—"Burn all, kill all, destroy all"—in which the destruction of villages and crops and the massacre of all villagers and even animals was common procedure. It is estimated that in the region of greatest Communist strength, in north China, the population dropped in those years from an estimated forty-four million to twenty-five million. China scholars have debated whether the Communist Party's popular support was due more to their program of land reform or more to their resistance to the Japanese—whether more to revolution or more to nationalism. Whatever the answer, the salient point for the evolution of modern warfare is that in both revolution and national resistance "politics" was an essential source of military power.

The thoroughgoing politicization of war, which lent the Communists the strength that so surprised their Chinese and Japanese foes, was accompanied, however, by an equally thoroughgoing militarization of politics. For while it was true that "the better the political reform, the more enduring the War of Resistance," as Mao said, so also was it true that "the more enduring the War of Resistance, the better the political reform." While military "simpletons" had to be taught to place politics first, politicians had to learn to place war first, for "the whole party must pay attention to war, learn military science and be ready to fight." (In Mao's hands, militarized politics would soon come to mean totalitarian politics, whereby enemies were crushed, critics "reeducated," and citizens required to follow a political line determined by the government.)

It is illuminating to compare the formulas of Mao with those of Clausewitz, whose works Mao had studied. On one occasion, for example, Mao, quoting Clausewitz, said, "War is the continuation of politics; in this sense, war is politics and war itself is a political action, and there has not been a single war since ancient times that does not bear a political character." But even as he approves Clausewitz's dictum, he goes on to reverse it: "It can therefore be said that politics are bloodless war while war is the politics of bloodshed." In Clausewitz, the philosopher of conventional war, war seems to take over where politics leaves off. In Mao, the originator of full-scale people's war, war and politics are intermixed. This *fusion* of war and politics, so disturbing to the liberal conscience—torn between admiration for the political restraints placed on the communist soldiers, whose proper treatment of civilians and prisoners was legendary, and horror at the revolutionary brutalization of politics, including the lavish coercion and violence of the totalitarian regime to which people's war often gave birth—is the distinctive contribution that the Communist Party of China made to modern war.

Clausewitz and Mao

In the Western military tradition, it would have been considered absurd to introduce *political* activities onto the field of battle: whatever decisions they led to would instantly be overruled by arms. Wherever guns were doing the arguing, the last word was conceded to them. In the words of the Roman general, "Don't speak to me of laws; here the sword rules." Only when the fighting was over could the diplomats reach agreements, which, within certain limits of maneuver, would be ratifications of the new, military "facts on the ground."

In the world of Maoist thought and practice, however, it's obvious that no such priority can be given to force. For Mao, politics meant, above all, the activities and the interests, as he conceived them, of common people—and above all, as it turned out, the interests of the peasants. If anything, politics is the final arbiter, with force playing only an assisting role. All the special strengths of a people's army—its invisibility to the foe, its knowledge of enemy plans, its spirit, its indigenous sources of supply and recruitment—are likewise bound up with the local people and the local territory. It was political struggle that would enable "weak" China eventually to defeat "strong" Japan. Faced with superior political strength, superior military strength would over the long run (in "protracted war") slowly yield. Mao derided those who, as he said, proclaimed that "China's weapons are inferior and she will certainly be defeated in war." Rather, "Our view is opposite; we see not only weapons but also the power of man." In Mao's vision, political action without a military arm attached was at least think-able, if unwise in the extreme, but military action without a politi-cal foundation was an absurdity.

However, the Chinese Communists' belief that political power was greater than military power was not unqualified. For all their hammering away at the folly of military action without political preparation, they still held on to the idea that the last stage of vic-tory could be accomplished in a conventional battle. In the same essay in which Mao asserted the primacy of man over weapons he set forth a three-stage program for war: "mobile war," then "guer-rilla war," and finally "positional"—that is, conventional—war. Mao rejected the idea that "the concept of guerrilla war is an end in itself and that guerrilla activities can be divorced from those of the regular forces."

And so it happened. Beginning in late 1948, the Communists, having mobilized more than two million peasants into their armies, embarked on a series of conventional campaigns against the Kuomintang (now backed by American money and arms), which carried them to victory, in 1949. Even in these final, conven-tional battles of the Chinese civil war, however, the dividends of political activity poured in, in the form of abundant support from the countryside and vast desertions by disillusioned Kuomintang soldiers. By the last months, it was hard to say which was occur-ring faster, the collapse of the government or the advance of the rebels.

The Forest of Political Defeat

The new relationship between political power and military power that had emerged in people's war was displayed to even more startling effect in the war in Vietnam. The world was slow to absorb the military lessons of people's war in China—just as, in the nineteenth century, it had been slow to absorb the lessons of people's war in Spain. The Second World War had been the greatest conventional war of all time, and guerrilla fighting—whether in China, Yugoslavia, Russia, or elsewhere—had been of secondary importance. When the Japanese occupation of China was cut short by the atomic bomb—an unparalleled display of brute firepower—it seemed clearer than ever that Churchill's "weapons of science," not Mao's irregular peasant armies, were to dominate military affairs.

There was in any case little inclination to reflect on the phenomenon of people's war. The defeated Japanese, living under American occupation, were scarcely in a position to launch a "Who lost China?" debate, which might have illuminated the nature of the Communist victory. That privilege was reserved for the United States, which had supported the Kuomintang until its defeat in 1949. But even then American officialdom, instead of studying the reasons for the Communist success, responded by hounding out of the foreign service as Communist sympathizers the few American firsthand observers who had made such a study. It was an act of willful blindness that, as many historians have noted, prepared the way for the American debacle in Vietnam. In retrospect, we can see, this self-inflicted wound, which occurred in the early 1950s, was part of a deeper policy mistake. Just at the moment when people's war was about to become the principle instrument of political change in the Third World, the United States turned its attention toward the sterile, changeless field of nuclear strategy, where the policy of "massive retaliation" became the order of the day.

It was in Vietnam—the hottest as well as the longest of the Cold War's limited wars—that the West's post–Second World War education in people's war got under way in earnest. After the Japanese were forced out of Vietnam, the French proceeded, with American help, to restore control over their former colony. The United States, which regarded the anticolonial struggle of the Vietnamese as the leading edge of "world communism," soon began to provide the French with supplies. Among all the Western powers, the French had had the most experience with people's war. Although Napoleon's experience in Spain was mostly forgotten, France had faced sporadic anticolonial opposition not only in Vietnam before the war but in its northern African colonies of Tunisia, Morocco, and, above all, Algeria.

The Vietnamese leaders, too, were veterans of people's war, having been steeped in Chinese revolutionary politics for two decades. Ho Chi Minh had lived in China in the twenties and thirties, and had even spent time in prison there. Many of the strategies the Vietnamese were to use against the French had already been battle-tested in China. They included concentration on the rural village as the essential unit of political organization; the foundation of multiple associations (the Peasant Association, the Women's Association, the Youth Association, and so forth) that drew everyone in the village into a tight network of participation and control; the fusion of communist revolution and nationalism; the targeted use of terror against the functionaries of the government; the appeal to popular sentiment together with the suppression of individual thought and opinion; a determined application of land reform; and, most important, an insistence, from start to finish, on the subordination of military action to political goals. The following quotations are a few among a superabundance that express this subordination. (In the first, the ritual bow to Clausewitz is worth noting.)

> Politics forms the actual strength of the revolution: politics is the root and war is the continuation of politics.—*Resolution of the Central Committee of the National Liberation Front.*

> Our political struggle is the manifestation of our absolute political superiority and of the enemy's basic weakness.—*Captured N.L.F. document, 1963.*

Douglas Pike, who served as an official of the U.S. Information Agency in Vietnam, agreed that the key to the N.L.F.'s strength was its political organization. In his book *Viet Cong*, which was written while the war was still in progress, he wrote:

> The purpose of this vast organizational effort was not simply population control but to restructure the social order of the village and train the villagers to control themselves. This was the N.L.F.'s one undeviating thrust from the start. Not the killing of A.R.V.N.'s [Army of the Republic of Vietnam's] soldiers, not the occupation of real estate, not the preparation for some great pitched battle at an Armageddon or a Dien Bien Phu but organization in depth of the rural population through the instrument of self-control—victory by means of the organizational weapon. The Communists in Vietnam developed a sociopolitical technique and carried it to heights beyond anything yet demonstrated by the West working with developing nations. The National Liberation Front was a Sputnik in the political sphere of the Cold War.

But it was French observers—among them the writers Jean Lacouture and Bernard Fall—who, among Westerners, were the first to come fully to terms with the nature and significance of people's war as it was being waged by the Vietnamese. Fall—an eyewitness to both the French and the American phases of the war—was in a position to compare the two. In *The Two Vietnams*, published in 1967, he stated boldly that North Vietnam's victory over the French lay "in the effective control of much of the countryside—*despite its occupation by a large Western army*—through the establishment of small but efficient administration units that duplicated the existing Franco-Vietnamese administration." This, of course, was precisely what the Chinese Communists had done behind Japanese lines in the 1940s. Fall called these Vietnamese administrative units *"hiérarchies parallèles,"* and said that it was they rather than "the existence of guerrilla battalions" that were "the source of France's defeat." So important was the point that Fall, a political writer immune to pseudoscience, went as far as to distill the essence of what he had learned into a formula. It was

$$RW = G + P$$

where *RW* is revolutionary war, *G* is guerrilla warfare, and *P* is political action. This formula called for violence, he noted, yet "the 'kill' aspect, the military aspect, definitely always remained the minor aspect: the political, administrative, ideological aspect is the primary aspect."

Of particular interest are Fall's applications of the lessons he learned in Vietnam to France's war in Algeria, where the Front de Libération Nationale had launched a guerrilla campaign to free its country from French colonial domination. The war had begun to heat up just as the French war in Vietnam was ending, in 1954. In the next several years, Fall noted, the French generals, by now steeped in the tactics of Mao Zedong that they had ignored in Vietnam, actually succeeded, to all intents and purposes, in militarily defeating the Algerian F.L.N., which, by 1958, had been reduced to a fraction of its former strength. Nevertheless, when Charles de Gaulle, the former leader of the Free French Force in the Second World War, returned to power as the president of the Republic, he understood that the native population of Algeria remained united in opposition to the French, and that as long as this remained the case French rule would be untenable. Fall comments pithily, "This is where the word 'grandeur' applies to President de Gaulle. He was capable of seeing through the trees of military victory to a forest of political defeat, and he chose to settle the Algerian insurgency by other means." Fall did not say so, but the Algerian story suggested a revision of his formula, for if revolutionary war could triumph even after the defeat of guerrilla operations, then political action alone might sometimes be enough for victory, and we would obtain

RW = P

in which force was missing altogether from the equation of revolution.

Notwithstanding the importance of revolutionary politics, the fall of the French in Vietnam, like the fall of the Kuomintang in China, came in a conventional engagement, the battle of Dien Bien Phu, in 1954, in which superior Vietnamese forces surrounded and decisively defeated the French. Once again, the underlying realities, though not themselves military in character, were given final expression in a set-piece battle, in accord with Mao's three-stage program. At the Geneva conference in 1954, the northern half of Vietnam was ceded to the revolutionary Viet Minh, and South Vietnam, destined soon to become a dependency of the United States, embarked on its brief, doomed existence.

A comment made by de Gaulle after he agreed to give Algeria its independence sheds further light on the contradictions explored by his countryman Fall. De Gaulle remarked that France could have prevailed in Algeria if she had been "a mastodon," and added that "only Russia, with its communist methods," could have won such a struggle. In fact, just two years earlier, in 1956, the Soviet Union had suppressed an uprising against it in Hungary. France, it seemed at the time, had suffered a failure, while the Soviet Union had enjoyed a success. However, de Gaulle's use of the word "mastodon," an extinct animal, proved accurate. He appears to have understood that the Soviet Union's reliance on terror as the method of rule, although a seeming strength, might be a fatal weakness in the end.

His comment is one of the few on record in that era hinting that the Soviet empire might collapse. But before that could happen, the United States intervened in Vietnam.

The Wills of Two Peoples

Much of the American experience on the ground in Vietnam consisted of bloodily learning the lessons that the French had already bloodily learned. Above all, the United States had to discover that the crucial war in Vietnam was not military but political. The immense American military buildup—a half million men at its peak, backed by a naval armada and the most powerful air force ever assembled for a single campaign—could not remedy the political failure but only mask it. In the words of Marine General Victor (Brute) Krulak, the big-unit battles with the National Liberation Front and the North Vietnamese "could move to another planet today, and we would still not have won the war," because "the Vietnamese people are the prize."

But if on the Vietnamese side the war remained the struggle for independence it had always been, the American war was quite different from the French. The United States saw it as just one of many theaters in its global struggle against communism—in the war that had to remain cold because hot war might mean the end of the world. As such, the Vietnam War for the first time brought face-to-face the two new kinds of power that stood at the end of the long, double transformation of war we have described. On the one side was the military power of the nuclear-armed—and nuclear-paralyzed—"superpower," seeking to create and maintain the elusive appearance of deliverable might summed up in the word "credibility." On the other side was the political power of a small nation waging a people's war.

In the broader picture of American strategic policy, the conceptual slot that Vietnam occupied was limited war, as distinct from "general war," which meant unfightable nuclear war. Limited war—as long as it did not get out of control, sending the antagonists back to the brink of nuclear war—*could* be fought, and in Vietnam it was. Limited war was thus the product of two, opposing strategic pressures. The first was the need to confine fighting to the nonnuclear level—meaning, probably, the "periphery." (On several occasions during the Vietnam War, military advisers to the president considered and recommended the use of nuclear weapons or the adoption of policies, such as attacking North Vietnam, that might have drawn Chinese troops into the war, and so precipitate nuclear war; but repeatedly the presidents, fearful of general war, refused.) The second, contrary pressure was the will to actively resist the communist foe—more particularly, to answer the challenge thrown down by Nikita Khrushchev when, in a speech in 1961, seeking to offset his nuclear weakness, he had vowed to support "wars of national liberation." In affirming this policy, which conformed to the long-standing Soviet opposition to Western colonialism, Khrushchev was aligning himself with one of the most durable and powerful movements of the twentieth century—the self-determination movement.

It was the misfortune of the United States that, by misnaming the national movements for independence in Vietnam and elsewhere as the advance guard of "world communism," it placed itself on the losing side of these struggles, and so, in Vietnam as elsewhere, found itself on the defensive. On the campaign trail in 1960, Kennedy had already identified Third World revolutions as Soviet emanations. "Their missile power," he had said of the Soviets, "will be the shield from behind which they will slowly but surely advance—through Sputnik diplomacy, limited brush-fire wars, indirect non-overt aggression, intimidation and subversion, internal revolution, increased prestige or influence, and the vicious blackmail of our allies. The periphery of the Free World will slowly be nibbled away. . . . Each such Soviet move will weaken the West; but none will seem sufficiently significant by itself to justify our initiating a nuclear war which might destroy us." On other occasions, invoking the two-century-old fear of global domination by a single power, he called this unconventional conflict a "twilight struggle"—blazing, high-noon war being inadvisable. (In an age when total war was ruled out, fear of indirect techniques, such as "subversion" and spying, became obsessive on both sides.)

The pressures that collided in America's Vietnam policy were more complex still. Although limited war had been conceived as an escape from the paralysis of nuclear deterrence, the Vietnam War in fact became tangled in it. In Vietnam, it turned out that limited war, just because it was supposed to be a surrogate for the unfightable all-out nuclear war at the center, became charged with an apocalyptic importance that it otherwise would have lacked. For if "indirect" fighting on the periphery was the only kind possible, then the country that mastered it might gradually win the Cold War, as the domino theory predicted. And if that were so, Vietnam was not a refuge from the Third World War, it *was* the Third World War.

Thus did Vietnam, a real war, acquire a symbolic importance in the war of appearances that now dominated nuclear strategy. In this thinking, collapse in Vietnam could lead to nuclear war, or to the collapse of the United States, or both—for all of this supposedly stood at the end point of a long row of collapsing dominos that would leave the United States at bay in a hostile, communized world. It would lead to "our ruin and almost certainly to a catastrophic war," in the words of Secretary of State Dean Rusk in June of 1965.

The consequence was that although the superpowers had gone to the periphery of their global struggle in order to liberate themselves from the futility of nuclear paralysis, they ended up importing that futility into the peripheral situations, to the high cost and sorrow of the resident peoples. In retrospect, it's easy to see that the two blocs were superimposing their struggle onto anticolonial struggles. The outcomes were sharp comeuppances for all concerned. The United States was not only defeated in Vietnam but suffered grievous domestic political harm. Yet it was the Soviets who were to experience the most bitterly ironic consequences. No doubt genuinely believing that they were supporting "international communism" in Vietnam (an illusion both superpowers shared), they were in fact supporting the final stages of a revolt against colonial rule. It apparently never occurred to the Soviet leaders that, in a world of triumphant national liberation, their own empire and union, which held half a dozen Eastern European nations in forcible subjection, and was itself composed of more than a dozen distinct major nationalities, might be a target for insurrection. They apparently thought they were to be the exception to the verdict history had rendered on all other empires of the modern age. They were wrong.

The differences between the geopolitical roles and strategies of France, a fading colonial power, and the United States, a global superpower, were reflected in the way each country fought its war in Vietnam. The most obvious difference was the incomparably greater firepower at the disposal of the United States. Vietnam was a limited war only in the sense that certain expansions of the war (for example, a ground invasion of North Vietnam) were ruled out. Within South Vietnam, the American military effort was unconstrained. By the end of 1966, the United States was pouring more explosive power day by day into that small territory than all the allies together had been using against Germany and Japan at the height of the Second World War. The B-52, an intercontinental bomber designed for a nuclear war with the Soviet Union, was retooled to drop a mile-long path of conventional bombs. Herbicides defoliated thousands of square miles of the country. Other large, populated areas were designated "free-fire zones," in which anything that moved was considered a target.

The immensity of the American military machine confronted the Vietnamese revolutionaries with a strategic problem that the French had never posed. In 1954, the French were defeated at Dien Bien Phu in a classic conventional siege and battle, but there was no hope of defeating American forces by these means. How—to give just one example—were the Vietnamese, who had no planes in the air in South Vietnam, even to touch the B-52s whose flights originated thousands of miles away, on the Pacific island of Guam, and loosed their payloads from an altitude of thirty thousand feet? No amount of political organizing in the Mekong Delta could have the slightest effect on these raids. In reserving the final act of people's war for a conventional victory on the battlefield, Mao, for all his insistence on the supremacy of political over military struggle, had kept one foot in the Clausewitzian world of conventional war, and Vo Nguyen Giap had done the same in his war against the French. Now Mao's blueprint for a three-stage war, culminating in a conventional victory, had to be thrown out. For the first time, the Vietnamese faced the question of how to eject a foreign power without a conventional finale.

The United States, on the other hand, was still unable even to begin to win the political victory without which all its battlefield successes were valueless. By about 1967, the war had reached a perfectly asymmetrical stalemate, from which no Dien Bien Phu could release the antagonists. Each side was supreme in its own sphere of activity—the Vietnamese communists in the sphere of politics, the United States in the sphere of force. Once the United States had committed ground troops in the hundreds of thousands, there was no chance that the Vietnamese could beat the Americans militarily. On the other hand, there was equally little possibility that the Americans and their client Vietnamese, who had all but destroyed the country they were supposedly saving, could win the political allegiance of the Vietnamese people. The two sides, each victorious in a different struggle, lacked, it appeared, any common playing field on which the match could be decided. Political victories won by the N.L.F. and the North Vietnamese in villages, which then were wiped off the face of the earth by American bombing, were as worthless as American military successes won without political support from Vietnamese villagers. In the meantime, everyone involved—the American soldiers, the South Vietnamese soldiers, the N.L.F., the North

Vietnamese Army, and, above all, the civilian population of Vietnam—was being killed in growing numbers.

The force that broke the stalemate came from without. It was a
change of heart by yet another player in the game, the American
public. The event that precipitated the change was the Tet offensive, in February of 1968. The Vietnamese revolutionaries, faced
with unbeatable American military superiority, modified Mao's
three-stage plan, with its conventional finale, and came up with a
new idea—the general uprising. At Tet they sought to put it into
practice. The concept was bold and original. The immediate target
would be not United States forces but the South Vietnamese government. Military attacks at all points of the country would sweep
aside this weak reed. Simultaneously, a general uprising among the
urban population would demand the establishment of a new government. The Americans, though still undefeated militarily, would
be left in a sea of visibly hostile Vietnamese, and would be forced
to withdraw.

Measured by its own goals, the offensive failed disastrously.
The military attacks did not spark a general uprising among the
urban population, which remained, for the most part, passive. For
once, the N.L.F. had made a huge political miscalculation. The
South Vietnamese government did not fall, nor did its members
defect to the N.L.F. Finally, in the absence of the uprising, the military attacks, although well coordinated and daring, were driven
back by American forces, with high losses for the N.L.F. (In the
process, the imperial capital of Hue was almost leveled, and parts
of Saigon were bombed.) The attacks did not even pay political
dividends in the Vietnamese countryside. A number of writers
have shown that the N.L.F., badly weakened, lost organizational
ground there.

And yet the offensive did bring the long American withdrawal,
leading to the eventual victory of the Vietnamese. How, we need
to ask, did this unequivocal battlefield defeat win a war? In the old
Clausewitzian dispensation, in which force was the final arbiter,

defeats in battles were the path to losing a war. But those rules were no longer in effect. In the new world of politically committed and active peoples, it was not force per se but the collective wills of those peoples that were decisive. And, in such a context, even a battlefield defeat could be a decisive victory for the losing side. So it was at Tet. When Richard Nixon was preparing to take office as president in 1968, he asked Rusk, "Where was the war lost?" Rusk answered, "In the editorial rooms of this country."

In March of 1968, President Johnson ducked defeat in the Democratic primaries by resigning his candidacy, stopping the bombing of North Vietnam, and opening peace talks. The Tet offensive had knocked an American president out of office. The war was to continue under Presidents Nixon and Ford for another seven years, yet the decision had been made. After Tet, in the regretful words of Henry Kissinger, Nixon's national security adviser and then secretary of state, "no matter how effective our actions, the prevalent strategy could no longer achieve its objectives within a period or with force levels politically acceptable to the American people." In 1958, President de Gaulle had seen through the trees of military victory to the forest of political defeat in Algeria, and had granted the country its independence. In the United States in 1968, it was not the head of state but the public at large that came to the same conclusion with regard to Vietnam.

However accidentally, the Vietnamese communists had added a new chapter to the annals of people's war: a war that is won not because the enemy is defeated in a conventional showdown but because the people on the other side, made to understand at last that the cause is ill-conceived and hopeless, *decides* to abandon the effort. Though relying on arms, such an outcome cannot be called a decision by arms. Mao had an inkling that political opinion in the country of the invading army might be decisive in people's war, and in 1938 predicted that revolution in Japan would eventually put an end to its invasion of China—a hope that, of course, was unrealized. It wasn't until the invader was a constitutional democracy that dissension on the home front could prove decisive. The United States lacked a de Gaulle, possessed of sufficient "grandeur" (a word impossible to apply to Richard Nixon), to write a quick finish to the tragedy, and the war staggered on to its humiliating conclusion; but the shift in opinion against the war was never reversed. Military force had played an important role on both sides, but in the last analysis it was the political will of the two peoples involved that was the *final* arbiter of the Vietnam War.

Beyond the Final Arbiter

In many respects, nuclear deterrence and people's war, each appearing at the end of the twofold metamorphosis of war that we have been tracing, were at opposite poles. One was a fruit of the scientific revolution, and depended on new technical instruments of unlimited destructive power; the other was mainly a fruit of the democratic revolution, and depended on the aroused will of peoples. One was a strategy of the powerful, the other a strategy of the wretched of the earth. One was geopolitical in scope, the other local. Yet in some respects the two strategies were interestingly akin. In both, a certain dematerialization of power occurred. In deterrence, it was the decline of actual war-fighting in favor of creating fearful appearances—credibility—that became the coin of military might in the nuclear age. In people's war, it was the eclipse of the power that flowed "from the barrel of a gun" by the political power that flowed from the hearts and minds of the people. In both shifts, violence became not so much an instrument for producing physical effects as a kind of bloody system of communication, through which the antagonists delivered messages to one another about will. In both, the intangible effect upon hearts and minds was paramount, and the tangible effect upon the opposing military forces was secondary. In both, we seem to see the human will detaching itself from physical fighting, as if getting ready to make a break and turn to other means, though without doing so.

In both, the capacity of force to decide political issues is thrown into doubt. In both, in short, the old final arbiter has lost its finality, and some new arbiter seems to be acting in the background. It is because of these developments, somehow occurring simultaneously at the apex and the base of the world's system of military power in the middle decades of the twentieth century, that it is more than a paradoxical phrase to speak of a kind of nonviolence, or at least a turn away from violence, that was occurring *within* war in this period.

The similarities between deterrence and people's war should not, however, unduly surprise us. Both were responses to the same broad, underlying historical development—the steady increase throughout the modern age of the violence at the disposal of military forces. Through people's war, non-Western peoples found a way to defend themselves against the awesome technical superiority of the superpowers. Through the strategy of nuclear deterrence, those superpowers themselves, finding that their weapons had become too destructive to be used against one another, tried as best they could to accomplish the old purposes with mere threats. The twentieth century had produced the most extreme violence that the human species had ever visited upon itself. It was natural—indeed, it was a necessity—that, in different ways, people would react against it, would seek ways to overcome it, to escape it, to go around it, to replace it. In earlier times, violence had been seen as the last resort when all else had failed. "Hallowed are those arms where no hope exists but in them," Livy had written. But in the twentieth century, a new problem forced itself on the human mind: What was the resort when that "last resort" had bankrupted itself? Nuclear deterrence and people's war were two groping, improvised, incomplete attempts to find answers to this question.

It is also true—to state what is perhaps more obvious—that nuclear deterrence and people's war marked two extremes of physical violence, two apogees of total war. Deterrence promised peace only at the price of threatening the world with annihilation.

People's war sought to assert the people's interests, but only by turning every section of the population, including women and children, into fighters and victims. Both strategies simultaneously evoke admiration and horror. Even as we are pleased with the peace that deterrence takes as its goal, we are revolted by the unlimited slaughter it menaces. Even as we are awed by the epic of human courage that people's war presents and the nobility of its goal of serving the interests of the least fortunate, we are disgusted by its frequent use of terror and by the totalitarian governments, with their various gulags and "reeducation camps," to which it has often given birth. Deterrence is only a stay of execution, not a reprieve. People's war immerses the people in the violence from which it seeks to deliver them. And yet, I suggest, in reaching each of these ambiguous extremes, we can, for the first time, catch a glimpse of a true rejection of the twentieth century's terrible legacy of violence, as when climbers, upon reaching a mountain-top, and able to climb no higher, first see the new land beyond, and turn their steps down the other side.

PART TWO

Nonviolence

4

Satyagraha

For most of history, military victory has been the royal road to political rule over a rival country, a sequence crystallized in the single word "conquest." The reason was no mystery. If, as Clausewitz said, an enemy was defeated only when he was ready to "do our will," then obviously military victory made rule possible by turning bold, angry enemies into frightened, obedient subjects. It was the genius of the inventors of people's war to challenge this deceptively self-evident proposition by discovering, in the very midst of battle, the power of politics. What if, the inventors of people's war asked, the people on the losing side declined to do the will of the conqueror and, taking a further step, organized itself politically to conduct its own business? In people's war, political organization did not stand on its own; it was interwoven with the military struggle into Mao's seamless fabric. Yet Mao and others placed politics first in the order of importance and military action only second, and this ranking at least suggested the question of whether, if the fabric were unraveled, political action alone might thwart an occupying power. Did revolutions have to be violent? Could nonviolent revolution—that is, *purely* nonviolent revolution—succeed?

The main schools of Western political theory in the modern age answered the question, with one voice, in the negative. Most thinkers, whether left, right, or center, agreed that revolution was in its nature violent. They believed, with Max Weber, that "politics operates with very special means, namely power backed up by *violence.*" For many, the resort to violence was the defining feature of the revolutionary act. Liberals no less than conservatives took it for granted that, as John Locke said, when the government uses "force without right upon a man's person," and "the remedy is denied by a manifest perverting of justice and a barefaced wresting of the laws to protect or indemnify the violence of injuries of some men," then people "are left to the only remedy in such cases—the appeal to heaven"—that is, to arms. For "in all states and conditions, the true remedy of force without authority is to oppose force to it." The upholders of absolutist monarchy had denied a right to revolt even in that case, but they certainly agreed that revolution was in its nature a bloody affair. Revolution, in the words of the eighteenth-century conservative parliamentarian and writer Edmund Burke, "becomes a case of war, and not of constitution. Laws are commanded to hold their tongues amongst arms; and tribunals fall to the ground with the peace they are no longer able to uphold."

The left-wing revolutionaries of the nineteenth and twentieth centuries more than agreed with the liberal contractarian thinkers who preceded them. "*Aux armes, citoyens!*" was the cry of the left from the time of the French Revolution down to the day of Mao and Ho. At the beginning of the nineteenth century, Napoleon, in exile on St. Helena, laid down the law in the following dictum: "General rule: No social revolution without terror. Every revolution is, by its nature, a revolt which success and the passage of time legitimize but in which terror is one of the inevitable phases." Karl Marx's famous formulation was "Violence is the midwife of every old society pregnant with a new one." (We must add that he didn't regard violence as the essence of revolution, which in his view was prepared above all by economic developments.) The leader of the Russian revolution of 1917, Vladimir Ilyich Lenin, asserted that "Not a single question pertaining to the class struggle has ever been settled except by violence." In a still broader generalization, he said, "Great problems in the life of nations are decided only by force."

Voices disagreeing with this wide consensus—the voices of a smattering of anarchists, some moderate Marxists and other socialists, and a few writers, including, above all, the Russian novelist and pacifist Leo Tolstoy—were rarely taken seriously by those who were in power, or even thinking about power. Lenin sneered at Tolstoy's "imbecile preaching about not resisting evil with force." And Max Weber, having declared that "the decisive means for politics is violence," added that "anyone who fails to see this is a political infant." It's hardly necessary to add to this list such right-wing enthusiasts of violence as Joseph de Maistre, who proclaimed, "All greatness, all power, all subordination rest on the executioner. He is the terror and the bond of human association." And when the right, turning revolutionary, produced fascism, it not only justified violence but reveled in it.

This consensus survived all but unshaken until recently, and undoubtedly played a role in the nearly universal failure to predict the downfall of the Soviet Union. The Soviet regime's monopoly on all the instruments of force seemed to render it invulnerable. If revolution had to be violent in order to succeed, then it seemed to have no chance against such a regime, which would thus have been well justified in its expectation (shared by so many of its awed detractors) that it would last, in effect, forever. The conviction that force was always the final arbiter was not in truth so much an intellectual conclusion as a tacit assumption on all sides—the product not of a question asked and answered but of one unasked. Only in the aftermath of the Soviet collapse have people been ready, perhaps, to open their minds to the idea that some power other than force can prevail in revolution and war. That was the utterly unexpected accomplishment of activists in Eastern Europe and the Soviet Union; but the man who first put the question fully to the historical test was Mohandas Karamchand Gandhi.

A Question of Life and Death

The inventors of people's war rewrote the rules governing the connection of politics to war. Gandhi, whose campaign to end Britsh rule in India was contemporaneous with Mao's revolution, was an even more radical tamperer with the relationships among basic human activities. He was a tireless workman in the shop in which new forms of human action and living are forged. He entered public life as the defender of a small, immigrant minority in a dusty corner of a global empire, but before he was done he had led a movement that, more than any other force, dissolved that empire, and in the process had proposed a way of life in which the constituent activities of existence—the personal, the economic, the social, the political, the spiritual—were brought into a new relationship.

Most important in our context was his fusion of politics and religion. Gandhi believed that to drive the gun out of politics he had to invite God in. It was an operation that, in his day of mostly secular politics, raised an array of new questions and problems even as it offered new solutions to old ones. But in order to better understand Gandhi's vision, in all its originality, strangeness, and greatness, we must first place it in its historical context.

As a youth, Gandhi, who was born in 1869 in the Indian city of Porbandar, on the Indian Ocean, exhibited no extraordinary talents of the testable kind. He takes his place on the long list of remarkable people who performed indifferently at school. His biographer Judith M. Brown titles her chapter on his young manhood "An Indian Nonentity." Sent by his family from India to London to study the law, he continued not to shine. He couldn't learn to dance; he couldn't master the violin; he failed his bar examinations on the first try, succeeding only on the second. Back in India, he couldn't get a law practice going. When he was finally given a case, in Bombay, he was struck dumb with shyness in the cross-examination and felt obliged to refund his client's fee. Proper employment did not come until 1893, when he accepted an invitation to handle a legal case for an Indian merchant in South Africa. In the new land, however, the mediocre student and failed barrister promptly demonstrated that he possessed at least one human quality to a superlative degree, and that was the capacity and the will to translate his beliefs into action.

Everyone forms opinions and beliefs, but most act on them only up to a certain point, beyond which fears, desires, doubts, prudence, laziness, and distractions of all kinds take over. Gandhi, as it turned out in South Africa, belonged to the small class of people, many of them religious or political zealots, who are able to act according to their beliefs almost without condition or reservation. On several occasions, he would read some advice in a book, or arrive at some new idea on his own, and put it into practice the next day. On a train from Durban to Pretoria, a white man had him thrown out of the first-class compartment for which he had paid, and when he protested the conductor dumped him onto the station platform. "I should try if possible," as he later wrote, "to root out the disease [of color prejudice in South Africa] and suffer hardships in the process." It was a decision, as things turned out, that would guide his actions for the next twenty-one years.

In 1894, having completed the legal business for which he had come, he had decided to leave South Africa, and a farewell dinner was held in his honor. That day, he had noticed an article in the *Natal Mercury* reporting that the British colony of Natal was about to pass a bill to disenfranchise Indians. His colleagues at dinner implored him to stay to fight the ordinance, and on the spur of the moment he decided he would. A decade later, he read

John Ruskin's *Unto This Last* during a twenty-four-hour train ride from Johannesburg to Durban. The book recommended a life of austerity, material simplicity, and self-control. "I arose with the dawn," he wrote later, "ready to reduce these principles to practice." The result was Phoenix Farm, the first of several experimental communities he was to found.

The political and racial issues in South Africa that Gandhi had committed himself to solving were many-layered. South African society was arranged in a four-tier, multinational, multiracial hierarchy. At the bottom was the completely unenfranchised and virtually rightless native black majority, outnumbering everyone else put together by about four to one. Next in the scale were Indians, who, by the turn of the century, were slightly more numerous than whites. Next were the local dominant whites, divided among Boers, who were the descendants of Dutch settlers, an English population, and a scattering of others. (In 1897 in Natal there were about four hundred thousand blacks, forty thousand Indians, and forty thousand whites.) At the top were the British imperial masters, trying to exercise ultimate control from London. In this hierarchy, the British, who would wage the Boer War at the turn of the century to prevent the Boers from seceding from the empire, were logical allies for the Indians, who suffered oppression at the hands of the local whites. South Africa was one of those complicated imperial situations in which a passion for self-rule by one group (the Boers, who by and large were more thoroughly racist than the British) meant even more severe repression for other groups.

Conflict arose when the Indians, imported to South Africa in the late nineteenth century under a system of indenture solely to serve as easily managed labor, began to acquire the aspirations of a normal human community: they began to buy and sell goods, to acquire land and farm it, to trade, to practice their religions, even to enter onto the fringes of political life. The local whites, Boer and English, were resentful and afraid of this new competition. Indian farming, they thought, would bring down the prices of agricultural goods by adding to the supply of food; Indian traders would take business from whites; Indian entry into politics would threaten white supremacy (though the modest Indians were far from having any such ambition).

Seized by a terror, which had no basis in fact, that millions of Indians would inundate South Africa, destroying the foundations of white rule, the whites took steps to suppress all the new signs of vigor and life in the Indian community. They passed bills that disenfranchised the few Indians who could vote; imposed exorbitant taxes on free Indians, to force them to re-indenture themselves; hampered and destroyed Indian traders by entangling them in a rigmarole of licensing and other restrictions; limited the areas in which freed Indians could live; restricted their travel; forbade them to use public facilities, including sidewalks; and even passed legislation to make non-Christian marriages illegal. In the background was the implicit threat that the Indian community would be driven out of South Africa altogether. "I clearly saw that this was a question of life and death for them," Gandhi wrote of his fellow Indians.

Lover of the British Empire

In theory, the ideals of the British Empire were liberal. In 1858, Queen Victoria had issued a proclamation declaring her wish that "our subjects, of whatever race or creed, be freely and impartially admitted to offices in our service." It was therefore not only to the local government but to London that the Indians of South Africa sent their numerous petitions and delegations for redress. A nascent black movement followed a similar strategy.

In 1903, we find the following characteristic peal of praise from Gandhi for the British Empire:

The Empire has been built up as it is on a foundation of justice and equity. It has earned a worldwide reputation for its anxiety and ability to protect the weak against the strong. It is the acts of peace and mercy, rather than those of war, that have made it what it is.

In 1905, on Empire Day, he is still eulogizing Queen Victoria:

By her large heart and wide sympathy; by her abilities and queenly virtues; above all, by her personal goodness as a woman, she has forever enshrined herself in the hearts of every nation under the British flag.

At times, he seems a more eager imperialist than the British. On the eve of the Boer War, which aroused broad protest among liberals in England and was not popular with all South African Indians, either, Gandhi wrote to an English friend, "We are all fired with one spirit, viz., the imperial." Gandhi had made a decision to support the empire on the ground that although "justice is on the side of the Boers," the Indians, as citizens seeking to enjoy the rights promised by the empire, should "accord their support to acts of state." His enthusiasm was more for what he hoped the empire might become than for what he currently found it to be. His strategy was to shame the imperialists into living up to their professed ideals. He backed up his words by organizing an ambulance corps of Indians to support the British army in the war. In 1906, when war broke out with the Zulus, he repeated the performance.

Somehow coexisting with this enthusiasm for the British Empire, however, was a growing dislike for modern, technological civilization, of which England was obviously the chief global representative and disseminator. He called the "wonderful discoveries and the marvelous inventions of science, good as they undoubtedly are in themselves," an "empty boast," as they did nothing to advance the spiritual life. He denounced "the invention of the most terrible weapons of destruction, the awful growth of anarchism," and the "frightful disputes between capital and labor." His enthusiasm for the British Empire and his mounting dislike of the modern civilization that it embodied were obviously headed for a collision, and it was not long in coming.

Like many other Asian reformers of the late nineteenth and early twentieth centuries, Gandhi had begun by distinguishing between a strong, materialist West and a weak but spiritual East. He recognized that England's power did not depend on technology alone. It depended also, he firmly believed, on the individual courage, martial and civic, of its people. As a national characteristic, that courage was, he thought, a product in part of England's gradual democratic revolution. In 1906, we find him paying tribute to the sacrifices of heroes of England's struggle for religious toleration, parliamentary supremacy, and the rule of law. "The English honor only those who make such sacrifice," he wrote in *Indian Opinion*, a newspaper he founded and ran. "Their shining glory has spread just because great heroes have been and are still among them. Such were Wat Tyler, John Hampden, John Bunyan and others. They laid the foundations of England's supremacy. We shall continue to be in our abject condition till we follow their example." Cultivating a spirit of civic responsibility and courage was a kind of Westernization of which Gandhi approved.

Gandhi's list of English people to admire is pointedly selective. Missing are such names as Isaac Newton, founder of classical physics; James Watt, inventor of the steam engine; Richard Arkwright, inventor of the power-driven loom; the Duke of Wellington, who defeated Napoleon at Waterloo; or any of the other creators of nineteenth-century England's scientific, industrial, and military dominance. Gandhi wanted only one of the two great modern revolutions. He wanted democracy but not science. It's well known that Gandhi, champion of the spinning wheel, rejected Western technological civilization, but less often appreciated is that, even as a young man, he ardently admired the habits of civic virtue that he believed he saw in the West and associated with the democratic revolution. Those virtues were, in fact, more than anything else the foundation of his program and of his hopes for

South Africa and then India. Like the ancient Greeks, he regarded courage as the most important virtue, because it was the prerequisite for all the others.

In the first years of the twentieth century, he seems to be ransacking both history and the contemporary world for examples of courage to set before the Indian community of South Africa. He pens eulogies of, among others, George Washington, Giuseppe Mazzini, Socrates, Maxim Gorky, Abraham Lincoln ("the greatest man of the last century"), Tolstoy, and Thoreau. All were held up as models of the virtue he found wanting in his countrymen. In 1905, when Japan administered its defeat to Russia, Gandhi was overjoyed. "No one ever imagined that Japan was capable of such bravery," the budding pacifist wrote. "But in scouting and watchfulness, Japan surpassed all the others. Admiral Togo's spies were very accurate in their intelligence, and pounced upon the Russian fleet just when it was most vulnerable." As late as 1908 he could still write, "When Japan's brave heroes forced the Russians to bite the dust of the battle-field, the sun rose in the East. And it now shines on all the nations of Asia. The people of Asia will never, never again submit to insult from the insolent whites." Gandhi thought he knew the "secret" of the Japanese success. It was "unity, patriotism and the resolve to do or die," he said, in the tropes of late-Victorian nationalist fervor.

Yet even in these years Gandhi's interest in nonviolence was developing. In 1896 he had read Tolstoy's Christian pacifist manifesto *The Kingdom of God Is Within You* and was "overwhelmed" by it. A few years later, he entered into correspondence with Tolstoy, who celebrated Gandhi's work in *Letter to a Hindu*. As early as 1902, Gandhi gave a speech in Calcutta in which he said that although the "hatred" of the colonials against the Indians was great, what he proposed was "to conquer that hatred by love." His voracious consumption of the news of the day yielded useful examples of nonviolent action. He praised a Chinese boycott of American goods to protest anti-Chinese discrimination in the

United States. He saluted a Bengali boycott of British goods to protest the partition of Bengal by the English viceroy, Lord Curzon. He lauded the Irish movement against English rule.

The example that inspired him most, however, was the Russian revolution of 1905, whose first stages were largely nonviolent. For some years, he observed in *Indian Opinion,* the Russian revolutionaries had resorted to terrorist attacks. He admired the courage of the attackers, including "fearless girls, actuated by patriotism and a spirit of self-sacrifice, [who] take the lives of those whom they believe to be the enemies of the country, and themselves meet an agonizing death at the hands of officials." Nevertheless, their method was "a mistake." Now they had discovered a new method:

> This time they have found another remedy which, though very simple, is more powerful than rebellion and murder. The Russian workers and all the other servants declared a general strike and stopped all work. They left their jobs and informed the Czar that unless justice was done, they would not resume work. What was there even the Czar could do against this? It was quite impossible to exact work from people by force.

In these years, Gandhi's religious faith was deepening. He did not, however, connect spirituality with any one religion or civilization. In the late 1890s, Anglicized Indian that he was, he had become the South African representative of a group called the Esoteric Christian Union, which taught an eclectic faith.

Finding God in Political Action

In the first years of the twentieth century, the chief elements that made up Gandhi's outlook on the world hung together uneasily, if they hung together at all. Shortly, under the pressure of events, they were to rearrange themselves convulsively in his mind. The crisis, which spanned three years and amounted to a kind of full-scale revolution in the life of a single man, swept together his social program for his local community, his personal spirituality, his political activity on the South African stage, and his view of the British Empire and the world.

The revolution in Gandhi's local community came with the creation of Phoenix Farm, in November of 1904. Gandhi took nothing in this little community as given, but subjected everything, from the activities of daily life (how to brush your teeth, how to clean the latrine) to the most general and fundamental structures of politics and faith, to scrutiny and revision. Because this scrutiny took the form of experimentation, not obedience to any fixed scripture or dogma, the revision was endless. It included an aspect of his life that has baffled and often repelled many of his admirers—his lifelong tinkering with his austere diet and his Christian Science–like home cures, to both of which he directed great attention.

The turning point in Gandhi's personal life came in 1906, while he was leading his ambulance corps during the Zulu war. It struck him that only someone who was pledged to celibacy and poverty could lead a life of unfettered public service. He "could not live both after the flesh and the spirit," he decided. At the time, he wrote later, he had begun to ask himself some questions: "How was one to divest oneself of all possessions? . . . Was not the body possession enough? . . . Was I to destroy all the cupboards of books I had? Was I to give up all I had and follow Him?" Forthwith, he became celibate—renouncing sex even with his wife, though he remained married—and poor, and remained so for the rest of his life.

Vows of poverty and celibacy were, of course, no novelty. Priests and monks had been taking them throughout history. It was the use to which Gandhi put the life thus disciplined that was new. In the religious traditions of both East and West, holy vows have usually been accompanied by a withdrawal from the world and especially from politics. Gandhi proceeded in exactly the opposite direction. He took his ascetic vows in order to free himself for action.

Significantly, Gandhi likened the common British soldiers—the "Tommies"—he met in the Zulu war to Trappist monks. "Tommy was then altogether lovable," he wrote, and went on to compare them to Arjun, the hero of the Indian epic the Mahabarata. "Like Arjun, they went to the battlefield, because it was their duty. And how many proud, rude, savage spirits has it not broken into gentle creatures of God?" Gandhi's admiration for soldiers was lifelong. Like a monk, he would devote his life to God; but like a soldier he would fight for his beliefs in this world. Of his pursuit of God, he said, "If I could persuade myself that I should find Him in a Himalayan cave, I would proceed there immediately. But I know that I cannot find Him apart from humanity." The aim of his life would be to "see God," but that pursuit would lead him into politics. "For God," he said, reversing centuries of tradition in a short sentence, "appears to you only in action."

To the question of whether political power alone might win out over military power, Gandhi answered without equivocation that it could. His answer, however, raised another question that was of the first importance for the future of nonviolent action. If politics was to be free of violence, must it become religious? The objections to the wedding of secular and spiritual power are of course ancient, dating in the East as far back as Gautama Buddha and in the West as far back as Jesus, another religious activist who lived and taught in a backwater of an empire. Universal Christian love, expressed in the sayings "Love your enemy" and "Forgive those who trespass against you," is the spiritual underpinning of his advice of nonviolence to Simon Peter, "Put up thy sword." Certainly, faith in God and ethical responsibility toward others were inseparable for Jesus. On the other hand, although Jesus was caught up in the politics of his time and place, he conspicuously stopped short of rebellion, nonviolent or otherwise. He steered clear of any claim to political leadership (refusing to accept the title "King of the Jews," which his crucifiers affixed to his cross), and he advised payment of taxes to the Roman authorities, saying, "Render unto Caesar what is Caesar's." In other sayings, too, he seemed to place the realm of faith apart from the realm of politics. When Pilate asked him whether he claimed to be a king—a claim that would have been an offense to Caesar—Jesus answered that he was not "a king of this world." If he had been making a claim of temporal power, he went on, his disciples would have used violence to release him. That they did not showed that his kingship was otherworldly. His prophecy that the world would end soon and the kingdom of heaven come also drew a line of separation between Christian love and politics. What need was there to prescribe a rule for a political realm that was about to be destroyed? It was on the basis of these sayings that the disciple Paul and, much later, St. Augustine founded their far sharper separation of the City of God from the City of Man.

To these Christian ideas we may contrast a few of Gandhi's. As he began a nonviolent campaign in 1930, he declared of the Raj, "I am out to destroy this system of Government. . . . Sedition has become my religion." Gandhi admitted no distinction between the City of God and the City of Man. He installed a political conscience in religion and a religious conscience in politics, and called the two the same.

The objections to such a union have come over the years from both saints and politicians. Faith, saints have said, is a domain of purity that is in its nature unworldly, and will be corrupted and destroyed by association with politics, which is in its nature brutal. Rule, politicians have added, is a rough pursuit that will be enfeebled by any introduction of spiritual rules of conduct. (An object lesson—in the eyes of the eighteenth-century historian of ancient Rome Edward Gibbon—was the Christianization and fall of the Roman Empire.) Or else politics, which requires a spirit of tolerance if its natural, ineradicable violence is at least to be moderated, may, if inspired by faith, become fanatical, and even more brutal than it has to be.

To these objections, Gandhi proposed explicit or implicit answers. The most important was nonviolence itself, which he called ahimsa—literally, non-harm, or harmlessness—in Hindi. If the ardor of the spiritual, with its tendency toward absolute demands, was to be permitted to inspire political action, then it had to be purged of violence. The spirit must check its guns at the door, so to speak, before entering the saloon of politics. Otherwise, saints would prove more murderous than sinners. He required the intellect, meanwhile, to undergo a parallel renunciation. It had to rid itself of dogmatic certainty. Shedding dogma was the counterpart in the intellectual world of nonviolence in the physical world: it was mental disarmament. Only if the faithful were ready to open their minds to the worth and validity of other faiths were they likely to be able to hold to the vow of nonviolence. The test of the "absoluteness" of faith became not adherence to the exact prescriptions of any sacred text—what today we call fundamentalism—but the willingness to make sacrifices, including the sacrifice of one's life, for one's admittedly fallible beliefs. Sacrifice and suffering without violence ("self-suffering," as Gandhi put it), not doctrinal purity, was the evidence and "proof" of faith.

These were all ways to permit spiritual love to fuel politics; but they did not answer the question of whether politics, in order to be nonviolent, *required* a spiritual basis. The issue is important, because such a requirement would obviously restrict the appeal of nonviolence. It seems almost in the nature of things that only a small minority can ever take Gandhi as a model for their lives—just as only minorities have ever been drawn to the priestly or monastic life. In particular, Gandhi's asceticism—and especially his vow of celibacy even within marriage—which he regarded as essential to the practice of satyagraha, seems unlikely to serve as a model for very many. The question is what it is about religious faith that enables it to serve as a foundation for nonviolence and whether, outside religion, there may be other foundations.

Something Strange Happens

The transformation in Gandhi's political program in South Africa came just a few months after his vows of celibacy and poverty during the Zulu war. In August of 1906, the Transvaal Legislature announced a so-called Asiatic Law Amendment Ordinance. Its main provision required all Indians above the age of eight to be registered with ten fingerprints and to carry a residency permit thereafter, on pain of fine, prison, or deportation. In combination with other restrictions already in place, the act in effect reduced the Indian community to the status of criminals. Its acceptance, Gandhi believed, "would spell absolute ruin for the Indians in South Africa." In response, Gandhi led the South African Indian community to cross the line from petitioning or otherwise seeking redress within the law to nonviolent lawbreaking.

On September 11, 1906, some three thousand Indian men met at the Empire Theater, in Johannesburg. Gandhi writes, "I could read in every face the expectation of something strange to be done, or to happen." On the agenda was an item resolving that the members of the Indian community would go to jail rather than submit to the Ordinance. One man, Sheth Haji Habib, suggested that the meeting should not only vote for the resolution but publicly vow before God that they would abide by it. Gandhi supported the suggestion in a speech. Such a vow was far different from a mere resolution, he said. It could not be enforced by majority vote; each person had to decide for himself whether to take it and abide by it. But, having once taken the vow, each person was obligated thereafter to keep it, no matter what others did, for "a man who lightly pledges his word and then breaks it becomes a man of straw." All present rose and took the vow.

The "strange" thing had happened. Gandhi knew, he said later, "that some new principle had come into being." Before a year was out, several hundred Indians had gone to jail. This revolution in action, significantly, was born in action. "The foundation of the first civil resistance under the then-known name of passive resistance," he wrote later, "was laid by accident. . . . I had gone to the meeting with no preconceived resolution. It was born at the meeting. The creation is still expanding."

Gandhi was dissatisfied with the term "passive resistance" for what the Indians were doing, and as an alternative came up with the new coinage "satyagraha," which combined the Sanskrit word *sat*, meaning "that which is," or "being," or "truth," with *graha*, meaning "holding firm to" or "remaining steadfast in." It is usually translated as "truth force" or "soul force"—terms that, without further elucidation, are almost as mysterious to the English reader as "satyagraha." Concretely described, satyagraha is direct action without violence in support of the actor's beliefs—the "truth" in the person. The philosophy of satyagraha prescribes nonviolent action in which the actors refuse to cooperate with laws that they regard as unjust or otherwise offensive to their consciences, accompanied by a willingness to suffer the consequences. For the Indian community in Transvaal it meant deliberate violation of the Amendment Ordinance and a commitment to fill the local jails.

Sermon on the Sea

The final step in the revolution in Gandhi's life in these years—the reversal of his appraisal of the British Empire—came in 1909, after he had spent several months in England at the head of an Indian delegation fruitlessly pleading with the imperial government for relief from Boer repression in South Africa (which was now about to become the Union of South Africa). Gandhi had already led one delegation to London, right after the passage of the Ordinance, and on that occasion Lord Elgin, the colonial secretary, had played a trick on the Indians. He had informed them that the imperial government would disallow the legislation. Halfway home, they discovered to their joy that it had done so. When they arrived, however, they learned what Elgin had known all along—that the Transvaal would shortly be granted "responsible government," and would then be permitted to adopt the act at will, without imperial challenge, as it soon did.

The second visit was no more productive. The imperial government wished to uphold the appearance of liberalism without paying the price. From the Indian point of view, the problem was not autocratic or arbitrary use of the empire's strength but default and weakness. Notwithstanding the empire's victory in the Boer War, its power in South Africa was waning. Lord Morley, the secretary of state for India, told the Indians that the empire—which, he startlingly said, was "miscalled an imperial system"—could not "dictate to the colonies." The English strategy in South Africa was to shore up overarching imperial power by yielding increased grants of authority to the local whites. For the Cape of Good Hope, like Egypt and the Sudan, was one of those "roads to India" that had to be defended at all costs. Global power politics took precedence over the grievances of the local black majority and the Indian minority, which were hardly a speck on the great imperial horizon. "I have now got fed up," Gandhi wrote home in *Indian Opinion* toward the end of his 1909 visit. "I think the reader, too, must have grown tired of reading uncertain news." At the Empire Theater, Gandhi had broken with the Boers. Now his patience with the British was coming to an end.

The historical predicament faced by Gandhi and other Indian leaders, barred from influence and power in South Africa as well as their own country, was, in its broadest outline, similar to that facing the leadership of all the colonialized countries: how to oppose domination by a foreign state wielding the incomparably superior weapons of the modern West. India's "Omdurman" had been the battle of Plassey, fought in 1757 between English forces under Robert Clive, and those of Siraj-ud-daulah, the nawab of the Mogul Empire. Clive's victory was one of the earliest to show the extreme imbalance that would become such a regular feature of modern imperial war. The nineteenth-century British military historian Colonel Malleson was not exaggerating when he wrote, "The work of Clive was, all things considered, as great as that of Alexander." For after the battle of Plassey, with its loss to England of a handful of soldiers, the power of England over India was not to be seriously challenged again until Gandhi's time.

The power of imperialist Europe presented the Eastern countries with a dilemma that was cultural and psychological as well as military and political. Everywhere in Asia, nascent movements to resist Europe were national, just as, earlier in the century, the European resistance to Napoleon had been national. However much these movements battened on enthusiasm for their own cultures, the most obvious solution to the crisis in which Asia found herself was to abandon her ways and adopt those of the powerful, dangerous West—in short, to "modernize." Nor could this adoption be halfhearted or superficial. The foundations of traditional society, it seemed, had to be uprooted.

In China, the Ottoman Empire, Japan, India, and elsewhere, innumerable variations of this solution to the dilemma were tried out. Science, evidently, was a source of Western power. Why not, then, learn science, and graft it onto Eastern society, combining the strength of the "material" West with the wisdom of the "spiritual" East? Such was the thinking of early Chinese reformers, who, however, soon noted what Clausewitz had discovered—that democracy, too, was a source of Western military power. "Science and democracy" then became the rallying cry of an important school of reformers. Chen Duxiu, a moderate, wrote, "The basic task is to import the foundation of Western society, that is, the new belief in equality and human rights." These Chinese, goaded by their country's humiliation, were perhaps the first anywhere, East or West, to understand and clearly state that at the base of modern power were the scientific and democratic revolutions. But in the early twentieth century it became obvious to them that neither revolution could grow in a vacuum. Both had roots in the emancipation of the individual. In order to be strong, China would have to alter its culture, even its family structure—the very things that, according to earlier reformers, China had been seeking to protect by adopting science. The further one went in Westernizing in order to protect China, it turned out, the less of "China" there was to protect. Not far down this path lay the wholesale condemnation of Chinese tradition that would be expressed by the Chinese Communist Party. The Asian nations, in order to survive in the social Darwinist, adapt-or-die war system that Europe had imposed on the world, seemed to be faced with a choice between watching Europeans destroy their traditional societies or doing the job themselves. It was hard soil in which to grow what later came to be called "national identity."

On a steamer back to South Africa in November of 1909, Gandhi, writing in his native tongue of Gujarati, poured out the longest and most inflammatory political pamphlet he would ever write, *Hind Swaraj: Indian Home Rule*—also called *Sermon on the Sea*. It dealt head-on with the issue of Westernization. If violence is truly the midwife of revolution, as Marx said, then this pamphlet was the closest Gandhi ever came to preaching it. He portrayed the civilization of England and her empire as an unmitigated evil. Gone now was the praise for Queen Victoria, gone the praise for British justice, gone the vision of a harmonious union of "different sections of ONE mighty empire." The larger villain of the story, however, was not England herself but modern technical civilization, of which England was only one representative. He anathematized it with fundamentalist fury. "This civilization is irreligion," he declared. "According to the teachings of Mahomed this would be considered a Satanic Civilization. Hinduism calls it the Black Age. . . . It must be shunned." To imitate this civilization, as Japan had done and China was trying to do, would be madness. "The condition of England at present is pitiable. I pray to God that India may never be in that plight." He excoriated modern ways. Railways only enabled "bad men [to] fulfil their evil designs with greater rapidity," he said, with primitive logic. English prime ministers had "neither real honesty nor a living conscience." The English Parliament was "a prostitute." The civilization of modern Europe as a whole was a mere "nine-days' wonder" that shortly would destroy itself; one had only to wait.

Indian civilization, he now found, was the opposite of all this. "The tendency of the Indian civilization is to elevate the moral being," he claimed, "that of the Western civilization is to propagate immorality. The latter is godless, the former is based on a belief in God." The foundations of Indian civilization arose, he insisted, from religious roots, when her great religious men had established pilgrimages to holy places, such as the Ganges.

Gandhi's rejection of the West and embrace of his own land was more radical by far than that of other anti-Western leaders of the time. The idea that the East should protect her spiritual treasures by means of a judicious borrowing of Western material techniques had been the stock-in-trade not just of the Chinese and Japanese but of Indians as well. For instance, the religious leader Vivekananda, who in other ways foreshadows Gandhi, said, "It is . . . fitting that when the Oriental wants to learn about machine-making, he should sit at the feet of the Occidental and learn from him. When the Occident wants to learn about the Spirit, about God, about the Soul, about the meaning and the mystery of this universe, he must sit at the feet of the Orient." Gandhi, by contrast, turns his back entirely on Western material techniques, placing his faith in Eastern spirituality alone.

Gandhi's sweeping rejection of modern technology, let us note, was never put into practice in India, except by himself and a few of his followers. And even Gandhi, though remaining true to his belief, did not propose a wholesale program of deindustrialization, and at times confessed that certain industries might be necessary, as long as they were strictly devoted to the benefit of the people. It is in the arena of nonviolence that Gandhi's repudiation of technology has so far proved historically fruitful. By associating technical progress with violence and both with the West and, on the other hand, technical simplicity with nonviolence and both of these with India, Gandhi and his colleagues forged a nationalistic pride in nonviolence that was to endure from about 1920, when the Congress Party adopted Gandhi's program, until 1948, when India gained independence. Thus was nationalism, which usually feeds on self-aggrandizement and militarism, wedded in India to a principle of self-restraint. (Once independent, the Indian state promptly abandoned nonviolence and immediately went to war with the newly created state of Pakistan over the territory of Kashmir; and it now possesses a large military establishment and a nuclear arsenal.)

Gandhi's embrace of nonviolence provided an escape from the discouraging choice between imitation of the West and defeat by the West. Nonviolence was a method for fighting the West *without* imitating her. As Gandhi put it in *Hind Swaraj,* "My countrymen . . . believe that they should adopt modern civilization and modern methods of violence to drive out the English. *Hind Swaraj* has been written in order to show that they are following a suicidal policy, and that, if they would but revert to their own glorious civilization, either the English would adopt the latter and become Indianized or their occupation in India would be gone."

The idea that India possessed a priceless, spiritually superior civilization was a welcome salve to the injured pride of a people that had been taught for some two hundred years to regard everything English as superior. In the words of India's first prime minister, Jawaharlal Nehru, Gandhi wrought in the consciousness of India "a psychological change, almost as if some expert in psychoanalytic methods had probed deep into the patient's past, found out the origins of his complexes, exposed them to his view, and thus rid him of that burden." In Gandhi's Manichaean celebration in *Hind Swaraj* of one civilization and condemnation of another, there is a note of chauvinism of a kind he later avoided. (Although he never repudiated *Hind Swaraj*, he would declare, "East and West are no more than names . . . there is no people to whom the moral life is a special vocation.") Yet we note at the same time a new clarity and firmness of tone in the pamphlet. Anything of the Uncle Tom that may have clung to the frock-coated, silk-hatted Gandhi as he made the rounds of the ministries of the British Empire has been purged. Soon he would adopt the simplest Indian dress. The disparate elements that composed the worldview of this rootless, much-traveled, English-trained, Esoteric Christian, immigrant to Africa, had fused in a new unity. The verbal "violence" of *Hind Swaraj* was perhaps the violence needed to rend the emotional tie with the empire. Gandhi had discovered a way to serve as a true son of India—at one, he was sure, with the spirit of his forefathers.

The Power of Nonviolence

There was practical as well as moral calculation in Gandhi's satyagraha. The West possessed means of violence that India could not hope to match. Gandhi later said, "Suppose Indians wish to retain by force the fruits of victory won through satyagraha. Even a child can see that if the Indians resort to force they can be crushed in a minute." Sensibly, he did not want to play a losing hand. As he explained, "The Whites were fully armed. It was clear that if the Indians were to come into their own, they must forge a weapon which would be different from and infinitely superior to, the force which the white settlers commanded in such ample measure. It was then that I introduced congregational prayer in Phoenix and

Tolstoy Farm as a means for training in the use of the weapon of satyagraha or soul force." In 1909, contemplating the might of the British Empire, he wrote:

> You [British] have great military resources. Your naval power is matchless. If we wanted to fight with you on your own ground, we should be unable to do so, but if the above submissions be not acceptable to you, we cease to play the part of the ruled. You may, if you like, cut us to pieces. You may shatter us at the cannon's mouth. If you act contrary to our will, we shall not help you; and without our help, we know that you cannot move one step forward.

Gandhi's nonviolence, too, is a chapter in the story that began with Clausewitz's Prussia, which, faced with the superiority of the French revolutionary armies, had embarked on its policy of conscious imitation of the French innovations, and continued with the attempts of so many nations to "catch up" with more "modern" powers.

By the time Gandhi wrote *Hind Swaraj*, he had in effect nationalized the principle of nonviolence. He brought it down from the ether of universal beliefs and gave it a terrestrial home—India. Violence, meanwhile, seemed to have taken up residence in the modern West. But where, if anywhere, in Gandhi's newly moralized geography did his *prime* virtue, civil courage, now reside? Previously, he had found it mainly in England, and scolded his countrymen for lacking it. In *Hind Swaraj*, it seems to have been left geographically homeless. Inspiring his countrymen to take active responsibility for their own social and political lives was *the* Gandhian program, yet since India had been defined as the home of the spirit, courage in her case must not take a martial shape (brute force) but must be of a nonviolent kind (soul force). So just when Gandhi's diatribe against the satanic West reaches its highest pitch in *Hind Swaraj*, as if to justify and prepare the way for anti-

Western violence, the restraining hand of nonviolence seems to reach in and turn the criticism and toward the passivity of his own countrymen. Psychologically speaking, we can almost watch the anger at the hated "other" being checked and directed back toward the self, which is excoriated with double fury.

Whatever pleasures of national pride Gandhi may have offered his countrymen when he called their ancient civilization the most godly of all he now more than took back. He dashed the sweet cup of national self-congratulation from the thirsting lips of the humiliated Indians. It is in the passages explaining England's domination of India that *Hind Swaraj* began to chart new political territory. Gandhi held Indians, not Englishmen, responsible for India's colonial dependency. "The English have not taken India," he wrote, "we have given it to them." He explained:

> They came to our country originally for purposes of trade. Recall the Company Bahadur. Who made it Bahadur? They had not the slightest intention at the time of establishing a kingdom. Who assisted the Company's officers? Who was tempted at the sight of their silver? Who bought their goods? History testifies that we all did this. In order to become rich all at once we welcomed the Company's officers with open arms. We assisted them.

Gandhi later elucidated his point:

> It is because the rulers, if they are bad, are so not necessarily or wholly by reason of birth, but largely because of their environment, that I have hopes of their altering their course. It is perfectly true . . . that the rulers cannot alter their course themselves. If they are dominated by their environment, they do not surely deserve to be killed, but should be changed by a change of environment. But the environment are we—the people who make the rulers what they are. They are thus an exaggerated edition of what we are in the aggregate. If my argument is sound, any violence done to the rulers

would be violence done to ourselves. It would be suicide. And since I do not want to commit suicide, nor encourage my neighbors to do so, I become nonviolent myself and invite my neighbors to do likewise.

Liberal-minded people have often held that society's victims are corrupted by a bad "environment" created by their privileged masters. Gandhi was surely the first to suggest that the victims were creating a bad moral environment for their masters—and to preach reform to the *victims*. Even allowing for a certain raillery and sardonicism in these passages, there can be no doubt that Gandhi is in earnest. Here we touch bedrock in Gandhi's political thinking. All government, he steadily believed, depends for its existence on the cooperation of the governed. If that cooperation is withdrawn, the government will be helpless. Government is composed of civil servants, soldiers, and citizens. Each of these people has a will. If enough of them withdraw their support from the government, it will fall.

This idea had admittedly occurred to political thinkers in the past. For instance, the sixteenth-century French writer Étienne de La Boétie had observed of tyrants, "the more is given them, the more they are obeyed, so much the more do they fortify themselves," and therefore "if nothing be given them, if they be not obeyed, without fighting, without striking a blow, they remain naked, disarmed and are nothing." The philosopher of the English enlightenment David Hume likewise believed that all government, even tyranny, rested on a kind of support. "The soldan of Egypt or the emperor of Rome," he wrote, "might drive his harmless subjects like brute beasts against their sentiments and inclination. But he must, at least, have led his *mameluks* or *praetorian bands*, like men, by their opinion." And James Madison once wrote, "All governments rest on opinion."

Gandhi, however, was the first to found upon this belief a thoroughgoing program of action and a radically new understanding of the relationship of violence to politics. The central role of consent in all government meant that noncooperation—the withdrawal of consent—was something more than a morally satisfying activity; it was a powerful weapon in the real world. He stated and restated the belief in many ways throughout his life:

> I believe and everybody must grant that no Government can exist for a single moment without the cooperation of the people, willing or forced, and if people withdraw their cooperation in every detail, the Government will come to a standstill.

Gandhi's politics was not a politics of the moral gesture. It rested on an interpretation of political power and was an exercise of power. From his surprising premises Gandhi drew a conclusion more surprising still:

> The causes that gave them [the English] India enable them to retain it. Some Englishmen state that they took and they hold India by the sword. Both these statements are wrong. The sword is entirely useless for holding India. We alone keep them.

Gandhi does not merely say that English rule is made possible by Indian acquiescence; he goes a step further and charges that Indians "keep" the English, almost as if the English were struggling to get away and the Indians were pulling them back. Gandhi's claim flies in the face of the one conviction on which everyone else in the imperial scheme, whether ruler or ruled, agreed—that, in the words of the *London Times,* it was "by the sword that we conquered India, and it is by the sword that we hold it." (We cannot prove that Gandhi had read the *Times* editorial, but the similarity in wording of the passage above suggests that he had.) Some enthusiastically approved of this supremacy of the sword, some bowed to it, and some despised it, but only Gandhi denied that it was a fact. Not only was force, in Gandhi's thinking, not the "final arbiter," it was no arbiter at all. What arbitrated was consent, and the cooperation that flowed from it, and these were the foundation of dictatorship as well as of democratic government.

More Active Than Violence

Governments do not normally fall simply of their own weight. Action is required. The obligation to act, in Gandhi's view, took precedence over even the obligation to remain nonviolent. "Non-cooperation is not a passive state," Gandhi said, "it is an intensely active state—more active than physical resistance or violence." Satyagraha was *soul* force, but equally it was soul *force*.

Asked to choose between violence and passivity, Gandhi always chose violence. "It is better to be violent, if there is violence in our breasts," he said, "than to put on the cloak of nonviolence to cover impotence. Violence is any day preferable to impotence. There is hope for a violent man to become nonviolent. There is no such hope for the impotent." "Activist" is a word that fits Gandhi through and through. "I am not built for academic writings," he said. "Action is my domain." Indeed, if he was a genius in any field, that field was action. "Never has anything been done on this earth without direct action."

In 1917, soon after he returned to India, he would say, "There is no love where there is no will. In India there is not only no love but hatred due to emasculation. There is the strongest desire to fight and kill side by side with utter helplessness. This desire must be satisfied by restoring the capacity for fighting. Then comes the choice." In 1918, he would shock his followers by enlisting as a recruiting sergeant for Indian troops to fight for the British in the First World War. How, his colleagues wondered, then and later, could the advocate of nonviolence recruit soldiers for this war—a mechanized slaughter of millions that surely had to rank as the prime exhibit in Gandhi's indictment of modern technical civilization for its "violence of the blackest sort"? His campaign, which proved almost fruitless, can be explained only by his belief that what India needed even more than nonviolence was the will and courage that would propel its people into action—even if this meant serving in war under the British.

Intuitively, nonviolence appears to have a restraining or crippling influence on action. To Gandhi, however, nonviolence appeared in exactly the opposite light. Nonviolent action had nothing to do with quietism or passivity. Noncooperation was, Gandhi believed, supremely energetic. "Another remedy [to injustice] there certainly is, and that is armed revolt," he acknowledged, but "Civil disobedience is a complete, effective and bloodless substitute." If Gandhi embraced nonviolence, it was not because, in the interest of an ideal, he accepted a competitive disadvantage. Satyagraha was not some pale sister of violence, embraced for her virtue alone. For Gandhi such acceptance would have constituted an unacceptable abdication of responsibility.

But how could someone who checked his energy be called more energetic and more powerful than someone who unleashed it without restraint? Weren't Gandhi's two dictates—that one must *act* directly, unhesitatingly, and fearlessly and that one must do so nonviolently—at war with one another? The kinship of action and violence, indeed, seems natural, and it's tempting to see Gandhi's nonviolence only as an attempted remedy for the danger. In this view, nonviolence would be seen as a reduction of freedom in which a certain passivity and loss of energy is the price paid for keeping the peace. And certainly Gandhi did see nonviolence as a cure for the danger inherent in mass action. He often said that in his time the rising tide of action would irresistibly occur whether leaders like him encouraged it or not, and that his job was to help guide it into peaceful channels. "A new order of things is replacing the old," he wrote as he embarked on a campaign of satyagraha on behalf of mill workers in his home city of Ahmedabad. "It can be established peacefully or it must be preceded by some painful disturbances. . . . I presumptuously believe that I can step into the breach and may succeed in stopping harmful disturbances during our passage to the new state of things. . . . I can only do so if I can show the people a better and more expeditious way of righting wrongs." He adamantly denied that the price of restraining violence entailed a reduction of energy and power. On the contrary, he claimed that satyagraha, far from being a restriction on action, was action at last unrestricted and unbound—action grown to the full height of its potential. "Nonviolence," he said, "is without exception superior to violence, i.e., the power at the disposal of a nonviolent person is always greater than he would have if he was violent."

Any action, Gandhi knew, called above all for willpower—for the sort of courage that was especially conspicuous in soldiers. But nonviolent action required even more courage of this sort. Gandhi was fond of a statue of Charles Gordon, a British general of imperial fame, which shows him carrying a mere riding crop instead of a weapon. Gandhi commented:

> The practice of *ahimsa* calls forth the greatest courage. It is the most soldierly of a soldier's virtues. General Gordon has been represented in a famous statue as bearing only a stick. This takes us far on the road to *ahimsa*. But a soldier who needs the protection of even a stick is to that extent so much the less a soldier. He is the true soldier who knows how to die and stand his ground in the midst of a hail of bullets.

Action, moreover, flourishes, Gandhi believed, in freedom; and nonviolent action, precisely because it requires the highest possible degree of courage, exhibits the largest freedom. Violence, although initiated in pursuit of political goals, can take on a life of its own, which distracts from the original goals, and may eventually compete with them or supplant them entirely. On the local scale, this leads to vendetta, which can outlast by generations any political or other purposes that gave rise to a quarrel. On a much wider scale, the logic of war can, as Clausewitz warned with such clarity, entirely supersede the political purposes that lend war whatever sense it may have. On each of these levels, the actors surrender their freedom of action to a process over which they have lost control.

The nonviolent actor exhibits the highest degree of freedom also because his action originates within himself, according to his own judgment, inclination, and conscience, not in helpless, automatic response to something done by someone else. He is thus a creator, not a mere responder. It is not digressive to recall a passage from a writer who might at first appear to be pretty much a polar opposite of Gandhi yet also associated nonviolence not with weakness but with a superabundance of energy and power. Friedrich Nietzsche, asking himself whether such a thing as a Christian turning of the other cheek was really possible, said that, if it were, it would be for only the strongest natures. He wrote:

> To be incapable of taking one's enemies, one's accidents, even one's misdeeds seriously for very long—that is the sign of strong, full natures in whom there is an excess of the power to form, to mold, to recuperate and to forget. . . . Such a man shakes off with a *single* shrug many vermin that eat deep into others; here alone genuine "love of one's enemies" is possible—supposing it to be possible at all on earth. How much reverence has a noble man for his enemies!—and such reverence is a bridge to love. . . . In contrast to this, picture "the enemy" as the man of *ressentiment* conceives him—and here precisely is his deed, his creation: he has conceived "the evil enemy," "THE EVIL ONE," and this in fact is his basic concept, from which he then evolves, as an afterthought and pendant, a "good one"—himself!

If such magnanimous characters—free alike of fear and lust for revenge, and braver than soldiers—had not found an appropriate arena for their kind of activity, they might have passed through history without leaving any mark but the admiration of a few people around them. Their arena could not, of course, be war. In fact, it was the arena of nonviolent action, soon to be strewn with the debris of the world's empires and some of its mightiest and most violent regimes.

Noncooperation in India

In 1915, Gandhi brought his battle-tested instrument of nonviolence from little Natal and Transvaal to great India. In South Africa, the forty thousand Indians had been a small minority, amounting to less than 10 percent of the total population. In India, they were a huge majority, of more than three hundred million, ruled over by a mere hundred thousand or so English. When forty thousand refused cooperation, it was a serious crisis for the imperial rulers; but if the three hundred million refused cooperation it was the end of the Raj, and probably of the British Empire as well. That, at least, was the view of Winston Churchill, who said in Parliament in 1931, "The loss of India would be final and fatal to us. It would not fail to be part of a process that would reduce us to the scale of a minor power." Gandhi agreed. "Through deliverance of India," he wrote, "I seek to deliver the so-called weaker races of the earth from the crushing heels of Western exploitation in which England is the greatest partner." History proved both men right.

Gandhi began modestly. Following the suggestion of his political mentor in India, the National Congress Party leader Gopal Krishna Gokhale, he maintained a public silence for a year, contenting himself with traveling throughout India in third-class railway compartments, in order to acquaint himself with the state of the country. Beginning in 1917, he engaged in a series of local satyagraha campaigns. One was in opposition to the exploitation of peasants cultivating indigo, out of which dye is made, in Bihar, in the Champaran district; a second was in support of decent wages for the mill workers in his native city of Ahmedabad; a third was in opposition to a British-imposed tax that was ruining the peasants of the Kheda district. Each campaign was a grueling, self-contained, high-stakes drama, pitting the willingness of peasants and workers and of Gandhi himself to suffer for their cause against the will of powerful factory owners and state authorities. "A series of passive resistances is an agonizing effort," he wrote of these campaigns to a friend, Henry Polak. "It is an exalting agony. I suppose the agony of childbirth must be somewhat like it." His modus operandi in these and subsequent campaigns included, as his biographer Judith M. Brown has written, "the search for a peaceful solution at the outset, the sacred pledge as the heart of the struggle, strict discipline and self-improvement among the participants, careful publicity and the generation of an ambience of moral authority and pressure, and finally a compromise solution to save the face and honor of all concerned." In the Ahmedabad strike, he fasted in support of a cause for the first time since arriving in India. His aim was twofold—to bring the pressure of "self-suffering" to bear on his opponent and to purify himself spiritually. A few years later, he explained, "I can as well do without my eyes . . . as I can without fasts. What the eyes are for the outer world, fasts are for the inner." Gandhi's methods and style, which made the privileged, moderate leaders of the Congress Party deeply uncomfortable, appealed strongly to masses of ordinary Indians, and Gandhi became India's first truly national figure.

In 1917, in the most discouraging days of the First World War, England had announced a series of liberal reforms that would increase Indians' participation in the administration of their own country. Yet when the war ended, in November 1918, these hopes were thwarted by the passage of the repressive Anarchical and Revolution Crimes Act, known also as the Rowlatt Act, imposed after an investigation by the British authorities of the possibilities for terrorism and "sedition" in India. In Gandhi's eyes, the Rowlatt bills were for the India of 1918 what the Amendment Ordinance of the Asiatic Act had been for the South Africa of

1906. He called both "black acts," and resisted both with full-scale campaigns of noncooperation. He called the Rowlatt bills evidence of "a determined policy of repression," and announced that henceforth "civil disobedience seems to be a duty imposed on every lover of personal public liberty," declaring that he was ready to fight "the greatest battle of my life."

Noncooperation was to continue in India, on and off, for the next three decades. In February of 1919, Gandhi announced his first nationwide act of resistance—a *hartal,* or strike, against the Rowlatt legislation. The *hartal* was observed throughout the country. This was Gandhi's answer to Omdurman and the weapons of civilization—not India heaping the ground with English corpses but masses of Indians withdrawing cooperation from English rule. A few days after the *hartal,* however, the British arrested him, whereupon riots broke out in Ahmedabad, and Gandhi found himself facing a problem he had not faced in South Africa—violence by his own supporters. An English policeman and others were killed.

Gandhi's response was to launch *"satyagraha* against ourselves," by fasting for three days. "In the place I have made my abode I find utter lawlessness bordering almost on Bolshevism," he now wrote to the viceroy's private secretary. "Englishmen and women have found it necessary to leave their bungalows and to confine themselves to a few well-guarded houses. It is a matter of the deepest humiliation and regret to me. I see that I overcalculated the measure of permeation of satyagraha amongst the people. . . . My satyagraha . . . will, at the present moment, be directed against my own countrymen." In 1922, shortly after launching noncooperation on an even wider scale, he again suspended it, after mobs of protesters burned a police station in the city of Chauri Chaura, and hacked several policemen to pieces. "All of us should be in mourning," he said. "May God save the honor of India." He fasted for five days in penance and the protest never was resumed.

In a campaign of noncooperation against the salt tax in 1930—probably the most renowned of his actions—Gandhi marched with seventy-five or so followers to the sea to make salt, in defiance of an English monopoly on salt making, and then was jailed, after which his followers marched nonviolently upon the saltworks at Dharasana, suffering many dozens of casualties at the hands of police wielding clubs. The upshot was an invitation to meet the viceroy, Lord Reading. The two men agreed that Gandhi would represent India at a constitutional conference in London. The conference failed, and another decade of resistance and repression began. The final nationwide noncooperation campaign—the Quit India campaign—was launched in 1942, in the third year of the Second World War, and was quickly and violently repressed; India did not attain her independence until the war ended, when England's grip on all her imperial possessions was weakening.

It is not certain that it was satyagraha that broke England's grip on India. The great hoped-for day never came on which all India refused cooperation with the English rulers, who therefore, finding themselves barking orders at an indifferent population, had nothing left to do but pull up stakes and leave. The English weathered all the individual satyagraha campaigns. It's also true that many factors other than satyagraha conspired to drive the English out. English trade with India declined in importance. The depression and the two world wars weakened England, forcing her finally to yield her position of global preeminence to the United States.

On the other hand, satyagraha unquestionably succeeded in winning the battle for the hearts and minds of the people of India. When the Second World War ended, although the back of the Quit India campaign had been broken, the viceroy, Lord Wavell, was well aware that "while the British are still legally and morally responsible for what happens in India, we have lost nearly all power to control events; we are simply running on the momentum of our previous prestige." Just as de Gaulle came to understand in

Algeria that victories through repression and violence were in the long run as useless as conventional battlefield victories in a people's war, so now Wavell acknowledged that technical victories against nonviolent opponents would in the long run prove equally useless. All these imperial defeats pointed to a lesson, which was spelled out clearly in Gandhi's writings: in a struggle for independence in our democratic age, the decisive contest, whose essence is political and therefore nonviolent, is not for control of any piece of territory but for the loyalty and cooperation of the people. Violence, where it is present, plays only a supporting role. It was Gandhi's discovery that violence did not need to play any role at all.

The Shadow

That lesson, however, is in fact a secondary one. When Gandhi arrived back in India in 1915, he knew he faced not only the evil of British rule but also the mountainous social ills of India, most of which had predated the Raj and would outlast it. The most important tasks, he believed, were providing a decent life, including adequate food, shelter, and sanitation, for India's "dumb millions," establishing a system of active self-government in the country's seven hundred thousand villages, ending the Hindu system of untouchability, raising the status of women, and making and keeping peace among Hindus and Muslims. Although *swaraj*—"self-rule"—included ejecting the English, he always believed that addressing these ills was its deeper and more important task.

Noncooperation, taken by itself, was useless for this purpose. It could do nothing to feed the hungry, to relieve the oppressed, to make peace among India's quarreling ethnic and religious groups. For these purposes, positive action was required. Gandhi gave it the unostentatious name of "the constructive program." Noncooperation embodied the obligation to reject participation in oppression. The constructive program embodied the obligation to actively pursue social betterment—"truth." As such, it was closer than noncooperation to the central meaning of "satyagraha," which is "to hold fast to truth." The story of Gandhi's satyagraha has traditionally concentrated on the three great noncooperation campaigns; but his most persistent efforts were his unceasing work in support of the constructive program. It's notable, for instance, that all of his "fasts unto death" (from each of which he was released by progress in solving the issue about which he was fasting) were launched in the name of one plank or another of the constructive program—of bringing justice to the workers of Ahmedabad, of ending untouchability, of making peace between Hindus and Muslims. "Satyagraha," he said, "is not predominantly civil disobedience, but·a quiet and irresistible pursuit of truth. On the rarest occasions it becomes civil disobedience."

A constructive program to address social ills may seem so elementary as scarcely to be an idea; yet few things caused more controversy in the Congress Party than Gandhi's dedication to it. In one of the lulls between noncooperation movements, Gandhi joked that in Congress "I stand thoroughly discredited as a religious maniac and predominantly a social worker." Most of the Congress leaders wanted to concentrate first on winning power and only then on addressing India's social ills. Gandhi reversed this order of business. He wanted Congress to address India's ills immediately and directly without regard to the English and their Raj. (The similarity between this program and the strategy of people's war is clear. In Gandhi's scheme, noncooperation was the nonviolent counterpart of guerrilla war while the constructive program was the counterpart of the Vietnamese *hiérarchies parallèles*.)

His thinking on the relationship of the constructive program to power was revealed in an answer to a letter from a reader of his journal *Indian Opinion* in 1931. The reader had written to protest that his constructive work was getting in the way of the attempt to take political power. "To me," the reader wrote, "political power is the substance, and all the other forms have to wait." Gandhi answered that "political power is not an end but only a means enabling people to better their condition in every department of life." Therefore, "Constructive effort is the substance of political power [while] actual taking over of the government machinery is but a shadow, an emblem." Five years later, at a time when he was devoting himself almost entirely to the constructive program, he wrote:

> One must forget the political goal in order to realize it. To think of the political goal at every step is to raise unnecessary dust. Why worry one's head over a thing that is inevitable? Why die before one's death? . . . That is why I can take the keenest interest in discussing vitamins and leafy vegetables and unpolished rice. That is why it has become a matter of absorbing interest to me to find out how best to clean our latrines.

If the goal was the renovation of India, why not proceed to it directly? Why not pick up a broom and sweep a latrine—as Gandhi in fact did at the first Congress meeting he attended, in 1915. If one concentrated too much on seizing the means of betterment, he feared, one might forget the goal. And in fact when India did achieve independence, this, in Gandhi's view, is exactly what happened. The Congress leaders took power but forgot what power was for. On October 2, 1947, when offered birthday congratulations, he answered, "Where do congratulations come in? It will be more appropriate to say condolences. There is nothing but anguish in my heart."

This is by no means to say, however, that Gandhi did not value political power, or did not believe in winning it or exercising it. He aimed at both throughout his life, though never as a government official. He did not say that the Congress Party should not take power; rather, he said that this was inevitable. Power might be only a "shadow"; on the other hand, there never was a thing that lacked its shadow.

He frequently suggested, indeed, that the constructive program was as effective a path to political power as noncooperation. Political power, he wrote, would in fact increase in "exact proportion" to success in the constructive effort. Whereas noncooperation drained power away from the oppressors, the constructive program generated it in the hands of the resisters. "When a body of men disown the state under which they have hitherto lived," he said in 1921, "they nearly establish their own government. I say nearly, for they do not go to the point of using force when they are resisted by the state."

Gandhi's view that winning state power, though necessary, should not be the supreme goal of India's political activity was also expressed in his arguments against adopting independence from England as the primary aim of Congress. As late as 1928, he opposed—successfully—a Congress independence resolution in response to the appointment by the English of a Statutory Commission for India. He had made his reasons clear as early as the publication of *Hind Swaraj.* Independence meant expelling the English and taking the reigns of government. But did India want "English rule without the Englishman"? Gandhi rejected this vision, as was not surprising for someone who at the time regarded the condition of modern England as "pitiable." He explained, "My patriotism does not teach me that I am to allow people to be crushed under the heel of Indian princes if only the English retire."

Independence meant dissociation—a merely negative goal. *Swaraj* meant building up something new. "Not only could *swaraj* not be 'given' to Indians," he said, "but rather it had to be created by them." Gandhi wanted action by Indians to better their own lives, not concessions or grants of authority from foreigners. *Swaraj*, as distinct from independence, must proceed from within each Indian. "Has independence suddenly become a goal in answer to something offensive that some Englishman has done?" he asked. And he went on, in simple words that seem to me to come close to the core of this arch-innovator's view of action and its proper place in the scheme of life, "Do men conceive their goals in order to oblige people or to resent their action? I submit that if it is a goal, it must be declared and pursued irrespective of the acts or threats of others." For Gandhi, ending untouchability, cleaning latrines, improving the diet of Indian villagers, improving the lot of Indian women, making peace between Muslims and Hindus—through all of which he believed he would find God—were such goals.

5

Nonviolent Revolution, Nonviolent Rule

Most of the formative revolutions of modern Western history were violent in one degree or another. They have been consigned—in political theory, if not in historical writing—to the anarchic state in which violence has always been assumed to be the final arbiter of events. The extreme violence of the French Revolution of 1789 and the Russian Revolution of 1917 is in fact probably the chief historical basis for the rarely doubted proposition that in revolution violence rules. We may inquire, though, in light of Gandhi's experience, to what extent the political theorists have been correct. In the chapters that follow, we will reflect upon a pivotal moment in four revolutions—the Glorious Revolution in England in 1689, the American Revolution, the French Revolution, and the Russian Revolution—and then we will turn to the recent Soviet collapse. Our purpose, needless to say, will not be to suggest that these revolutions were lacking in violence. It will be to ask what the roles of violent and nonviolent action were.

One point is clear at the outset: the possibility of nonviolent revolution is rooted in the democratic revolution of modern times.

Violence is a method by which the ruthless few can subdue the passive many. Nonviolence is a means by which the active many can overcome the ruthless few. In this respect, it is like people's war. If the people are not politically conscious—if they have not "risen to the height of political being," in the phrase of the German revolutionary Rosa Luxemburg—they can be neither a nourishing sea for the guerrilla fish nor a mighty army of non-cooperators. This is not to say that acts of civil disobedience by a few people, or even a single person, are unimportant. "I know this well," the American pioneer of civil disobedience Henry David Thoreau wrote in the 1840s: "If one thousand, if one hundred, if ten men whom I could name—if ten honest men only—ay, if one HONEST man, in this State of Massachusetts, ceasing to hold slaves, were actually to withdraw from this co-partnership, and be locked up in the county jail therefor, it would be the abolition of slavery in America." Yet in the long run the influence of such individuals will depend on the participation of the many. War cannot be waged without guns, tanks, and planes. Nonviolent resistance cannot be waged without active, steadfast, committed masses of unarmed people. The civil-rights movement led by Martin Luther King in the United States provides an illustration. The courageous campaign of a minority, mostly black, touched the conscience of an inactive majority, mostly white, who provided the political support necessary for the movement's historic judicial, legislative, and social victories.

It is also helpful to keep in mind the classic observation that revolutions pass through two distinct stages—overthrow of the ancien régime and foundation of a new one. Political theory as well as common sense suggests that overthrow, an act of destruction, should require violence. It seems equally obvious that the subsequent stage of foundation of the new regime, an act of creation, should be peaceful. However, the historical record shows that the reverse has much more often been the case. The overthrow has often been carried out with little or no bloodshed, while the foundation—and the revolutionary rule that follows it—has been bathed in blood.

The "Battle" of Salisbury Field

On Sunday, November 5, 1688, when the Dutch stadtholder, William of Orange, landed at the head of fifteen thousand troops at Brixham on Torbay, on the southern coast of England, there was every reason to suppose that the ensuing contest with King James II of England would be a bloody one. Still fresh in everyone's mind was the civil war of the 1640s, in which parliamentary armies had defeated the royal forces of Charles I, and in 1649 beheaded him. William, the head of the Dutch state, was James's nephew and son-in-law, and he had been invited to invade by powerful disaffected British nobles and clergy. The fundamental issues underlying the conflict—whether king or Parliament would be politically supreme and whether Protestantism would prevail in England—had first come to a head in the civil war.

James mustered his troops and sent them to Salisbury field, where they awaited William's army. The stage was set for a classic decision by arms. But no battle occurred, nor would one during the Glorious Revolution, also known as the Bloodless Revolution. Within a week, James, still in command of numerically superior forces, retreated from the field. A week later he ordered his commander in chief, Lord Feversham, to disband his force, but by then James's army was already dissolving as rapidly as if it had suffered decisive military defeat in classical Clausewitzian combat. James then ordered the destruction of the writs by which parliaments were summoned, threw the Great Seal—emblem of royal authority—into the river Thames, and fled.

What had happened? A contest not of arms but of defection and allegiance had taken place. The tide had run in one direction: the defection was almost all on the side of James, the allegiance on the side of William. The defectors included Colonel Cornbury, the son of Lord Clarendon, one of the king's principal advisers, John Churchill (the future Duke of Marlborough and ancestor of Winston Churchill), and, finally, King James's daughter, Princess Anne. Thomas Macaulay, the nineteenth-century historian and Member of Parliament, wrote in his seminal history of the revolution, "It was true that the direct loss to the crown and the direct gain to the invaders hardly amounted to two hundred men and as many horses. . . . But where could the King henceforth expect to find those sentiments in which consists the strength of states and armies?" He continues, "That prompt obedience without which an army is merely a rabble was necessarily at an end." For, "The material strength of the army were little diminished: but its moral strength had been destroyed." In the first epic battle for hearts and minds of the modern period, the decision had gone, bloodlessly, to the insurrectionary forces.

William did not frame a plan of nonviolent action; but he didn't quite stumble into his nonviolent victory, either. From the beginning, *waiting* had been his calculated strategy. He was an inveterate, zealous soldier—soon he would marshal a coalition of forces that would defeat the expansionist continental plans of Louis XIV, the Sun King of France—but in 1688 he calculated that combat with James would hurt his cause. Actual battle, he feared, would rouse the national spirit of the English against his mostly foreign troops. James, on the other hand, understood that the mere fact of battle would favor his cause. "The king was eager to fight," Macaulay explains, "and it was obviously in his interest to do so. Every hour took away something from his own strength, and added something to the strength of his enemies. It was important, too, that his troops should be blooded." Win or lose, James knew, a battle in which English soldiers were wounded and killed would stoke the patriotic ire of the English. Unfortunately for James, "All this William perfectly understood, and determined to avoid an action as long as possible."

Commanders in the field naturally weigh the strength of the

opposing forces. The two sovereigns who pondered battle at Salisbury, however, had a prior question to consider: *which* forces were the ones that would count, and *where* would the decisive struggle take place? Would it be on the field of combat, where soldiers wounded and killed each other, or would it be on that other, silent "battlefield," the hearts and minds of the people, where allegiance is won or lost? According to Macaulay, James and William somehow understood that the second field was the important one, and so combat played almost no role in the Glorious Revolution. "That great force," Macaulay writes of James's army, "had been absolutely of no account in the late change, had done nothing towards keeping William out, and had nothing towards bringing him in."

Much of what Macaulay—the great purveyor of liberal "Whig history"— wrote in the nineteenth century about the seventeenth has been challenged by historians in the twentieth, but his assessment of the role of violence in the revolution, on the whole, has not. In the 1930s, for example, G. M. Trevelyan wrote, "No encounter of the least military importance took place," and added, "the war was won and lost in the camp at Salisbury, and in the mind and heart of James." And the contemporary historian J. G. A. Pocock has described William's progress as follows: "William of Orange, a powerful European prince, landed in the west of England at the head of an army in campaign order, composed of regiments of long-service professionals in historic transition from the status of *condottieri* [mercenary commanders] to that of a national army. . . . The campaign of 1688 . . . had no military solution, only a political and revolutionary one; by 'revolution' would here be meant the dramatic collapse of a power structure and the overthrow of its head."

Pocock's words suggest that William found himself wrestling with the same distinction between military and political power that arose in people's wars in our century. If the Americans in Vietnam illustrated the negative proposition that military victory can be worthless without political victory, William illustrated the complementary proposition that political victory can be complete without military victory. That is why, whereas no amount of fighting could bring the Americans victory, no fighting at all was necessary to bring victory to William. In both cases, political victory was paramount. (What is perhaps most surprising to modern sensibilities about these pre-national or proto-national events is that William, a foreigner, was the popular, patriotic choice of the English, whereas the native James was spurned.)

William's popularity had not sprung out of nowhere. James's political support had ebbed among the people long before his armies melted away at Salisbury field. Two years earlier, James had sent his army to intimidate London, which was in a state of virtual rebellion against him. "The King ... had greatly miscalculated," Macaulay tells us. "He had forgotten that vicinity operates in more ways than one. He had hoped that his army would overawe London: but the result of his policy was that the feelings and opinions of London took complete possession of his army." London was in fact the first of many modern capitals whose rebellious spirit was to infect and destroy the allegiance of an army of an ancien régime.

The outcome of this contagion had been prepared by what can aptly be called a protracted, nationwide movement of noncooperation. The principal issues in the civil struggle between the English Parliament and James II had been in contention throughout his reign: first, whether James, a Catholic, could impose his faith on the largely Protestant English and, second, whether the prerogatives of a king were to be subordinate to the rights and powers of Parliament in particular and of law in general, or whether James was to be an "absolute" monarch, like Louis XIV. The key events in the struggle against James were acts of nonviolent resistance by men ready to pay a high price for their disobedience. Their storied deeds included the refusal of Magdalen College at Oxford to accept the king's arbitrary attempt to impose a Catholic rector on that Protestant institution and the resistance of seven Anglican bishops to his demand that they read a declaration of indulgence, which was offensive to most Anglicans and other Protestants, in their churches. The bishops' resistance was followed by their trial and dramatic acquittal, all leading directly to the decision by the great lords, on the very day of the acquittal, to invite William to invade. When King James, attempting to create a submissive parliament, ordered his lords lieutenant to scour England for subservient electors, Lord Bath was forced to report back, "No one of note will accept." He went on, "Sir, if your Majesty should dismiss these gentlemen [then sitting in Parliament], their successors would give exactly the same answer."

When the king ordered the public reading by the rest of the Anglican clergy of his declaration of indulgence, the result was similar. Macaulay describes what happened in the king's own palace: "The minister who had officiated at the chapel in Saint James's Palace had been turned out of his situation, and a more obsequious divine appeared with the paper in his hand: but his agitation was so great that he could not articulate. In truth the feeling of the whole nation had now become such as none but the very best and noblest, or the very worst and basest, of mankind could without much discomposure encounter." Macaulay's enthusiastic summary is a portrait of the politically engaged portion of the country united in de facto nonviolent resistance to its ruler. "Actuated by these sentiments," Macaulay concludes, "our ancestors arrayed themselves against the government in one huge and compact mass. All ranks, all parties, all Protestant sects, made up that vast phalanx." Here was the victory that put William on the throne, though he was not to arrive in England until a year later. If Macaulay was right, then the face-off at Salisbury was the last act of a long nonviolent struggle that had been waged in civil society. What need was there for a battle if, with the mere passage of time, one side would throw down its arms?

Conquest or Consent?

It was one thing for William to defeat James, another to take the English crown. William's approach to foundation was entirely of a piece with his approach to overthrow. In both, he relied for success not on arms but on consent by those Englishmen who had the power to decide the matter. Macaulay explains:

> His only chance of obtaining the splendid prize [the British crown] was not to seize it rudely but to wait till, without any appearance of exertion or stratagem on his part, his secret wish should be accomplished by the force of circumstances, by the blunders of his opponents, and by the free choice of the Estates of the Realm.

William convened a Revolutionary Convention, composed of lords, representatives of the House of Commons, and city magistrates, to deliberate and decide the disposition of the crown and the constitutional shape of the future. The debates revolved around the question of how, in a political system in which most agreed that the throne was and should remain hereditary, an alteration in the line of succession could be justified.

Two factions, already known as Whigs and Tories, put forward their solutions. The Whigs, who had long favored parliamentary power and had led the resistance to James from the beginning, proposed a contract theory of governing, according to which the subject's oath of allegiance to the king must be reciprocated by a royal oath of service to the people and allegiance to the law of the land. A modest, deliberate breach in the succession (William being the son of James's sister), they alleged, would merely bring the underlying contractual character of kingship out into the open—a good thing, in their eyes, for their party and its predecessors had been agitating for a contractual basis for government for more than half a century. The Tories, who denied that there could be any contractual foundation for royal rule or *any* right of resistance to a king's commands by a subject, were in a quandary. They, too, had been driven into opposition to James—by his attack on Anglicanism, among other things. They had done in fact what they had disavowed in theory: they had resisted and then driven out their king. The question was how they could justify this. For some, William's joint investiture with his wife, Mary, James's elder daughter, and the nearest *Protestant* heir to the crown, provided some legitimacy to the deed. Others suggested that they were simply submitting to conquest; for, as Macaulay notes, "No jurist, no divine, had ever denied that a nation, overcome in war, might, without sin, submit to decisions of the God of battles." The advantage to the Tories of claiming that William had conquered England was that it delivered the country from any taint of the hated contract theory. What contract could there be when a people had submitted at swordpoint?

Unfortunately, the claim was clearly contrary to fact. True, armies had marched. True, they had arrayed themselves for battle. But they had never fought. In what sense, then, had the English been conquered? Everything William had won had been delivered to him by willing Englishmen, many of whom were Tories. In effect, the English had chosen a new king. William, ever the realist, declined the temptation to misinterpret his success as a conquest. "For call himself what he might," Macaulay comments, "all the world knew that he was not really a conqueror. It was notoriously a mere fiction to say that this great kingdom, with a mighty fleet on the sea, with a regular army of forty thousand men . . . without one siege or battle, had been reduced to the state of a province by fifteen thousand invaders. Such a fiction . . . could scarcely fail to gall the national pride . . ."

William chose the contractual solution. The choice was anything but arbitrary. More than half a century of struggle between Parliament and the king pointed in that direction. In his announcement of his invasion, he had sworn to defend "a free parliament." Now he would accept the crown only with the agreement of the Revolutionary Convention, on terms that it set forth.

They turned out to include a Declaration of Right, later formalized as the Bill of Rights. This decision by William, in turn, laid the foundation for government based on the supremacy of Parliament over the king and of law over both. Overthrow based on consent had made possible foundation based on consent, which in turn made possible government based on consent. Although no balloting had occurred, the English had chosen their political future freely, and they would continue, in greater and greater measure, to do so from then on. The basis for the creation of a government that was to become, after a long development, the liberal democratic rule we know today was, in fact, a nonviolent revolution.

It would be preposterous to present William of Orange—that great warrior-king—as any sort of pacifist. Nevertheless, the revolution he brought about rested not on fear but indeed on a kind of consent. William, who may have merely happened upon the power of nonviolence, was shrewd enough to seize the opportunity. But having seized it, he found himself subject to its laws. William was not a dreamer. His biographers describe him as "cold," "taciturn," "reserved," "gloomy." A Dutchman, he spoke English imperfectly and had little emotional attachment to England. "To him she was always a land of exile, visited with reluctance and quitted with delight." "What the king wanted was power," his recent biographer Stephen B. Baxter writes, "power enough to bring England into an alliance against Louis XIV and to keep her there." But the means to this end, he understood, was not to establish absolute rule in England, even supposing it were possible.

For most of the seventeenth century, William's Stuart predecessors had battled over the power of the purse with Parliament, which had responded at several key junctures by severely curtailing the king's resources for war on the continent. It was their strongest weapon in their fight with the king. William grasped that a free parliament might be willing to loosen its purse strings to an extent that a coerced, manipulated one would not. From his point of view, granting Parliament its freedom was a recipe for more, not less power in pursuit of his aim of fighting Louis on the continent. Thus for a second time William increased his power through an act of restraint. In deciding on both of these policies, he took his bearings from the same underlying fact: his support among the English public. And both policies were richly rewarded in exactly the coin he sought: power. What is more striking still, the system of government thus established proved a fountainhead of new power for the country that established it. England at that moment began the long rise to an international preeminence that lasted through the first several decades of the past century. It is true that England's power was based on other strengths as well, including its central bank and trading system, its technical genius, which placed it in the forefront of the industrial revolution, and its early development of the free-market system, but it may be doubted that any of these would have served England as they did if not reared on the foundation of the unique system of government created in 1689. In the words of Trevelyan, "The Revolution gave to England an ordered and legal freedom, and through that it gave her power."

The Glorious Revolution and Political Theory

The nonviolence of the Glorious Revolution, although plainly described and acknowledged in the dominant, Whig school of English history, failed to find reflection in English political theory, in which the conviction persisted that tyrannical rulers could be overthrown only by violence. Pocock has written an essay that bears on the neglect by Whig theorists of the nonviolence of 1689. John Locke's famed *Second Treatise on Government*, which appeared after the revolution, with a dedication to "our great restorer, King William" whose crown was rooted in "the consent of the people," was accepted over time as the classical statement of the principles of the revolution as well as a founding document of liberal thought. However, Pocock notes, the *Treatise* was written before the revolution—probably in the early 1680s. Locke defined conditions under which the "dissolution of government"—i.e., popular rebellion—was justified. The clear reference was to the extremely violent civil war between parliamentary and royal forces that had resulted in the overthrow and beheading of Charles I and the arrival in power of Oliver Cromwell in the 1640s. As Pocock points out, "There is no way of reading Locke's scenario of appeal to heaven [to battle], dissolution of government, and reversion of power to the people except as a scenario of civil war." And yet when revolution came, there was no civil war.

The failure of prophecy was hardly Locke's alone. It was as universal as the failure in our day to predict the nonviolent fall of the Soviet Union. For some, the consequences of the misjudgment were dire. Louis XIV, for one, was badly misled, and at a high cost. "For twenty years," the historian Lord Acton writes, "it had been his desire to neutralize England by internal broils, and he was glad to have the Dutch out of the way [in England] while he dealt a blow at the Emperor Leopold [of Austria]." But as Trevelyan, who quotes this passage, comments, Louis's hopes were "defeated by the unexpected rapidity, peacefulness and solidity of a new type of Revolution." Louis was calculating according to the Realpolitik of his day. How could he guess that a phoenix—the force of modern revolution based on the consent of the governed—would rise up from those obscure and peripheral English quarrels and, in violation of the political principles he and his "realist" advisers knew so well, thwart his continental ambitions? For as Trevelyan has said, "What happened was contrary to all precedent."

The failure of theory to come to grips with the nonviolence of 1689 left both the Whigs and the Tories without adequate terms to account for what had happened. The Whigs and a few moderate Tories, eager to claim the respectability of tradition for their actions, denied that any "dissolution" of the government had in fact occurred. According to them, everything had happened according to fully constitutional processes—in keeping with the "ancient constitution"—which supposedly had been in operation since the Magna Carta. This interpretation enlisted history on the side of contract theory but at the cost of denying that any revolution had occurred. "In 1689, both William's 'conquest' and James' 'treason' could have been read as dissolutions of government," Pocock notes, "but these were unacceptable interpretations, appealing to no more than a handful of radicals, and rejected unceremoniously by the Convention and the political nation at large." The claim that the continuity of royal governance was unbroken would prove especially appealing a hundred years later, when the French launched their bloody revolution, to which the peaceful English "restoration" could be smugly contrasted. As Macaulay boasted, "Because we had a restoration, we did not have to have a revolution."

Some Tories, engaging in an opposite sort of obfuscation, acknowledged that the dethronement of James and his replacement by William were indeed revolutionary but denied, for that very reason, that the events could have been "constitutional" or "bloodless." That is why they revived the idea, rejected by William himself, that the decision by force had in fact taken place. As the conservative Burke wrote later, "The Revolution of 1688 was obtained by a just war, in the only case in which war, and much more, a civil war, can be won." Calling the revolution an outcome of war, Burke could sidestep the detested conclusion that overthrowing kings was in any way provided for in the English constitution.

The idea of nonviolent revolution, although corresponding to the facts of 1689, would have to wait more than two hundred years, until the Indian community in South Africa took its oath in the Empire Theater in 1906. Looking back from the 1850s, Macaulay marveled at the apparent anomaly: "Never, within the memory of man, had there been so near an approach to entire concord among all intelligent Englishmen as at this conjuncture," he wrote, "and never had concord been more needed. Legitimate authority there was none."

"The appeal to heaven meant the drawing of the sword," Pocock aptly comments. "The only alternative for us to imagine is some Tolstoyan or Gandhian process whereby the people dissolve government and revert to natural society by means of purely passive disobedience, and this was not available in an England where subjects who possessed arms were expected to use them." But isn't the history of James II's reign, in which the English stood, as Macaulay says, "in one compact mass" against its king, replete with scenes from just such a process? And didn't this long movement of civil disobedience prepare the way for the defections from James to William at Salisbury? A theory of nonviolent revolution was missing but something close to the fact of it was present.

John Adams and the Jurors of Massachusetts

Like England's Glorious Revolution, the American Revolution laid the foundation for lasting constitutional government. There could, however, be no Salisbury field in the United States. The surprising turn of events by which the Glorious Revolution was peacefully accomplished—the dissolution of the army of one side—was not possible in America. When the English in 1688 switched their allegiance en masse from one prince to another, they in fact made the nation whole again under a new ruler and a changed system of government. "Treason" turned out to be the path to national unity. It was not likely, however, that the Americans would accomplish a similar miracle among the redcoats, who, in order to defect, would have had to switch national as well as party loyalties. In the United States, a radically new stake was on the table. Not just a new government but a new nation, separated from the old by thousands of miles of ocean and a hundred and fifty years of semiautonomous development, was being born.

Here, at least, battles would be fought; but what would be their role in deciding the outcome of the revolution? George Washington hinted at an answer when, en route to his victory over the English at Yorktown, in September of 1781, he stopped in Philadelphia to report to Congress. "I have been your faithful servant so far as it lay within me to be," he said. "I have endured." A seemingly modest claim—yet to endure had been the heart of Washington's strategy. As long as the army remained in the field, the will of the American people to prevail remained intact; as long as the will of the American people was intact, the British could not militarily defeat the United States; as long as the British could not militarily defeat the United States, the war would go on indefinitely—a burden that the British were not ready to shoulder. Eventually, they had to tire and leave. Washington defined what it meant to endure more precisely in a remark to a crowd of bystanders. "We may be beaten by the English ... but *here* is an army they will never conquer," he said. Washington's fine but all-important distinction between an army that might be "beaten" and a people that could never be "conquered" expressed the essence of his strategy—a strategy that would have a long and rich history in the people's wars and nonviolent revolutions of the future.

To be sure, General Washington never deprecated victories and, even as he conducted a long series of retreats, won several, including the one at Trenton, New Jersey, following his renowned counterattack across the Delaware River. The war ended, of course, with the triumph at Yorktown, won with the assistance of the French navy. Yet Washington was always aware that his most important task was to insure the survival of his own forces—not strictly for military purposes but to personify the unconquerable will of the American people. The winter at Valley Forge—that epic of endurance, in which the enemy was not the British army but snow, cold, and short rations, and during which Washington invited his troops to read Tom Paine's *American Crisis,* praising these "winter soldiers"—has rightly gone down in American legend as a decisive event in the revolutionary war. Paine stated in clear terms what Washington, as leader of the revolutionary army, could only hint at—that British military victories might be useless to the

British cause. In one of the earliest and most succinct formulations of the strategy of nonviolent revolution, he said, " 'Tis not in numbers but in unity that our great strength lies; yet our present numbers are sufficient to repel the force of all the world." Therefore, "In the unlikely event that the British conquered the Americans militarily the victory would be utterly fictional." In Paine's view, his biographer John Keane comments, "Rulers can rule only insofar as they have the tacit or active support of the ruled. Without it, they become impotent in the face of citizens acting together in solidarity for the achievement of their own common goals." What is perhaps more surprising is to find the same point being made on the other side of the Atlantic by members of England's antiwar faction, led in Parliament by Edmund Burke. Burke was soon to enter into world-renowned debate with Paine over the nature of the French Revolution, but in the matter of the American Revolution the two men were in substantial agreement. Burke understood early that a policy of force in America was futile. As the British general Howe drove the Continental Army across New Jersey, Burke warned, in words that would be echoed for the next two hundred years by commanders seeking to quell people's war, "Our victories early on in the war can only complete our ruin."

In 1777, after the Americans defeated General Burgoyne at Saratoga, Burke introduced a Bill for Composing the Present Troubles in America. His argument for a quick settlement of the war on terms favorable to the colonies went to the heart of the distinction between power based on force and power based on popular consent, or "love"—a term Burke did not shy from using. The British government, he noted, wanted to obtain revenue from America through taxation. The terms of the tax legislation, however, could be guaranteed only by one of two possible means: "force" or "the honor, sincerity, and good inclination of the people." He argued, "If nothing but force could hold them, and they meant nothing but independency, as the Speech from the throne asserted, then the House was to consider how a standing army of 26,000 men, and 70 ships of war, could be constantly kept up in America. A people meaning independency, will not mean it the less, because they have, to avoid a present inconvenience, submitted to treaty."

There was more. The choice between force and consent was inseparable from the choice that England had made a century earlier for its own government, which, Burke said, was and must continue to be based not on fear but on "the love of the people." He wrote:

> Do you imagine ... that it is the Land-Tax Act which raises your revenues? that it is the annual vote in the Committee of Supply which gives you your army? or that it is the Mutiny Bill which inspires it with bravery and discipline? No! Surely, no! It is the love of the people; it is their attachment to their government, from the sense of the deep stake they have in such a glorious institution, which gives you your army and your navy, and infuses into both that liberal obedience without which your army would be a base rabble and your navy nothing but rotten timber.

Before a Drop of Blood Was Shed

John Adams, who appointed the committee that wrote the Declaration of Independence, served as the first vice president and second president of the United States, and was called "the colossus of independence" by Thomas Jefferson, penned some reflections late in his life that form a perfect complement to those of Washington, Paine, and Burke. If these three had defined negatively what could *not* decide the outcome of the revolution—namely, force—Adams defined positively what it was that *did* decide it: the combination of noncooperation and a constructive program now familiar to us.

Adams, in his late seventies, lacked the time and strength, he said, to write a history of the revolution; and so he offered his reflections only in letters to friends. He was prompted to write by the news that one Major General Wilkinson was penning a "history of the revolution," which was to begin with the battle of Bunker Hill, in 1775. Wilkinson, Adams wrote, would "confine himself to military transactions, with a reference to very few of the civil."

Such an account, Adams protested, would falsify history. "A history of the war of the United States is a very different thing," he claimed, "from a history of the first American revolution." Not only was Wilkinson wrong to concentrate on military affairs; he had located the revolution in the wrong historical period. The revolution, Adams claimed, was over before the war began:

> General Wilkinson may have written the military history of the war that followed the Revolution; that was an effect of it, and was supported by the American citizens in defence of it against an invasion of it by the government of Great Britain and Ireland, and all her allies . . . but this will by no means be a history of the American Revolution. The revolution was in the minds of the people, and in the union of the colonies, both of which were accomplished before hostilities commenced.

To his correspondent, Thomas Jefferson, a former political antagonist, he made the point emphatically: "As to the history of the revolution, my ideas may be peculiar, perhaps singular. What do we mean by the revolution? The war? That was no part of the revolution; it was only an effect and consequence of it. The revolution was in the minds of the people, and this was effected from 1760 to 1775, in the course of fifteen years, before a drop of blood was shed at Lexington."

Adams described an event that for him was a true turning point in the revolution. The English crown had decided to pay the judges of the Massachusetts Supreme Court directly. The colonists were indignant, and, at the suggestion of John Adams, voted to impeach the judges in the Massachusetts House of Representatives. The crown ignored the impeachment. Then came the decisive step. Jurors unanimously refused to serve under the embattled judges.

Adams, who likes to use military metaphors to describe great deeds of peaceful noncooperation, remarks, "The cool, calm, sedate intrepidity with which these honest freeholders went through this fiery trial filled my eyes and my heart. *That* was the revolution—the decisive blow against England: In one word, the royal government was that moment laid prostrate in the dust, and has never since revived in substance, though a dark shadow of the hobgoblin haunts me at times to this day."

Adams's gallery of heroes are all civilians, his battles nonviolent ones. When he learns that Congress has appointed a national painter, he recommends paintings, to be executed in the grand style, of scenes of protest—a painting, for example, of Samuel Adams, his cousin and a sparkplug of the revolution, arguing with Lieutenant Governor Hutchinson against standing armies. "It will be as difficult," he remarks lightly, "to do justice as to paint an Apollo; and the transaction deserves to be painted as much as the surrender of Burgoyne. Whether any artist will ever attempt it, I know not."

Acts of noncooperation were one indispensable ingredient of what Adams calls "the real American revolution"; acts of association were another. At their center were the Committees of Correspondence, through which, beginning in the mid-1760s, the revolutionaries in the colonies mutually fostered and coordinated their activities. "What an engine!" Adams wrote of the Committees. "France imitated it, and produced a revolution. England and Scotland were upon the point of imitating it, in order to produce another revolution, and all Europe was inclined to imitate it for the same revolutionary purposes. The history of the world for the last thirty years is a sufficient commentary upon it. That history ought to convince all mankind that committees of secret correspondence are dangerous machines." Here, plainly, is another predecessor of the *hiérarchies parallèles*.

The decisive revolution, according to Adams, was thus the process by which ordinary people withdrew cooperation from the British government and then, well before even the Declaration of

Independence, set up their own governments in all the colonies. The war that followed was the *military defense* of these already-existing governments against an attack by what was now a foreign power seeking to force the new country back into its empire. In his view, indeed, independence was nothing that could be *won from* the British; it had to be *forged by* the Americans. "Let me ask you, Mr. Rush," he wrote to his friend Richard Rush in April of 1815, in phrases that startlingly resemble Gandhi's later denial that Indian independence could be "given" her by England, "Is the sovereignty of this nation a gift? a grant? a concession? a conveyance? or a release and acquittance from Great Britain? Pause here and think. No! The people, in 1774, by the right which nature and nature's God had given them, confiding in original right, assumed powers of sovereignty. In 1775, they assumed greater power. In July 4th, 1776, they assumed absolute unlimited sovereignty in relation to other nations, in all cases whatsoever; no longer acknowledging any authority over them but that of God almighty, and the laws of nature and of nations."

In a recent description of the process Adams described, the historian Gordon Wood has written, "The royal governors stood helpless as they watched para-governments grown up around them, a rapid piecing together from the bottom up of a hierarchy of committees and congresses that reached from the counties and towns through the provincial conventions of the Continental Congress." On May 15, 1776, Adams notes, the Continental Congress declared that "every kind of authority under the . . . Crown should be totally suppressed," and authorized the states to found "government sufficient to the exigencies of their affairs." "For if," Wood comments, "as Jefferson and others agreed, the formation of new governments was the whole object of the Revolution, then the May resolution authorizing the drafting of new constitutions was the most important act of the Continental Congress in its history. There in the May 15 resolution was the real declaration of independence, from which the measures of early July could be but derivations." James Duane, a delegate to the first congress, called this process "a Machine for the fabrication of Independence." Adams responded, "It was independence itself."

It is interesting to observe that another very notable authority on American political history also located the foundation of the Republic before July 4, 1776. "The Union is much older than the Constitution," Abraham Lincoln said in his First Inaugural. "It was formed in fact by the Articles of Association of 1774."

If we accept Adams's view, then both the overthrow of the old regime, laid in the dust (as Adams said) through a series of acts of noncooperation, and the foundation of the new one, accomplished the moment the Americans set up governments to govern themselves, were, like the overthrow and the foundation in 1688–89, nonviolent events, and the war that followed could be seen as a war of self-defense. In that war, Adams wrote to Rush, "Heaven decided in our favor; and Britain was forced not to give, grant, concede, or release our independence, but to acknowledge it, in terms as clear as our language afforded, and under seal and under oath."

6

The Mass Minority in Action: France and Russia

It might seem perverse to mention nonviolence in connection with the French Revolution, a notoriously blood-soaked event that produced, along with much else, the first instance of large-scale, organized revolutionary terror of the modern age. Let us nevertheless consider the best known of all the days of the revolution, July 14, 1789, commemorated in France as Bastille Day.

In June of that year, the Estates-General, an assembly representing the aristocracy, the clergy, and the bourgeoisie, had been summoned, as all French schoolchildren know, by the king to meet for the first time in one hundred and seventy-five years. Louis XVI hoped that if he granted the three "estates" an advisory voice in the country's affairs, their members would agree to raise the new taxes needed to reduce the royal government's perilously high debt, run up during the recent Seven Years' War. Upon meeting, however, the Estates-General immediately passed beyond the issues of taxes and budgets to launch a full-scale challenge to the absolute rule of the king. The representatives of the third estate, the bourgeoisie, declared themselves to be "the nation," and demanded that all three orders vote together, creating a body in which the third estate's large numbers would give it the decisive voice. The king, in alarm, locked the third estate out of its meeting hall, and the body proceeded to the famous tennis court, where it took the solemn Tennis Court Oath, declaring that henceforth they were a National Assembly. Within days, the other two estates yielded to this fait accompli and joined the third, whereupon the king also acceded.

On July 11, however, the king reversed course, firing his minister of finance, Jacques Necker, who was popular in the estates and among the people, and summoning royal troops from the frontier. The stage seemed set for a decision by arms, pitting the royal forces against the Parisian rebels. In fact, however, such a contest would no more occur than had a battle on Salisbury field. Mirabeau, the renowned orator and schemer of the early years of the revolution (and something of a student of the Glorious Revolution), predicted in one of his speeches to the Assembly the course that events actually took. "French soldiers are not just automata," he declared. "They will see in us, their relatives, their friends, and their families. . . . They will never believe it is their duty to strike without asking who are the victims." The French commander in Paris, the Baron de Besenval, apparently was aware of the uncertain loyalty of his troops, because instead of sending them forth to defeat the enemy, he confined them to their barracks. There, some took a secret oath not to act against the Assembly. The king's cavalry briefly got ready to attack a crowd in the Place Vendôme, but Besenval's Gardes Françaises appeared in the crowd's defense and the cavalry fled.

On the fourteenth came the celebrated "storming" by the rebellious Parisians of the infamous royal prison the Bastille. The nineteenth-century French historian of the revolution Jules Michelet describes, with almost a touch of embarrassment, what it actually consisted of: "The bastille was not taken; it surrendered. Troubled by a bad conscience it went mad and lost all presence of mind." After a confused negotiation and a brief skirmish, the governor of the fortress turned it over to the angry crowd. Michelet describes the mood of the prison's French defenders—called *invalides*—among whom were intermixed a few Swiss mercenaries:

> Shame for such cowardly warfare, and the horror of shedding French blood, which but little affected the Swiss, at length caused the *Invalides* to drop their arms.

The Parisian rebels had been ready for a violent showdown but it never materialized; nor did the mighty ancien régime, for all its "absolute" power, ever pull itself together to strike a serious military blow against the revolution. Itself a kind of *invalide*, it in effect dropped its arms without a battle. The nineteenth-century historian of the revolution Thomas Carlyle commented acutely on the reason.

> Good is grapeshot, Messeigneurs, on one condition: that the shooter also were made of metal! But unfortunately he is made of flesh; under his buffs and bandoleers, your hired shooter has instincts, feelings, even a kind of thought. It is his kindred, bone of his bone, the same *canaille* that shall be whiffed [fired upon with grapeshot]: he has brothers in it, a father and mother—living on meal husks and boiled grass.

It was with excellent reason that the Romantic poet Chateaubriand, in a comment that strongly resembles Adams's observations on the American Revolution, later remarked, "The French revolution was accomplished before it occurred." To the degree that a revolution in hearts and minds had taken place, his comments suggested, violence was unnecessary. Rifles were not fired but thrown down or turned over to the revolution. How can there be shooting if no soldiers will defend the old regime? Individual hearts and minds change; those who have changed become aware

of one another; still others are emboldened, in a contagion of bold-
ness; the "impossible" becomes possible; immediately it is done,
surprising the actors almost as much as their opponents; and suddenly, almost with the swiftness of thought—whose transformation has in fact set the whole process in motion—the old regime, a
moment ago so impressive, vanishes like a mirage.

Must we conclude, then, that all revolutions are over before they
begin—or, at least, before they are seen to begin? If so, revolutions
would all be nonviolent. In France, however, the revolution soon
descended into carnage, signaled on the very day of the Bastille's
fall by the beheading of two officials and public display of their
heads on pikes. Still to come were the massacres in the prisons in
September of 1792, the brutal war of repression in the Vendée, the
wars against the other European dynastic powers, the execution of
the king, the repeated intimidation of the new legislature by the
Paris Commune, and, of course, the Jacobin terror. The revolutionaries would be more violent toward one another than they had
been toward the old regime.

In the French Revolution, as in the English and the American,
the stage of overthrow was nearly bloodless; but the stage of foundation was bloody—establishing a pattern that was to be repeated
in more than one revolution thereafter, and never with more fearful consequences than in the Russian Revolution of 1917. (Let us
here recall, too, that the foundation of the independent Indian
state was violent. It precipitated the partition of India and Pakistan, which cost almost a million lives.)

Nonviolent Revolution, Violent Rule

The Bolsheviks seized power in October 1917, through direct
action in St. Petersburg, the capital of Russia. Their aim was to
relieve the desperate poverty and humiliation of the workers and
peasants of Russia by overthrowing the czarist regime and establishing communism—all as a prelude to a wider revolution that

would bring communism to the rest of Europe and, in the not-too-distant future, the world. Little, if any, blood was shed in the revolution, although the Bolsheviks were quite prepared to shed it. However, having seized state power without violence, they instantly began, like the French revolutionaries, to defend and consolidate it with extreme violence, directed against not only their adversaries from the overthrown Provisional Government and the former czarist regime but also their fellow socialists. The Jacobin regime of Maximilien Robespierre ruled by terror for a little more than a year, then was overthrown in the reaction of Thermidor, in 1794. The regime founded by Lenin in 1917 did not meet its Thermidor for seventy-four years.

The sequence in which an unexpectedly nonviolent overthrow of Russia's ancien régime produced an unexpectedly violent new regime has given rise to unending interpretive debates, which have been all the more difficult to sort out because the principal actors, including, above all, Lenin, stuck with political theory rather than the facts of the case in their interpretation of their deeds. The Bolsheviks doggedly insisted they had unleashed force to seize power, even sponsoring a movie, the Soviet director Sergei Eisenstein's film *October*, that showed the imaginary battles they believed theoretically necessary. And, to complete the confusion, they falsely denied that, once in power, they ruled by force—a far more sweeping lie.

The regime's legions of subsequent detractors strove to disprove the claim that Bolshevik rule was based on consent but tended, on the whole, to confirm the claim that the takeover had been violent. As happened after the revolution of 1689, historians plainly recorded that the revolution had succeeded almost without bloodshed but theorists insisted that battles had been decisive. Especially problematic has been the assertion, made by many of the Bolsheviks' opponents, that the revolution wasn't a revolution at all but a mere coup d'état—a procedure that by definition is characterized by violence. (According to Webster's, a coup d'état is "a sudden decisive exercise of force in politics; *esp:* the violent over-throw or alteration of an existing government by a small group.")

The issue does not admit of easy resolution. The Bolsheviks, an armed minority party, did indeed unilaterally seize power without seeking permission from anyone. When it was suggested to Lenin that he await the outcome of the forthcoming Russia-wide elections to a Constituent Assembly, his answer was, "No revolution waits for *that.*" The Bolsheviks were believers in violent revolution, even in flat opposition to the will of the majority. In July 1917, Lenin wrote, in words that scarcely could have been plainer, "In times of revolution, it is not enough to ascertain the 'will of the majority'—no, one must *be stronger* at the decisive moment in the decisive place and *win....* We see countless instances of how the better-organized, more conscious, better-armed minority imposed its will on the majority and conquered it."

In February 1917, in the fourth year of the First World War, protests against shortages of bread in the capital city of Petersburg led to workers' strikes; the strikes led to demonstrations, and the demonstrations led to mass protest against both the war and the Romanov dynasty. For the second time since the new century began, the Russians were rebelling against the czar's rule. In 1905, after political concessions by the regime had failed to appease the protesters, the government put down an impending revolution by force. In 1917, however, the troops would not fight. They were receptive to the revolutionaries' socialist message of justice for the poor. Like many of James II's troops in 1688 and the Gardes Françaises in Paris in 1789, they went over to the side of the rebels. Once again, the revolutionary spirit of a capital city spread to troops, rendering them useless to the old regime. Once again, defections were pivotal, and Czar Nicholas II abdicated the throne, ending the dynasty.

Leon Trotsky, who had been a leader of the Petersburg soviet, or council, that had sprung up in 1905, had foreseen these defections and the reasons for them. In a speech he gave at his trial for his participation in the events of 1905, he proclaimed:

No matter how important weapons may be it is not in them, gentle-men the judges, that great power resides. No! Not the ability of the masses to kill others but their great readiness themselves to die—this secures in the last instance the victory of the popular rising.

For:

Only when the masses show readiness to die on the barricades can they win over the army on which the old regime relies. The barri-cade does not play in revolution the part which the fortress plays in regular warfare. It is mainly the physical and moral meeting ground between people and army.

These Gandhi-like predictions (let us recall that the revolution of 1905 inspired Gandhi as he forged satyagraha in South Africa just one year later) came true in the revolution of February 1917. The defection of the Petersburg garrison played a decisive role. In its wake, leaders of Russia's consultative congress, the Duma, and the military command joined in counseling the Czar's abdication. From start to finish, the February revolution took less than a week. In the words of the socialist Sukhanov, a firsthand observer of and actor in the revolution, it occurred with "a sort of fabulous ease." The description of these events by Aleksandr Kerensky, the second leader of the government that succeeded the Czar's, shows a remarkable resemblance to descriptions of the more recent col-lapse of the Soviet regime: "A whole world of national and politi-cal relationships sank to the bottom, and at once all existing political and tactical programs, however bold and well conceived, appeared hanging aimlessly and uselessly in space."

The Romanovs were succeeded by a system of "dual power," consisting of two ambiguously connected governing bodies: a Soviet, which was the successor to the Petersburg soviet of 1905, and a Provisional Government, composed chiefly of liberals and socialists, some of them leaders of the old Duma, which had melted away. The Soviet, though already exercising functions of government in the capital (to the extent that anybody did), was unwilling to claim full power, and invited the Provisional Government to share it. Broadly speaking, the Soviet directly represented workers, soldiers, and peasants, and the Provisional Government was the hope of the middle classes. In fact, both bodies were formally provisional, for both had agreed to yield to the Constituent Assembly, which was to be elected by all Russia in the fall and then was to establish a democratic, constitutional government for the nation.

The February revolution had revealed that the allegiance of the military—a largely peasant army, eleven million strong—was indispensable to victory. Other forces in society had, of course, played essential roles: members of the Duma eager to liquidate czarism, a radically disaffected intelligentsia, a peasantry eager and able to seize the land that it tilled, workers in the factories of Petersburg, Moscow, and other cities, and, of course, the radical political parties, including the Bolsheviks, Lenin's centralized "party of a new type." Yet "the decisive revolutionary agent," in the words of the historian Martin Malia, was "the peasant in uniform," for "it was his refusal to obey that neutralized the Imperial government."

The Overthrow

While Russia waited for the election of the Constituent Assembly, the country's politics swung between the extreme right and the extreme left. Although violence constantly threatened in this period, first from one side and then from the other, it never broke out to any great extent. The first and shortest swing was to the left. In late March, the Provisional Government sent its allies in the First World War a note that appeared to support imperialistic and annexationist war aims that were anathema to the left, which was dominant in the Petersburg Soviet, and demanded and obtained the resignation of Minister of War Aleksandr Guchkóv and Foreign Minister Pavel Milyukov. (In the politics of the time, pursuing the war was the position of the right and ending it was the position of the left.) In June, another attempt to revive the war effort was made by the new minister of war, Kerensky (later prime minister of the Provisional Government), who sought to rebuild the prestige of the new revolutionary government by launching an offensive against Austria and Germany. It failed catastrophically, creating conditions for the next swing to the left—the "July days," in which the Bolsheviks led armed demonstrations in the capital that, until the last moment, when the Bolsheviks backed off, gave every appearance of being an attempt to seize power. Now the pendulum swung back with equal force to the right. Lenin went into hiding, while much of the rest of the Bolshevik leadership, including Trotsky, was arrested. A right-wing czarist general, Lavr Kornilov, pursued tangled negotiations with the Provisional Government and then launched an insurrection against it. However, the forces he dispatched suffered a fate familiar to the student of revolutions: they melted away. In Trotsky's words, "After the February days the atmosphere of Petrograd becomes so red hot that every hostile military detachment arriving in that mighty forge, or even coming near to it, scorched by its breath, is transformed, loses confidence, becomes paralyzed, and throws itself upon the mercy of the victor without a struggle."

The way was open for the Bolshevik takeover, and the Party, whose most important leaders were now out of jail, began a debate on how to proceed. Lenin's recommendation was simple and clear. He championed an immediate "armed insurrection"—in other words, a straightforward coup d'état.

> We can (if we do not "await" the Congress of Soviets) strike *suddenly* from three points: Petersburg, Moscow, and the Baltic Fleet . . . we have the technical capability to take power in

Moscow . . . we have *thousands* of armed workers and soldiers who can *at once* seize the Winter Palace.

However, Lenin encountered strong opposition, not only from other socialist parties when they got wind of his planned coup but also from other Bolshevik leaders, two of whom, Aleksandr Zinoviev and Lev Kamenev, resigned from the Party in protest. The Bolsheviks had "no right," the pair wrote publicly, "to stake the whole future of the present moment upon the card of armed insurrection." The Party, they observed, faced a basic choice between "the tactic of conspiracy and the tactic of faith in the motive forces of the Russian revolution." The latter path was peaceable; the former led to rule by force, for without a broad coalition, as the Central Committee member Nogin wrote, the regime would "eliminate the mass organizations of the proletariat from leadership in political life . . . and can be kept in power only by means of political terror." At one point, Lenin stood alone in the Central Committee in his championship of an immediate coup.

It was Trotsky who broke the impasse. More mindful of the importance of mass support than Lenin, he proposed an armed insurrection under the auspices of the upcoming second All-Russian Congress of Soviets, in which the political strength of the Bolsheviks was then on the rise. In other words, he proposed that the Provisional Government be overthrown by a Bolshevik armed insurrection legitimated by the Soviet assemblies. (Hence the legendary slogan "All power to the soviets.") But first Trotsky had to take over the Soviets. He promptly launched a successful effort to convene unilaterally an unauthorized, all-Russian Soviet that would be controlled by the Bolsheviks.

Events, however, played havoc with the expectations of all three factions of the Bolshevik Central Committee. Neither Lenin's naked armed coup, nor Kamenev and Zinoviev's peaceful, gradual acquisition of power, nor even Trotsky's subtler, Soviet-sanctioned coup came to pass. Instead, something unplanned by anyone occurred. With Lenin still in hiding, the chief improviser on the spot was Trotsky. In a meeting of the Petersburg Soviet on October 9, a worker affiliated with the Menshevik Party, Mark Broido, proposed the foundation of a Committee of Revolutionary Defense to prepare Petersburg against the advancing German army. The Bolsheviks opposed the plan until it occurred to Trotsky that the committee, which came to be known as the Milrevkom, would, if taken over by the Bolsheviks, be an ideal instrument for overthrowing the Provisional Government. The committee was then established. So important did Trotsky consider the foundation of the committee that he later claimed its creation was in fact a "dry" or "silent" revolution that won "three quarters, if not nine-tenths, of the victory." He meant that, without a shot being fired, the Bolsheviks now had in their hands a military instrument in the capital with which, as soon as they chose to employ it, they could seize full power.

What happened next lays bare with particular clarity the process by which revolutionaries can neutralize or win over the armed forces of the existing government. (Of the revolutions discussed here, only the American, as noted, had no chance of winning over the opposing army.) The pivotal event—second in importance only to the foundation of the Milrevkom—was a meeting with the regimental committees of the Petersburg garrison, at which a motion by Trotsky was passed assuring the Milrevkom of "full support in all its efforts to bring closer the front and rear in the interest of the Revolution." In the independent socialist Sukhanov's words, "On October 21, the Petersburg garrison *conclusively acknowledged the Soviet as sole power, and the military revolutionary committee as the immediate organ of authority.*"

In Sukhanov's opinion, this decision was more than the prelude to the takeover: "In actual fact, the overturn was accomplished the moment the Petersburg garrison acknowledged the Soviet as its supreme authority." He marveled at the blindness of others to what was happening. An "insurrectionary act" had occurred. The Provisional Government did not respond. It was "busy with something or other in the Winter Palace" (its headquarters) and took no notice. But even the Bolsheviks, Sukhanov thought, were not quite aware of what they had done. "War had been declared," Sukhanov, sounding like Lenin, notes, "but combat activities were not begun." At such a moment, the "correct tactics" in the revolutionary guidebooks were to "destroy, shatter, paralyze" the enemy command, which in this case was the general staff of the army, still following orders from the Provisional Government. A mere "three hundred volunteers" could have carried out the task "without the slightest difficulty," Sukhanov thought. Instead, he observed with a note of scorn, the Bolsheviks merely sent a delegation to the commander, Georgi Polkovnikov, demanding his obedience to the Milrevkom. Polkovnikov refused, but then entered into talks with the Soviet—talks that were still in progress four days later, when the events that have gone down in history as the October 25 Bolshevik takeover occurred.

Of the seeming passivity of the Bolsheviks, Sukhanov rightly comments, "This, to put it mildly, was hardly according to Marx." To that observation, we can add only that it was hardly according to Locke, Hobbes, Rousseau, or almost any other major thinker on revolution, either, since virtually all of them had taught that revolutions had to be decided by the use of force. The whole weight of this tradition bore down on the minds of the actors.

Sukhanov showed greater appreciation of Trotsky's tactics in his report on another important episode in the preparation for the takeover. On October 23, the commander of the Peter-Paul Fortress in the center of Petersburg announced his refusal to obey a commissar sent by the Soviet. Here, surely, a military confrontation was called for, and indeed the Bolshevik Vladimir Antonov-Ovseenko did recommend sending a loyal regiment to disarm their reluctant comrades in arms. Trotsky had another idea. "He, Trotsky," Sukhanov records, would "go to the Fortress, hold a meeting there, and capture not the body but the spirit of the garrison." And he did. He made a speech there that won over the soldiers. Such was the true nature of the "fighting" that occurred in Petersburg in the days leading up to the October revolution.

Trotsky vs. Trotsky

In his book *The Russian Revolution*, Trotsky took note of Sukhanov's bafflement regarding the Bolsheviks' failure to unleash force immediately. "The Committee," he explained, "is crowding out the government with the pressure of the masses, with the weight of the garrison. It is taking all that it can without a battle. It is advancing its positions without firing, integrating and reinforcing its army on the march. It is measuring with its own pressure the resisting power of the enemy, not taking its eyes off him for a second. . . . Who is to be the first to issue the call to arms will become known in the course of this offensive, this crowding out." Then, making an addition to our list of observers in various ages who commented that the revolution was over before it seemingly began, he added that the Soviet's "declaration of October 23 had meant the overthrow of the power before the government itself was overthrown."

It was because so much had been accomplished beforehand that the twenty-fifth itself came and went with little violence. Sukhanov reports that on that day Trotsky boasted, "We don't know of a single casualty," and added, "I don't know of any examples in history of a revolutionary movement in which such enormous masses participated and which took place so bloodlessly." Trotsky identified this bloodless activity as the main engine of the revolution. "The unique thing about the October revolution, a thing never before observed in so complete a form, was that, thanks to a happy combination of circumstances, the proletarian vanguard had won over the garrison of the capital before the moment of open insurrection." In point of fact, the garrisons had also been won over before the moment of insurrection in both the Glorious Revolution and the French Revolution. The difference was that Trotsky had deliberately engineered what had happened spontaneously in England and France. Although he didn't put it in so many words, Trotsky had grasped what Mao and Ho would later formulate more explicitly—that even when the readiness and capacity to act violently is present, political action is still the most important factor in a revolutionary struggle.

Quotations from Trotsky attesting to the decisive importance of strictly political action in the revolution could be multiplied many times over. However, he also made statements of exactly the opposite import, claiming that revolutions could succeed only through armed insurrection. For example, after claiming that the main task of the insurrection—winning over the troops—had been accomplished before the twenty-fifth, he went on to add, "This does not mean, however, that insurrection had become superfluous. . . . The last part of the task of the revolution, that which has gone into history under the name of the October insurrection, was therefore purely military in character. At this final stage, rifles, bayonets, machine guns, and perhaps cannon were to decide." Elsewhere, he wrote, "Only an armed insurrection could decide the question." And quotations of this kind, too, could be multiplied many times over. These assertions, however, are unsupported by evidence.

Why, we must ask, would Trotsky wish to contradict his own clearly drawn conclusions as well as the facts of history? One likely reason is that Trotsky wrote his history in the late 1920s, at the end of a decade-long, losing struggle with Stalin to become Lenin's heir, and it was Leninist dogma that the October revolution had been the armed insurrection that Lenin had beforehand asserted it must be. As such it had already gone down in myth and story, including *October*, in which a proper battle is shown. (During the filming, several people were accidentally killed, leading one wit to remark that more people died in the filming of the storming of the Winter Palace than in the actual event.)

A comical episode on the day of the takeover suggests that Lenin, who resumed command of the Party only the day before, never did understand the nature of Trotsky's accomplishment. On the twenty-fourth of October, Bolshevik forces began to move through the capital, taking control of key points, such as the central telephone office. They encountered no resistance, leading one observer to liken the takeover to a mere "changing of the guard." Could this be the "armed insurrection" that revolutionary doctrine called for? Lenin thought not. Where was the gunfire? Where were the bodies in the streets? In his history, Trotsky notes how different from expectation events turned out to be. "The final act of the revolution seems, after all this, too brief, too dry, too businesslike—somehow out of correspondence with the historic scope of the events. . . . Where is the insurrection? . . . There is nothing of all that which imagination brought up upon the facts of history associates with the idea of insurrection."

Although Trotsky doesn't say so, one imagination brought up on these "facts of history" was Lenin's. Emerging from his hiding place in disguise, he could make out nothing that looked to him like the battles he had insisted upon. In despair at what he misjudged to be the irresolution of his colleagues, he harangued them to act. "We are confronting questions that are not solved by consultations, not by congresses (even by congresses of Soviets)," he railed, "but exclusively by the people, by the masses, by the struggle of the armed masses." Failing to see in Trotsky's having captured the spirit rather than the body of the garrison the victory that had been won, he cried out, on the day that the revolution was being accomplished without violence, for the violent revolution he had always believed in.

Trotsky's lip service to Lenin's afactual dogma would have been reason enough, in the late 1920s in the Soviet Union, for him to contradict his own plainly stated observations and conclusions, but there were other reasons as well. He had not shed blood in 1917, but by the time he wrote his history he had shed it abundantly—as commander and savage disciplinarian of the Red Army, as champion of "war communism," in which workers were subjected to military discipline, as a practitioner of and apologist for the "red terror" that was inaugurated in the first years of Bolshevik rule, and as the pitiless suppressor of the democratic Kronstadt rebellion against the Bolshevik dictatorship, in 1921. The day after the October 1917 overturn, the Bolsheviks carried out a wave of arrests and closed down all the opposition newspapers. The new rulers immediately made known their intention to monopolize power. It was on this occasion that Trotsky made an infamous threat to the non-Bolshevik socialist parties, who asked the Bolsheviks to share power with them. He said:

And now we are told: renounce your victory, make concessions, compromise. With whom? I ask: with whom ought we to compromise? With those wretched groups who have left us or who are making this proposal? . . . To those who have left and to those who tell us to do this we must say: you are miserable bankrupts, your role is played out; go where you ought to be: into the dustbin of history!

The Menshevik Party and others did in fact walk out of the meeting. Sukhanov, among those who left, later bitterly castigated himself for abandoning the field of the revolution to the Bolsheviks.

In short, while the Bolsheviks did not use violence to win power, they used it, instantly and lavishly, to keep power. Their insistence that they had needed violence to overthrow the Provisional Government provided cover of a sort for their unprovoked use of violence against their former revolutionary comrades who belonged to other parties. The repressive measures of the first days of Bolshevik rule were only the beginning of a wave of repression that almost immediately outdid czarist repression by an order of magnitude. If there was in fact a "coup," it was by the new revolutionary government against the other parties as well as opposition by ordinary citizens. The event was not so much a coup d'état as a *coup par l'état*—or a *coup de societé*—for it consisted not in the violent seizure *of* the state by military forces but in the destruction of society *by* the state once it had been taken over by the Bolshevik Party. Here, truly, were the origins of totalitarianism, to use Hannah Arendt's famous phrase.

The next step was taken in January, when the long-promised Constituent Assembly chosen in Russia's first nationwide election finally met and was promptly dispersed by Bolshevik troops. Eventually, the forcible takeover of society by the state proceeded from mere repression to Stalin's full-fledged totalitarian "war against the nation" (in the words of the Russian poet Osip Mandelstam).

But why would a party that had won power without bloodshed use it violently? The obvious answer is that the Bolsheviks' nonviolence was merely tactical. Indeed, it came as a surprise to them. Unforeseen in advance and forgotten later by Party theorists, the Bolsheviks' capture of the hearts and minds of the Czar's troops was an opportunity latent in events that the agile Trotsky had the wit to see and exploit. The nonviolence of October 25, you might say, belonged to the revolutionary situation, not to the ideology of the Bolsheviks, who believed in violence and used it unstintingly as soon as they deemed it necessary.

The curious record of the Bolsheviks' violence has a bearing on the question of whether October 25 was a mass revolution or merely a coup carried out by a small group of conspirators. Sukhanov, an anti-Bolshevik eyewitness, certainly believed that since the collapse of the Kornilov insurrection the workers of Petersburg had supported the Bolsheviks—"had been *their own people*, because they were always there, taking the lead in details as well as in the important affairs of the factory barracks." True, the Party had won its support because it had been "lavish with promises and sweet though simple fairy tales"; nevertheless, "the mass lived and breathed together with the Bolsheviks." Yet just a few years later the distinguished historian (and first president of Czechoslovakia) Tomáš Masaryk wrote in his work on the revolution, in direct contradiction of Sukhanov, "The October revolution was anything but a popular mass movement. That revolution was the act of leaders working from above and behind the scenes." And many historians have since followed Masaryk in his judgment.

In *The Russian Revolution,* Trotsky quoted and debated Masaryk. He claimed that the lack of street demonstrations and violent mass encounters was proof not of lack of mass support but of near-unanimity. Only because the Bolsheviks won every contest in the bloodless struggle for popular allegiance, he argued, could the takeover occur with so little commotion. All of this sounds very like John Adams describing the revolution in hearts and minds that preceded the Declaration of Independence. Trotsky likened the day of the twenty-fifth to an endgame in chess: "At the end of October the main part of the game was already in the past. And on the day of insurrection it remained to solve only a rather narrow problem: mate in two moves." He concluded, "As a matter of fact, it was the most popular mass-insurrection in all history."

In sorting out these contradictory claims, the most important data are probably the results of the national elections to the Constituent Assembly. They permit two conclusions: first, that in the country at large the Bolsheviks were a minority, commanding only 25 percent of the overall popular vote, and, second, that in Petersburg and Moscow—the two primary scenes of the revolution—they enjoyed a majority. (The Social Revolutionary Party, a rival revolutionary party with a large rural constituency, won 42 percent of the national vote, and the rest was divided among other parties. In the all-important Petersburg garrison, the Bolsheviks won 71 percent of the vote.) As a measure of public opinion, this election might be compared to a single photograph of a wrestling match taken with a flashbulb in a dark room, but its results are consistent with other evidence, such as elections to the Soviets in the period just before the takeover. There was factual support, in other words, both for Trotsky's and Sukhanov's claim that the masses supported the Bolsheviks and for Masaryk's claim that the Bolsheviks were in the minority. The Bolsheviks were, in fact, a *mass minority.* But that mass was concentrated where it most counted in 1917: in the revolutionary cities of Petersburg and Moscow, which were also the seats of government. (Much the same thing had happened in France, where the Parisian radicals assailed and dominated the National Assembly.) Thanks to the Bolsheviks, who evicted the Constituent Assembly at gunpoint, there are no other reliable election results to examine, but subsequent protests by factory and white-collar workers against the Bolsheviks strongly suggest that even urban support for them declined. Later, the leadership lost support among their own mass organizations, which they soon shut out of political life. What they did not lose—at least until late in the post–Cold War years— was the support of some hundreds of thousands or millions of Communist Party members and of the Red Army.

This pattern of minority mass support amid majority rejection or indifference, I suggest, is an important factor in explaining the paradox that a nonviolent revolutionary overthrow was followed by an act of revolutionary foundation that depended on violence beyond all historical precedent. If we fail to grant the Bolsheviks their measure of mass support, we cannot understand how they came to power in Petersburg *without* violence or why, once they were in power, they were able to impose their rule on almost the whole czarist empire *with* violence. In revolutions (as opposed to coups d'état), success in nonviolence depends on the extent of popular support—on the depth of what John Adams, Chateaubriand, and Trotsky (men so unlike in most respects) identified as the "revolution before the revolution," in hearts and minds.

The overthrow in Petersburg could be nonviolent, just as Trotsky said, because the Party enjoyed wide and deep mass support on that particular urban stage. The consolidation of the regime was violent because such support was absent in Russia at large, and therefore could be imposed only by force—force that the Bolsheviks could unleash because of the mass minority support that they *did* possess. In the first case, their support was strong enough that at the crucial moment effective opposition never arose in the locality of the takeover; in the second, it was strong enough to win the civil war and fuel the totalitarian engine of repression nationally—something that a small, isolated band of "conspirators" could not conceivably have done. For it is also true that terror is necessary for rule in the same proportion as support is limited—unless, of course, the party in charge is willing to yield its power to the majority. But this the Bolsheviks were never prepared to do.

Denial that the Bolsheviks enjoyed a degree of mass support may be born, in part, of an understandable wish to deny the last shred of legitimacy to their brutal rule, but this denial is won at the cost of historical accuracy. Their message of proletarian revolution in fact won support in the cities of Russia. Let me avoid any misunderstanding. Lenin and Trotsky were two of the most violent men of their supremely violent century. Together with Stalin, they were in fact the most important figures in the formation of totalitarian rule, which originates with them and only then proceeds, whether in imitation (Mussolini, Mao) or in reaction (Hitler), to spread around the world. Acknowledging all this, however, is no reason to deny the popular character of the revolution at the time it occurred in the particular cities in which it took place.

The Mass Minority in Power

By way of addendum, let us note that the story of Hitler's rise to power shows similar features. He first sought to win power in a violent coup—the Munich beer-hall putsch of 1923. When it failed, he turned, over time, to a "legal" strategy that carried him into the chancellorship in 1933. In certain respects, his strategy was one of building up *hiérarchies parallèles,* or even, in nightmarish reverse-image, a Gandhian constructive program. A comparison of these morally opposite characters of the twentieth century looks less outlandish if we recall that both Gandhi and Hitler were keen enthusiasts of direct action. Hitler, too, built up a sort of shadow government outside the existing regime. "We recognized," he explained in 1936, "that it is not enough to overthrow the old State, but that the new State must previously have been built up and be ready to one's hand. . . . In 1933, it was no longer a question of overthrowing a State by an act of violence; meanwhile the new State had been built up and all that remained to do was to destroy the last remnants of the old State—and that took a few hours." Grotesque as it might seem, Hitler even bragged about the nonviolence of his revolution. Sounding eerily like Trotsky on the day of his triumph, Hitler claimed that it had been "the least bloody revolution in history." Thereafter, his job was much easier than that of Lenin, who had to fight a civil war to consolidate his rule. Nevertheless, the procedures followed by the two men after arriving in power were of a kind: both mounted completely successful assaults by the state on the independent institutions of society, political and civil. Society, already partially enlisted in the mass movement, could not or simply did not resist.

Organizationally speaking, a disciplined, aggressive mass minority that had seized state power and was prepared to use any degree of violence to impose its will, in disregard of the will of the majority, was the dangerous new force. If by "democratic" we mean obedient to the will of the majority, then the Bolshevik mass minority was not democratic, and the Nazi movement may or may not have been (Hitler never won a majority in an election, but some historians believe that he gained majority support after coming to power); but if by "democratic" we mean propelled and sustained by the action of large masses of people, then both were democratic. Nevertheless, Trotsky's claim that the Russian Revolution was "the most popular mass-insurrection in all history" is certainly false. If he had been right, the Bolsheviks might well have achieved in all of Russia the bloodless triumph they achieved in Petersburg alone. (This larger miracle of nonviolence in fact had to await the *anti*-Bolshevik forces that in 1991 overthrew the regime Trotsky and Lenin had brought to power.) The English, the American, the French, the German, and the Indian revolutions all demonstrated the power of people to enervate and paralyze a regime by withdrawing support from it while at the same time building up parallel organizations. But unlike the English, the Americans, and the Indians, the French under Robespierre, the Russians under Lenin, and the Germans under Hitler disregarded or rejected the experience of nonviolence that their revolutions had accidentally brought to light, and turned instead—with a vengeance—to force as the method of their rule.

7

Living in Truth

The end of the regime founded by the Bolsheviks in 1917—the collapse, three-quarters of a century later, of the Soviet Union and its satellite regimes in Eastern Europe—presents the most sweeping demonstration so far of the power of "politics" without violence. The story combines many strands—economic, military, political. Among them, the failure of the Soviet economy, especially in comparison to Western economies, was of course especially important. Our subject, however, is chiefly the political processes involved. Two global developments already discussed were powerfully at work in the background. One was the nuclear paralysis of great-power war; the other was the global movement for self-determination. These two factors—one acting from "above," the other from "below," one rooted in the scientific revolution of modern times, the other in the democratic revolution—are basic to understanding the surprising manner in which the Soviet collapse unfolded.

The paralysis of great-power war imposed a stability on international relations that was new. A conviction, unknown perhaps since the days of the Roman Empire or certain dynasties of ancient China, took root that the current shape of things was likely to remain unchanged more or less forever. War itself became "cold." A moment of slightly reduced tension was a "thaw," when in a cooperative frame of mind the two powers aimed at "peaceful coexistence." In one of the acutest crises of the conflict, the Soviet Union's satellite government in East Germany built a wall around Berlin, and the United States acquiesced in the deed. "A wall is a hell of a lot better than a war," President Kennedy remarked to an adviser.

Nuclear strategy reinforced totalitarian strategy in important respects. In both nuclear deterrence and totalitarian rule, terror was used to paralyze. The men in power in Moscow, though putative revolutionaries, dreamed of stasis. In 1965, the Polish Party's first secretary, Wladyslaw Gomulka, asserted that once the Communists arrived in power in a country, they would never give it up. Even after Khrushchev's epochal secret speech denouncing Stalin's rule at the Soviet Party Congress in 1956, when the role of state terror was sharply reduced in the Soviet Union, political paralysis continued. Thereafter, the Soviet ruling class congealed into the privilege- and status-hungry *nomenklatura,* the "new class," or "Red bourgeoisie." The historian Adam Ulam has aptly called their philosophy *immobilisme,* and the state they ran a "bureaucrats' paradise." In 1968, the Soviet government formalized a principle of stasis in what came to be known, in honor of the chairman of the Communist Party of the U.S.S.R., as the Brezhnev Doctrine. On July 18, 1968, at the height of the movement for liberalization in Czechoslovakia called the Prague Spring, an open letter to the Central Committee of the Czechoslovakian Communist Party from a conclave of Communist Parties in Warsaw at which Brezhnev was present stated, "Never will we consent to allow imperialism, whether by peaceful or non-peaceful means, from within or without, to make a breach in the socialist system and change the balance of power in Europe in its favor."

However, it was Nadezhda Mandelstam, the widow of Osip Mandelstam, who penetrated to the heart of the matter. "There was a special form of the sickness—lethargy, plague, hypnotic trance or whatever one calls it," she wrote in the late sixties, in her memoir *Hope Against Hope,* "that affected all those who committed terrible deeds in the name of the 'New Era.' All the murderers, provocateurs, and informers had one feature in common: it never occurred to them that their victims might one day rise up again and speak. They also imagined that time had stopped—this, indeed was the chief symptom of the sickness. We had, you see, been led to believe that in our country nothing would ever change again, and that it was now up to the rest of the world to follow our example and enter the 'New Era.'" George Orwell was another who worried that the new form of rule might be impervious to resistance. "The terrifying thing about the modern dictatorships is that they are something entirely unprecedented," he wrote. ". . . In the past every tyranny was sooner or later overthrown, or at least resisted, because of 'human nature,' which as a matter of course desired liberty. But we cannot be at all certain that 'human nature' is a constant. It may be just as possible to produce a breed of men who do not wish for liberty as to produce a breed of hornless cows."

As Orwell's shaken faith in freedom and loss of confidence in human nature show, the apparent success of totalitarianism in suppressing popular will in the name of that same will produced a crisis of faith in the liberal West. Had the will of the people, nemesis of aristocrats, kings, and emperors in the eighteenth and nineteenth centuries, been nullified in the twentieth by Gauleiters and commissars? Had the totalitarians discovered what had eluded the tyrants of every previous age, a foolproof antidote to human freedom? Had they, with the reinforcement of nuclear terror, wrestled Father Time himself to the ground? Cold indeed was the Cold War, whose dominant note, especially in its first decade, seemed to be this double obedience to terror. No global war, of course, broke out, yet force and the threat of force reigned over the world, all-pervading and ever-present. While the totalitarian leaders were hoping that, metaphorically, time had stopped, they and their Western antagonists were wheeling into place the nuclear machinery that could actually cut short historical time.

And yet the universal conviction proved wrong—stupendously wrong. Human freedom had not died under totalitarian rule. It was about to make a spectacular demonstration of its power. The Cold War, paralyzed at the summit of the world order, was moving along unnoticed, circuitous pathways toward its amazing denouement. Resistance, blocked in the time-tested arteries of military action, was forced into the world's unremarked-on capillary system, where, disregarded, it quietly advanced. And then it gushed forth in mass protest by entire societies. In retrospect, it's apparent that the long series of rebellions against the Soviet empire in Eastern Europe—in East Germany in 1953, in Poland and Hungary in 1956, and in Czechoslovakia in 1968—which at the time looked like exercises in noble futility, were actually stages on the way to the Soviet collapse. The actors were, among others, workers on factory floors, rebellious students, intellectuals talking to one another over kitchen tables or "writing for the drawer," dissidents who were promptly dispatched to concentration camps or psychiatric hospitals, disaffected technocrats, and even bureaucrats in the state apparatus. Every step they took was ventured without a chart or a clear destination. Yet the revolution they made was peaceful, democratic, and thorough.

The nonviolent popular resistance that brought down the Berlin Wall was as historically consequential—as final an arbiter— as either of the two world wars. It ended Soviet communism and its shadow, the specter of "international communism." It finished off an empire whose origins predated the communists. It initiated the creation of more than a dozen new countries. It was the equivalent of a third world war except in one particular—it was not a war.

A Better Today

It's often said, with good reason, that the Soviet collapse proceeded from the top down. It is no less correct to say that it trav-
eled from the outside in—from the Eastern European periphery to
the Soviet center. And in Eastern Europe it decidedly flowed from
the bottom up. In the first stage of the collapse, the Solidarity
movement of the early 1980s in Poland in effect dissolved the local
communist system from within, demonstrating once and for all its
previously unsuspected radical weakness of the entire structure
of Soviet power. In Czechoslovakia and Hungary, quieter, more
gradual movements were under way. It was not the first time that
the occupied western territories of the empire proved to be its
Achilles' heel. In 1945, in a cable from the American embassy in
Moscow to the State Department, George Kennan noted that in
the nineteenth century Russian repression had turned Poland into
a "hotbed out of which there grew the greater part of the Russian
Social Democratic Party which bore Lenin to power." Kennan
was one of the few who understood that the Soviet Union's occupation of Eastern European nations after 1945 posed a lethal danger to Moscow. "Successful revolts on their part against Moscow
authority," he wrote, "might shake the entire structure of Soviet
power." Totalitarian rule, it was turning out, had not endowed the
Soviet empire with immunity to the fever for self-determination
and freedom that had by then overturned the Western colonial
empires. It wasn't until the second stage of the collapse, when
Mikhail Gorbachev came to power in Moscow and adopted his
radical policies of perestroika and glasnost in the Soviet "center,"
that change from the top down led to the final dissolution.

Until the late 1970s, the idea that Soviet power might be challenged from within had been largely discarded, and the progress of
the revolution from the edges of the empire to its heart caught
almost everyone, observers and participators alike, by surprise.
Until very late in the day, not even the activists who founded Soli-

darity imagined that they were inaugurating the collapse of their local, satellite governments, much less the downfall of the whole Soviet system. On the contrary, one of their most original achievements was to discover a way to act and fight for more modest, immediate goals *without* challenging the main structures of totalitarian power head on. Their ambition—itself widely condemned as utopian by Western observers—was merely to create zones of freedom, including free trade unions, within the Soviet framework. And yet once the disintegration at the edges of the empire began, it proved to have no stopping point. The contagion, which combined a longing for national self-determination with a longing for freedom, proceeded, in an unbroken progression from the Eastern European satellites to the peripheral republics of the union (in particular, Lithuania), and from there to Moscow itself, where, to the amazement of all, Russia joined the company of rebels against the Soviet Union, which, lacking now any territory to call its own, melted into thin air.

One of the puzzles of the Soviet downfall is how it happened that a peaceful revolution described by its authors as "self-limiting" (because it did not aim at state power) brought about this unlimited result. As guides to the Eastern European stage of the anti-Soviet revolution, we shall adopt three writer-activists—Adam Michnik, of Poland, Václav Havel, of Czechoslovakia, and Gyorgy Konrád, of Hungary. In the 1970s, the walls of the Kremlin fortress rose impregnable, as it seemed, before their eyes. Fresh in their minds was the succession of defeated rebellions against Soviet domination in East Germany (1953), Poland (1956), Hungary (1956), and Czechoslovakia (1968). From these routs the three writers drew a lesson that might have seemed a counsel of despair but in fact was the basis for a revival of hope and activity. They decided to accept the brute existence of the system as an unchangeable fact of life for the time being. "To believe in overthrowing the dictatorship of the party by revolution and to consciously organize actions in pursuit of this goal is both unrealistic and dangerous,"

Michnik wrote in 1976, in a pivotal essay called "A New Evolutionism." For "the Soviet military and political presence in Poland is the factor that determines the limits of possible evolution, and this is unlikely to change for some time."

In the mid-1980s, after a declaration of martial law in 1981 had temporarily suppressed Solidarity in Poland, Konrád was still writing, in his book *Anti-Politics*, "It is impossible to alter the . . . system from inside East Europe by means of dynamic, uncontrolled mass movements . . . because the limits of social change are fixed by the military balance, and by a Soviet power elite which labors to preserve the military status quo and has considerable means with which to do it—means that are political as well as military." The division of Europe that had been decided at the summit meeting at the Soviet Black Sea resort of Yalta at the end of the Second World War—an iconic event for Eastern Europeans, known to them simply as "Yalta"—symbolized, Konrád observed, the ancient idea that force has the last word in political affairs:

> The morality of Yalta is simple: those who have the bombs and tanks decide the social and political system. Since the United States and the Soviet Union had the most bombs and tanks, they were called to lead the world. Later—by the fearful light of Hiroshima— their calling was confirmed, for only these two giant nation-states had the resources to build arsenals of nuclear weapons.

Havel, commenting in a similar vein, wrote that what he called the "post-totalitarian" dictatorships of the Soviet empire were "totally controlled by the superpower center and totally subordinated to its interests." He, too, cited the nuclear standoff. "In the stalemated world of nuclear parity, of course," he wrote, "that circumstance endows the system with an unprecedented degree of external stability." Havel, it must be added, was considerably less impressed with the durability of the Soviet edifice than most of his colleagues in resistance. He was one of the very few who suggested that the worldwide self-determination movement, which the Soviets blindly believed to be working in their favor, might undermine the Soviet Union. In an essay in 1978, he took note of the rebellions that in one country after another had rocked the empire, and commented, "If we consider how impossible it is to guess what the future holds, given such opposing trends as, on the one hand, the increasingly profound integration of the [Communist] 'bloc' and the expansion of power within it, and on the other hand the prospects of the USSR disintegrating under pressure from awakening national consciousness in the non-Russian areas (in this regard the Soviet Union cannot expect to remain forever free of the worldwide struggle for national liberation), then we must see the hopelessness of trying to make long-range predictions."

Havel's agnosticism, however, led him to the same practical counsel that Konrád and Michnik were giving: it was a mistake to try to overthrow the system. Activism should be directed at achieving immediate changes in daily life. He proposed unshakable commitment to achieving modest, concrete goals on the local level. "Defending the aims of life, defending humanity," he asserted, "is not only a more realistic approach, since it can begin right now and is potentially more popular because it concerns people's everyday lives; at the same time (and perhaps precisely because of this) it is also an incomparably more consistent approach because it aims at the very essence of things." The three men in effect lowered their field glasses from the remote heights of state power and turned their gazes to the life immediately around them. Gandhi had faced neither totalitarian rule nor nuclear stalemate, yet he, too, had arrived at a decision to aim not at state power directly but at immediate local improvement of life, to be achieved through direct action in the form of the constructive program, which he, too, saw as the essence of things. When Eastern Europeans did this in their own way, a rich field of activity opened up to them, in what they soon began calling civil society.

Neither the term nor the fact of civil society was new. Tom Paine, who so greatly appreciated the power of nonviolent popular resistance during the American Revolution, was, according to his biographer John Keane, the first to fully elucidate the distinction between civil society and civil government. Until Paine, the terms had been used interchangeably. The key distinction had been the much older one between the wild, contractless, stateless state of nature and the orderly civil state, which was the fruit of the "original contract" among the people. Paine now asserted the existence of two contracts—the original contract, by which the people quit the state of nature and entered *society*, and a second one, by which people in civil society created a *government*. The consequence was the addition of a third state, a purely social state (hence civil "society"), between the traditional state of nature and the civil state. In language that foreshadows the distinctions the Eastern Europeans would draw, Paine praised society at the expense of government:

> Society is produced by our wants, and government by our wickedness; the former promotes our happiness *positively* by uniting our affections, the latter *negatively* by restraining our rule. The one encourages intercourse, the other creates distinctions.

For Paine, the foundation of civil society was an almost entirely benign first step, the foundation of government a regrettably necessary second step.

In the hands of the Eastern European activists, the idea of civil society underwent further development. It was turned into a rival—almost an alternative—to government. Their new rule of thumb was to act not *against* the government but *for* society—and then to defend the accomplishments. In 1976, in "A New Evolutionism," Michnik asserted that the suppression of the Prague Spring and of a Polish student-protest movement in March of 1968 had spelled the end of any hope of reforming the state from within. The new generation must learn to act in a new way: "I believe that what sets today's opposition apart from the proponents of those ideas [of reform in the past] is the belief that a program for evolution ought to be addressed to an independent public, not to totalitarian power. Such a program should give directives to the people on how to behave, not to the powers on how to reform themselves." Michnik later set forth what he called a "philosophy of political activity in a post-totalitarian system." "Why post-totalitarian?" he asked. "Because power is still totalitarian, whereas society isn't any more; it is already anti-totalitarian, it rebels and sets up its own independent institutions, which lead to something we could call civil society, in Tocqueville's sense. That is what we tried to build: civil society."

Michnik's words of 1976 fell on fertile ground. They anticipated (and helped to produce) a blossoming of civic and cultural activity in Poland. An early example was the Worker's Defense Committee. Its purpose was to give concrete assistance to workers in trouble with the authorities—assistance that the organization referred to as "social work." Help was provided to the families of workers jailed by the government. Independent underground publications multiplied. A "flying university," which offered uncensored courses in people's apartments and other informal locations, was founded. Organizations devoted to social aims of all kinds—environmental, educational, artistic, legal—sprouted. In both form and content, these groups were precursors to the ten-million-strong Solidarity movement that arose in 1980.

The Explosive Power of Living in Truth

What Michnik called a new evolutionism or building civil society Havel called "living in truth"—the title of an essay he published in 1978. Living in truth stood in opposition to "living in the lie," which meant living in obedience to the repressive regime. Havel wrote:

We introduced a new model of behavior: don't get involved in dif-
fuse general ideological polemics with the center, to whom numerous concrete causes are always being sacrificed; fight "only" for
those concrete causes, and fight for them unswervingly to the end.

Why was this living in truth? Havel's explanation constitutes one
of the few attempts of this period—or any other—to address the
peculiarly ineffable question of what the inspiration of positive,
constructive nonviolent action is. By living within the lie—that
is, conforming to the system's demands—Havel says, "individuals
confirm the system, fulfill the system, make the system, *are* the
system." A "line of conflict" is then drawn through each person,
who is invited in the countless decisions of daily life to choose
between living in truth and living in the lie. Living in truth—
directly doing in your immediate surroundings what you think
needs doing, saying what you think is true and needs saying, acting the way you think people should act—is a form of protest,
Havel admits, against living in the lie, and so those who try to live
in truth are indeed an opposition. But that is neither all they are
nor the main thing they are. Before living in truth is a protest, it is
an affirmation. Havel, who sometimes makes use of philosophical
language, explains as follows:

> Individuals can be alienated from themselves only because there is
> *something* in them to alienate. The terrain of this violation is their
> essential existence.

That is to say, if the state's commands are a violation deserving of
protest, the deepest reason is that they disrupt this *something*—
some elemental good thing, here called a person's "essential existence"—that people wish to be or do for its own sake, whether or
not it is opposed or favored by the state or anyone else.

This is the point, it seems to me, that John Adams was getting at when he said that the American Revolution was completed before the war, and that Gandhi was making when he suggested that, if independence is a goal, then "it must be declared and pursued irrespective of the acts or threats of others." Like them (and like Nietzsche), Havel rebels against the idea that a negative, merely responding impulse is at the root of his actions. He rejects the labels "opposition" and "dissident" for himself and his fellow activists. Something in *him* craves manifestation.

Of those labels he writes:

> People who so define themselves do so in relation to a prior "position." In other words, they relate themselves specifically to the power that rules society and through it, define themselves, deriving their own "position" from the position of the regime. For people who have simply decided to live within the truth, to say aloud what they think, to express their solidarity with their fellow citizens, to create as they want and simply to live in harmony with their better "self," it is naturally disagreeable to feel required to define their own, original and positive "position" negatively, in terms of something else, and to think of themselves primarily as people who *are* against something, not simply as people who are what they are.

For Havel, this understanding that action properly begins with a predisposition to truth—often considered a merely private or personal endowment—has practical consequences that are basic to an understanding of political power:

> Under the orderly surface of the life of lies, therefore, there slumbers the hidden sphere of life in its real aims, of its hidden openness to truth. The singular, explosive, incalculable political power of living within the truth resides in the fact that living openly within the truth has an ally, invisible to be sure, but omnipresent: this hidden sphere.

Havel is describing, in words that anticipated the fall of the Soviet Union before that event had occurred, a secular variant of what Gandhi had called "truth force." If Michnik's words anticipated the sudden rise of Solidarity, Havel's bore fruit in the rise of the resistance movement in Czechoslovakia called Charter 77 and in the "velvet revolution" that put an end to communist power in Czechoslovakia.

Konrád offered what might be called a Hungarian version of living in the truth. Having witnessed the slow but surprisingly broad liberalization of the Hungarian system in the 1970s and eighties, he hoped that the changes under way in society would infect the communist functionaries, who would come to see "that their interests were better served by forms of government other than dictatorship." Konrád, who in such passages obliquely debated his Polish and Czech contemporaries on how change might occur, urged "confidence in this growing complexity—in the fact that a society can gradually slough off dictatorship, and that the prime mover in that process is a growing middle class." In his scheme, this liberalization, called "goulash Communism" by some, would gradually turn into goulash decommunization. Konrád wanted society to "absorb" the regime in a "ripening social transformation." He wanted the "iceberg of power . . . melted from within." He cited the historical precedent of the surrender of the dictatorial, right-wing regime of Francisco Franco in Spain to democratic forces in the 1970s. "Proletarian revolution didn't break out in any country of southern Europe," he commented. "If it had, the military dictatorships would only have hardened."

In all three of the Eastern European movements, the strategy was to bypass the government and tackle social problems directly, as Gandhi had done with his constructive program. But whereas "social work" presented no challenge to the Raj, it did challenge the Soviet regime. Within the class of repressive regimes, the Raj was an authoritarian regime, and left vast areas of Indian life untouched. The Raj had no difficulties with Gandhi's constructive program, to which it offered no rival; it was compelled to react only when he practiced noncooperation with the state. To the totalitarian Soviet regime, which sought to control almost every aspect of life, very much including the social, on the other hand, any independent activity looked like the beginnings of a rival governing power. Gandhi had said that once people disown the state under which they live they have "nearly" established their own government. On rare occasions, leaders of totalitarian regimes have also shown that they also understood the danger. In his memoirs, Khrushchev described his fear of the thaw he had started by his secret de-Stalinization speech of 1956. "We were scared—really scared," he wrote. "We were afraid the thaw might unleash a flood, which we wouldn't be able to control and which could drown us. It could have overflowed the banks of the Soviet riverbed and formed a tidal wave which would have washed [away] all the barriers and retaining walls of our society."

We have noted the central role in revolutions of defections among the troops of the old regime. Under a totalitarian regime, which seeks to mobilize the entire population in support of its ideological cause, the people become a sort of army on whose obedience the regime relies. But the very immensity of this army presents a target of opportunity for the opposition. If the essence of totalitarianism is its attempted penetration of the innermost recesses of life, then resistance can begin in those same recesses—in a private conversation, in a letter, in disobedience of a regulation at work, even in the invisible realm of a person's thoughts. Havel gives the example of a brewer he knew who, putting aside official specifications for making beer, set about making the best beer he could. Such was a brewer's living in truth.

Once the unraveling of the single, indivisible fabric of totalitarianism began, the rapidity of the disintegration could be startling. In Havel's prophetic words, "Everything suddenly appears in another light, and the whole crust seems then to be made of a tissue on the point of tearing and disintegrating uncontrollably."

Totalitarian rule made constructive work and noncooperation difficult and costly but at the same time was especially vulnerable to those tactics. The pessimistic stock observation that Gandhi could never have succeeded against a totalitarian regime had an optimistic corollary. If such a movement could ever get going, as it did in the Soviet empire, the unraveling would be sudden and irresistible. The "Salisbury field" of a totalitarian regime was its entire society.

The radical potential of constructive work was implicit in a famous saying of Jacek Kuron, an intellectual adviser to Solidarity, who in the late 1970s counseled angry workers, "Don't burn down Party Committee Headquarters, found your own." And that is what they did, in August of 1980, when a spontaneous strike by workers in the Baltic shipyards spread like wildfire through Poland. Soon something like a general strike was under way, and the regime was forced to come to terms by granting, among other concessions, the right to form an independent trade union. The regime would not collapse for another nine years, but its death throes had already begun.

Even before the rise of Solidarity, Havel had reflected on the potential for developing power by founding new associations and organizations. The natural next step for an individual already trying to live in truth in his individual life, he advised in 1978, was to work with others to found what the writer Václav Benda called "parallel structures." These could be expected to arise first, Havel writes, in the realm of culture, where a "second culture," in the phrase he borrows from the rock musician Ivan Jirous, might develop. The step beyond that would be the creation of a "parallel polis" (another phrase of Benda's). This was the Czech version of Kuron's advice to the Polish workers to build their own headquarters.

In 1980, when Solidarity sprang into existence, it preferred on the whole to soft-pedal these radical possibilities, which, its leaders believed, might well provoke the Soviet Union to intervene, as it had in the past in Eastern Europe. They proposed instead a novel division of functions. "Society" would run itself democratically, but "power," which is to say the central government (and especially that part of it in charge of foreign affairs), would be left in the hands of the Communist Party dictatorship, whose survival would serve as a guarantee to the Soviet Union that its security interests would not be challenged. Long debates within the Solidarity movement were devoted to negotiating and fixing the boundaries of such a compromise. The debates came to an end only with the imposton of martial law, in December of 1981.

The similarities between the Eastern European movements and Gandhi's movement in India are obvious. If there were evidence that Havel had pored over Gandhi's works, we might suppose that his phrase "living in truth" was an inspired translation of "satyagraha"—a term so difficult to render into other languages. In both movements, we find a conviction that the prime human obligation is to act fearlessly and publicly in accord with one's beliefs; that one should withdraw cooperation from destructive institutions; that this should be done without violence (Gandhi endorses nonviolence without qualifications; each of the Eastern European writers enters some qualifications); that means are more important than ends; that crimes shouldn't be committed today for the sake of a better world tomorrow; that violence brutalizes the user as well as his victim; that the value of action lies in the direct benefit it brings society; that action is usually best aimed first at one's immediate surroundings, and only later at more distant goals; that winning state power, if necessary at all, is a secondary goal; that freedom "begins with myself," as Michnik said, is oriented to love of truth, and only then discovers what it hates and must oppose; and that state power not only should but actually does depend on the consent of the governed.

The differences are also obvious. The Eastern Europeans demonstrated that revolution without violence did not have to depend on religious faith or an abstemious life. Whereas Gandhi's movement was spiritual in inspiration, the Eastern European movements were largely secular (although the Catholic Church played an important role in Poland). Whereas Gandhi called for a strict renunciation of selfish desires in favor of civic obligation, the Eastern Europeans sought to separate the private and other realms of life from political intrusions, of which they were heartily sick after decades of totalitarian rule. (The last thing they would have wanted was a single standard, whether imposed by God, "truth," or anything else, to which people had to subordinate every realm of their existence.) Whereas Gandhi was radically antimaterialistic, the Eastern Europeans were, variously, either only moderately so or hugely interested in material abundance for society. (There can be no such thing as goulash satyagraha.) Whereas Gandhi was an ascetic, the Eastern European leaders tended, in their personal lives, to be *hommes moyens sensuels*. Whereas Gandhi dreamed of a village-based cooperative society unlike any ever seen, then or since, the Eastern Europeans wanted to adopt the kind of parliamentary democracies and free-market economies already functioning in much of the world.

Although nonviolence was not an article of dogma for the Eastern Europeans, it was an essential element of their chosen form of action. "The struggle for state power," Michnik wrote, "must lead to the use of force; yet . . . according to the resolution passed at the memorable Solidarity Congress in Gdansk, the use of force must be renounced." One reason for the choice of nonviolence was pragmatic. The totalitarian state's monopoly on the instruments of violence required a search for some other means. "Why did Solidarity renounce violence?" Michnik asked while in prison after the imposition of martial law. He answered, "People who claim that the use of force in the struggle for freedom is necessary must first prove that, in a given situation, it will be effective, and that force, when it is used, will not transform the idea of liberty into its opposite. No one in Poland is able to prove today that violence will help us to dislodge Soviet troops from Poland and to remove the Communists from power. The USSR has such enormous power that confrontation is simply unthinkable. In other words: we have no guns." But in a comment that adds to our collection of remarks from various times and places claiming that the real revolution has occurred before the fighting (if any) breaks out, Michnik wrote, "Before the violence of rulers clashes with the violence of their subjects, values and systems of ethics clash inside human minds. Only when the old ideas of the rulers lose their moral duel will the subjects reach for force—sometimes."

Also like Gandhi, the Eastern Europeans shunned violence for moral reasons: they did not wish to become like the enemies they despised. The point was not to change rulers; it was to change the system of rule, and the system they opposed had been based on violence. Michnik again: "My reflections on violence and revolution were sparked by my puzzlement about the origins of totalitarianism. I searched for clues in the writings of George Orwell, Hannah Arendt, Osip Mandelstam, and Albert Camus, and I came to the conclusion that the genesis of the totalitarianism system is traceable to the use of revolutionary violence."

Havel concurred. He and his colleagues had "a profound belief that a future secured by violence might actually be worse than what exists now; in other words, the future would be fatally stigmatized by the very means used to secure it." In *Anti-Politics*, Konrád expressed full agreement, and drew an important conclusion. His mention of an active search for an alternative to the traditional ultima ratio is especially noteworthy:

The political leadership elites of our world don't all subscribe equally to the philosophy of a nuclear *ultima ratio*, but they have no conceptual alternative to it. They have none because they are professionals of power. Why should they choose values that are in direct opposition to physical force? Is there, can there be, a political philosophy—a set of proposals for winning and holding power— that renounces *a priori* any physical guarantees of power? Only antipolitics offers a radical alternative to the philosophy of a nuclear *ultima ratio.* . . . Antipolitics means refusing to consider nuclear war a satisfactory answer in any way. Antipolitics regards it as impossible in principle that any historical misfortune could be worse than the death of one to two billion people.

Violence, the Eastern Europeans found, was to be shunned for another reason: it was useless—more or less beside the point—for the sort of action they had resolved to pursue. Someone once remarked to Napoleon that you can't mine coal with bayonets. Neither are bayonets helpful for writing a book, cleaning a room, designing a microchip, or dressing a wound. Violence might or might not be useful for overthrowing a state, but Solidarity had renounced this ambition.

What Is and What Ought to Be

The comments of Michnik, Havel, and Konrád bring into the open a question never far from the surface when people choose nonviolent over violent action. Should nonviolence be chosen more for moral and spiritual reasons or more for practical ones? The issue is important because the believer in nonviolent action seems, to an unusual degree, to be ready to suffer defeat rather than abandon his chosen means. For Gandhi, nonviolence was foremost a moral and spiritual requirement. No mere circumstance—least of all the approach of defeat—could justify abandoning it. That is what he meant when he said that nonviolence was for him a creed, not a policy. For Michnik, by contrast, nonviolence was more a policy. He said he wanted the Russians to know that if they used force to put down the Polish movement, they would find themselves "spitting up blood." These are words that Gandhi could never have spoken. On the other hand, as we've seen, Gandhi's nonviolence was founded in part upon the recognition that in a violent fight with the English, the Indians would be "crushed in a minute." In other words, as Michnik said of the Poles, the Indians had no guns. And Gandhi had used language close to Michnik's when he declared that the Indians therefore must create a weapon "which would be different from and infinitely superior to the force which the white settler commanded." In these words, too, there is a kind of ambiguity. Gandhi sought spiritual victory above all else, yet he wanted to win in this world as well.

With Gandhi, we might say, the moral motive is primary, the pragmatic secondary, while with the Eastern Europeans the reverse is true. Either way, it seems to be in the very nature of principled nonviolent action that it tends to combine moral and practical calculation—just as it seems to be in the nature of violent action that, justifying means by ends, it tends to separate the two. That nonviolent action won more and more impressive successes even in the violent twentieth century has, I suggest, a meaning. Isn't it entirely fitting that, in a time when violence has increased its range and power to the point at which the human substance is threatened with annihilation, the most inventive and courageous people would cast about for something better to use? But the wonder of it is not that they have sought but that they have found. Michnik and his colleagues told themselves that they and others had discovered the political equivalent of the "atomic bomb," and they were right—except that their invention in fact accomplished what no actual atomic bomb could accomplish, the defeat of the Soviet Union. When they began their agitation, the iron law of the world dictated that revolution must be violent because violence was the foundation of power, and only power enables you to storm that citadel of violence and power, the state, and so to *take power*. When they were finished, and state after repressive state had been dissolved with little or no use of violence, a new law of the world had been written, and it read: Nonviolent action can be a source of revolutionary power, which erodes the ancien régime from within (even if its practitioners don't aim at this) and lays the foundation for a new state. If totalitarianism is a perversion of the democratic revolution, then the rise of nonviolent revolution is totalitarianism's antidote and cure, pointing the way to a recovery of democracy and, perhaps, to a deeper and truer understanding of democracy's nature, which is bound up with the principle of nonviolence.

Hanging over these political issues are questions of a more philosophical character, having to do with whether or not people are to suppose that the conduct they require of themselves is patterned upon, or takes its cue from, some underlying order of things, natural or divine, or whether, on the contrary, human beings live in an alien, inhuman universe. The tendency of philosophers at least since Nietzsche has been to take this latter view. Neither Gandhi nor Havel considered himself a philosopher, but both plainly thought otherwise. It is striking, for instance, that both chose the word "truth"—perhaps the key word for philosophy— as the touchstone for their actions. Each had very concrete, even mundane, things in mind—for example, the good beer the Czech brewer wanted to brew or the sanitary conditions in India's villages that absorbed Gandhi so much. But each also occasionally touched on metaphysical issues. Describing the illness and death after a jail term in South Africa of a *satyagrahi* called Valliama, Gandhi said, "The world rests upon the bedrock of *satya* or truth. *Asatya,* meaning untruth, also means non-existent, and *satya* or truth also means that which *is.* If untruth does not so much as exist, its victory is out of the question. And truth being that which is can never be destroyed. This is the doctrine of *satyagraha* in a nutshell." For Gandhi, this "truth" was God. In the essay "Politics and Conscience" Havel, a secular man, wrote in terms that were quite different yet conveyed a similar meaning:

> At the basis of this world are values which are simply there, perennially, before we ever speak of them, before we reflect upon them and inquire about them. It owes its internal coherence to some-

thing like a "pre-speculative" assumption that the world functions and is generally possible at all only because there is something beyond its horizon, something beyond or above it that might escape our understanding and our grasp but, for just that reason, firmly grounds this world, bestows upon it its order and measure, and is the hidden source of all the rules, customs, commandments, prohibitions. . . . Any attempt to spurn it, master it, or replace it with something else, appears, within the framework of the natural world, as an expression of *hubris* for which humans must pay a heavy price.

To live in accord with this "something" was to live in truth. A similar confidence was expressed in the saying that, in the Western tradition, must be considered the foundation stone of any philosophy of nonviolence, namely Jesus' "They that live by the sword shall die by the sword." The advice does more than prescribe conduct; it makes a claim about the nature of the human world. We cannot suppose Jesus means that everyone who kills will be killed. But we can suppose he means that violence harms the doer as well as his victims; that violence generates counterviolence; and that the choice of violence starts a chain of events likely to bring general ruin. What Gandhi, Havel, and most of the others who have won nonviolent victories in our time believed and made the starting point of their activity was a conviction—or, to be exact, a faith—that if they acted in obedience to certain demanding principles, which for all of them included in one way or another the principle of nonviolence, there was, somewhere in the order of creation, a fundament, or truth, that would give an answering and sustaining reply.

Revolution from the Side

The rise of Solidarity, in which millions of Poles actively and naturally opposed a Soviet-sponsored communist regime, foreshadowed the collapse of the Soviet Union a decade later. Solidarity laid bare the previously invisible weakness of Soviet rule. The trance of totalitarian power of which Nadezhda Mandelstam had spoken was broken. And yet the collapse of the Soviet Union itself—"the center," as it was called—proceeded along a different path. Moscow was two steps behind Poland in 1980. The formative events for Soviet liberals had been the Prague Spring of 1968, which aroused their hopes that communism could acquire a "human face," and the intense disappointment, bordering on despair, they felt when Soviet tanks rolled into Czechoslovakia. The leaders of the Czech Party, who were trying to liberalize the Party from within, had spoken the language of "reform communism," which Soviet officialdom understood, whereas the Poles in the 1980s already spoke the language of a post-communist era, which not even Soviet dissidents could yet imagine. Moscow had not experienced even Czech-style reformism, much less anything like Michnik's new evolutionism or Havel's living in truth. Khrushchev's reformist de-Stalinization of 1956 had been the limit of their experience of liberalization, and Khrushchev had been deposed by hard-liners. Such heroic oppositional figures as the novelist and author of *The Gulag Archipelago* Aleksandr Solzhenitsyn, the father of the Soviet H-bomb and leader of the human-rights movement Andrei Sakharov, his wife Yelena Bonner, and the dissident scientist Yuri Orlov had served as moral tuning forks for many who shared their beliefs, if not their almost superhuman courage; but in the face of repression they had not been able to spark a mass political movement. The recovery of civil society in the Soviet Union began only in the late 1980s, after Gorbachev's reforms had been under way for a few years. Nevertheless, the two processes had something in common. The nonviolence of the mass movement at the bottom permitted a largely nonviolent, reformist response. If Solidarity and Charter 77 had been violent, the nonviolent Gorbachev reforms would have been unthinkable.

The specific events in the Soviet Union that led directly to its collapse thus started with drastic reform at the top, not with a mass movement at the bottom of society. Revolution from the top, which dates from Peter the Great's attempts at Westernization, has a long history in Russia. In his memoirs, Gorbachev explained his thinking. "By the mid-1980s," he said, "our society resembled a steam boiler. There was only one alternative—either the Party itself would lead a process of change that would gradually embrace other strata of society, or it would preserve and protect the former system. In that case an explosion of colossal force would be inevitable." To head off the explosion, he made sure—for much too long, his critics assert—that he remained the leader of the Communist Party, the better to keep it under control. At the same time, he embarked on his programs of glasnost and perestroika—of introducing market reforms, decentralizing the state, liberalizing the press, and gradually democratizing the political process.

In order to understand the importance of the movements in Eastern Europe for the collapse of the Soviet Union, we must recall that the union, like the czarist regime before it, was not only an empire but an empire that ruled an empire. (The Soviet Union proper, that is, was an empire long before it acquired its Eastern European satellites, which were held in subjection by Moscow but never incorporated into the union.) Under the czars, Russia had never experienced a national revolution of the kind that had occurred throughout Western Europe in the late eighteenth and nineteenth centuries. One reason had been precisely that Russia, as an empire, ruled over many nationalities. "For the tsars," the historian Richard Pipes writes, "the imperial principle meant that loyalty to the dynasty, and to the Orthodox faith, took priority over Russian nationalism in the hierarchy of values." Had Russian nationalism become the basis for the state in 1917, it might have caused the breakup of the empire, just as Turkish nationalism under Kemal Ataturk spelled the end of the Ottoman Empire only a few years after the Bolshevik revolution. In 1917, the empire did briefly break up into several independent nations. Its restoration under the Bolsheviks—Stalin's job, accomplished in the civil war and in the years immediately following—was an act of imperial reconquest carried out in the name of revolution. The high tide of this effort was reached in the unsuccessful Bolshevik war against Poland in 1920, which Trotsky, showing a lingering respect for the idea of popular will, opposed, on the ground that revolution cannot be imposed "at the point of a bayonet." Not until the Second World War, when Stalin wished to stir Russian—as distinct from Soviet—patriotism against the German invaders, did the Party explicitly play the national card in Russia, the largest of the union's republics. Even then, it refused to provide Russia with its own "national" communist party.

It would be a mistake, however, to regard the Soviet Union as simply an instrument of Russian domination over imperial colonies—a domination similar, say, to Britain's over its empire. Even though Russians had a preeminent role in governing the union, Russia was to a certain extent one more nation oppressed by a multinational central government, which was at the same time oppressing Ukraine, Armenia, Georgia, and so on. (Stalin, let us recall, was a Georgian.) After the Second World War, when Eastern Europe was incorporated into the socialist "bloc," Russians were often resentful that Russia was subsidizing the Eastern European satellites, many of which did in fact enjoy living standards higher than those in Russia.

Owing to this unique history, there was no clear dividing line in the Soviet Union between "domestic" rule and external conquest, and the methods used in both were extremely similar, if not identical. In *Revolution from Abroad,* the historian Jan Gross observes that the techniques the Soviets used to subjugate Polish society when they invaded Poland in 1939 were the ones they had employed to subjugate their own society in the "war against the nation" in the thirties. The repression that the totalitarian state imposed abroad was a domestic export. The resulting consistency of rule at home and in the satellites meant that a crack in any part of the edifice was more likely to rend the whole. The indivisibility of Soviet rule underlay the indivisibility, from rim to rim of the great empire, of the Soviet collapse.

Nonviolence from the Top Down

When Mikhail Gorbachev came to power in 1985, he embarked on his epic attempt to reform Soviet communism through perestroika and glasnost. He soon realized that reform at home could not succeed if at the same time he was trying to crack down in Eastern Europe. He therefore made a radical decision that few had foreseen, and that even today stands out as remarkable. In a rare act of what we might call nonviolence from the top down, he withdrew the threat of Soviet military invasion that, throughout the Cold War, had been the final guarantee of the survival of the Eastern European communist regimes. In December of 1988, in a speech at the United Nations, he said, "Necessity of the principle of freedom of choice is clear. Denying that right of peoples, no matter what the pretext for doing so, no matter what words are used to conceal it, means infringing even that unstable balance that it has been possible to achieve. Freedom of choice is a universal principle, and there should be no exceptions." His decision marked an acceptance of the new political reality that had been created by Solidarity, Charter 77, and other protest movements in Eastern Europe. (A history of unforced surrender of imperial possessions would make a slender volume. De Gaulle's relinquishment of Algeria even after the military defeat of the F.L.N. would be another of its few chapters.) Military crackdowns in the new conditions might or might not have eventually succeeded. What is certain is that they would have been savage and bloody, and it is for avoiding this that Gorbachev is justly admired. What Gorbachev did not foresee was that by withdrawing the invasion threat, he was pulling the plug on the communist regimes and that their collapse would pull the plug on the Soviet Union itself. Exactly a year after the U.N. speech, the first partially free elections were held in Poland, and the results amounted to a death warrant for communism. Not a single communist running for a contested seat won office. Poland was on its way to full independence and freedom—and after Poland came, in rapid succession, Czechoslovakia, Hungary, East Germany, Bulgaria, and Romania.

Why did the unraveling not stop there? When Britain lost its empire, its domestic system did not collapse. Neither did that of France in the wake of the liquidation of the French empire—although after de Gaulle had announced his readiness to grant Algeria independence he did face a coup attempt by military forces stationed in Algeria. Had the Soviet Union been a nation-state, founded, like England and France, upon the consent of its people, it, too, might well have survived. Soviet rule "at home," however, was too much of a piece with Soviet rule "abroad," and the corrosion in the outer empire jumped over into the inner empire. Armenia, Azerbaijan, and Georgia all stirred, but the portal through which the Eastern European sickness (or cure, as we might prefer) entered the union was the Baltic lands, of which the first to rebel was Lithuania.

Having enjoyed semiautonomous status under the czars, the Lithuanians were given their independence after the First World War. In 1939, owing to the Molotov-Ribbentrop pact, in which the U.S.S.R. and Nazi Germany agreed to partition Poland, the Lithuanians were forced to join the Soviet Union. Though living under direct Soviet rule, their memory of an independent national existence was recent and strong. In 1990, they demanded independence. Now the Soviet Union itself was threatened. If the Lithuanian independence movement were crushed, it was unlikely that perestroika could be saved in Russia: the use of the repressive apparatus "abroad" would very likely strengthen it decisively at home. On the other hand, if Lithuania were let go, its release would be a precedent that any or all of the other republics might follow. Now the indivisibility of the choice facing the entire union and empire—a choice, at bottom, between government based on force and government based on consent—became obvious to all. No less clear at that moment was what consent meant: the dissolution of the union. Gorbachev's reforms had activated forces that, if not violently suppressed, were bound to sweep simultaneously from the periphery of the empire into its center and from the bottom of society to the top.

An appeal launched at this hour shed a clear light on the significance of the Lithuanian events for the future. It came from Boris Yeltsin, then president of the Russian Parliament, and it amounted to a call for Russian forces to refuse to participate in a Lithuanian coup. Speaking from the territory of Lithuania's neighbor Estonia, Yeltsin addressed his appeal to the "soldiers, sergeants, and officers of the Soviet Union." He declared, "Today . . . you may be given the order to act against legally created state bodies, against the peaceful civilian population that is defending its democratic achievements. Before you undertake the storming of civilian installations in the Baltic lands, remember your own homes, the present and the future of your own republic, and your own people. Violence against the people of the Baltics will bring new serious crisis phenomena in Russia itself." What gave Yeltsin's words weight was the popular support he had been given in Russia after he had been drummed out of the Party leadership in 1988 and then had quit the Party, paving the way for his election as Russia's president. The last act of the collapse was, naturally, the Russian act.

As the movement spread from the edges into the center, it did not gain in popular intensity and strength. Resistance to Soviet rule was never as strong in the Soviet lands as it was in Eastern Europe. In Poland, there was an explosion; in Russia there was an implosion. Yeltsin, a careful student of the structure of the Soviet Union, had taken note of Stalin's fear of Russia and his refusal to establish a Russian communist party. "God forbid it should rise up and be a counterweight," Yeltsin said in a 1990 interview in the magazine *Soyuz*, elucidating Stalin's thinking. "Understandably, a small republic could not affect the entire Union," he said. "But with giant Russia, if it were to assume its real position, it would be difficult to fight it, or, rather, impossible." Politically, Yeltsin noted, Stalin had made "a precise calculation." Yeltsin made a precise calculation, too. He would use Russia to destroy the Soviet Union. He did not conceal his intention. "It was clear to me," he said, "that the vertical bureaucratic pivot on which the country rested had to be destroyed, and we had to begin a transition to horizontal ties with greater independence of the republic-states. The mood of the people, the democratization of society and the growth of that people's national self-awareness led directly to this."

Yeltsin's opponents, including his rival Gorbachev, have taken him to task for using his support in Russia to break up the union. He used his presidency of Russia, they charge, as a mere instrument for opposing Gorbachev, the union president. And yet the rebellion of Russia against the union—perhaps the least-predicted event in the entire chain of unpredicted events—was of a piece with the story from start to finish. For the last act in Russia, like the first in Poland and most of those in between, was at once democratic, national, and nonviolent. In truth, Russia's self-assertion, putting an end to the Soviet empire, was the final act in the much longer drama of the two-century-long world revolt of nations against the immense empires that ruled over them.

The end came with the failed coup against both Gorbachev and Yeltsin by conservative communist forces, in 1991. While Gorbachev was held captive by the plotters in his summer retreat in the Crimea, it was left to Yeltsin to win the necessary battle for hearts and minds in Moscow. He had already consolidated his position as the first elected president of Russia in its history. When Gorbachev had sought to bar the election in which he was chosen, tens of thousands of demonstrators had assembled in Moscow in support of Yeltsin, and Gorbachev had backed down. Now, with Gorbachev in captivity and many of his own ministers and aides launching a coup against him, the question was whether the people would obey orders given by the self-appointed coup leadership or those given by Yeltsin. They chose Yeltsin. The decisive factors, it appears, were the crowd that assembled at the risk of its lives in support of democracy in front of the parliament building and the refusal of soldiers and security forces to attack them. As in so many revolutions, including the one in Russia in 1917, the changed mood of the population had spread to the troops, who then went over to the opposition.

When Russia rebelled, "the center" was left suspended in air. Center of what? Where was it? Was it in the Kremlin—a sort of "Kremlinistan"? Or in outer space, where the Soviet Union's manned space station was still orbiting the globe? In Soviet times, Russia, lacking a communist party to call its own, had been called a "ghost state" in the union. Now it was the Soviet Union that would prove the ghost. A few months later, it was gone.

8

Cooperative Power

The professionals of power, in or out of government, were consistently caught off guard by the failures of superior force and the successes of nonviolence. In 1930, when Gandhi was in negotiations with the Raj, Winston Churchill announced that he found it "nauseating and humiliating" that Gandhi, "formerly a Middle Temple lawyer, now posing as a fakir of a type well-known in the East," was to be seen "striding half-naked up the steps of the Viceroy's palace to confer with the representative of the King-Emperor." (Upon hearing of the comment Gandhi wrote, "Dear Prime Minister, You are reported to have the desire to crush the 'naked fakir,' as you are said to have described me. I have been long trying to be a fakir and that naked—a more difficult task. I, therefore, regard the expression as a compliment, though unintended. I approach you, then, as such, and ask you to trust and use me for the sake of your people and mine, and through them those of the world. Your sincere friend, M. K. Gandhi.") Several American administrations were unable to fathom the political power that, in conjunction with inferior instruments of force, was overmatching their military superiority in Vietnam. Soviet leaders soon had a similar experience in Afghanistan. Later, Soviet hard-liners watched in astonishment as state power slipped out of their hands and their empire crumbled with scarcely a shot being fired, and even the nonviolent rebels who brought about this result were startled by their own accomplishment. Most contemporary political theory, wedded to the ageless idea that force was the final arbiter in politics and war, was equally barren of tools for understanding these events, which it could neither foresee nor explain after the fact.

One thinker who did shed light on the new phenomena was Hannah Arendt, whose description and analysis of revolution anticipated the antitotalitarian movements in Eastern Europe with remarkable precision. (Her writing also had a modest influence upon several of the more intellectual-minded Eastern European activists.) Arendt did not oppose violence on principle, and in her book *Eichmann in Jerusalem* she supported the death penalty for Adolf Eichmann, the Nazi bureaucrat who ran the transportation system for Hitler's program to exterminate the Jews of Europe. Nor was she given to underestimating the role of violence in politics. Born in 1906 into a secular Jewish family in Hanover, Germany, she spent a week in a German prison in 1933 for involvement in a Zionist organization, and shortly fled the country for Prague. She remained stateless for the next eighteen years. In her pioneering work *The Origins of Totalitarianism*, which she wrote in this period, she became one of the first to describe and analyze the full dimensions of the role of terror in totalitarian rule. Nevertheless, in the years that followed she broke decisively with the tradition of political thought that held that the foundation of power is the sword.

Violence vs. Power

In approaching the question of power, Arendt followed a procedure characteristic of her thought. Her frequent method was to boldly take sides in debates on the meanings of certain words. Her advocacy of a given meaning might be seen as a bid to push the word in question in one direction or another. The operation proceeded toward both a clarified understanding of the meaning of the word and a new interpretation of historical events. Such was the method she followed when, in the teeth of a tradition as long as history, she asserted that violence, far from being the essence of power, was in fact antithetical to it. It was not enough, she wrote in *On Violence* (1969), to say that "violence and power are not the same." Rather, "Power and violence are opposites; where the one rules absolutely, the other is absent." Therefore, "to speak of nonviolent power is actually redundant." To appreciate just how unorthodox, even shocking, this claim was, we only have to recall A. J. P. Taylor's definition of the great powers of the nineteenth century as "organizations for power, that is, in the last resort, for war." His assumption that an organization for power is "for war" was, of course, perfectly in keeping with the conventional wisdom of his time and ours. Or we can recall the assertion by Max Weber, quoted by Arendt, that the state can be defined as "the rule of men over men based on the means of legitimate, that is allegedly legitimate, violence."

By contrast, Arendt held that power is created not when some people coerce others but when they willingly take action together in support of common purposes. "Power," she wrote, "corresponds to the human ability not just to act but to act in concert." Such action requires "the making and keeping of promises, which in politics may be the highest human faculty." The human endowment Arendt was pointing to was not something mysterious or rare. One of her favorite examples was the Mayflower Compact, in which a small company of people on the high seas swore to "solemnly and mutually in the Presence of God and one another, covenant and combine ourselves together into a civil Body Politic." The idea that power is born out of action in concert had not gone unnoticed in political thought. Burke summed it up in a sentence when he said, "Liberty, when men act in bodies, is power." Tocqueville said much the same in his analysis of the vibrant civil society he witnessed in the United States in the 1830s. "There is no end which the human will despairs of attaining," he asserted, "through the combined power of individuals united into a society." Referring to the "power of meeting," he remarked, "Democracy does not confer the most skillful kind of government upon the people, but it produces that which the most skillful governments are frequently unable to awaken, namely an all-pervading and restless activity, a superabundant force, and an energy which is inseparable from it, and which may, under favorable circumstances, beget the most amazing benefits." We have already noted that Adams's characterization of the peaceful, rebellious civil activity before the revolutionary war—especially in his beloved Committees of Correspondence—is a portrait of the power generated by peaceful association. Gandhi's claim that through acts of noncooperation *satyagrahis* "nearly establish their own government" obviously refers to the same phenomenon, as does his view that political power, though not necessarily a goal of constructive social action, was its inevitable by-product. Havel's "living in truth" and Benda's creation of a "parallel polis" were incarnations of cooperative power. Examples given by Arendt were the "revolutionary councils" that arose, repeatedly and spontaneously, at the beginning of almost all the modern revolutions, including the popular societies of the districts of Paris in the French Revolution, the soviets in the Russian Revolution (in her view, the soviets were promising and positive institutions that were manipulated, abused, and eventually liquidated by the Bolsheviks to win and keep dictatorial power), and the German *Räte* that briefly came into existence in the socialist rebellion of 1918–19. The Interfactory Strike Committees, which coordinated the protests in factories in Poland in 1980 to create the powerful national Solidarity movement, were the very model of the power of concerted action, though Arendt did not live to witness them.

Arendt's conception of power was different in important respects from the liberal conception. The liberal thinkers generally located power in government, and went on to ask what its foundation should be. Some answered with Weber that at bottom it was and had to be fear, inspired by the ever-present threat of violence, while others answered that it should be popular consent. Arendt, by contrast, located power not in government but in societies, whose people generated it by their action in concert, and then might go on to vest it, for a while, in a particular government. Like freedom, which was its foundation, power was not to be found in all societies. It existed only latently, until activated by deeds such as the Mayflower Compact and the activities of the revolutionary councils. If citizens became passive, power would evaporate. For, "Where power is not actualized, it passes away, and history is full of examples that the greatest material riches cannot compensate for this loss." When a government was based on the concerted action of its citizens, its power, on the other hand, would be at its maximum. For this to happen, the council system, by which society would organize itself into spontaneous deliberative local bodies, would have to become the foundation of a system of government—something that, to Arendt's regret, had never been accomplished. (An example she cited was Thomas Jefferson's proposal after the American Revolution to divide the counties into town meeting–like "wards.")

In this view, power did not reside, as is usually said, in officials who issue commands but in citizens who follow them. A long tradition had identified the officials as the powerful ones. Arendt quoted her contemporary, the political thinker Bertrand de Jouvenal: "To command and to be obeyed: without that, there is no Power—with it no other attribute is needed for it to be." Or as Weber put it, "Power means every chance within a social relationship to assert one's will even against opposition." Arendt answered, with Hume, Burke, Gandhi, and Havel, that in a deeper sense power is in the hands of those who obey the commands, which is to say with society. Power is indeed "never the property of an individual," she writes; "it belongs to a group and remains in existence only so long as the group keeps together." If society withdrew its obedience, the commander's rule was at an end. Even Clausewitz, let us recall, was of this opinion, for he understood that military victories were useless unless the population of the vanquished army then obeyed the will of the victor. The resolute society that dislikes its ruler can find another ruler; but where would a ruler who had lost the obedience of his society find another society?

If power was the force that is created by action in common and sustained by mutual promises, then it followed that violence, which is the action of one person against another, was in fact destructive of it, inasmuch as violence breaks up the relationships of trust on which power is based. A violent state or group, Arendt well knew, could defeat a more "powerful" rebellion of people acting together peacefully, at least in the short run: "In a head-on clash between violence and power, the outcome was hardly in doubt." What violence could never do was create power: "While violence can destroy power, it can never become a substitute for it. From this results the by no means infrequent political combination of force and powerlessness, an array of impotent forces that spend themselves often spectacularly and vehemently but in utter futility."

Surprisingly, perhaps, Arendt's principal example of the powerlessness of violence was the totalitarianism she had studied so deeply. Precisely its unprecedented dependence on violence, she asserted, deprived it of what she defined as power. "Nowhere is the self-defeating factor in the victory of violence over power more evident," she wrote, "than in the use of terror to maintain domination, about whose weird successes and eventual failures we know perhaps more than any generation before us." Terror, even as it keeps its practitioners in office for a time, destroys the foundation of their power. "The climax of terror is reached when yesterday's executioner becomes today's victim," she observes. "And this is also the moment when power disappears entirely."

Such were the insights that underlay her prophetic comments regarding the long-term fate of Soviet totalitarianism. They permitted her, for example, to perceive that each time the Soviet Union used its tanks to crush a rebellion in Eastern Europe, it was diminishing its power, not increasing it, as most observers thought. In *The Origins of Totalitarianism*, she had taken the full measure of the totalitarian evil, yet she was one of the few writers of the Cold War years to perceive the Soviet Union's underlying weaknesses. It's one thing to grasp in hindsight that the succession of rebellions against Soviet rule in Eastern Europe were shocks portending the fall; it was another to write in 1969, just after the suppression of the Prague Spring, that "the head-on clash between Russian tanks and the entirely nonviolent resistance of the Czechoslovak people is a textbook case of a confrontation between violence and power," and to comment, "To substitute violence for power can bring victory, but the price is very high; for it is not only paid by the vanquished, it is also paid by the victor in terms of his own power." For even as this use of violence restored rule, it destroyed the last reserves of support—even if these amounted only to a minimal, grudging acquiescence or tolerance—that the regime required. The ground was prepared for the later rebellions in Eastern Europe, in which millions of ordinary people, acting together for what they believed in and so creating genuine power in Arendt's sense, precipitated the final convulsion of the Soviet system. Arendt indeed foresaw a more general "reversal in the relationship between power and violence, forshadowing another reversal in the future relationship between small and great powers."

In a passage that both portrayed the collapses of the anciens régimes that she knew from history and dramatically anticipated the Soviet collapse, she described what happens when, behind the unchanging, impressive facade of violence, the reserves of power run too low. Then, "the situation changes abruptly. Not only is the rebellion not put down but the arms themselves change hands—sometimes, as in the Hungarian revolution, within a few hours. . . . The dramatic sudden breakdown of power that ushers in revolution reveals in a flash how civil obedience—to laws, to rulers, to institutions—is but the outward manifestation of support and consent."

The commonalities between Arendt and Gandhi are obviously many. Her observation that the power of a government depends wholly on civil obedience and evaporates if this is withdrawn is virtually identical to Gandhi's many observations on the subject. Like Gandhi, Arendt also believed not only that revolution can be nonviolent but, among other things, that any politics worth its salt must be rooted in direct action; that the obligation to act is therefore a paramount requirement, after which the mode of action can be considered; that at the heart of action lies freedom, which both inspires action and lends it meaning, and, in fact, lends life meaning; that courage is the sine qua non of freedom and action; that action must proceed by agreement among equals, not through suppression by violence of one party by another; that rule based on violence is in its nature not only destructive but in the long run self-destructive; and that authentic, enduring power must be based on nonviolent action—that, in Arendt's memorable words, "Power is actualized only where word and deed have not parted company, where words are not empty and deeds not brutal, where words are not used to veil intentions but to disclose realities, and deeds are not used to violate and destroy but to establish relations and create new realities."

This closely connected complex of ideas not only is shared by Arendt and Gandhi but is shared, as far as I'm aware, by them alone among twentieth-century analysts of political power. (The nearest exceptions, perhaps, are the Eastern European writers I have cited.) And yet Arendt mentions Gandhi even less often than the Eastern Europeans did. In all of her work, there are only a handful of references to him, and she never quotes him. (All of the mentions, it is true, are admiring. For example, she refers to "Gandhi's enormously powerful and successful strategy of nonviolent resistance"—although she joins those who surmise that it would have failed against a Stalin or a Hitler. Elsewhere, without mentioning Gandhi, she nevertheless seems to refer to him. "Popular revolt against materially strong rulers . . . may engender an almost irresistible power," she writes, "even if it forgoes the use of violence in the face of materially vastly superior forces. To call this 'passive resistance' is certainly an ironic idea; it is one of the most active and efficient ways of action ever devised, because it cannot be countered by fighting, where there may be defeat or victory, but only by mass slaughter in which even the victor is defeated, cheated of his prize, since nobody can rule over dead men.")

On at least one fundamental point, however, Arendt couldn't have differed from Gandhi more sharply. Whereas he turned to spiritual love as the source and inspiration of nonviolent action, Arendt was among those who argued strenuously against introducing such love into the political sphere. Her objections were not those of the realist school, which holds that love is too weak a force to be effective in politics, which is and must be governed by force. Rather, she regarded love as extraordinarily powerful, and expressed intense admiration for those who, like Jesus, she believed were capable of it. It is in part for this reason, she urges, that the wall of separation between the City of God and the City of Man must be left intact.

Politics wrecks love, in her version of the venerable argument, because love's proper domain is the hidden world of the spirit and the heart, and publicity, which is necessary for politics, will coarsen and corrupt it by turning it into a public display, a show. Love wrecks politics also because the demands of the spirit and the heart are peremptory, and cannot endure the legal restraints that must prevail in a sound political order. She cites Robespierre's "terror of virtue" and its Bolshevik epigones. Robespierre's virtue counts for her as "love" because its inspiring motive was "pity" for the suffering of the poor, which she saw as a kind of love. Such pity may be admirable in itself but, if "taken as the spring of virtue, has proved to possess a greater capacity for cruelty than cruelty itself."

Gandhi, the uniter of religion and politics, asserted, "A *satyagrahi* has no other stay but God, and he who has any other stay or depends on any other help cannot offer *satyagraha*." He admitted that a nonbeliever could still be "a passive resister" or a "noncooperator," but "not a true *satyagrahi*." Echoing the liturgy of many faiths over many centuries, he added, "Only in His strength are we strong." The political secularist, however, will answer with Arendt that there is something forbidding, even tyrannical, in the fact of subordinating every sphere of life to the demands of religion. The secularist will be more at home with her careful separation of these spheres and her search within each for virtues proper to each. "Moderation is best in all things," the secularist will say with Montesquieu, "even virtue."

Although Arendt was not as thoroughgoing an opponent of violence as Gandhi, her views were in one respect even more radically subversive than his of any political justification for violence. Gandhi mounted an attack upon violence, so to speak, from outside politics, demanding that politics live up to divine law. Accepting that violence might indeed be a source and instrument of power, he rejected it on moral and spiritual grounds. Arendt, on the other hand, finds all she needs for rescuing politics from violence in politics itself. She calls for no rescue by God. On the contrary, she merely lets the political man know that if he relies on violence he may score successes but in the long run will lose what he most wants, namely power.

Arendt, however, leaves many questions raised by Gandhi unaddressed. Gandhi, we recall, proposed to answer the objections to the spiritualization of politics by placing his *satyagrahis* under two severe restraints as they entered public life: the renunciation, on the physical plane, of violence and, on the intellectual plane, of any claim to absolute truth. Gandhi showed he was in earnest about these restraints by ending satyagraha whenever his followers violated them. Might these two renunciations make "love" safe for political expression? Arendt left us without her reflections on the subject, citing only instances in which the politicization of spiritual love bred fanaticism and violence. What she did leave was her daring bid to redefine politics and, with it, a deeply thought-through approach to nonviolent action that is distinctly un-Gandhian. To the question what the usefulness of violence was and was not, Arendt answered that violence, even when used in the service of goodness, lies outside politics and is destructive of it. And to the question what the role of nonviolent action in politics is, her answer was: politics *is* nonviolent action.

What Do We Love?

Even as Arendt's distinction between power and violence illumines not only the sudden Soviet collapse but aspects of all the revolutions we have discussed, it creates a conceptual problem. It seems to leave dictatorship dangling, linguistically speaking, in midair, without any political properties to call its own. "Tyranny prevents the development of power, not only in a particular segment of the public realm but in its entirety," Arendt wrote. Yet if tyrants—including the totalitarian variety—were not "powerful," what were they? The Bolsheviks' loss of power did not catch up with their dependence on violence for seventy-four long years. What word was appropriate for the sway they exercised in that period?

Gandhi was a more thoroughgoing advocate of nonviolence than Arendt, yet he spoke, as we've seen, of the existence of two kinds of power. "One is obtained by the fear of punishment," he said, "and the other by acts of love." His power based on love closely resembled in practice what Arendt simply called "power." Its methods were noncooperation and constructive action, both of course nonviolent. His power based on fear—what he called *dura-*

graha (bodily, or coercive, force)—corresponded to what she called violence. But Gandhi's distinction has the advantage over Arendt's of acknowledging the existence of a kind of power based on support without outraging common usage by denying, as Arendt does, the title of "power" to rule by force and fear.

I suggest that the power that is based on support might be called cooperative power and that the power based on force might be called coercive power. Power is cooperative when it springs from action in concert of people who willingly agree with one another and is coercive when it springs from the threat or use of force. Both kinds of power are real. Both make things happen. Both are present, though in radically different proportions, in all political situations. Yet the two are antithetical. To the extent that the one exists, the other is ruled out. To the degree that a people is forced, it is not free. And so when cooperative power declines, coercive power often steps in to fill the vacuum, and vice versa. Society's need for power of one kind or another is so great that in the absense of popular government people will often accept dictatorship, creating a sort of desperate "consent" that is quite different from the "liberal obedience" (in Burke's phase) that is the bedrock of a system of cooperative power. Likewise, when coercive power weakens, cooperative power may suddenly appear, as it did in the latter days of the Soviet empire.

In this distinction between two kinds of power, love and fear are functional equivalents (both are sentiments, and both produce obedience, on which, all schools agree, government depends). In a coercive system, fear, of course, is the product of force. But of what, in a cooperative system, is love the product? What summons up the love that produces the consent, the support, the willing agreement on which cooperative power depends?

The answer to this question, obviously of fundamental importance to any politics based on cooperation rather than coercion, is curiously elusive. The things that inspire fear—death, threat of injury—as well as the behavior it prompts have a monotonous uniformity, like the bending of blades of grass in a wind, which is the oldest of metaphors for obedience to oppressive power. But if we ask ourselves what inspires love in the public realm the possible specific answers seem unlimited. For if no one forces us to do his bidding, we are simply free to desire and do anything we may get it into our heads to desire or do, for any reason whatsoever, trivial or grave, wicked or virtuous: build a school, take a bribe, eat an apple, kill a neighbor, save a neighbor's life at the cost of our own. We are left not with a particular goal but with the latitude to choose any goal. In other words, we are left with freedom. According to Tocqueville, a passionate believer in political freedom, it was indeed unworthy of the ideal to identify any particular good as freedom's aim. In his words, "What has made so many men, since untold ages, stake their all on freedom is its intrinsic glamour, a fascination it has in itself, apart from all 'practical' considerations. For only in countries where it reigns can a man speak, live, and breathe freely, owing obedience to no authority save God and the laws of the land. The man who asks of freedom anything other than itself is born to be a slave."

Gandhi, of course, gave a clear and unequivocal answer to the question. The love that should guide political action, he believed, was the love of God, or truth, which for him were the same. "If God who is indefinable can be at all defined," he wrote, "then I should say that God is TRUTH. It is impossible to reach HIM, that is TRUTH, except through LOVE." Havel, too, resorted to the word "truth," but in a secular definition, though now and then he ventured metaphysical explanations. Many other political figures have, without resorting to religion or metaphysics, also drawn a distinction between love, always associated with freedom, and fear. John Adams was drawing it in 1776, when he wrote that in an independent American republic "love and not fear will become the spring of their [the people's] obedience." And Montesquieu stated that "government is like everything else: to preserve it, we must love it." The love he had in mind was "love of the laws and of our country"—a love, he added, "peculiar to democracies." None other than the arch-realist Machiavelli also linked love and freedom. In a passage in *The Prince*, he commented, "Men love at their own free will but fear at the will of the prince." (He therefore recommended *fear* as the basis of government, for "a wise prince must rely on what is in his power and not on what is in the power of others.") Hard as it is to fix any bounds on what people may spontaneously admire, we know how to identify a free person. We call that person free who, in disregard of force and fear, acts in accord with what his soul prompts him to love.

Opinion

One political thinker who reflected on the dual character of political power was the liberal English thinker par excellence of the nineteenth century, John Stuart Mill. In *Representative Government* he put the question, "What is meant by power?" He answered, "Politically speaking, a great part of all power consists in will." "Will" here obviously refers to the capacity for spontaneous, willing allegiance and action that is at the root of cooperative power. Because will was politically important, "opinion," which guides the will, was also important. "Opinion is itself one of the greatest active social forces," he observed, and those who, by teaching or example, could offer people something they admire or believe in therefore may be the most powerful figures on the social landscape. For "They who can succeed in creating a general persuasion that a certain form of government, or social fact of any kind, deserves to be preferred, have made nearly the most important step which can possibly be taken towards ranging the powers of society on its side." He gave two examples. One was the first Christian martyr, St. Stephen, who was "stoned to death in Jerusalem while he who was to be Apostle to the Gentiles [St. Paul] stood by 'consenting unto his death.'" "Would anyone," Mill asked of these first Christians, "have supposed that the party of that stoned man were then and there the strongest power in society? And has not the event proved that they were so? Because theirs was the most *powerful* of then existing beliefs." The other example was Martin Luther at the Diet of Worms, who, because he founded a faith that the people freely chose, was "a more powerful social force than the Emperor Charles the Fifth, and all the princes there assembled."

If, as Mill pointed out, opinion guided the will, and the will moved people to give political support, and political support was the foundation of power, then the most powerful people seemed to be those who, whether in government or out, had the capacity to create or do something that inspired the respect, admiration, loyalty, faith—all of which, again, is to say the love—of others. Power, according to this conception, which dovetails closely with Arendt's, begins with the capacity to create or discover something (including, for example, a republic) that other people cannot help but love—a definition about as far as one can get from A. J. P. Taylor's "organizations for war" or Jouvenel's "to command and be obeyed."

Yet in speaking of someone as more "powerful" than those stoning him to death, or than the princes of his day, because later generations were persuaded by his teaching and example, don't we reach the boundaries of what can be understood by the word "power"? Don't we begin to speak in mere conundrums? If this is the measure of power, then is anyone who catches the attention of the world in one way or another politically "powerful"? The inspiring example of a human being stoned to death is only one ingredient even of cooperative power, which depends on the responding active support of many, and to call such a person powerful is admittedly to flirt with paradox. Why insist on *this* word to describe the phenomenon? Wouldn't it be better to reserve the word, as is so often done, for those who occupy high positions in government or command tank divisions, and leave it at that?

The events of our time, however, rule out this reversion. For in our day the dual aspect of power lies not only in the uses of the word but in the new phenomena it must describe. The power that flows upward from the consent, support, and nonviolent activity of the people is not the same as the power that flows downward from the state by virtue of its command of the instruments of force, and yet the two kinds of power contend in the same world for the upper hand, and the seemingly weaker one can, it turns out, defeat the seemingly stronger, as the downfall of the British Raj and the Soviet Union showed. Therefore, although it may lead to paradox and linguistic tangles to speak of martyrs as being more "powerful" than the authorities who put them to death, the exercise is inescapable. For it is indeed a frequent mistake of the powers that be to imagine that they can accomplish or prevent by force what a Luther, a Gandhi, a Martin Luther King, or a Havel can inspire by example. The prosperous and mighty of our day still live at a dizzying height above the wretched of the earth, yet the latter have made their will felt in ways that have already changed history, and can change it more.

PART THREE

The Civil State

9

The Liberal Democratic Revival

Everything we have discussed so far—conventional war, nuclear war, people's war, and revolution—falls under the heading of what the contract theorists of the seventeenth century called the state of nature: their term for conditions, domestic or international, that lie outside the protection of states and their laws. For most of these thinkers, the state of nature was indistinguishable, or scarcely distinguishable, from a state of war, and was the last place they would have gone searching, as we have done, for an escape from political violence. The unexpected appearance in these normally chaotic, blood-spattered precincts of new and historically potent forms of nonviolent action is one measure of the radical difference between their time and ours. Now in the same quest we turn, more conventionally, to the ordered realm of the civil state, and its underpinning, law, to which not only theorists but ordinary people have long looked to give relief from anarchy and violence—to pacify the warring tribes, to prevent the attack of neighbor upon neighbor, to fix the boundaries of states and regulate weights and measures, to mete out justice and provide for the common good.

Most visions of world peace, indeed, have traditionally been based on some notion of extending the structures of civil rule to the international realm. The idea that the foundation of a universal state—world government—would put an end to war has been a perennial dream.

One development in the civil sphere that holds promise as a foundation for peace is the liberal democratic revival of the late twentieth century. This revival, however, has been so tightly entangled with contrary forces, including the traditional imperial proclivities of many democratic states, that its potential contributions to peace may be foreclosed before even being offered.

If satyagraha, living in truth, and the spontaneous foundation of institutions of civil society are the forms that cooperative power takes in the state of nature, then liberal democracy is the chief form it takes in the civil state. We have already noted the association of nonviolent revolution and democracy. No less striking is the tendency, noted by recent scholars, of liberal democracies to refrain from war among themselves. This disposition found one of its first articulations in Immanuel Kant's essays "Perpetual Peace" (1795) and "Idea for a Universal History" (1784), in which he called for "a universal civic society," and named the goal "the highest problem Nature assigns to the human race." He advocated a "civic union" of republics that would establish universal and perpetual peace in the world. However, the liberal revival must have a central place in any discussion of nonviolence for a deeper reason: the goal of taming violence is written into liberalism's genetic code.

According to the contract theorists (whose thinking stands behind the rise of liberal government), the choice between force and consent is perennial, because of the ineradicable fact of human existence that human beings are many but inhabit together a world that is one. It was hardly necessary, of course, to postulate an "original" state of nature (which even in Locke's time was proposed more as a thought-experiment than as a description of historical reality) or to travel to a war zone to confirm the truth of this commonsense observation. A visit to any playground, family living room, office, or street corner—not to speak of any company boardroom, university department, or legislature—would do. "The latent causes of faction," James Madison wrote, "are . . . sown in the nature of man." Or, in the words of Thomas Hobbes, who, though no liberal, must be classed among the contractarians, "If any two men desire the same thing, which nevertheless they cannot both enjoy, they become enemies; and . . . endeavor to destroy, or subdue one another." Thus arose his "war of all against all."

Broadly speaking, the contractarians identified two possible solutions to the dilemma. The first was that one party imposed its will on the others by force; the second was that the parties found their way to agreement. The first saved the freedom of one party at the expense of the others'; the second saved the freedom of all parties, because all had given their approval—had, though perhaps surrendering a portion of their ambitions, given their consent to the final result. The first was an institutionalization of what we have called coercive power and the foundation of authoritarianism, the second—the liberal program—an institutionalization of cooperative power and the foundation of civil freedom.

Any constitution based on freedom must of course be complex, yet its essential requirements have been defined with remarkable consistency over the more than two thousand years of the democratic tradition. They were summarized in the riposte that, according to Greece's first great historian, Herodotus, the Spartan Demaratus gave to the Persian king Xerxes, who challenged him to explain how Greece, which endowed its citizens with freedom, could produce obedient, steadfast soldiers. "They are free—yes—but not entirely free," Demaratus answered, "for they have a master, and that master is Law, which they fear much more than their subjects fear you." Cicero described the citizen of a free Rome in similar terms. "He obeys the laws not, of course, because of fear," he wrote; "he complies with them and respects them because he judges that such a course is extremely advantageous. He says nothing, does nothing, thinks of nothing except in a free and voluntary manner. All of his plans and all of his acts proceed from himself, and he himself is also the judge of them."

The connection between nonviolence and freedom in a liberal democratic constitution, a moment's thought will show, lies in the nature of both. Freedom is twofold. In the first place, it is a power inherent in the human being to decide to do things and to do them. Shall I eat a pear or a peach? Shall I vote for this candidate or that? Shall I start a school? Yet, having made my decision and embarked on a course of action, I may encounter some obstacle—perhaps prison walls, or a police barricade. If the obstacle is removed, then I am "free" to proceed. And so in the second place freedom is the lack of an external obstacle to my action once I have embarked on it. "Liberty, or freedom," Hobbes wrote, defining this second aspect of freedom, "signifieth, properly, the absence of opposition; by opposition, I mean external impediments of motion."

In the political sphere, the innate human power of doing things is displayed in what has been called positive freedom, which is the capacity to participate in political life, by such acts as voting, demonstrating, even rebelling against the government. Its exercise satisfies the human desire to be an active agent of one's own fate, not just the passive object of the wills of others. The second aspect of freedom—Hobbes's absence of external impediment—has been called negative freedom, which is the citizen's freedom from coercion by the state, typically codified in bills of rights and the like.

The two aspects of freedom are tightly connected in the liberal democratic scheme of government. Negative freedoms such as bills of rights and other legal protections of citizens do not come into existence by themselves; they are creations of those same citizens as exercisers of positive freedom, who either make the laws or choose those who will do so. Negative freedoms represent a collective decision by the citizenry not to use the state's monopoly to coerce themselves as individuals. In a word, negative freedoms are institutional acts of restraint, which is to say acts of nonviolence. By participating in politics, citizens exercise their positive freedom; by institutionally restraining their collective violence, they show respect for the positive freedom of other citizens. But at the same time such restraints on the state's coercive power are precisely what we mean by negative freedom. On the side of the receiver, negative freedom is what Hobbes said it was, absence of impediment. On the side of the bestower, negative freedom is nonviolence.

The nonviolent revolutionary exercises the same restraint, and for the same reason, although in an utterly different context. By declining to coerce his opponent, he grants him a kind of raw negative freedom. Of course, in the midst of a revolutionary contest for power, this freedom cannot take the form of legal guarantees but merely that of leaving the opponent safe from violent harm at one's own hands. Yet nonviolent revolution and liberal government both restrain violence in the name of freedom—the freedom, that is, of *others,* including opponents. Those who "live in truth," and so refrain from violence, even against their oppressors, for fear of reproducing tyranny, are receiving ideal training for office (including the office of citizen) in the liberal state, which must refrain from any violence against the political opposition.

Although Gandhi emphasized love more than freedom—just as he emphasized social service more than politics—he, too, believed that freedom was essential to any healthy political order. "No society can possibly be built on a denial of individual freedom," he said. "It is contrary to the very nature of man. Just as man will not grow horns or a tail so he will not exist as man if he has no mind of his own." The beauty of satyagraha is that it saved the freedom of both the doer and the done to. It is a system of respect for individual freedom without benefit of the civil state. In both satyagraha and liberal democracy, nonviolence reconciles the individual's freedom with his exercise of power. Herein lies the inextricable—indeed the definitional—connection of freedom and nonviolence. These two are inseparable and their union is rooted in the very nature of action and of every scheme so far invented, whether within the civil state or outside it, that seeks to reconcile the exercise of positive freedom with enjoyment of its negative partner.

To the degree that the ideal is realized, a country's constitution and its laws in fact become a hugely ramified road map for the peaceful settlement of disputes, large and small. For if it is true, as the Romans said, that *inter arma silent leges* (when arms speak, the laws fall silent), it is equally true that when the laws speak arms fall silent. Otherwise, who would bother with laws? Every peaceable transfer of power in accord with the decision of an electorate is a coup d'état avoided. Every court case—however acrimonious the lawyers—is a possible vendetta or bloodbath averted. And so the spread of democracy, if it rests on a solid foundation, is an expansion of the zone in which the business of politics is conducted along mainly nonviolent lines. In this basic respect, the long march of liberal democracy is a "peace movement"—possibly the most important and successful of them all.

It is not, of course, liberal government alone that seeks to give society relief from its violent tendencies. Every form of government accepts this responsibility, at least in theory. However, the liberal commitment to nonviolence is deeper than the authoritarian promise to end the war of all against all. Whereas the authoritarian promises only to deliver society from its own "natural" violence, the liberal wants to protect it also from the violence of the state. Beginning by saving human beings from their mutual violence through the establishment of government, it then tries to save them from the savior, by guaranteeing the negative freedoms of the citizen. Why, Locke asked, would men fear violence from one another but not fear the violence of Leviathan? To imagine that, he said, would be to think men are "so foolish that they take care to avoid what mischiefs may be done them by polecats or foxes, but are content, nay, think it safety, to be devoured by lions."

Authoritarian rule is in fact not so much an escape from violence as a rearrangement of it, in which the violence at the disposal of each person is pooled in the hands of the state. Locke took the critical next step. By insisting that government be rooted in the willing support of the people, he sought to change their relationship to it to one of consent—or love, if Montesquieu and Burke speak truly. The fundamental change occurs in what Montesquieu described as "the spirit" of the laws, and what others have called hearts and minds. It is the spirit of consent—this willing disposition of the people, Burke's "liberal obedience"—that is, wherever it exists, the true foundation of the liberal democratic state, just as it is the true foundation of nonviolent direct action. The inner moral change in hearts and minds from fear to consent is the specific genius of liberal democracy, permitting its citizens to remain free even as they obey the commands of the law.

In the teeth of this venerable tradition, many observers have, of course, continued to insist that the foundation of all state power is force. Pointing out that governments claim the power to enforce the laws, they conclude that political power always and everywhere rests on a foundation of violence. Their mistake is to confuse police power with political power—or, in Arendt's terms, violence with power. These two are in fact the same only in a police state. In newly democratic South Africa, for example, the police are called on to enforce the law. Indispensable as enforcement is, its existence doesn't mean that the authority of Parliament, the ministers, and the courts rest on a foundation of police power. On the contrary, their political power obviously depends on the willing support and obedience of the great majority of the public, expressed in free elections. By comparison, the power of the police is a marginal affair. Much less does the domestic power of the government rest on the military, whose abstention from politics is essential to the democratic contract. The instant that the majority of citizens withdrew their support from the system of government, the South African state would cease to be democratic, and revolution or dictatorship would ensue.

An American Reformation

In reality, of course, liberal governments live up to their ideals only to a limited extent. Gross, long-lasting, injustices commonly exist alongside real freedoms. The United States—to give one illustration—has been a genuine republic for more than two hundred years, but for its first eighty years it was also a slave power and for a century after that systematically denied fundamental human and democratic rights to its black minority. In the segregated South, blacks were held in subjection by an interlocking system involving the states, local government, and economic and social repression. Protest was met with economic sanctions, petty humiliation, beatings, imprisonment, lynching, and other forms of abuse. Not until the civil-rights movement of the 1950s and sixties were legal remedies enacted, and even then social and economic discrimination remained facts of American life. That movement— the most successful expansion of freedom during the past hundred years in the United States (only the labor movement and the women's movement are in the same class)—was nonviolent. It illumines in practice the kinship of democratic government and nonviolent direct action.

In certain respects, the position of blacks in the American constitutional order was like the position of the Indians of South Africa in the English imperial order. Both groups appealed to the highest constituted authority—the federal government of the United States in the first case, the imperial government in London in the second—for relief from local oppression. Both restricted themselves to nonviolence. Neither had any hope of securing its rights through the establishment of an independent nation. (Gandhi's movement in India, on the other hand, aimed at and achieved independence.) The black minority in the United States had suffered far more at the hands of the dominant white majority than that majority had ever suffered at the hands of the English in the years leading up to independence, impelling the Americans "to separation," as the Declaration of Independence says. The Muslim black nationalist Malcolm X, who believed that "there can be no revolution without bloodshed," was certainly correct when he pointed out that the founders of the United States had not hesitated to resort to violence under far milder provocation.

Yet however justified by white precedent, the plan of separation and violence was impractical for the black American minority, if only because it amounted to no more than 15 percent of the population. What Gandhi came to understand in South Africa and Michnik came to understand in Poland—that violence would be self-defeating—was even more obviously true for the black minority in the United States. As Lawrence Guyot of the Student Nonviolent Coordinating Committee put it, "They'll shoot us quicker if we're armed." In these demanding, confining circumstances, an accommodation with the white majority was the only route to equal rights. If blacks could not *separate,* as the white American colonists had done in their revolution, then they must *integrate.*

The strategy of the movement was direct nonviolent action by masses of people in defiance of the Jim Crow laws of the South. The response of the white-run state and local governments and of allied white vigilante groups such as the Ku Klux Klan was ferocious repression. Movement activists asserting their legal rights were hosed, jailed, beaten, bombed, tortured, and murdered. A civil-rights protester in the South of the democratic United States in the early 1960s was almost certainly in more danger of physical violence than an activist in totalitarian Eastern Europe in the 1970s or 1980s. (On the other hand, jail terms were more common and much longer in Eastern Europe, and other basic freedoms, such as freedom of speech, were absent.)

"Unearned suffering is redemptive," said the movement's pre-eminent leader, Dr. Martin Luther King, Jr. Those to be redeemed by this suffering were, in the first place, the black protesters themselves. One who acts nonviolently in support of justice "lives in the kingdom NOW, and not in some distant day," King declared. And the Birmingham civil-rights leader the Reverend Fred Shuttlesworth asserted that the black preacher was "the freest man on earth." "They can't enjoin us from being free," he pointed out. Those to be redeemed were, in the second place, the white majority, who were challenged to live up to their professed ideals. By bringing the unearned suffering imposed by the system into the light of day, the civil-rights movement forced the white majority to make the choices that it had ducked for a century—either to embrace and fully institutionalize repression or to lift it. Not until public opinion had thus been changed did the national politicians act. It would be wrong, however, to deprive them of credit. On several occasions, they rose above political expediency, and took risks for what they had come to believe in. For example, on June 9, 1963, in the midst of the desegregation crisis in Birmingham, Alabama, President Kennedy decided spontaneously to appear on national television to support an omnibus civil-rights bill. Resisting dismayed advisers who pointed out that he had no carefully prepared text, Kennedy delivered what the *New York Times* called "one of the most emotional speeches yet delivered by a president who has often been criticized as too 'cool and intellectual.'" Kennedy's words "rose from the twin moorings that anchored King's oratory at the junction of religious and democratic sources," Taylor Branch, a chronicler of King and his movement, has written. "We are confronted primarily with a moral issue," Kennedy said. "It is as old as the Scriptures and is as clear as the American Constitution." And President Johnson, whose support for desegregation was stronger than Kennedy's, fought to pass the decisive Civil Rights Act of 1964 in the face of distinct warnings that the political price could be immense for the Democratic Party. "I think we just gave the South to the Republicans," he said prophetically after signing the civil-rights bill.

The civil-rights movement took its stand at the crossroads of democracy and nonviolence. Nonviolence acts upon totalitarianism from without, as a corrosive agent. Under totalitarian rule, the radical suppression of the freedom, or "truth," inhering in each person renders nonviolent action not only exceptionally costly to practice, but, once under way, exceptionally powerful. Precisely because totalitarian control is so thoroughly based on coercive power, nonviolence possesses the capacity, once it appears, to unravel an entire system with breathtaking suddenness. The influence of nonviolent action on democracy is different. Because both are based on cooperative power, nonviolent action can, if successful, strengthen democracy. Under a totalitarian system, nonviolence is revolutionary; under a democratic system it is an agent of reform. For the one it is lethal, for the other curative, as it was for the United States in the time of the civil-rights movement.

King and his colleagues understood the inner unity of democracy and nonviolence more deeply, perhaps, than any earlier leaders of a social movement. They were virtuosos in the art of summoning the American republic to live up to its declared principles. In that sense, they were American conservatives. But because the deepest principles of the American polity—that all men are created equal, that all should live in freedom—are, if taken seriously, radical, the civil-rights leaders were also radicals.

The movement's strategy was to break the law in the name of the law—to practice civil disobedience of the repressive laws of the Southern states in the name of constitutional law. In King's words in his "Letter from a Birmingham Jail," "I submit that an individual who breaks a law that conscience tells him is unjust and who willingly accepts the penalty of imprisonment in order to arouse the conscience of the community over its injustice, is in reality expressing the highest respect for law."

Nonviolence had little to do with moderation. The civil-rights protesters were fearlessly militant. "We mean to kill segregation or be killed by it," said Shuttlesworth. "You know my friends, there comes a time when people get tired of being trampled over by the iron feet of oppression," King told his audience in his first major speech in support of the famed bus boycott against segregation in Montgomery, Alabama. But when the crowd thundered its approval, he immediately went on, "Now let us say that we are not here advocating violence. We have overcome that." And, "There will be no crosses burned at any bus stops in Montgomery. There will be no white persons pulled out of their homes and taken out on some distant road and murdered. There will be nobody among us who stand up and defy the Constitution of this nation." For "If we are wrong—the Supreme Court of this nation is wrong. If we are wrong—God Almighty is wrong! . . . We are determined here in Montgomery—to work and fight until justice runs down like water, and righteousness like a mighty stream!"

King's nonviolence, of course, had foundations deeper than mere legal strategy. It was rooted in the Christian faith of the black churches of the South, which were both a point of origin and a mainstay of the movement, as were Gandhian political methods, which King and a number of other leaders of the movement, including James Lawson, James Bevel, Robert Moses, Bayard Rustin, and Diane Nash, had carefully studied. Gandhi's example was especially important for the youthful Student Nonviolent Coordinating Committee, which was the source of many of the movement's most successful specific techniques of direct action, such as sit-ins and voter-registration drives. King liked to say that Jesus gave him "the message," and Gandhi gave him "the method." King did not distinguish between a City of God and a City of Man any more than Gandhi had, and he moved back and forth between the two realms with singular dexterity. Like Gandhi, he based his political action squarely on love, the polestar of both his faith and his politics. "Standing beside love," he said at twenty-six, "is always justice."

However, the message of Gandhi—a man as little known to the black minority in the United States as to the white majority—was overshadowed by the message of faith, which offered a bond between the two races. Just as King the legal activist called on America to live up to its Constitution, King the preacher called on it to live up to its Christian and Jewish faiths. (The importance of the Old Testament, and especially of the book of Exodus, to the black community created a tie of particular warmth between the civil-rights movement and the American Jewish community.) In any case, King, a Baptist minister, found all that he needed to say about love in the Bible. When his house was bombed during the boycott in Montgomery, and an angry crowd of black supporters assembled, he counseled, "Don't get panicky. Don't get your weapons. If you have weapons, take them home. He who lives by the sword will perish by the sword. Remember that is what Jesus said. We are not advocating violence. We want to love our enemies. I want you to love your enemies. Be good to them. This is what we must live by. We must meet hate with love." Later he said, "Somebody must have sense enough and morality enough to cut off the chain of hate and the chain of evil in the universe. And you do that by love." When an officer who had just called Shuttlesworth a "monkey," then kicked him in the shin and was taking him off to jail, asked him—perhaps in disappointment—"Why don't you hit me?" Shuttlesworth replied, "Because I love you," and smiled.

Democratic Revival

The kinship of nonviolence and democracy—and of both with peace among nations—was put on more extensive display in the parade of democratic revolutions of the last quarter of the twentieth century. The threads of liberal development that had been snapped by the global descent into violence in 1914 were picked up in the century's final years. Time after time—as in England in 1689—the power of nonviolent action showed itself, and time after time it led to democratic government. Like the self-determination movement, the liberal revival included defeat of dictatorial governments of every political shape and form—right as well as left, totalitarian as well as authoritarian—and on every continent. Its centerpiece was the democratization of Eastern Europe and, we can still hope, Russia; but it began in southern Europe in the 1970s. In 1974, a junta of Greek colonels, who had overthrown the democratic government of Constantine Karamanlis in a coup in 1967, yielded power to civilians, after the military intervention in Cyprus in support of the Greek community. Next came the overthrow in Portugal of the autocratic regime of Marcello Caetano, successor to the dictator Salazar, by pro-democratic Portuguese military officers abetted by a powerful civil movement. It's a suggestive historical detail that this second in the series of liberal democratic revolutions brought the downfall of the last of the Western European colonial empires in Africa. It might appear a paradox that the feeble, backward, superannuated regime founded by Salazar was able to hold on to its empire longer than the other, more impressive colonial powers. Portugal was hardly mightier than France or England, or more adept at the imperial arts. Rather, its advantage was precisely its backwardness. Its repressive rule abroad was fully consistent with its repressive rule at home. The regime, wedded equally to both, lost both at once. It was a story not to be repeated until the Soviet empire and the Soviet state collapsed in a single cloud of dust. In both Portugal and the Soviet Union, the home population rebelled in the aftermath of colonial revolt as if its country had been just one more colony of the empire.

After Portugal came its neighbor, Spain. In 1975, following Franco's death, the regime, increasingly deserted by important elements in the Catholic Church and by the king, Juan Carlos, yielded without violence to democratic government. Although the liberal revival so far was largely a southern European affair, the fall of Franco foreshadowed the Soviet collapse in certain respects. Among many right-wing dictatorial regimes founded in Europe in the 1930s, only Spain's and Portugal's had survived into the postwar period. Spared the destruction visited by the Allies on Nazi Germany and Fascist Italy in the Second World War, they, like the Soviet Union, were permitted to live out (so to speak) their natural lives. In Spain, the Francoist Cortes, or parliament, helpfully smoothed the path to its own extinction by providing for a free election in which most of its members were defeated. It was not surprising that as the Soviet empire headed toward history's dustbin the Portuguese and Spanish events attracted the attention of Eastern European observers. All three of these violent regimes defied expectation by giving up the ghost with a minimum of violence, or even struggle. By the end of the century, all Europe was under democratic government—the culmination of a remarkable transition on the continent that had given birth to both the right-wing and left-wing versions of totalitarianism and as recently as the late 1930s had been ruled mostly by dictatorships.

Similar events unfolded in Latin America. In 1982, the draconian regime of Argentina's generals surrendered power after suffering defeat by Great Britain in the war over the Falkland Islands, and a year later a civilian president, Raul Alfonsín, came to power in an election. In 1985, a military regime was removed in neighboring Brazil. In 1989, the military dictator of Chile, Augusto Pinochet, also yielded power to an elected government (a successor government later considered prosecuting him). In the same years and in the years following, a profusion of more or less democratic governments replaced outright military dictatorships in most of the other countries of Latin America.

Meanwhile, in Asia several authoritarian governments were giving way to democracies. The dictatorship of Ferdinand Marcos in the Philippines yielded in 1986 to a vigorous, peaceful, popular resistance, led by the Catholic Church and a rebellious faction in the military. Pressure from allies, including the United States, which had previously supported Marcos, played a role. Two years later in South Korea, the autocratic Chun Doo Hwan agreed to an election that led to his replacement by his rival Roh Tae Woo. In Taiwan, the first multiparty legislative and local elections were held in 1989, after four decades of one-party rule by the Nationalist Party that had once governed mainland China.

In the late 1990s, the autocratic regime of General Suharto fell in Indonesia; free elections were held in Nigeria in 1999; and in Iran a strong opposition challenged the autocratic rule of Islamic mullahs who had installed themselves in power in the revolution of 1978–79, against the regime of Shah Mohammad Reza Pahlavi. In 2001, seventy-one years of unbroken rule by the People's Revolutionary Party in Mexico was ended in a free election won by the presidential candidate of the National Action Party, Vicente Fox. In October of that year, the murderous regime of Slobodan Milosevic in Serbia was overthrown by a nonviolent, democratic movement. In this revolution, the affinity of nonviolence and democracy was demonstrated with particular clarity, for the movement arose in support of election results that had given victory to the democratic forces but had then been falsified by the Milosevic regime. In all previous nonviolent revolutions, the revolt had preceded the elections; in Serbia, the procedure was reversed.

Of all the peaceful transfers of power from tyranny to democracy of the late twentieth century, however, perhaps the most remarkable was the one in South Africa. There, almost every kind of major strife of the twentieth century seemed to be tangled in a single inextricable knot. The conflict was racial: a white minority ran an all-white government along democratic lines but ruled and oppressed a black and "colored" majority under the system of apartheid. (In 1958, Prime Minister Hendrik Verwoerd had announced, "Our motto is to maintain white supremacy for all time to come over our own people and our own country, by force if necessary.")

It was national: most whites and more than one group of blacks considered themselves a nation. It was colonial: the whites had installed themselves in Africa in several waves of imperial invasion. It was ideological: the dominant, white government believed in capitalism, but the dominant black organization, the African National Congress (A.N.C.), was socialist, and many of its leaders were communists. As if all this were not enough, the white regime introduced nuclear arms into the picture. In the mid-seventies, South Africa became Africa's sole possessor of nuclear weapons, and this complication, too, required resolution. (Among the deadly poisons of the era, only religious hatred was largely missing.)

The leader of the African National Congress, Nelson Mandela, was not a believer in Gandhian nonviolence; in the early 1950s, in fact, he explicitly rejected it. In 1951, the A.N.C. had declared a defiance campaign that called for nonviolent disobedience of racial laws; in the face of government repression, it faltered, and the A.N.C. embarked on a reappraisal of its tactics. Gandhi's influence was strong, especially among the A.N.C.'s Indian members; the organization's black president, Albert Luthuli, a Christian, was a Gandhi admirer. "The urge and yearning for freedom springs from a sense of DIVINE DISCONTENT," Luthuli wrote, "and so, having a divine origin, can never be permanently humanly gagged." He argued for a continuation of peaceful resistance. But Mandela argued for armed insurrection, and prevailed. He then went underground to create the Umkhonto we Sizwe, Spear of the Nation. "The attacks of the wild beast," he said, quoting an African proverb, "cannot be averted with only bare hands." Later, he explained, "I saw nonviolence on the Gandhian model not as an inviolable principle but as a tactic to be used as the situation demanded."

In South Africa, however, violent rebellion somehow never developed into full-scale people's war. The government was easily able to withstand Umkhonto we Sizwe's attacks, which were few and far between. Mandela was arrested with other leaders of the

A.N.C. in July of 1963, sentenced to prison for life, and sent to a jail on Robben Island. The protest of the fifties was followed by what came to be known as "the silent sixties." (South Africa appears to have been one of the few countries on earth that was quiet in that noisy decade.) "Luthuli, Mandela and [the A.N.C. leader Walter] Sisulu were perceived dimly, as if they belonged to another time, long past and long lost," the *Washington Post* writer Jim Hoagland wrote at the time.

Political protest against South Africa's apartheid system revived in the 1970s, and this time it developed, without any particular reference to Gandhi, into something resembling the mass-based civic action that would break out in Eastern Europe a few years later. It engaged mainly in local boycotts and protests in support of concrete causes, such as rent abatement and better sanitation, or in protest against concrete injustices, such as the government's attempt to force all South Africans to learn the white Afrikaners' language, Afrikaans. In 1982, a few years after Havel and Michnik had first argued for resolute activism for limited social objectives, the Soweto Civic Association leader Popo Molefe was urging boycotts and other actions for local objectives that were "essential, real and vital." These, he said, would give people "the confidence that through their united mass action they can intervene and change their lives on no matter how small a scale." Only then could they "start to build progressively more political forms of organization—a process which would culminate in the development of a national democratic struggle." In 1983, this new wave of protest led to the foundation of the United Democratic Front, an umbrella group of more than five hundred civic organizations.

Meanwhile the imprisoned Mandela's influence was growing. By sheer force of courageous and restrained personal example, he established a kind of ascendancy over both his fellow prisoners and his prison guards. He and the other prisoners held marathon political discussions, read literature (Shakespeare was their favorite), and studied for correspondence degrees. While the Polish activists were establishing a flying university, the A.N.C. prisoners on Robben Island were establishing a captive one. Here the new generation of activists of the seventies and eighties, many of whom knew little of the A.N.C., received an unexpected education from their elders. Mandela's reputation spread and grew. Seemingly powerless in jail, he was on his way to becoming the fulcrum and pivot of South African history.

Behind the myth of the great man—the A.N.C. propaganda, the hero worship—there was in fact a great man. The government, under pressure from spreading disturbances, and from a growing international movement to impose economic sanctions on the apartheid regime, began to meet with their prisoner Mandela, probably hoping to divide the movement by entering into separate agreements with him. Those hopes foundered on Mandela's unswerving commitment to full majority rule. Nevertheless, Mandela's oppressors found reassurance in the qualities of the person. Instead of finding a broken, pliable man, they encountered the giant who, in spite of them, had grown in stature in their prisons. The first to meet with Mandela, Hendrik Coetsee, the minister of justice, recorded his impressions. "It was quite incredible," he said. "He acted as if we had known one another for years, and this was the umpteenth time we had met. . . . He was like the host." Coetsee continued, "He came across as a man of Old World values. I have studied Latin and Roman culture, and I remember thinking that this is a man to whom I could apply it, an old Roman citizen with *dignitas, gravitas, honestas, simplicitas.*" Most surprising was Mandela's lack of bitterness and his capacity for forgiving those who had caused him so much suffering—a capacity that not only was to be writ large in the final settlement of the conflict but perhaps was to make it possible. "Mandela had become famous above all as the man who forgave the enemies who had jailed him," his biographer Anthony Sampson writes. But he goes on to add, "It was not an obvious role for him to play."

The ability to forgive is a spiritual quality, but in Mandela it was not rooted in religion. He was a stoic, as Coetsee's comments suggest, but not an ascetic. "Gandhi took off his clothes," Mandela's friend Fatima Meet has commented. "Nelson *loves* his clothes." Regarding religion, there is no reason to doubt Mandela's assessment of himself—"I'm just a sinner who keeps on trying. I am not particularly religious or spiritual. I am just an ordinary person trying to make sense of the mysteries of life."—or to doubt the assessment of the Nigerian poet Wole Soyinka, who commented that Mandela's character was "the unselfconscious manifestation of uncluttered humanity."

The refusal of bitterness was a matter of both prudence and conviction. "When one is faced with such situations [of provocation and brutality]," Mandela has remarked, "you want to think clearly, and obviously you think more clearly if you are cool, you are steady, you are not rattled. Once you become rattled you can make serious mistakes." He also said, "Bitterness would be in conflict with the whole policy to which I dedicated my life." Of his forgiveness, he once commented, "Courageous people do not fear forgiving, for the sake of peace." Commenting on this stance, Anthony Sampson observes, rightly and factually, "Forgiveness was an aspect of power."

Few countries seemed to have less in common in the late 1980s than South Africa and the Soviet Union, yet the paths to democracy the two of them took have a surprising resemblance, as if the world, at certain moments, were indeed guided by a secret Zeitgeist, just as Hegel said. In both countries, the leader of the ruling establishment—in the Soviet Union, Gorbachev; in South Africa, President Frederik de Klerk—made an astonishingly bold commitment to change that led, against his expectation, to the dissolution of the regime he headed. Both leaders, it appears, stayed faithful to *principles,* even when it turned out that in the name of them they had to surrender cherished *goals*—in the case of Gorbachev, it was a humanistic communist Soviet Union, and in the case of de Klerk, who wound up becoming vice president under

President Mandela, it was a regime of power sharing that would have preserved a white veto over legislation. Of de Klerk after Mandela's release, Allister Sparks, a chronicler of the A.N.C.-government negotiations, commented, "His own process of change kept pace with events, which is what has saved him—and South Africa. And so he remains on the scene, although in a lesser role." De Klerk's acceptance of the outcome of the process he unleashed, even more than the original decision to end apartheid, is, as Sparks wrote, "the real measure of the man's reflective intelligence."

In both countries, violence on the grand scale was averted—although in South Africa over the four years of negotiation between the A.N.C. and the regime several thousand people were killed, most by the government or its agents. In both, the opposition discovered the virtues of restraint and "self-limiting revolution." In both, "truth and reconciliation" won out over revenge. People have often spoken of a "South African miracle." The government negotiator Albie Sachs has protested the use of the phrase. The settlement, he accurately claims, was "the most predicted and consciously and rationally worked-for happening one could ever have imagined, and certainly the most unmiraculous." But that of course was precisely the miracle.

The Western Settlement

The Washington think tank Freedom House keeps a record of countries it considers to be democracies. In 1971, it counted thirty; in 2001, after a quarter century of the liberal revival, it counted one hundred and twenty-one. The question is what such a development portends for peace. Gigantic claims have been made, the most grandiose of which was probably the assertion in 1989 by the American political scientist Francis Fukuyama that the liberal democratic revival heralded the "end of history." He did not mean, naturally, that no new events were to be expected. He was only suggesting that the widespread adoption of liberal democracy constituted humanity's final judgment that, among all the forms of government, this one had shown itself to be the best.

A more modest and defensible claim—itself sufficiently sweeping—is that the revival constituted a grand settlement along liberal lines of what might be called the Western civil war of the twentieth century. This civil war began in 1914, with the outbreak of the First World War; paused for two decades after 1918; and resumed with the Second World War, followed of course by the Cold War. At issue was which of the three dominant models of government of the period—fascism (and its various offshoots, such as Japanese militarism and Spanish Falangism), communism, or liberal democracy—would prevail. The first stage of the settlement came when, following their defeat, Germany and Japan enthusiastically took to the democratic systems imposed upon them by the victorious Allies. By making democracy their own, they robbed fascism of almost all of its glamour and appeal for the rest of the century. (What country, upon overthrowing a regime and establishing a new one, has announced that it will model itself on Hitler's Germany or Mussolini's Italy?) The second stage was the overthrow from within of the Soviet Union by the peoples over whom it had ruled, which left liberal democracy standing alone in the Western ring.

In the light of twentieth-century history, the potential importance of this settlement for world peace appears great, even if liberal democracy does not continue to spread, and even if it turns out that its existing spread has in many places been superficial and reversible. Since it was the Western world, after all, that, thanks to its creation of the global adapt-or-die war system and imperialism, twice turned its local wars into world wars, settlement of the Western civil war at least removes the prime specific cause of the world's most violent wars of the last century. Whatever the cause of war in the future, it is unlikely to be a conflict between Germany and France. The emergence of a political consensus in the West on *any* form of government would have reduced the likelihood of intra-Western war; but a consensus on liberal democracy was especially promising. It laid the basis in Europe for the now–burgeoning European Union, which institutionalizes liberal democratic principles on the regional level.

However, if in the wake of September 11, pacification of the West turns out to set the stage for conflict with an Islamic "East," or a bid for American military hegemony over the entire world, there may be no net gain. The Western settlement also leaves open the question of its relations with the generally poorer, weaker countries of the rest of the world. Once called the Third World, these countries are now more often called the South, while the West, in another shift in quadrant of the world's political compass, has been renamed the North. By the end of the twentieth century, the South had driven back and destroyed the territorial empires that the North had forced upon them. Didn't this reversal deliver the West a blow that undercut its global preeminence? As it turned out, just the opposite has been the case. It is true that the global influence of several European nations—most notably England and France—was reduced (while that of the United States grew). But if we consider the Western world as a whole, it responded to the loss of its territorial empires as if throwing off a burden.

For one thing, territorial imperialism, even as it advanced the market system, had been a source of wars that had impeded that system's smooth spread and weakened democracy at home. (World trade, which had reached a historical high point in the first decade of the twentieth century, steeply declined in the twenties and thirties.) For another, no sooner did the South drive out its imperial oppressors than it found itself reincorporated into the Northern market system, now more pervasive and less escapable than ever. Imperialism had always been economic as well as military. Whether trade was following the flag or vice versa (and the history of imperialism offers abundant examples of both), the two had marched together almost everywhere.

The liquidation of the colonial regimes by no means meant liquidation of economic influence. On the contrary, a united West—a North—was in certain respects more formidably powerful in the Third World than the old, divided West, whose powers were often played off against one another by the countries they ruled. Nor did those countries manage to confront this united, liberal West with any rival political or economic model that held wide appeal, even to one another, much less to the world. After the Soviet collapse, socialism lost ground almost everywhere. The most prominent new political model, the theocracy of Islamic fundamentalism, first embodied in revolutionary form in the Iranian regime of the Ayatollah Khomeini, could by its nature appeal only to Islamic countries. Even in these it proved more attractive as an inspiration for rebellion than as an actual form of government. (Today, a majority of Iranians regularly vote for moderate candidates who seek to soften the repressive rule of the mullahs.) Of course unliberal governments of all types are still to be found in the Third World, but none of them have been widely imitated. Now that "there is no alternative," as people like to say, the original elements of the West's predominance—its science, its arms, its capitalism, and to some extent its liberal democracy—have become harder than ever to reject.

Precisely because the post–Cold War market system—sometimes called "the Washington consensus," sometimes simply globalization—has become so pervasive, it exerts the sort of irresistible, impersonal, adapt-or-die pressure that the war system exerted in its heyday. The international currency speculators who pulled the rug out from under the Mexican and Argentinean pesos, the Thai baht, the Indonesian rupiah, and the Russian ruble had no interest in humiliating or weakening Mexico, Argentina, Thailand, Indonesia, or Russia; they were seeking only to fatten their bottom lines. The New York Times columnist Thomas Friedman has called this system "the golden straitjacket." Golden it may or may not be (Russians, Mexicans, Indonesians, Thailanders, Argentineans, and most Africans, among others, have excellent reasons for finding it less than golden); a straitjacket it certainly is. The paradox of the global market system is that while it offers a wide choice of goods to many consumers within the system, it closes off choice among systems. Countries going shopping for economic systems will find only one product on the shelf. This theoretical enemy of monopoly has itself become a global monopoly. If in the birth canals of the future, some other, better system is getting ready to be born, it is in acute danger of being aborted by the monopolistic pressure of the existing system.

Totalitarianism, in the view of some of its most penetrating analysts, was a monster created from the rib of the predominantly liberal European civilization of the nineteenth century. "If it is true," Hannah Arendt wrote in *The Origins of Totalitarianism*, "that the elements of totalitarianism can be found by retracing the history and analyzing the political implications of what we usually call the crisis of our century, then the conclusion is unavoidable that this crisis is no mere threat from the outside, no mere result of some aggressive foreign policy of either Germany or Russia, and that it will no more disappear with the death of Stalin than it disappeared with the fall of Nazi Germany. It may even be that the true predicaments of our time will assume their authentic form—though not necessarily the cruelest—only when totalitarianism has become a thing of the past."

That day has come. Imperialism, whose tradition is as long in the West as the tradition of democracy, was one of the points of origin of totalitarianism that Arendt identified. Imperialism began not with conquest but with trade, and with corporations licensed by royalty to exploit faraway lands. Economic globalization has so far widened the global gap between rich and poor. "Our British colonizers stepped onto our shores a few centuries ago disguised as traders," the Indian writer Arundhati Roy notes. "Is globalization about 'eradication of world poverty,' or is it a mutant variety of colonialism, remote-controlled and digitally operated?" she asks. On the answers the prosperous countries give to such questions will depend in considerable measure the ability of the liberal nations of the North to make a contribution to the peace of the world.

The Imperial Temptation

It would be tempting to suppose that imperialism is an alien product imposed upon the liberal democratic political system by the global market system. And it is certainly true that in many places the market system distorts and threatens to overwhelm democracy, which has proved highly vulnerable to the inroads of corporate power. The record suggests, however, that republican political systems have by no means been perverted only by economic pressures. The tendency of republics to engage in imperialism existed before the modern age and the rise of capitalism. Periclean Athens, the birthplace of democracy, was both democratic and energetically imperial. The Roman republic was the only power that has ever conquered almost the whole known Western world. Holland of the seventeenth century had both quasi-republican institutions and a global empire. Not long after France became a republic, Napoleon sent its armies out to conquer Europe. England was both the "mother of parliaments" and the ruler of the most extensive empire the world had ever known. The United States is a republic that now styles itself the "world's only superpower" and increasingly claims the mantle of global hegemony.

There is something in republicanism itself, it appears, that is prone to imperialism. It is equally true, however, that imperialism has been a menace to republican government, destroying the institutions out of which it arose. The conflicts have been persistent and deep. They were described by the historian of the Peloponnesian wars Thucydides, who attributed democratic Athens' downfall to its imperial overreaching, which culminated in its disastrous, unsuccessful invasion of the city of Syracuse. The Roman republic fell victim to the Roman Empire—an event symbolized forever by Julius Caesar's decision to send his imperial army across the Rubicon to intervene in the domestic affairs of Rome. The intellectual founders of modern democracy were fully conscious of the lesson. In Jean-Jacques Rousseau's words, "Whoever wants to deprive others of their freedom almost always ends by losing his own; this is true even of kings, and very much more true of peoples." According to Montesquieu, who wrote a book analyzing the downfall of the Roman republic, "If a democratical republic subdues a nation in order to govern them as subjects, it exposes its own liberty, because it entrusts too great a power to its magistrates sent into the conquered provinces." Both opponents and supporters of the European empires also reflected deeply on the contradiction. For example, in his classic *Imperialism* (1902), which had a strong influence on Lenin, J. A. Hobson wrote, "Imperialism and popular government have nothing in common: they differ in spirit, in policy, in method."

As long as colonial peoples remained politically passive, the contradiction could be ignored. But when they began to demand their freedom, a decision was forced. In the 1920s, Leonard Woolf, who had served in the British colonial service in Ceylon, described what this clash of principles led to in practice. "European civilization, with its ideas of economic competition, energy, practical efficiency, exploitation, patriotism, power, and nationalism, descended upon Asia and Africa," he wrote. "But with [nationalism] is also carried, involuntarily perhaps, another set of ideas which it had inherited from the French Revolution and the eighteenth-century forerunners of the French Revolution." These—he meant the ideas of liberty, equality, and fraternity—embodied the principles of democracy. He concluded, "The question imperialism posed was whether or not these [democratic] ideas were really universal. If not, they were discredited at home. If so, imperialism was discredited abroad."

An unusually interesting pro-imperial analyst of the problem, the Frenchman Jules Harmand, who served as the commissioner general in Tonkin (later North Vietnam) in 1884, and in 1910 published *Domination and Colonization,* came to similar conclusions. Imperial conquest, he frankly declared, was based on coercion. "The two ideas of true empire and of force, or at least of constraint," he wrote, "are correlative or complementary. According to the time, circumstance, and procedures, force can be more or less strong or weak, open or hidden, but it can never disappear. On the day when constraint is no longer required, empire will no longer exist. . . . What was taken by force," he went on, "had to be held by force"—indeed, by the "uninterrupted use of force." On the other hand, democracy at home, he well knew, was based on "political liberty" and "equality" of all. Accordingly, imperial conquest was necessarily "disturbing to the conscience of democracies."

Harmand had defined the choices that, over the long run, faced the citizenry of a republic bent on imperialism. They must either reconcile themselves to the uninterrupted use of force, in which case their republic, like that of the Romans, might be lost, or they must "stay at home." Few champions of imperialism have had the frankness to acknowledge this choice. Most have preferred to bridge the gulf between their principles and their actions with what Hobson called "a sea of vague, shifty, well-sounding phrases, which are seldom tested by close contact with fact," while hoping vainly that some respectable and dignified middle course would present itself.

In the internal politics of dozens of liberal democratic countries, governments really do regularly succeed one another without intervention by armies or secret police; decisions *are* made by elected representatives, freedom of speech and assembly *are* realities, the news media *do* operate with some independence, and most disputes *are* settled by legal means. However, in their foreign dealings many of those same countries have backed dictatorships, supported or sponsored massacres and terrorism, and engaged in imperialism. To the extent that democratic procedure is simply corrupted or overridden by military ambition or economic interest—and no one can doubt that this frequently happens—there is no paradox. However, to the extent that the contradiction emerges from the political system itself, then the question becomes why republics so often generate imperial policies that are destructive of their own domestic institutions. The country that today faces the choice between republic and empire is the United States, of which we will have more to say later.

Democracy and Militarism

The military historian Victor Hanson has recently argued, in a series of books, that the association of democracy and military aggression predates the modern age. Democratic Athens, he has shown, invented the savage set-piece battles between disciplined infantries that we have come to call conventional war. (Previously, war had been a more disorganized affair, consisting of a series of opportunistic sallies and retreats by cavalry and mounted bowmen, often with little bloodshed.) "Shock battle," as Hanson calls it, gave Western arms a superiority they have never lost. It was not only in modern times that Western armies won lopsided victories. The epochal naval battle at Salamis, at which the Persians lost some forty thousand men, mostly by drowning, and the Greeks probably only a few thousand, revealed a pattern that would often be in evidence from then on.

The decisive advantage, Hanson suggests, was freedom. Because the soldiers of a free state were also citizens and fought for their own freedom as well as that of their city, their morale was high. Because they were leagued with their fellow citizens, they fought with discipline and were ashamed to flee the battlefield. ("Infantrymen of the *polis* think it is a disgraceful thing to run away, and they choose death over safety through flight," Aristotle wrote. "On the other hand, professional soldiers, who rely from the outset on superior strength, flee as soon as they find out they are outnumbered, fearing death more than dishonor.") Because they and their fellow citizens enjoyed free speech, their military campaigns could be discussed and harshly criticized in their assemblies, and so they could learn from their mistakes. Because they could write freely, they could record their own histories. Until recent times, Hanson notes, military history was close to being "an exclusive Western monopoly." (At Omdurman, for example, there was no Sudanese equivalent of Churchill, whose recording eye and hand may have been as important an element of Britain's long-term military superiority as Kitchener's gunboats.) Because their political constitutions were strong, they were able to preserve their communal will and quickly replenish their forces. When the Greek historian Polybius sought the cause of Rome's rise to "universal dominion" in the fifty-two years between 220 B.C. and 167 B.C., he found it in Rome's constitution.

A recurring tragedy of republics has been that freedom, far from enervating the state, as authoritarians have claimed, in fact generates power, which then can be converted into force, which, as in classical tragedies, not only creates nightmares for other nations but recoils upon its possessors, extinguishing the freedom from which it arose. Arendt's precept that violence is inimical to power comes into play, and the empire destroys the republic. James Madison, who was acutely aware of the danger, put it well in a comment on the destruction of the Roman republic that seems pertinent to the United States today: "The veteran legions of Rome were an overmatch for the undisciplined valor of all other nations, and rendered her mistress of the world. Not the less true is it that the liberties of Rome proved the final victim to her military triumphs; and that the liberties of Europe, as far as they ever existed, have, with few exceptions, been the price of her military establishments." The danger, now as in other times, is that democracy's basic nonviolent principles, so promising for the peace of the world, can be undermined by the very power the system generates, bringing itself as well as its neighbors to ruin.

10

Liberal Internationalism

When Caesar crossed the Rubicon, he resolved the contradiction between empire and republic in favor of empire. Others have tried to resolve it the other way around: instead of sending soldiers across the Rubicon into the republic, they have sought, so to speak, to send jurists and citizens from the republic across the Rubicon to tame the savage international arena. The martial tendency of democracy to evolve into empire has its mirror image in the pacific dream that all the world can be turned into a republic. This has been the program of the liberal internationalists. If imperialism and war are lethal to liberalism, they have asked themselves, does not liberalism contain within it a principle that, if extended to international affairs, could be lethal to imperialism and war? For the plan of the liberal democratic state is based on a formula that seems to beg for application in the international sphere. Might not nations enter into a social contract just as individuals supposedly once did? Why should domestic governments alone be founded on nonviolent principles? Why stop at national borders? Shouldn't a system of cooperative power, the key to resolving disputes without violence, be extended to the limits of the earth? Thought glides smoothly and easily to this conclusion. The mechanism is known, its procedures proven within many national states. Liberalism, moreover, lays claim, as science and religion do, to universal principles (that "all men are created equal," that all must enjoy the "rights of man") and feels itself confined and incomplete on a merely national stage. Having asserted the dignity of man against the arrogance of aristocrats and kings, it looks in vain in its stock of principles for any good reason to confine this benefit to just *one* people. (Conservatism, by contrast, looks only to a particular place and circumstance, and proclaims not the rights of man but, with Burke, the "inherited . . . rights of Englishmen.")

Wherever liberalism has flourished domestically, it has been accompanied by visions of liberal internationalism. With few exceptions, the thinkers and statesmen of the liberal tradition have dreamed such dreams or sought to make them a reality. As early as the late seventeenth century, William of Orange was already "busy with a scheme remarkably like the ideal which the League of Nations [attempted] to achieve," in the words of his biographer G. J. Renier. William envisioned a system of collective security that would keep the France of Louis XIV in check. Disputes would be arbitrated by an impartial court, and "recusants would be brought to reason by force of arms."

In the age of revolution, scarcely any of the contract theorists failed to champion some liberal scheme for international harmony. In May 1776, Tom Paine proposed a "European Republic," to be guided by a "General Council," to which nations would submit disputes for arbitration. In *Common Sense,* published in the same year, he recommended, as everyone knows, a union of states to the American colonies—with more telling effect. In his work we find, perhaps for the first time, the belief that republics will be more peaceful abroad than monarchies. But it was in England in the nineteenth century that liberal internationalism took root most deeply. When Jeremy Bentham, the founder of utilitarianism, wrote *The Principles of International Law* (thereby introducing the word "international" into common usage), he included a "Plan for a Universal and Perpetual Peace." To the liberal English mind of the nineteenth century, civil liberties at home, enlargement of the franchise, championship of national movements for independence, like those of Greece, Italy, and the Balkan states, and support for the arbitration of international disputes belonged together, because all were expressions of the fundamental liberal faith in popular self-government under the rule of law. Indeed, a conviction that it is possible to base all policy, foreign and domestic, on the same basic principles, and therefore on a single moral standard, has been one of the enticements of liberal thought since its birth. (This conviction has also been from the beginning a butt of criticism from conservatives, who have regarded it as foolishly idealistic or utopian.)

The statesman with whose name liberal internationalism was most closely associated in the nineteenth century was the Liberal prime minister William Gladstone, who, together with his Tory rival Benjamin Disraeli, dominated British politics in the century's latter half. Gladstone's opposition to Disraeli's policies of imperial expansion and Realpolitik in European affairs had its origins in his belief in the self-determination of nations, which he associated with England's own independence and freedom. His desire for a single standard for judging all conduct was evident in his reaction to news that a British general was carrying out executions of Afghans who resisted British rule. Wasn't it "monstrous," he asked, to "place ourselves in such a position that when the Afghan discharges the first duty of a patriot—namely, to endeavor to bring his countrymen to resist the foreign invader—that is to be treated as a sin?" Each person's right—and patriotic duty—to seek self-government was also the keynote of his epic, unsuccessful campaign to pass a home-rule bill for Ireland. Laws passed in England for Ireland might, he conceded, sometimes be "good laws," but that was beside the point. For "the passing of good laws is not enough in cases where the strong permanent instincts of the people, their distinctive marks of character, the situation and history of their country, require not only that these laws should be good but that they should proceed from a congenial and native source and besides being good laws should be their own laws."

On the moral foundation of self-determination Gladstone built a strategic vision. It emerged most clearly in his response to the crisis in the Balkans in the late 1870s. The strategic problem for Britain in the area was the expansion southward of Russia, which the English regarded as a potential threat to their rule in India. (The Balkans were seen as another of the "roads to India.") At the same time, several Balkan peoples, whose populations were largely Christian, stepped up their resistance to the Ottoman imperial master. The Turks responded with massacres. Russia intervened militarily and, after initial failure, prevailed over the Turks.

Britain's traditional policy, based on keeping the Russians' Balkan road to India shut, had been support for Turkey, a policy that became morally awkward once Turkey, a Muslim power, began butchering Christians. Gladstone's archrival Disraeli nonetheless favored support for Turkey in order to defend the empire. To the intense indignation of Gladstone, he belittled accurate reports of the massacres as "coffee-house babble." "What our duty is at this critical moment," Disraeli said, "is to maintain the Empire of England."

In his election campaign of 1880, Gladstone wove all the strands of liberal internationalism into an appeal that, more than anything else, carried him into office. On the ground of conscience alone, the massacres had to be condemned: "There is not a criminal in a European jail; there is not a cannibal in the South Sea Islands whose indignation would not arise and overboil at the recital of that which has been done." His policy was also strategic. A string of independent Balkan states, Gladstone believed, would form a stronger barrier against Russian expansion than the faltering Ottoman Empire. "Give those people freedom and the benefits of freedom," he said; "that is the way to make a barrier against despotism." Giving voice in familiar terms to the bedrock faith of liberalism that the will of peoples will prevail over tyranny and force, he added, "Fortresses may be levelled to the ground; treaties may be trodden under foot—the true barrier against despotism is in the human heart and the human mind."

At the same time, he championed an extension of the principle of law to the world at large. He proposed a strengthened Concert of Europe, which would be empowered to adjudicate "disturbances, aggrandizements, and selfish schemes." In 1880, he wrote, "Certain it is, that a new law of nations is gradually taking hold of the mind, and coming to sway the practice of the world; a law which aims at permanent authority... the general judgment of civilized mankind."

Gladstone's liberal internationalism proved easier to preach than to practice. He had excoriated Disraeli's imperialism as "dangerous, ambiguous, impracticable, and impossible." In particular, he called for an "Egypt for the Egyptians." And yet two years later he found himself, to his dismay, ordering military intervention in Egypt (which set the stage for the farce at Fashoda nearly two decades later). He would have been happy to let the Egyptians have Egypt if he had believed that Egypt was the only stake on the table; but Egypt, too, was seen as a station on Britain's road to India—a country to which even Gladstone was unwilling to apply the cherished principle of self-determination. Without dropping out of the Great Game altogether (that is, giving up India), he discovered, he could not indulge his liberalism in Egypt. Whatever its other merits, liberal internationalism made a poor adjunct to the Realpolitik of imperial strategy. Either Egypt was a hitching post on the road to India, or it was a nation, with a right to determine its own affairs. It could not be both.

Not for the first or the last time, the two expansionary tendencies of liberalism—imperialism and liberal internationalism—were in collision. Imperialism extended power by coercive means; liberal internationalism did so by cooperative means. Not for the first or last time, either, empire prevailed.

The Wilsonian Apogee

The fullest expression of liberal internationalism, however, came not in Britain but in the United States, in the statesmanship of President Woodrow Wilson. The political climate of the United States was even more promising than England's for the growth of liberal internationalism. Whereas the English constitution had evolved over hundreds of years, the American constitution had been written at a single convention. Whereas England possessed a global territorial empire, in the 1910s the United States was still mainly a regional power. It was easier for Americans, lacking experience with other countries, to imagine that their constitutional miracle could be repeated on a global scale. The lines of connection between Gladstone's liberalism and Wilson's are nevertheless clear and direct. In September 1915, one year after the outbreak of the First World War, the British foreign secretary, Lord Grey, dispatched a telegram to Wilson. In words that might have been taken directly from Gladstone's speeches in 1880 regarding the Concert of Europe, he inquired, "Would the President propose that there should be a League of Nations binding themselves to side against any Power which broke a treaty . . . or which refused, in case of dispute, to adopt some other method of settlement than that of war?"

The President would. He began a process of reflection that led to his proposal for the League of Nations, which would embody the liberal international program in full. He argued for nothing less than a sudden, complete, systemic change in the international order, which would do for nations in the current anarchic international state of nature what the social contract, according to liberal theory, had done for particular peoples in the primeval state of nature. Wilson intended to revolutionize the international system—to "do away with an old order and to establish a new one," as he said in London as the war was ending. "The question upon which the whole future peace and policy of the world depends," he had declared in January of 1917, "is this: Is the present war a struggle for a just and secure peace, or only for a new balance of power? ... There must be not a balance of power but a community of power; not organized rivalries, but an organized common peace." The next year, he called for "the destruction of every arbitrary power anywhere that can separately, secretly and of its single choice disturb the peace of the world; or, if it cannot be presently destroyed, at the least its reduction to virtual impotence...." "Trustees of peace," he said not very convincingly, would shoulder this task. In short, Wilson proposed a wholesale liquidation of the war system and its replacement by a structure of cooperative power framed, like the Constitution of the United States, on liberal democratic principles.

The All-or-Nothing Choice

The watchwords of Wilson's vision were democracy, freedom, self-determination, the rule of law, and peace—principles that still command assent. Yet Wilson of course failed utterly. He failed in his own country, whose Senate rejected the League of Nations, on the ground that Article 10 of its charter, requiring collective action to prevent aggression, would abrogate Congress's constitutional power to declare war. And Wilson failed in the world, which proceeded, as he had warned it would, to a second, even more destructive bout of global war. His scheme foundered upon the huge, interlocking structures of violence—imperialism, totalitarianism, and the war system itself—that were to produce the carnage of the twentieth century. His principle of self-determination would have required dismantling not only the European empires but also the United States' imperial acquisitions of the turn of the century—

the Philippines, Hawaii, and Guam. "All the great wrongs of the world," he said, "have their root in the seizure of territory or the control of the political independence of other people." The second of his renowned Four Principles, announced on January 29, 1917, as a basis for settling the war, was "that people and provinces are not to be bartered about from sovereignty to sovereignty as if they were mere chattels and pawns in a game, even the great game, now forever discredited, of the balance of power." Rather, in the words of his fourth principle, "all well-defined national aspirations shall be accorded the utmost satisfaction."

America's allies, England and France, however, had no intention of relinquishing their empires. Neither, for that matter, did the United States propose to give up its new colonies. The victorious powers' chief interest was in parceling out Germany's few colonies among themselves. Western imperialism was at its zenith. The English were still rulers of an empire on which the sun never set. During the war, England, France, and Italy had been secretly and shamelessly bartering peoples from sovereignty to sovereignty. England and France, for example, had signed the secret Sykes-Picot agreement, in which they divided up large chunks of the Middle East between them without consulting either the peoples of the region or their leaders. Japan demanded and received promises of fresh colonial acquisitions in China's Shandong Peninsula in payment for its contributions to the Allied war effort—an outrage that spurred a protest movement in China that turned out to be the precursor to the rise to power of the Communist Party. Italy presented a similar bill for services in the war, in the form of a demand for the Balkan territories of Trieste and Dalmatia. Near the end of the peace conference at Versailles, after Wilson had surrendered ground to his allies on many colonial issues while publicly holding fast to his general principles, the English prime minister, David Lloyd George, remarked with a chuckle to an aide, "He has saved his precious principles, but we got our colonies."

Well might Lloyd George chuckle. Neither Wilson nor the

League of Nations that he championed would put the smallest dent in the European colonial empires. The empire that *had* already collapsed in 1918 was the Austro-Hungarian one, in the heart of Europe, and it was here that the Allies could all agree to apply the newly trumpeted principle of self-determination. Unfortunately, this was a part of the world in which such a principle faced immediate, insuperable obstacles. Self-determination calls for each people, or nation, to take sovereign power over the territory in which it lives, but in the lands of the former Austro-Hungarian Empire national populations were mixed. No matter how the boundaries might be drawn, they divided some people from their national brothers, while intermixing nationalities that did not wish to share a common state. If, in one of these territories, one people claimed national sovereignty, others necessarily were deprived of their rights.

If imperialism was a mature, well-developed structure of violence, totalitarianism, born in and of the late war, was just coming to life. The liberal ideology that had seemed so securely rooted at the turn of the century was about to suffer its worst reversal since the late eighteenth century. Since then, liberal principles had steadily gained ground. In countries with popular suffrage, the franchise was slowly widened and extended, and civil liberties were consolidated. Even in places, including Germany and Russia, in which dynasties remained in power, popular participation in government had steadily increased. The First World War gave birth to an opposite trend. Never had the damage of war to liberalism been more catastrophic. In Russia and Germany, the combination of unprecedented casualties with destruction or defeat created social conditions essential for the rise of totalitarianism. Even in the democracies, the war produced a general disillusionment and bitterness that put democratic institutions on the defensive. In a word, the blow that the war system had already landed on liberalism turned out to have been incomparably more powerful than a staggering liberalism's answering blow. Wilson was in this respect like a man who proposes the construction of additional floors of a building at exactly the moment that the floor he's standing on is collapsing under his feet.

The most intractable of the structures of violence that Wilson faced, however, was the one he had targeted directly, the war system. It was in its prime. The nation in arms, the industrialization of war, and heavy artillery, the tank, the modern battleship, the submarine, the machine gun were already in existence. The full panoply of air war, including the aircraft carrier and strategic bombing, was already under preparation.

Wilson spoke for many in his time when he identified the causes of the First World War as systemic. The origins of the war lay not so much in the ambitions of one actor or another as in the precariousness of an international system that could tip the world into catastrophe if the slightest imbalance of power appeared. In 1898, the imbalance had been at Fashoda, but war had somehow been averted. In 1914, the imbalance had been in the Balkans, and war had come. As Wilson put it, "War had lain at the very heart of every arrangement of Europe—of every arrangement of the world—that preceded the war." But now "Restive peoples . . . knew that no old policy meant anything else but force, force—always force. . . . They knew that it was intolerable."

Sometimes, a revolution can be accomplished in stages. That was not possible with Wilsonism. A fatally flawed global system required a full systemic substitute—a new "constitution for the whole world produced in eight days," as the French Prime Minister Georges Clemenceau, who opposed the plan, described it mockingly. The choice was all or nothing. In the words of the diplomat Harold Nicolson, who attended the Versailles conference as a member of the British delegation and at first was an ardent supporter of Wilson, "Instinctively, and rightly, did we feel that if Wilsonism was to form the charter of the New Europe it must be applied universally, integrally, forcefully, scientifically." If the Wilsonian palace were to be built, the edifice of the war system had to be torn down.

If the war system were to survive, it could not be adulterated with Wilsonism. In the Wilsonian system, the sovereignty of nations had to be abandoned, but in the war system sovereignty was inviolable except by force. In the Wilsonian system, the safety of nations required disarmament, but under the war system safety required arms. Wilsonism called for a league of all nations in a system of cooperative security; the balance of power called for specific alliances against specific enemies. Wilsonism hearkened to considerations of equity and justice; the war system attended only to calculations of force.

The best illustration of the stark character of the choice forced upon the conferees at Versailles was the potential threat to victorious but exhausted France from prostrate Germany, whose population and industrial capacity were nevertheless still the greatest in Europe. France wanted guarantees that these strengths would not be brought to bear against it one day in another war. There were two possible solutions to the problem—Wilson's League and a continuation of the balance-of-power policy that belonged to the war system. Each precluded the other. Wilson's plan called for generous treatment of Germany and reconciliation with it. A balance of power required harsh measures—a permanent, enforced second-class status for Germany and ironclad defense guarantees for France by England and the United States. The exorbitant and unrealistic demand for reparations from an impoverished Germany in the Versailles treaty and France's occupation of the German Ruhr in 1923 were elements of such a policy. Ineffective as they were, they nonetheless created a two-tier system of nations based on force, which ruled out Wilson's solution of a concert of equal nations, including Germany, based on a shared conception of international justice. Likewise, the balance-of-power solution would have been ruined by Wilsonian measures—disarmament and conciliation with Germany were hardly compatible with Germany's enduring subjugation.

Wilson's insistence upon a systemic solution may have been

hopeless, but it was not gratuitous. He had located the source of the problem at its true depth, and outlined a solution on the scale necessary to solve it. That the cure was beyond the will or capacity of the world of his day does not impeach the accuracy of the diagnosis. Wilson has often been taken to task for the naïveté of his solution, but his analysis of the problem was more realistic—and more prophetic—than that of his detractors. Unfortunately, the flaws in Wilson's system did not mean that the alternative, realist system—the system that had already brought on the First World War and the death of millions—had suddenly become a formula for peace and stability. Clemenceau spoke in Parliament of "an old system which appears to be discredited today, but to which I am not afraid of saying I am still faithful." But his faith, too, was tragically misplaced. The balance of power was never righted. The world was not rescued from another world war by its rejection of Wilsonism.

There is, as George Kennan has remarked, a naïveté of realism as well as a naïveté of idealism. Clemenceau's realist successors fell victim to it. It could, of course, be no comfort to idealists that realism was as unrealistic as their idealism. The interwar period, it appears, was one of those unfortunate times when each school is shrewd in its critique of its rival's plan but credulous regarding its own. There is such a thing as a disease that cannot be cured, and in the first half of the twentieth century the growing cancer of the war system may have been one of them.

In fairness to both the realists and the idealists of the time, however, it must be admitted that neither of their medicines was administered in a full dose. France neither received the real security guarantees that might conceivably have prevented the revival of the German threat nor was given the protection of any genuine system of collective security. What actually happened was that England and the United States offered rhetorical assurances of collective security to France while the League of Nations dissolved. In the 1930s, halfhearted realism vied with quarter-hearted idealism, and the curative effects of neither, even if they were available, were experienced.

In any case, when the participants of Versailles came to understand that Wilson's vision, of which they were already skeptical, might not be backed by the United States, they retreated with alacrity to the known and familiar. "The defensive value of armaments, strategic frontiers, alliances, and neutralization," in Harold Nicolson's words, "could be computed with approximate accuracy: the defensive value of 'virtue all round' could not be thus computed. If in fact Wilsonism could be integrally and universally applied, and if in fact Europe could rely upon America for its execution and enforcement, then indeed an alternative was offered infinitely preferable to the dangerous and provocative balances of the European system."

The puzzle was how, without writing a constitution for the world in eight days, to tackle the war system that had brought disaster. Even Nicolson was impaled on the dilemma. The political credo he offered in *Peacemaking 1919* remained a summation of the liberal internationalist faith.

> In spite of bitter disillusionment, I believe [in the principles of Wilson] today. I believed, with him, that the standard of political and international conduct should be as high, as sensitive, as the standard of personal conduct. I believed, and I still believe, that the only true patriotism is an active desire that one's own tribe or country should in every particular minister to that idea. I shared with him a hatred of violence in any form, and a loathing of despotism in any form. I conceived, as he conceived, that this hatred was common to the great mass of humanity, and that in the new world this dumb force of popular sentiment could be rendered the controlling power in human destiny. "The new things in the world," proclaimed President Wilson on June 5, 1914, "are the things that are divorced from force. They are the moral compulsions of the human conscience."

Yet having delivered himself of this anathema against force and in favor of the human conscience, Nicolson declared in almost the next breath that force must be the linchpin of the system he had wanted Wilson to build. Asking himself how he had placed his faith in Wilson at the beginning of the conference, he answered unequivocally that it was not the originality of Wilson's ideas, for Wilson "had not . . . discovered any doctrine which had not been dreamed of, and appreciated, for many hundred years." Rather, "The one thing which rendered Wilsonism so passionately interesting at the moment was in fact that this centennial dream was suddenly backed by the overwhelming resources of the strongest Power in the world." For "Here was a man who represented the greatest physical force which had ever existed and who had pledged himself openly to the most ambitious moral theory which any statesman had ever pronounced." Therefore, he possessed "the unquestioned opportunity to enforce these ideas upon the whole world."

Here was a contradiction to contend with. Force was to be expunged from world affairs by the greatest force that had ever been known. Yet if enough force was assembled to overpower the most powerful aggressors, then the question naturally arose what else might be done with that force. The "war to end war" would have to do its job, it seemed, with as much war as it ended. Liberalism called domestically for a limitation on the force in the hands of the state, but here would be force without limit. In reality, the League of Nations never came remotely near to posing such a threat, yet the central quandary had been posed.

On the one hand, there was the likelihood that the League's powers of enforcement would not be strong enough to prevent aggression. On the other hand, there was the danger that if the League did become strong enough, it would have to become something like a world government. Yet a world government based on force would be a global Leviathan. No halfway house, no mere reformist program could resolve this quandary. And given a choice between international anarchy, no matter how bloody, and global Leviathan, how could anyone who loved liberty—that is, how could any *liberal*—choose Leviathan?

The liberal tradition, which had broken the state's reliance on the sword in domestic affairs, seemed full of promise for peace in the world, but Wilsonism was unable to deliver on it. In order to have any part of the Wilsonian program, you had to have all of it, but all of it was too much. This was the unsolved riddle that the liberal internationalist project placed before the world in 1919.

11

Sovereignty

The objections to Wilson's international liberalism had a name, in which the mountainous impediments to its enactment were summed up: national sovereignty. The conflict between Wilsonism and sovereignty was fundamental. No international organization could preserve peace in the world without a grant of immense power, but the principle of sovereignty reserved ultimate power to the national authorities. The American senators who kept the United States out of the League of Nations accordingly asserted that membership in the League would abridge America's sovereign right to decide when to go to war. Would the League or Congress, they demanded to know, make this life-and-death decision? In vain did Wilson argue that the decisions of the League's council would be merely advisory and had to be unanimous in any case, so that the United States could by itself prevent any unwanted outcome. The opposing senators countered that if the United States did not mean to keep its pledge to enforce world peace it should not make it in the first place. "Guarantees must be fulfilled," Senator Henry Cabot Lodge explained. "They are sacred promises—it has been said only morally binding. Why, that is all there is to a treaty between great nations."

The events of the twentieth century that require a rethinking of the sources of political power also require a rethinking of the nature of sovereignty. To this end, we need to return to the intellectual roots of sovereignty, in sixteenth-century Europe. Both the fact and the idea of sovereignty have undergone deep changes. In essence we will see that the idea that power is indivisible, which is at the core of the concept of sovereignty, and has been the greatest of the obstacles to liberal internationalism, turns out to belong to coercive power alone. In the 1920s, the historian E. H. Carr said, "All power is indivisible." He should have said, "All coercive power is indivisible." For cooperative power, the story of democracy shows, can be divided. And this possibility, together with the radical changes in the war system that we have already described, opens up large new possibilities for cooperative action in international politics.

The Sovereignty of Kings

When the idea of sovereignty arose, it did not create a new political reality; rather, at a particular moment in history it legitimatized a preexisting conception of the state that proved to have remarkable appeal and endurance, not least because the stewards of the state found it to their liking. From the beginning, sovereignty faced in two directions—inward, toward the domestic arena, in which the monarchs of continental Europe were beginning to assert their absolute power, and outward, toward the foreign arena, where, around the time of the Treaty of Westphalia, in 1648, the war system assumed the form of the "Westphalian system" of sovereign states. Since then, sovereignty has, until recently, undergone remarkably little evolution in the foreign sphere; but in the domestic sphere of many countries it has changed a great deal.

The widely acknowledged intellectual father of the concept of sovereignty is Jean Bodin, a French political thinker of the late six-teenth century whose work provided a theoretical basis for the absolute rule of the French monarchs, then in its formative stage. He asserted with unblushing frankness that state power has only one basis: force. "In matters of state the master of brute force," he wrote, "is the master of men, of the laws, and of the entire com-monwealth." And so, "An absolute sovereign is one who, under God, holds by the sword alone." In short, according to Bodin, sovereign power was a name given to what we have called coercive power. He knew well that such a thing as cooperative power, based on consent, existed, but he deliberately denied it any role in the state. If cooperation by anyone else were solicited, Bodin asserted, then sovereignty was lost, for if the sovereign "holds of another, he is not sovereign."

What logically followed was the second chief characteristic of sovereignty—that the power of the state must be "indivisible," and must therefore be held entirely in the hands of a single author-ity, which meant the king. Bodin deduced this aspect of sover-eignty from the nature of politics and government, without appealing to any higher authority or sanction. In the words of the scholar Julian H. Franklin, he presented the indivisibility of sover-eignty not as an ideal or goal but as "an analytic truth." The indi-visibility of sovereignty ruled out consent because consent requires a division of power—between the ruler and those upon whose consent he relies. And so "the principle mark of absolute sover-eign majesty, absolute power," is "the right to impose laws regard-less of their consent." For, "If the prince can only make law with the consent of a superior he is a subject; if of an equal he shares his sovereignty; if of an inferior, whether it be a council of magnates or the people, it is not he who is sovereign."

Bodin believed his rule was valid for all forms of government, not just monarchy. The sovereign might be a king, a body of aris-tocrats, or even the people, but it had to be *one* of these. Bodin argued with particular vehemence against the ancient Greek and

Roman concept of "mixed" government, in which power was divided among a people, an aristocracy, and a king. In a mixed system Bodin saw only a recipe for civil war. (The civil strife between aristocrats and kings in the France of his time provided a vivid example.) Conflicts between the parties, he wrote, "could only be resolved by an appeal to arms, until by this means it was decided whether final authority remained in the prince, or a ruling class, or in the people." He added a telling analogy: "Just as God, the great Sovereign, cannot make a God equal to Himself because He is infinite and by logical necessity two infinities cannot exist, so we can say that the prince, whom we have taken as the image of God, cannot make a subject equal to himself without annihilation of his power."

The logic at work was simply the logic of force. Every violent conflict must run to extremes, at which point one side wins and the other loses, creating an extreme—an absolute—inequality between the two parties. Here indeed is the root of the all-or-nothing choice imposed by the idea of sovereignty. "All": whatever command I give, the others must obey—or be killed. "Nothing": whatever command I am given, I must obey—or die. In such relationships, there can be no question of consent or of mixed, divided, or balanced powers. It's no surprise, then, that in Bodin's view "Reason and common sense alike point to the conclusion that the origin and foundation of commonwealths was in force and violence."

Having placed all power in a single pair of hands, Bodin went on to identify a single function of government as the heart of sovereignty: the legislative power. The law, he observed, does not appear out of thin air; it requires a lawgiver. But someone who makes the law obviously cannot, like others, be under that same law. Ipso facto, there must be someone who is above the law, and that someone is the sovereign. Bodin's vision of an indivisible monarchical power came to life in seventeenth-century Europe in the growth of absolute rule, based on newly founded standing armies, centralized bureaucracies, and marginalization of the other estates of the realm, including the aristocracy. The absolute monarchs of the age also asserted a new independence from religion—a position captured in the comment by the chief minister of the French state, Cardinal Richelieu: "Man's salvation occurs ultimately in the next world, but States have no being after this world. Their salvation is either in the present or nonexistent."

The Sovereignty of Legislatures

Considering that Bodin's system rested without equivocation on force, it may seem surprising that his central concept of sovereignty would be adopted by the social-contract theorists, whose system was based on consent. Certainly, no self-respecting liberal could embrace the principle that government should rule "by the sword alone." The concept of sovereignty nevertheless survived in liberal thought. For example, Rousseau, who named the people as the new sovereign, placed them as high above the law as Bodin had placed kings, and this understanding of the matter was enshrined in the French Constitution of 1791, which declared that "Sovereignty is one, indivisible, unalienable and imprescriptible; it belongs to the Nation; no group can attribute sovereignty to itself nor can an individual arrogate it to himself." Even the English contractarians, who had defeated absolutism in 1689 and established exactly the sort of mixed, or "balanced," government Bodin had mocked, held fast to the idea of sovereignty, so obviously favorable to the centralized rule that they hated. Locke, for example, called for "one people, one body politic, under one supreme government," and Blackstone, the eminent exegete of English law of the eighteenth century, declared that "an absolute despotic power must reside somewhere." He located it in Parliament. "The power and jurisdiction of Parliament," he wrote, ". . . is so transcendent and absolute that it cannot be confined, either for causes or persons, within any bounds. . . . It hath sovereign and uncontrollable authority. It can change and create afresh even the constitution of the kingdom and of parliaments themselves. . . . True it is that what the parliament doth no authority upon earth can undo." Could Louis XIV have asked for more?

It is *not* surprising, however, that English liberal thinkers, having once decided that they needed an indivisible—even a "despotic"—sovereign in their system, identified it as Parliament, for they, in agreement with Bodin, believed that the essential power of government was the legislative. Here, too, there is unexpected continuity between the absolutists and the liberals. The French revolutionaries were of like mind. "What is a nation?" the French revolutionary constitutional theorist Emmanuel-Joseph Sieyès asked, and answered, "A body of associates living under one common law and represented by the same legislature." The foundation of the legislative power inspired even the normally reserved Locke to raptures. The legislature, he wrote, "is the soul that gives form, life, and unity to the commonwealth," for "from hence the several members have their mutual influence, sympathy, and connection, and, therefore, when the legislative is broken or dissolved dissolution and death follows."

The Sovereignty of Peoples

In the light of the agreement among absolutists and liberals that the legislative power is the core of sovereignty, we can ask with greater precision why it is that sovereignty is conceived as supreme and indivisible. The question becomes what it is about the legislative power that, in the opinion of so many thinkers of so many different persuasions, renders it impervious to division. One way to approach the question is by addressing the closely related question of minority rights. According to classical liberal doctrine, the rights of minorities are guaranteed by the protection of individual rights. The members of minority groups can, the liberal argues, fully satisfy their aspirations through the exercise of the same rights of free speech, assembly, and political participation that the majority enjoys. It would therefore in this view be a mistake to offer minorities "collective rights" in addition. Collective rights are ones that, to be realized, must be offered not to an individual but to a group—the right, for example, of an ethnic minority to choose what language will be spoken in the schools its children attend, or of the people of a particular ethnicity or religion to elect a certain proportion of Members of Parliament from their number. Collective rights, the liberal argues, are special privileges that, once granted to a group, will soon lead to a bidding war among all groups for special privileges that has no logical limit and can have no fair or just resolution. In other words, while every individual must have rights, groups must not. In fact, there is only one group that can enjoy rights collectively, and that is the sovereign people.

This solution has left many unsatisfied. One of the earliest and most lucid expositions of its weaknesses was made in 1934 by C. A. Macartney, who was secretary to the Minorities Committee of the League of Nations. In his book *National States and National Minorities,* he described and analyzed the failure of the Minorities Treaties established by the Treaty of Versailles to protect minorities in the states that, thanks to the treaty's sweeping application of the principle of self-determination, were born in Central Europe after the First World War. As he noted, no matter how small one chopped the pieces of the crumbled Hapsburg and Ottoman empires, the resulting units included unhappy national minorities. Macartney quotes Acton: "By making the State and the Nation commensurate with each other in theory, it reduces practically to a subject condition all other nationalities that may be within the boundary."

Strife arises if a minority, seeking more than individual rights, "aspires to political expression," as Macartney put it, or if the dominant nationality tries to make the state "the exclusive instrument of their own national self-expression," in which case "the rule of the majority, exercised, most often, under the title of democracy, is a true tyranny." Such tensions, moreover, had a dangerous tendency to spill across borders and trigger international war of the conventional kind, for the minority in one country "is usually nationally identical with the majority in another, which is often its neighbor." Therein lay the chief concern of the League—charged, above all, with maintaining the peace. It failed in fact either to protect the minorities *or* to prevent war. The ill-treatment of minorities continued and became an important factor in the outbreak of the Second World War.

The roots of the problem lay in the very concept of "self-determination." The "self" in question was, again, a collective self—the particular population that, distinguishing itself from the rest of mankind, announced itself as one of the world's peoples, possessing the right to form a government and so assume the "rightful station" among the peoples of the earth that had been promised so long ago in the American Declaration of Independence. It is this collective self—the nation—that international law endowed with sovereign rights. The formula could not fail to create conflict in those places, such as Central Europe between the world wars and since, in which individual selves in the same locality wished to belong to different collective selves. In our day, for example, when the Bosnian Serbs of the city of Banja Luka "determined" in the early 1990s that their city was to become part of the new collective self of the Republic of Srpska, they proceeded to "ethnically cleanse" their city of those who wished to be part of the collective self of the Bosnian state.

Such clashes are a symptom of a political dilemma of a fundamental character that bedevils sovereignty. It is a basic, structural fact of politics that humankind is divided into a multitude of peoples. The dilemma is how they should be formed. We can call it the separation question. Exactly how should the population of the earth be carved up into political units? First comes the issue of membership. Who shall belong to a given nation? Who's in? Who's out? Who decides? If a nation is to be democratic, the people must decide what their form of government shall be; yet in order to make that decision, they must first choose one another. Before there can be a constitution of the United States, there must be an American people corresponding to the "we the people" that, in the Constitution's preamble, "ordain and establish" the Constitution. What *is* a people, anyway? How can you—or they—tell when a collection of individuals is one? Is it a population that defines itself by preexisting, extrapolitical characteristics, such as race, language, or religion, and then goes on to found a state to protect those characteristics, sometimes called its "identity"? Is it simply any group that decides that it *is* a nation, no matter what the reason? Or is the nation perhaps defined by the state, so that anyone who agrees to the terms of citizenship may belong? But, in that case, what criteria should the state use to choose the population (for instance, when it comes to immigration)? For until the day comes that all humankind lives in a single body politic, every act of foundation—of self-determination—must at the same time be an act of separation, a kind of secession, or perhaps we should say "self-separation." And in this act of separation, dividing Us from the Other, often lie the seeds of murderous hatred and war. For inasmuch as the lines of separation divide one nation from another, the nature and method of this act is obviously of elemental importance for the character and tone of the relations among nations, which thereby become "inter-national" affairs.

In addition to choosing its members, a nation must decide what territory it claims. For just as each body politic lays claim to only a portion of humankind, so those people will occupy only a portion of the earth's surface. Having decided who is a Russian, the Russians must determine where Russians shall live. Where are the borders? Is Chechnya to be part of Russia? Don't the Chechnyans have the same right of self-determination that Russians have? But, if so, then why not any group, of any size or description, living anywhere in Russia?

The final basic issue to be resolved in answering the separation question is how peoples and the territory should match up with states. The preferred solution in modern times has been simple and clear: the people, the territory, and the state should be coextensive. *One* state should possess exclusive authority over *one* people residing in *one* territory. This is the formula for national sovereignty. For self-determination is nothing but sovereignty under conditions of democracy. "National sovereignty" means that the people, through the agency of their state, justifiably reject any interference in their affairs or on their territory. What the state may do to its own people—or what the majority of its people may do to some minority among them—is solely their own business and no one else's. The solution perfectly fits—and not by accident—the demands of military planning. Only well-consolidated nations living in well-defined territories can have clear, defensible borders. The system so constituted can accept no halfway houses, no dispersed populations, no divided or joint jurisdictions. Under this formula, there cannot be two states with jurisdiction over one territory, or one territory comprising two peoples, or one people on two territories. Under the name of national sovereignty, the absolutism of kings became the absolutism of peoples.

Such was the depth of the issues that Macartney faced when he tackled the minorities question in Central Europe between the wars. The liberal leaders of the victorious powers in the First World War were "guided by their own experience," he wrote. Schooled in "the traditional idealism of Western liberal and humanitarian thought," they naturally turned for models to the efforts of their own countries to provide "full civil and political rights" to Catholics and Jews, among others. Those rights—"liberty, equality, toleration"—were all that these minorities wanted. For example, Jews in the United States requested no special legislation (not to speak of a legislature) to manage Jewish affairs. Nor did Catholics in England demand any "collective rights." Full enjoyment of the individual rights possessed by everyone was all that either group asked for.

290 | The Unconquerable World

It was quite different with minorities in Eastern Europe, who (then and since) found themselves suddenly cut off from a majority of their group in a neighboring country and oppressed by an alien majority in the land and state to which they were assigned. They were not, could not be, satisfied with individual rights. They wanted, at the very least, some collective rights. But collective rights are, in fact, powers—the powers of a group to make decisions about itself. More precisely, they are legislative powers, for a legislative power is nothing but a decision taken by a group and binding upon all its members. A division of legislative powers, however, was exactly the thing that the entire European tradition of national sovereignty, including its liberal branch, ruled out as an abridgment of sovereignty. Liberal theory of the day left the minorities of Central Europe without recourse. They had to either accept repression or seek indivisible legislative rights of their own, which meant that they had to found a nation of their own, through partition, with all its customary bloodshed and horror.

Were these minorities greedy and overambitious? Shouldn't they have contented themselves with individual rights, themselves hard to come by in Central Europe in the 1930s? Weren't "universal" rights enough for them? The problem was that the things they wanted could not be obtained by an exercise of such rights. The right to get an education in a certain language cannot be secured by an individual; a legislature must decide it by majority vote, if the state in question is a democracy. The dilemma of the minorities was that in the states in which they found themselves they could never realistically hope to become a majority, and so could always be outvoted.

The liberals who argued that the minorities of Central Europe should be content with individual rights were in a false position. They had never been prevented from using their own languages or practicing their own customs. For they, *without quite being aware of it,* enjoyed full collective rights—that is to say, full legislative powers. They participated in nation-states in which they were either in the majority or could reasonably expect one day to be in the majority. For what is the democratic state itself but the full—indeed, the *sovereign*—expression of collective rights, in the form of national legislative rights? In other words, they were in full possession of immense powers a mere fraction of which the Central European minorities aspired to enjoy.

The bad faith of the liberal citizen who unconsciously enjoys full sovereign legislative powers but thinks that minorities are seeking special favors when they demand a fragment of these privileges leads into the heart of the whole complex of elemental issues raised by the idea of the indivisibility of sovereign legislative power. For to join a body politic is not merely to acquire rights but to join a body of co-legislators. The right of self-determination begins with the right to decide who those co-legislators, those co-sovereigns, will be. Liberal doctrine specifies that "the people" are to choose their form of government and their governors, but is silent on the matter of who is to choose the choosers, and by what procedure they are to do it. In territories of mixed populations seeking self-determination, people have generally found brutal answers: repression, expulsion, ethnic cleansing, genocide.

Stated theoretically, the idea of collective rights may at first sound either recondite or abstract. In practice, it is neither. It was to get these rights that former Yugoslavs drove each other out of their homes, locked each other up in concentration camps, and cut each other's throats. It was to get these rights, too, that the American colonies, the Irish, and the Indians, among others, battled for independence from the English.

In the nineteenth century, Ireland was represented in the English Parliament (as Northern Ireland still is). In that respect, the Irish enjoyed the rights of the citizens of a democracy. But it was not enough. They wanted also to enjoy the right of choosing their fellow nationals, their co-sovereigns. Americans had the same desire in 1776. They opposed, as every American schoolchild once knew, "taxation without representation." But that slogan did not in fact go to the heart of the matter. In the debates leading up to the Declaration of Independence, the question arose of whether, if the colonies were given due representation in the British Parliament, they might accept the taxation and stay within the British Empire. The answer was no. The Virginia Resolves, authored by Patrick Henry, after stating the principle that "no taxes be imposed" on the people "but with their own consent," added, "the people of these colonies are not, and from their local circumstances cannot be, represented in the House of Commons in Great Britain." To the famous slogan we should therefore add a second one: "And no taxation *with* representation, either"—at least, not if the representation was in England. For it was not merely the issue of representation that was decisive; it was the composition of the population that would send the representatives to the legislature. The critical phrase in Henry's Resolve was the unassuming "from their local circumstances." In that phrase was quietly contained the demand not just for universal "rights and liberties" but for a *nation*—a new body of citizens, on a new territory, assuming the full legislative power themselves. To be ruled by a foreign tyrant was one evil. But to be ruled by a foreign representative government—even *with* representation of one's own—was, in the colonists' opinion, another evil. They rejected both. They wanted "collective rights." They wanted full legislative power. They wanted self-determination. They wanted sovereignty.

As it happened, after independence an instance soon arose—trivial in itself but important for what it revealed—of a claim of a right to separate that the Americans chose *not* to honor. Certain towns in western Connecticut and Massachusetts took the position that each town, regardless of its size, should have one representative in its state legislature. In these towns, which were in a state of virtual insurrection in the years just before and after independence, "it was as if all the imaginings of political philosophers for centuries were being lived out in a matter of years," as the historian Gordon Wood has written. The objective was modest, but the reasoning behind it radical. "Every town government," one William Gordon wrote at the time, "is an entire body politic"—in effect, a nation. Weren't the towns "in the same situation with reference to the state that America is to Britain?" he wanted to know.

Some towns in New Hampshire made similar claims, in language that spelled out the underlying issues with exceptional clarity. The Declaration of Independence, they said, had "nullified all governmental authority." Therefore, their town incorporations were "miniature constitutions that made every one of the towns 'a state by itself,' able to justify binding its minority by the majority." But these claims, too, were rejected. What was a nation? Which bodies of people have the right to separate themselves from all others and lay claim to the sovereign power? No one could say. But somehow almost everyone knew that the United States of America might become a nation while the towns of western Connecticut, Massachusetts, and New Hampshire definitely could not.

National sovereignty can mean many things—the right to speak in one's own tongue, to worship one's own God, to decide to wage war, to be ruled by a native tyrant rather than a foreign one, to invade and occupy a neighbor, to participate in politics as an equal with one's fellow citizens. But in the framework of liberal thought the New Hampshire towns were right: sovereignty was the power to select, and separate from humanity at large, a population among whom a majority binds any minority, thereby exercising the legislative power.

Once we have clearly grasped that this is what sovereignty meant in a democratic context, we can better understand why the doctrine of sovereignty, which seems to trail so much illiberal, absolutist baggage in its wake, was nevertheless so firmly embraced by liberals in the eighteenth century. For in liberal no less than in absolutist doctrine, sovereignty is the foundation of the legislative power that performs the first and greatest of all political miracles. It lifts unprotected, aggressive, perpetually warring human beings out of the anarchic state of nature and places them under the shelter and protection of the civil state, which is meant, above all else, to provide peace. The virtue of the legislature is that it is the source of law, and the virtue of law is that *all* must obey it, submitting their disputes to its dictates, and so quelling the war of all against all that might otherwise break out. In Locke's words, the "union of the society consisting in having *one will*, the legislative, when once established by the majority, has the declaring and, as it were, keeping of that will." (Emphasis added.) This much Locke and Bodin had in common. If the legislative power is what we essentially mean by sovereignty, then to tamper with sovereignty would be to abort this miracle: to endanger the civil state, destroy the protection it affords the citizen, and consign society to anarchy—a prospect that horrifies the liberal as much as it does the conservative.

To divide the contract was to destroy the contract. To have two judges on earth, Bodin and Locke agreed, was to have no judge. Two judges meant war. One judge—and one alone—meant peace.

The reason neither the minorities of Eastern Europe nor the New Hampshire townships could be permitted to form a body politic within the nation, the reason nations have not been able to find a way to live peacefully together on a single territory in the Balkans, the Middle East, or elsewhere, and the reason neither the League of Nations nor the United Nations could form a supranational body politic was, at least as far as theory goes, the same: sovereignty could not be divided without courting disaster.

Sovereignty and Consent

One of the first events to open a breach in this remarkably broad embrace of sovereignty was the foundation of the United States of America. During the revolution, however, the American revolutionary leaders joined the consensus. For example, John Adams stated, in words that could have been penned by Bodin, that England and America were debating "the greatest question ever yet agitated," namely the question of sovereignty, which in his opinion dictated that in "all civil states it is necessary there should somewhere be lodged a supreme power over the whole." In the words of Gordon Wood, on whose account of the sovereignty question in the revolution and in the constitutional settlement I draw here, "The doctrine of sovereignty almost by itself compelled the imperial debate to be conducted in the most theoretical terms of political science." Blackstone's conception of the absolute sovereign power of the English Parliament obviously precluded any sharing of the legislative power with an American legislature or American legislatures. And when, in the course of the debate that led to independence, some suggested that America, while forming its own legislative bodies, could still remain in the empire through loyalty to the crown, thus creating a sort of dual, or joint, legislative sovereignty, it turned out that most Americans agreed with their English antagonists that sovereignty was indivisible, and the idea was rejected. All that was left was the all-or-nothing choice between full imperial rule and full independence, which the idea of sovereignty always imposes on international relations. As the republican John Adams wrote, in words that again echoed the absolutist Bodin, two legislatures could not coexist in one body politic "any more than two supreme beings in one universe."

The Latin phrase that referred to the supposed impossibility of dual sovereignty was *"imperium in imperio"*—or "sovereignty within sovereignty"—which was described by Adams as "the height of political absurdity." Benjamin Franklin—who had once sought colonial representation in Parliament—had now drawn the inevitable conclusion when he said that "no middle doctrine can well be maintained" between the proposition "that Parliament has a right to make *all laws* for us, or that it has a power to make *none* for us." (His "no middle" position crystallized in microcosm the dilemma faced by Wilson more than a hundred years later when he faced the decision between the war system and his new constitution for the whole world.) At the beginning of the debate, Americans claimed, with perfect sincerity, that all they demanded was their full "rights as Englishmen." But because those rights included exercise of sovereign legislative power, it turned out that they could enjoy the full rights of Englishmen only by becoming Americans.

One of the few significant voices to dissent from this grand transatlantic consensus among otherwise irreconcilable antagonists was Edmund Burke, champion of reconciliation with the colonies. Just as Burke, lover of the gradual and the organic, would later condemn the doctrine of the rights of man for its abstractness, so now he opposed the abstract character of the doctrine of sovereignty, which in the hands of the English ministers compelled England to make war on the colonies. In 1774, he advised England to keep its mind on concrete colonial issues, and "leave the rest to schools." Assertion of indivisible British sovereignty might provoke the rebellion in the United States that it was meant to suppress. "If, intemperately, unwisely, fatally, you sophisticate and poison the very source of government by urging subtle deductions and consequences odious to those you govern, from the unlimited and illimitable nature of supreme sovereignty," he warned, "you will teach them by these means to call that sovereignty in question." Many observers on both sides of the Atlantic opposed the war between England and America, but Burke was the only important voice, as far as I'm aware, to so much as whisper a word of criticism of the underlying doctrine of sovereignty that forced the two lands toward their irreparable division. Rarely asked—then as now—is whether there could have been another, more flexible conception of state power that would have permitted the American states to govern their own local affairs while remaining conjoined in a voluntary, multinational union.

It was not until the late 1780s, when the Americans turned from their act of separation to their act of consolidation, the framing of the Constitution, that the logic of sovereignty came under serious challenge. The old Latin axioms that had made separation from England seem necessary seemed to make the union of the states impossible. Invocation by the Constitution's opponents of the indivisibility of rule drove the Federalists into genuine political terra incognita. They were now proposing two distinct challenges to the traditional understanding of sovereignty. One was federalism, which divided power between the states and a federal government, and the other was the doctrine of the separation of the federal government's own powers. How, Federalist supporters of the Constitution had to ask themselves, could "sovereign" states combine to form a federal government if sovereignty could not be divided? Wasn't it logically necessary for the national legislature, for example, to make *all* laws or to make *none*? The Anti-Federalists certainly thought so, and did not fail to confront the Federalists with all the familiar arguments. For example, Samuel Adams, an Anti-Federalist, called the Constitution a plan for the absurd "*Imperia in Imperio,* justly deemed a solecism in politics."

James Madison now found his way to the middle ground that theory had so long forbidden as "absurd." He asserted, with uncharacteristic vagueness, that under the Constitution the government would be "not completely consolidated, nor . . . entirely federal." It would be "of a mixed nature," being made up of "many co-equal sovereignties." Alexander Hamilton called a federation "an assemblage of societies." Was there a "sovereign" in the United States? The Constitution remains silent on the point. The word nowhere appears in the document. Strangely, it was not the militant movement for independence of the 1770s but the supposedly "conservative" movement to found the national government in the 1780s that carried the United States into these chartless waters. The Declaration of Independence is the United States' most fiery document but the Constitution is its most radical.

The Dissolution of Domestic Sovereignty

The American formulation marked the beginning of a new chapter in the saga of sovereignty. Sovereignty had proved a pilgrim.

Invented for the use of kings, it migrated, in the hands of the English Whigs, to Parliament. Then, in American and French keeping, it descended to the people. In France, at first, sovereignty—*une et indivisible*—remained undividable. In the United States, events took a different turn. Just how, in "the crisis years" between the Declaration of Independence and the ratification of the Constitution, popular sovereignty came to be defined is a marvelous tale of action and thought told in Gordon Wood's *The Creation of the American Republic*. The important point for our purposes is that the Federalists clinched the argument in favor of their cause when they asserted that sovereignty in a republic resided not in the states or in the federal government—or, for that matter, in any governmental body—but in the people, who were therefore entirely free to add to existing political structures (such as the states) any other structures (such as the federal government) that they might desire. If sovereignty belonged to neither the federal government nor the states, then neither had to possess indivisible power, and a middle ground could be found between them. The institutional innovation that permitted this solution was the state constitutional convention, which, bypassing the state governments, enabled the citizens of each state to ratify or reject the federal constitution directly, in an unmediated exercise of their sovereign power. The constitutional conventions in each state did not so much override the state governments as simply circumvent them through a fresh, direct recourse to the power of the people.

Sovereignty was not like some precious heirloom that could pass unchanged from one pair of hands to another. It was transformed as it made its way from its royal pinnacle to the people. As it descended, it fragmented. The English had resorted to the ungainly phrase "King-in-Parliament" in order to go on imagining that their system, described by themselves as "mixed," nevertheless contained a single, indivisible sovereign. By the time sovereignty was in the people's hands, it had in fact lost its indivisibility.

If Bodin had proved that sovereign power—which for him was the same as coercive power—was indivisible, the American Federalists, founders of a national government based on consent, proved that cooperative power was divisible. Far from endowing any single authority with the power to make all decisions, the framers of the Constitution required the concurrence of many authorities in order to make almost any decision. They created a veritable maze through which power had to travel in order to achieve its appointed ends.

But perhaps, someone might argue, the power of the new sovereign, the people, was in fact indivisible. If that were so, however, it was hard to explain why, as Madison commented in *The Federalist Papers,* the "true distinction" of the American Constitution, "lies in the total exclusion of the people in their collective capacity from any share" in the government. It was a fact that the people, using their powers to amend the Constitution, could, both legally and peacefully, pull down the whole edifice, including their own amending power, and in that sense were supreme. Yet it was no less true that in the ordinary business of government the people were barred from directly making almost any decision. (The exceptions are referenda in certain states.) They could dynamite the whole building but were powerless to so much as change the curtains in any of the rooms. For instance, if the public dislikes a Supreme Court decision, it can try to elect three or four presidents in a row who might appoint a majority of justices who might reverse the decision (as the opponents of abortion have tried to do in recent years), or else the people can convene a constitutional convention and change the document to undo the court's work. But short of these cumbersome or drastic recourses, the people are powerless.

The American Constitution deliberately shuns the establishment of any single, indivisible organ of power. The whole document, one might say, is a device for heading off such a development.

Liberal thinkers adopted the doctrine of sovereignty from their absolutist forebears because it embodied what was *the* central requirement of the liberal civil state—namely, procedures for the peaceful arbitration of the disputes that are endemic in human existence. It's evident that the American Constitution provides such procedures. Laws *are* passed; they *are* obeyed; disputes among citizens *are* settled and do *not* lead to the war of all against all. Yet all this happens without concentration of indivisible power anywhere in the system.

Should the word "sovereignty," then, still be applied to name anything in the American system, or were the drafters of the Constitution right to shun the term? Wasn't the doctrine of the indivisibility of sovereignty disproven by the American experience? Hadn't the time come to search for new words? I suggest that the change has been so profound that the word should be dropped. In the United States, sovereignty—if we accept the definition of the word employed for hundreds of years—did not merely change its location or character but disappeared.

This is a linguistic point. The substantive point is that the claim that the power of the well-ordered state must be indivisible was a deeply entrenched theoretical mistake. The division of sovereignty, in the United States and other liberal democracies all over the world, does not belong merely to the rather large class of events that mainstream theory failed to predict; it belongs to the more select class that mainstream theory had ruled out as impossible but that then happened. The nonviolent collapse of the Soviet Union also belongs to this class. In both cases, an overestimation of the role of force in politics was involved. In fairness to the theorists, though, it has to be admitted that the successful division of state power was a possibility that not even the statesmen accomplishing the feat believed possible. They were almost as surprised by what they had wrought as anyone else.

The Persistence of International Sovereignty

The eclipse of sovereign, coercive power and the rise in our time of divided, cooperative power in the domestic affairs of dozens of governments suggest that a similar eclipse in the international sphere is possible. Isn't it conceivable that states no longer insisting on indivisible, centralized power at home could sooner or later stop insisting on it in their relationships abroad? In that case, might not the international sphere experience growth of the same variety of mixed and federalistic forms of power that the domestic sphere has witnessed in so many countries?

If sovereignty in international affairs were a mere concept, its decline would be a merely intellectual event. In reality it has been much more than that. Above all, it has been an intellectual and juridical crystallization of conduct imposed upon states by the tyranny of the war system. Its first principle—that power was based on force—was the first rule of life under the war system. Its second principle—that power was indivisible—was simply an obvious corollary. As long as the war system remained intact, the new forms of divided power were condemned to remain bottled up within national borders. There was no room in this framework, as Wilson was forced to recognize, for interesting federalistic experiments, or Madisonian "mixed sovereignty." There was room only for the wholesale, go-for-broke replacement of the war system with something like the League of Nations. But in actual practice, of course, it turned out that there was no room for this, either.

The war system, however, has now been revolutionized by the metamorphosis we have chronicled. The age of total wars and world-spanning territorial empires has ended. The implacable pressures of the adapt-or-die system that undid the league and have disabled the U.N. have been lifted. The question arises whether in this new world the new forms of power at home may not be extended to the world at large. There are already promising signs that they might be. The place where the most interesting experiments in divided power are occurring is not, however, the United States but the birthplace of modern sovereignty, Europe, where a quiet but powerful incremental movement is afoot to join the formerly warring lands of that continent into a body politic whose outlines are as unclear as they are unprecedented. But before turning to this matter, we need to discuss the fresh perils, which may prove no less implacable than the old, that have accompanied the new opportunities of our day.

PART FOUR

The Shapes of Things to Come

12

Niagara

Black and hideous to me is the tragedy that gathers, and I'm sick beyond cure to have lived on to see it. You and I . . . should have been spared this wreck of our belief that through the long years we had seen civilization grow and the worst become impossible. The tide that bore us along was then all the while moving to *this* as its grand Niagara—yet what a blessing we didn't know it. It seems to me to *undo* everything, everything that was ours, in the most horrible retroactive way—but I avert my face from the monstrous scene!—

HENRY JAMES, LETTER TO RHODA BROUGHTON, AUGUST 10, 1914

In these pages so far I have sought to trace, alongside the awful history of modern violence, a less-noticed, parallel history of nonviolent power. The chronicle has been a hopeful one of violence disrupted or in retreat—of great-power war immobilized by the nuclear stalemate, of brutal empires defeated by local peoples fighting for their self-determination, of revolutions succeeding without violence, of democracy supplanting authoritarian or totalitarian repression, of national sovereignty yielding to systems of mixed and balanced powers. These developments, I shall argue, have provided the world with the strongest new foundations for the creation of a durable peace that have ever existed. But first we must turn to the more familiar task of assessing the new violent dangers of our time—most of them present before September 11—that have the potential to make the twenty-first century even bloodier than the twentieth. Many of them are in fact connected with the new opportunities. Even as the self-determination movement was toppling the world's territorial empires, it was fueling a multitude of wars, some of them genocidal, among the successor states and peoples. Even as the Western liberal settlement ended the inter-Western wars that had disrupted the peace of the world for so long, the most prosperous nations were confronting the poorer ones with a new concentration of economic and military power that threatened to create a new line of conflict along a North-South axis. Even as liberal democracy was spreading, the most powerful of the liberal democracies, the United States, was, like ancient Rome, in danger of transforming itself from a republic into a fearsome empire. And, to say what is obvious but too often overlooked, even as nuclear terror paralyzed the old danger of total war, it created a new danger of annihilation—a danger, moreover, that was evolving, for in the post–Cold War period nuclear technology and other technology of mass destruction were rapidly spreading.

Wars of Self-Determination

In the post–Cold War period, the world boiled, as it always has, with local and regional wars, but in at least one respect their general character was different from those of the recent past. They were occurring almost entirely within nations rather than between them. In 2001, according to the Stockholm International Peace Research Institute, twenty-four wars were in progress, of which twenty-one were mainly within nations. Taken by itself, the decline of classic, conventional wars among full-fledged nation-states marks a profound, welcome change. Its causes include the dampening influence of nuclear arsenals; the collapse of the territorial empires, which historically have been a prolific cause of wars; and the absence of any worldwide ideological struggle among states in the post–Cold War world. (The American war on terrorism is so far the nearest thing to a new ideological cause.)

Some of the wars within national borders are turf battles among local warlords, some are civil wars, some are class wars, some are religious wars, some are ethnic wars, and most are a combination of several of the above. One category, however, stands out as prevalent. It is what we can call war of self-determination, in which the issue is the definition, ethnic composition, or birth of a nation. There are several kinds. One is the war of foundation. Historical examples include the three wars that the Prussian Chancellor Otto von Bismarck waged in the 1860s and seventies in order to found the German Reich and the wars waged by Slovenia, Croatia, Bosnia, and Kosovo in the 1990s to extricate themselves from the Yugoslavian federation and establish their independence. The war between Israel and the Palestinians has been a double war of national foundation: first, Zionists fought to found the state of Israel in Palestine; now Palestinians fight to found a Palestinian state in the lands conquered by Israel in 1967. Both parties are, in their own opinion, fighting for their national existence. Another kind is the war of secession—such as the American Civil War or the war of partition that accompanied the withdrawal of Pakistan from India in 1948—in which one part of a nation breaks away from the whole, either to join another or to establish its independence. Still another kind is the territorial war, in which two countries each lay claim to one piece of land that lies between them, as India and Pakistan do with respect to Kashmir. (In Kashmir, there is also an independence movement, adding a third dimension of self-determination to the conflict.)

Because the formula for self-determination—the exact congruity of people, state, and territory—is, in our democratic age, also the formula for national sovereignty, it would be equally appropriate to call wars of self-determination wars of national sovereignty.

The global self-determination movement, which has contributed so much to peace by ridding the world of its colonial empires, has in the postimperial world become a disturber of the peace. Expelling the imperial master turned out to be only the first step in self-determination. The liberated peoples then had to carve up the imperial territories among themselves. In short, imperial withdrawal confronted them with the separation question. In the eighteenth century, when the democratic revolutions occurred in the United States and Europe, many of the peoples involved had the good fortune already to belong to fairly well-defined national populations living within well-defined national borders. The revolutionaries who took to the streets in Paris in 1789 did not have to ask who qualified as a French person or what territory should be their homeland. Those questions had been largely answered by several centuries of dynastic war. The extent of the United Kingdom likewise was quite clear by the middle of the eighteenth century. (The remaining contested zone was Ireland.)

It was different in the lands evacuated in our time by the European empires, where, as in the Balkans, national populations were often mixed in one territory or dispersed among many territories. Most, as Macartney observed, were unable to find any means but warfare to create nation-states according to the approved formula for self-determination and sovereignty. *People's* wars (wars of the people against imperial overlords), you might say, gave way to *peoples'* wars (wars among newly liberated peoples). The latter have been as sanguinary as the former and certainly less tractable. In people's war against an imperial power, a clean resolution is at least possible. The occupier, once he has decided to leave, can pull up stakes almost overnight. A local people can hardly do the same. People's war ends when the conquerors have had enough and go home. Peoples' wars tend to go on indefinitely, because everyone already is at home.

The end of the British Empire alone touched off a multitude of wars of self-determination. The fall of the Raj led directly to the violent partition of Pakistan and India and set the stage for the three succeeding wars between the two countries. Britain's incomplete withdrawal from Ireland in 1922, which left six mainly Protestant northern counties under British control, created the conditions for the Catholic-Protestant violence that erupted in the late 1960s. Britain's surrender of its mandate over Palestine in 1948 left a political vacuum that was soon filled by Arab-Israeli strife. The British withdrawal from Cyprus prepared the ground, in time, for conflict between its Greek and Turkish communities (backed respectively by Greece and Turkey) and finally the enforced partition of the island. The fall of the Soviet empire also touched off several territorial wars—between Georgia and Abkhazia, between Armenia and Azerbaijan, and between Russia and Chechnya. The disintegration of Yugoslavia led to the multiple, interlocking wars of the 1990s on that territory. The Treaty of Sèvres of 1920, marking the end of the Ottoman Empire, promised the Kurdish people a state of their own but in actuality left them partitioned among and repressed by Iraq, Turkey, Iran, and Syria. Many of the wars now afflicting Africa also have postimperial aspects. Borders established by the imperial powers in the nineteenth century often reflected the outcome of inter-imperial jockeying more than local realities. The imperialists divided tribes by means of "national" boundaries, forced peoples hostile to each other together, and often ran roughshod over distinctions of language, religion, and culture. Often, the movements that won independence had little in common but their hatred for the imperial overlords, and began to fall apart soon after taking power, or even before. Sometimes, the imperial rulers deliberately set one tribe or ethnic group against another, dividing to conquer, and then left the locals to fight it out after they had withdrawn. For example, the Belgian rulers of Rwanda and Burundi fostered divisions between the Hutu and Tutsi tribes that led to the genocidal campaign waged by the Hutu against the Tutsi in Rwanda in 1994.

The anarchy that has often broken out in lands of what some have called "failed states," such as Somalia and Sierra Leone, may be regarded as misbegotten wars of national foundation. In those places of Hobbesian nightmare, no group—be it tribe, clan, religious sect, or political party—generates enough power, whether cooperative or coercive, to found a state, and the country is carved up by chieftains and warlords or simply preyed upon by armed bands or mafias with no clear political loyalties. The people may have had too little in common or too feeble a political will to found a nation. Not abuse of power but default of power is the problem. Whatever may be wrong with the nation-state per se, these cases remind us, its existence is nothing to be taken for granted. Where it does exist, it is an achievement, not a gift.

Inasmuch as the age of the territorial empires has ended, it is possible that the supply of wars of self-determination that often follow in their wake is slowly running out—that these are not the first stage of a new wave of anarchy about to engulf the world, as some have suggested, but rather the last stage of a long wave that will gradually recede. This hope, however, is small comfort for the near future, since wars of self-determination are among the most durable conflicts on record. For example, the conflicts between India and Pakistan and between Israel and the Palestinians, both of which broke out in earnest in the late 1940s, are still continuing a half-century later. And the conflict created by English colonization and domination of Ireland, which may finally be ending, has lasted for almost four hundred years—some would say longer. Shortly after the First World War, Winston Churchill marveled at its durability. "The integrity of their quarrel is one of the few institutions," he quipped, "that has been unaltered in the cataclysm that has swept the world."

Nations that have solved the separation problem by accomplishing the approved triple overlap of nation, state, and territory have been called "achieved" nations, while those that have fallen short in one way or another have been labeled "unachieved." When we witness the catastrophes that the wars of self-determination have brought to mixed populations, we can well appreciate the value of an achieved nation, such as France or England. Yet this solution to the separation problem has also come with a high price attached. For the homogeneity of peoples that has brought peace *within* state borders has encouraged jingoistic passions that support war *across* state borders. The mutual hatreds removed from the domestic sphere have again and again assumed the familiar form of chauvinistic resentment and hatred of another country, fueling straightforward, old-fashioned conventional war. This is what happened, for example, in South Asia, which has the unfortunate distinction of having run almost the entire gamut of possible forms of violence. Under the Raj, Hindus and Muslims frequently engaged in "communal" violence in their villages; then came "ethnic cleansing" during partition; then the series of conventional wars between the nation-states of Pakistan and India; and now the nuclear buildup and the nuclear confrontation.

It would in truth be hard to decide which was worse in the twentieth century—the killing at close quarters in the postimperial wars within unachieved nations or the wars fought across national borders by the achieved nations. Either way, the formula that required identity of state, people, and territory has brought catastrophe. The achieved nations of Germany and France, for instance, fell on one another with the utmost savagery in the world wars, bringing to bear all the concentrated violence that technical progress had put in their hands. The riddle is how to avoid both sorts of war, for both are forms of a single dilemma: How can the nation determine its collective self without cultivating murderous hostility toward others? This problem is the unsquared circle of international politics, and, though the frequency of interstate wars has now waned, the internecine variety are rife as the twenty-first century begins.

The Second Nuclear Age and the Last Man

The seeds of wars of self-determination are local or regional. The same is true of most revolutions, coups, and ethnic and religious strife, most terrorism and the quarrels of mafias and warlords out for power or lucre. These conflicts need no global war system to keep them going. Their persistent, smoldering flames burn in or under home soil, like peat fires, and can survive the rise and fall of international systems.

Nuclear arsenals, by contrast, are by nature global in their influence and, since the bomb's advent, have continuously been a prime factor shaping the structure of the international political and military systems of the era. It was of course the bomb's arrival that disabled the global war system at its upper levels and replaced it for the duration of the Cold War with the new system of nuclear deterrence. That system, we can see in retrospect, was a strategic adjustment to two dominant historical realities, one political, the other technical. The political reality was the division of the world into two ideologically hostile camps. The technical reality was the restriction of the newborn capacity to build nuclear weapons to just a few nations. (The eventual legal expression of this nuclear oligopoly was the Nuclear Nonproliferation Treaty, which created two classes of powers. One consisted of the five nuclear-weapon states—the United States, the Soviet Union, China, England, and France—who were permitted to retain their nuclear arsenals, on condition that they made good-faith efforts to reduce and then eliminate them, and the other consisted of all the other signatories, who agreed to forgo nuclear arsenals.)

Now both of these realities have been washed away. The world's bipolarity ended with the collapse of the Soviet Union, and the nuclear oligopoly has been steadily yielding to nuclear proliferation. In the late 1980s, Iraq came within perhaps a year of attaining nuclear weapons, but in the aftermath of its defeat in the Gulf War was required to dismantle its bomb-making facilities under the supervision of U.N. inspectors. In 1998, the inspectors were forced out. After September 11, 2001, the United States began to brandish its threats to overthrow the Iraqi government, and the inspectors were readmitted. In May of 1998, India had conducted five nuclear tests, and Pakistan responded with seven, and both nations pronounced themselves nuclear powers, creating the first nuclear confrontation entirely unrelated to the Cold War; in the spring of 2002, after terrorist attacks on the Indian Parliament that India blamed on Pakistan, the two countries went to the brink of nuclear war. North Korea and Iran both have nuclear programs, and in October 2002, North Korea announced that it possessed nuclear weapons. In our day, nuclear danger has been supplemented by the spread of biological and chemical weapons, not only to states but to terrorist groups. If bipolarity shaped the strategy of the first nuclear age, then proliferation, if it is not reversed, is destined to define that of the second.

In assessing nuclear proliferation, it is important to distinguish between the capacity to construct a nuclear arsenal and the deed of actually constructing one. By the count of the State Department, forty-four nations have the capacity, which is to say there are forty-four nations that, if they choose to build nuclear weapons, can be reasonably certain of success. Whereas developing nuclear weapons requires a political decision, acquiring the capacity happens almost of itself. Switzerland, for instance, has never made a decision to acquire the capacity, yet no one can doubt that Switzerland has it. Being a modern, technically competent nation is enough.

This excess of capacity over possession points to the fundamental fact of the nuclear age, known from the beginning to all who have worked on the weapons, that the basic building block of nuclear arms, which is the knowledge required to build them, was destined to spread. In 1945, for example, the physicist Leo Szilard, one of the discoverers of nuclear fission, predicted the terrorist threat that now so deeply worries the United States and other countries. "The position of the United States in the world may be adversely affected by [nuclear weapons'] existence," he wrote. "Clearly if such bombs are available, it will not be necessary to bomb our cities from the air in order to destroy them. All that is necessary is to place a comparatively small number in major cities and detonate them at some later time. . . . The long coastline, the structure of our society, and the heterogeneity of our population may make effective controls of such 'traffic' virtually impossible." In the long run, there can be no "secret" of the bomb. A historical period that, like the nuclear age, is defined by a technology has a natural life cycle. At its birth, the technology may be held by a single pair of hands—in this case, the United States'. In its youth, the technology may be confined to a few nations, as during the Cold War. But in its maturity, which comes with the mere passage of time, it is destined to be available to all. The reason is the innate mobility of scientific knowledge. An era of information and free trade is an especially difficult one in which to keep technical secrets. Like a battery that is slowly charging, the proliferation of nuclear capacity creates a growing potential—a potential that may or may not end in sudden, violent discharge but, as the years go by, *can* be released by an ever-increasing number of states or groups in an ever-increasing number of ways.

The Cold War may have retarded proliferation, but even its continuation probably could not have stopped it. (Would India and Pakistan have been *less* likely to nuclearize their conflict if the Cold War had continued?) The Cold War was in fact a sort of two-power disguise temporarily assumed by the nuclear predicament. This form of the dilemma depended on certain historical conditions that looked highly durable but turned out to be temporary. Its new form will be based on the universal availability of nuclear

know-how that is written into the predicament's makeup. To paraphrase Clausewitz, the Cold War was a restricted, "real" form of
the nuclear predicament, and now we are on our way to facing it in
its unlimited, hydra-headed, "ideal" form. "Ideal," in this context,
means that the threat is not only all-embracing but also originates
at all points of the compass. And this underlying change will occur
irrespective of any military and political decisions. I do not mean
that all nations will inevitably build nuclear weapons. I mean that
all will be *able* to do so and, in that restricted yet fundamental sense, emanate nuclear danger. The question is to what extent
nations will turn capacity into hardware—into nuclear bombs.

Chemical and biological weapons, which are easier to acquire
than nuclear weapons, are equally unconfinable. Both are banned
by international conventions, although these so far lack adequate
provisions for inspection and enforcement. In late September and
early October of 2001, three letters containing spores of the lethal
virus anthrax were sent to three addresses in the United States,
including the office of Senate Majority Leader Tom Daschle. It
was the first use in history—however limited—of an acknowledged weapon of mass destruction on American soil. Five people
died, Senate buildings were shut down, and the postal service
was disrupted for several months. If sophisticated delivery systems had been used, tens of thousands could have died. If the
pathogen released had been smallpox, which is contagious, rather
than anthrax, which is not, millions of people, experts say, might
have died.

During the Cold War, the capacities for violence of the great
powers were in effect compressed into a single integrated explosive device, to which a warning sign was affixed that said, "You
have the power to set off this device, but if you do, you, too, and
perhaps all humankind, are doomed." The doom was real enough,
but the compression could not last. As the Cold War ended, and
the compression began to weaken, the contents of the device
began to seep into the world. During the Cold War, a variety of

"thresholds," enforced by strong taboos, confined the danger to a certain extent. One was the clear distinction between the nuclear powers, few in number, and the many nonnuclear powers. Another was the threshold between conventional and nuclear war. Still another was "the brink" between the two superpowers. Today, all these boundaries have been breached or blurred. The line between conventional and nuclear war is being blurred by many developments—by the increasing power of conventional weapons, such as the fifteen-ton American "daisy-cutter" bomb, and by the miniaturization and refinement of American nuclear weapons, including the proposed so-called bunker buster, designed for use against caves deep underground, and by the rise of the chemical and biological threats. The single nuclear abyss on whose dizzying edge the nuclear-armed superpowers stood (and still stand) has, in effect, branched out to form innumerable smaller abysses. They run through Wall Street, where the September 11 attacks occurred; through Kashmir, dividing nuclear-armed India from nuclear-armed Pakistan; through Pyongyang and Beijing; through Peshawar, Manila, and Mindanao, or wherever Al Qaeda or its like may be preparing weapons of mass destruction for use against the United States or others; and through New Jersey suburbs and Washington post offices and wherever else the anthrax-laden letters may arrive.

Proliferation has still another dimension. Some scientists fear that new, even more deadly and more easily concocted instruments of mass destruction, based on the newly developed techniques of genetic engineering and nanotechnology, may be discovered before long. Bill Joy, a cofounder of Sun Microsystems, has noted that the production of nuclear, and even of today's biological and chemical, weapons of mass destruction requires the resources of states—or, at least, of large teams of scientists. However, the technologies of the future may well lie within the reach of far smaller teams, or even solitary individuals. In Joy's words:

As this enormous computing power is combined with the manipulative advances of the physical sciences and the new, deep understandings in genetics, enormous transformative power is being unleashed. These combinations open up the opportunity to completely redesign the world, for better or worse: The replicating and evolving processes that have been confined to the natural world are about to become realms of human endeavor. I think it is no exaggeration to say we are on the cusp of the further perfection of extreme evil, an evil whose possibility spreads well beyond that which weapons of mass destruction bequeathed to the nation-states, on to a surprising and terrible empowerment of extreme individuals.

Joy's fears, though fortunately still speculative, help to understand the novel character of the forces that are defining what we may call the second nuclear age. At the beginning of history, the homicidal "first man," to borrow a term from Nietzsche, confronted his enemy with only his bare hands. Then, at one of history's turning points, or possibly its origin, he availed himself of his first destructive instrument, perhaps a stick or a rock. From that time on, the curve of humanity's technical capacity for violence rose steadily until, in 1945, it invented a device with which it could exterminate itself as a species. Yet that moment, for all its seeming finality, was not the end of the story. Nuclear weapons were hard to make and remained in just a few hands. Since then, the line to watch has been the ascending curve of distribution, which places this apocalyptic power as well as new ones in ever more hands. Its logical end point would be the person—let us borrow another term of Nietzsche's and call him the "last man"—who could concoct and release an unstoppable, contagious bacterium that could end human life.

Nuclear weapons, as all believers in deterrence know, are instruments of *terror*. We should not be surprised to find that they are of particular interest to *terrorists*. Osama bin Laden has sought to acquire nuclear weapons and, soon after the September 11 attack, he announced that he possessed them—but only (shades of the Cold War) for purposes of "deterrence." It's likely that both parts of the statement were false, yet no one can rule out the possibility that Al Qaeda or another group will obtain nuclear weapons. Science is delivering the mass over to the whim of the individual. The bewildering dilemma that the last man—the terrorist with an instrument of annihilation in his or her (as we must add after the suicide bombings by young Palestinian women) hands—presents to the world is the ever-increasing likelihood that a small band of criminals, or even a single evildoer, even today can conceivably cause the death of millions and in a conceivable future could cause the death of all.

"*Liberal*" *Threats to the Peace*

Many observers in the prosperous democracies like to imagine that the post–Cold War world's disorder and violence arise only in poor, misgoverned, anarchic lands. Historically, of course, it has been otherwise: the West has been the world's most active military volcano, bringing destruction upon itself through war and on the rest of the world through imperial conquest and exploitation. (The cost of imperialism in human lives rivaled strictly inter-European slaughter. For example, it has been estimated that in the Congo Free State alone, the death toll under the colonial administrations of King Leopold of Belgium and his successors was between ten and twenty million.) Although the Western civil war has been stilled by the liberal settlement, and old-style Western colonial rule has been ended by the world revolt, economic exploitation is alive, active, and rapidly developing new forms, which could prove as destructive—to the natural environment of the earth as well as to its poorer inhabitants—as the old.

The issue of imperial exploitation now arises in the context of economic globalization. According to some, the end of the territorial empires meant the end of imperialism. In Francis Fukuyama's view, for example, imperialism is an anachronism—"an atavism, a holdover from an earlier stage in human social evolution." Others contend that globalization is in fact imperialism in a new guise—"neo-imperialism." An increasingly powerful popular movement has arisen to oppose it. Its members observe that in the era of globalization the gap between the rich and the poor has increased, along with the power of wealthy countries to dictate economic policies to poor ones, that international economic decisions increasingly escape democratic control, and degradation of the environment is proceeding at a gallop. Among the instruments of economic control are the International Monetary Fund, the World Bank, and the World Trade Organization, all of whose decisions are dominated by wealthy countries; but even more powerful pressure is brought to bear by the global market system itself. States that structure their economies along approved lines do so not because they fear that otherwise their capitals will be bombarded and their lands occupied, as in the days of gunboat diplomacy, but because they know that if they do not, international loans and investments will dry up, their currencies will crash, and the living standards of most of their people will nose-dive. A balance sheet of gains and losses to the poorer countries is difficult to draw up, but it's possible that these new strictures, imposing what some call "structural violence" on the poor, may in fact bring more suffering to ordinary people than overt imperial violence once did.

The prosperous nations themselves are, it is true, also subject to market pressures—although generally to a lesser extent, since the system's rules have been written in good measure to advance their interests. The overall health of the global market system depends, as the war system's once did, on a precarious balance that the great powers must exert themselves mightily to preserve. Whereas in 1914 the ministers of foreign affairs flew into a panic when the balance of military power began to tip one way or another, now the ministers of finance scurry to take action when the economic order is threatened by a plunge in the currency in Jakarta, Buenos Aires, or Phnom Penh. These are the Fashodas and Sarajevos of the global market system, which, like the war system, is placed at risk of collapse by local crises that have the potential to start a broader unraveling of the system.

The World's Only Superpower

Whether economic globalization will benefit the world or become a new kind of imperialism—a sort of global rule by the rich over the poor—is a question that will be decided by many countries. Whether overt force, as distinct from economic pressure, will be used to renew imperial domination will depend above all on a single country, the United States—the sole power that has military resources on the scale necessary to harbor such an ambition.

In the early years of the Cold War, the United States, born in rebellion against the British Empire, styled itself, as it had for most of its history, an opponent of the European sort of imperialism. But soon in the name of anticommunism the United States was supporting many colonial regimes, including, with notably disastrous results, that of the French in Vietnam. Before long, the United States became the supporter and often the installer of murderous right-wing dictatorships on every continent—a pattern of conduct that, in its brutality and indifference to the will of local peoples, strongly resembled the supposedly rejected European precedent. A short list of such regimes would include those of Shah Reza Pahlavi in Iran, the dictator Saddam Hussein in Iraq (until he invaded Kuwait), the House of Saud in Saudi Arabia, Mobutu Sese Seko in the Congo, Fulgencio Batista in Cuba, Park Chung Hee in South Korea, a succession of civilian and military dictators in South Vietnam, Lon Nol in Cambodia, Suharto in Indonesia, Marcos in the Philippines, the colonels' junta in Greece, Franco in Spain, and a long list of military dictators in Argentina,

Chile, Brazil, Uruguay, Guatemala, El Salvador, Nicaragua, and Pakistan. In supporting such governments, the United States was acting in pursuit of both Cold War geopolitical aims and economic advantage: the regimes in question were in general both anticommunist and friendly to American interests.

When the Cold War ended, the United States began to support the revival of democracy, and many of the repressive regimes it had backed, as we've seen, fell from power. At the same time, however, the unexpected collapse of the Soviet Union left the United States standing alone in the world as a military superpower. In economic strength, the United States had peers and near-peers—the European Union, Japan, China—but in military might it was in a class by itself. American military spending equaled that of the next dozen or so countries put together. In the 1990s, as the United States implemented a "revolution in military affairs," which applied information technology to warfare, its lead only increased. Never in history had any single power possessed such military advantage, qualitative as well as quantitative, over any or all other nations, and never had the likelihood of another nation catching up seemed more remote.

The emergence of this freakish imbalance, which came as quickly and unexpectedly as the Soviet collapse that was its proximate cause, posed a fundamental question for both the international order and the United States. The founders of the country had detested "standing armies"—an innovation of the despised absolutist monarchs of Europe. The founders feared that a large army with nothing to do would look for wars to fight. They also feared executive control of the military. In the words of John Jay in the *The Federalist Papers,* "absolute monarchs will often make war when their nations are to get nothing by it, but for purposes and objects merely personal, such as a thirst for military glory, revenge for personal affronts, ambition, or private compacts to aggrandize or support their particular families or partisans. These and a variety of other motives, which affect only the mind of the sovereign, often lead him to engage in wars not sanctified by justice or the voice or interests of his people." That is why the constitution they wrote declares, in one of its shortest and least equivocal statements, "The Congress shall have power to declare war."

The United States had often assembled great military forces, but always for a specific war, and had disbanded them when the war was over, as it did, for example, after the First World War. Even after the Second World War, American forces were reduced. (It's also true, however, that the effect of the reduction was more than offset by the creation of a growing arsenal of nuclear weapons—then an American monopoly.) With the end of the Cold War, the situation most feared by the founders came into existence. The nation was, for the first time in its history, in possession of a gigantic military force with no particular enemy to fight. Meanwhile, Congress had in practice yielded its power to declare war to the president.

In the 1990s, the question arose: Would the United States, having lost its global competitor, demobilize (as it had after the two world wars), or would it find some new mission for its military machine. If so, what would that mission be? These questions were especially acute in regard to the nation's thousands of nuclear weapons, whose deployment had been geared almost exclusively to Cold War purposes. Some in power asked (as Secretary of State Madeleine Albright, frustrated by American inaction in the Balkans, once did of Chairman of the Joint Chiefs of Staff Colin Powell), "What's the point of having this superb military that you're always talking about if we can't use it?" Others—distant from power—asked why, if there was little use for such military forces, the United States had to have them.

In the last decade of the twentieth century, the United States arrived at no clear answer: it neither dismantled its military machine nor found a mission for it. Overall military spending briefly dipped, and then resumed an upward curve. In the 1990s, the lone superpower was also a reluctant one. With regard to the two sources of most acute danger—local wars, including wars of self-determination, and weapons of mass destruction—the United States pursued vacillating policies. The American nuclear arsenal, literally deprived of its raison d'être by the disappearance of the Soviet target, fell into a sort of political vacuum. The policies of the United States in regard to nuclear proliferation were equally uncertain. An early decision to preserve the American nuclear arsenal indefinitely and a long hiatus in the START negotiations with Russia (owing in good measure to the decision to expand NATO to include Poland, the Czech Republic, and Hungary) helped prompt other, anxious or ambitious countries to seek or acquire their own arsenals. When the Soviet Union collapsed, the Clinton administration did succeed in brokering the denuclearization of Ukraine, Belorussia, and Kazakhstan, leaving Russia alone as the legatee of the Soviet Union's nuclear arsenal, but the exchange of nuclear tests by India and Pakistan in 1998, in disregard of weak American sanctions, left subsequent American nonproliferation policy in tatters.

A string of local and regional wars provoked American responses with no clear theme. President George H. Bush appeared to adopt a strongly interventionist stance when, in the name of a "new world order," he successfully reversed Iraq's annexation of Kuwait; but when violence of near-genocidal proportions broke out in Yugoslavia Secretary of State James Baker declared, "We have no dog in that fight," and the United States stayed out. The lesson seemed to be that the United States intervened only when its interests were at stake. As a presidential candidate, Bill Clinton castigated Bush for his inaction in the Balkans, but as president he, too, was at first inactive there. Only after Serbian forces had laid a long siege to Sarajevo did the United States conduct a bombing campaign under the aegis of NATO to protect the city. In 1999, Clinton ordered American forces to bomb Serbia to obtain its withdrawal from Kosovo. Meanwhile, in 1993, when American soldiers in a force that the United States had sent to stop a famine in Somalia were killed in a battle with a local warlord, Clinton promptly withdrew those troops, creating a strong impression that the United States would use its forces only when it could be sure they would not suffer casualties.

"Humanitarian intervention" was the official description of each of these interventions. Yet the Clinton administration did nothing to stop the worst atrocity of the era, the genocide in Rwanda. Nor did Clinton's Republican opposition—torn between its hawkish wing and its isolationist wing—offer a clear or consistent alternative policy. The reaction of the rest of the world to the uncertain superpower's use of its power was likewise equivocal. On the one hand, many nations—especially European nations—supported the use of American might in the crises in the Gulf, Somalia, and the former Yugoslavia; on the other hand, many nations (including some of the same nations) made clear their alarm that the use of such immense power, even if for ends defined as humanitarian, set a precedent that could soon be abused and was dangerous to the international order.

Then came the attack of September 11. Like the starting gun of a race that no one knew he was to run, this explosion set the pack of nations off in a single direction—toward the trenches. Although the attack was unaccompanied by any claim of authorship or statement of political goals, the evidence almost immediately pointed to Al Qaeda, the radical Islamist, terrorist network, which, though stateless, was headquartered in Afghanistan and enjoyed the protection of its fundamentalist Islamic government. In a tape that was soon shown around the world, the group's leader, Osama bin Laden, was seen at dinner with his confederates in Afghanistan, rejoicing in the slaughter. Historically, nations have responded to terrorist threats and attacks with a combination of police action and political negotiation, while military action has played only a minor role. Voices were raised in the United States calling for a global cooperative effort of this kind to combat Al Qaeda. President Bush opted instead for a policy that the United States alone among nations could have conceivably undertaken: global military action not only against Al Qaeda but against any regime in the world that supported international terrorism. The president announced to Congress that he would "make no distinction between the terrorists who commit these acts and those who harbor them." By calling the campaign a "war," the administration summoned into action the immense, technically revolutionized, post–Cold War American military machine, which had lacked any clear enemy for over a decade. And by identifying the target as generic "terrorism," rather than as Al Qaeda or any other group or list of groups, the administration licensed military operations anywhere in the world.

In the ensuing months, the Bush administration continued to expand the aims and means of the war. The overthrow of governments—"regime change"—was established as a means for advancing the new policies. The president divided regimes into two categories—those "with us" and those "against us." Vice President Cheney estimated that Al Qaeda was active in sixty countries. The first regime to be targeted was of course Al Qaeda's host, the government of Afghanistan, which was overthrown in a remarkably swift military operation conducted almost entirely from the air and without American casualties.

Next, the administration proclaimed an additional war goal—preventing the proliferation of weapons of mass destruction. In his State of the Union speech in January 2002, the president announced that "the United States of America will not permit the world's most dangerous regimes to threaten us with the world's most destructive weapons." He went on to name as an "axis of evil" Iraq, Iran, and North Korea—three regimes seeking to build or already possessing weapons of mass destruction. To stop them, he stated, the Cold War policy of deterrence would not be enough—"preemptive" military action would be required, and preemption, the administration soon specified, could include the use of nuclear weapons. Beginning in the summer of 2002, the government intensified its preparations for a war to overthrow the regime of Saddam Hussein in Iraq, and in the fall, the president demanded and received a resolution from the Security Council of the United Nations requiring Iraq to accept the return of U.N. inspectors to search for weapons of mass destruction or facilities for building them. Lists of other candidates for "regime change" began to surface in the press.

In this way, the war on terror grew to encompass the most important geopolitical issue facing the world: the disposition of nuclear weapons in the second nuclear age. The Clinton administration had already answered the question regarding American possession of nuclear weapons: even in the absence of the Soviet Union, the United States planned to hold on to its nuclear arsenal indefinitely. In 2002, the Bush administration gave an answer to the question regarding nonproliferation, which throughout the nuclear age had been dealt with exclusively by diplomacy and negotiation, or, on occasion, economic sanctions.

The new answer was force. Nuclear disarmament was to be achieved by war and threats of war, starting with Iraq. One complementary element of the new policy, embraced long before September 11, was the decision to build a national missile defense system to protect the United States against nuclear attack by "rogue nations." But the fundamental element was a policy of preemptive war, or "offensive deterrence." This momentous shift in nuclear policy called, in addition, for programs to build new nuclear weapons and new delivery vehicles; confirmed new missions for nuclear weapons—retaliation for chemical or biological attacks, attacking hardened bunkers unreachable by other weapons—in the post–Cold War world; and listed seven countries (Russia, China, North Korea, Iraq, Iran, Libya, and Syria) for which contingency plans for nuclear attack should be considered. To achieve all these aims, nuclear and conventional, the president asked for an increase in military spending of forty-eight billion dollars—a sum greater than the total military spending of any other nation.

The sharp turn toward force as the mainstay of the policies of the United States was accompanied by a turn away from treaties and other forms of cooperation. Even before September 11, the trend had been clear. Now it accelerated. The Bush administration either refused to ratify or withdrew from most of the principal new international treaties of the post–Cold War era. In the nuclear arena alone, the administration refused to submit to the Senate for ratification the Comprehensive Test Ban Treaty, which would have added a ban on underground tests to the existing bans on testing in the air; withdrew from the A.B.M. Treaty, which had severely limited Russian and American deployment of antinuclear defensive systems; and jettisoned the START negotiations as the framework for nuclear reductions with Russia—replacing them with the Strategic Offensive Reduction Agreement, a three-page document requring two-thirds of the strategic weapons of both sides to be removed from their delivery vehicles, but then stored rather than dismantled. In addition, the Bush administration withdrew from the Kyoto Protocol of the United Nations Framework Convention on Climate Change, which had become the world's principal forum for making decisions about reducing emissions that cause global warming; refused to ratify the Rome treaty establishing an international criminal court; and declined to agree to an important protocol for inspection and enforcement of a U.N. convention banning biological weapons.

The consequences of this revolution in American policy rippled through the world, where it found ready imitators. On December 12, the Indian Parliament was attacked by terrorists whom India linked to Pakistan. Promptly, nuclear-armed India, citing the American policy of attacking not only terrorists but any state that harbored them, moved half a million men to the border of nuclear-armed Pakistan, which responded in kind, producing the first full-scale nuclear crisis of the twenty-first century. In South Asia, nuclearization did not produce the cautionary effects that the theorists of deterrence expected. High Indian officials openly threatened Pakistan with annihilation. Rajnath Singh, the minister for the state of Uttar Pradesh, declared, "If Pakistan doesn't change its ways, there will be no sign of Pakistan left," and when India's army chief, General S. Padmanabhan, was asked how India would respond if attacked with a nuclear weapon, he answered that "the perpetrator of that particular outrage shall be punished so severely that their continuation thereafter in any form of fray will be doubtful." In Pakistan, the dictator General Pervez Musharraf stated that, in the event of an Indian conventional invasion of Pakistan, "as a last resort, the atom bomb is also possible." In March 2002, Israel, citing the same American precedent and calling for U.S. support for its policy on this basis, responded to Palestinian suicide bombings by launching its own "war on terrorism"—a full-scale attack on the Palestinian Authority on the West Bank.

The revolution in American policy had been precipitated by September 11, but went far beyond any war on terror. It remained to give the policy comprehensive doctrinal expression, which came in an official document, "The National Security Strategy of the United States of America," issued in September 2002. In the world, it stated, only one economic and political system remained "viable": the American one of liberal democracy and free enterprise. The United States would henceforth promote and defend this system by the unilateral use of force—preemptively, if necessary. The United States, the president said, "has, and intends to keep, military strengths beyond challenge, thereby making the destabilizing arms races of other eras pointless, and limiting rivalries to trade and other pursuits of peace." In other words, the United States reserved the entire field of military force to itself, restricting other nations to humbler pursuits. In the words of the "National Security Strategy," "Our forces will be strong enough to dissuade potential adversaries from pursing a military build-up in hopes of surpassing, or equaling, the power of the United States." If the United States was displeased with a regime, it reserved the right to overthrow it—to carry out "regime change." "In the world we have entered," President Bush has said, "the only path to safety is the path of action. And this nation will act."

Niagara

A policy of unchallengeable military domination over the earth, accompanied by a unilateral right to overthrow other governments by military force, is an imperial, an Augustan policy. It marks a decisive choice of force and coercion over cooperation and consent as the mainstay of the American response to the disorders of the time. If wars of self-determination and other kinds of local and regional mayhem multiply and run out of control; if the wealthy and powerful use globalization to systematize and exacerbate exploitation of the poor and powerless; if the poor and the powerless react with terrorism and other forms of violence; if the nuclear powers insist on holding on to and threatening to use their chosen weapons of mass destruction; if more nations then develop nuclear or biological or chemical arsenals in response and threaten to use them; if these weapons one day fall, as seems likely, into the hands of terrorists; and if the United States continues to pursue an Augustan policy, then the stage will be set for catastrophe. Each of these possibilities represents a path of least resistance. Local and regional conflicts have been the way of the world since history began. The spread of nuclear- as well as biological- and chemical-weapon know-how is an automatic function of technical progress, and the spread of nuclear arsenals is a self-feeding process of action and reaction. Continued possession of nuclear weapons by those who already have them is the path of inertia, of deep sleep. The imperial temptation for the United States is the path of arrogance and ignorance.

At the intersection of these tendencies is a Niagara higher and more violent than the one that a heartbroken Henry James lived to witness in 1914. It is of course impossible to predict how and where history might again go over the precipice. It could be nuclear war in South Asia, bringing the deaths of tens of millions of people. It could be the annihilation of one or several cities in the United States in a nuclear terrorist attack, or the loss of millions in a smallpox attack. It could be a war spinning out of control in the Middle East, leading by that route to the use of weapons of mass destruction in the Middle East. It could be war in Korea, or between the United States and China over Taiwan. It could even be—hard as it is to imagine now—intentional or semi-intentional nuclear war between Russia and the United States in some future crisis that we cannot foresee but cannot rule out, either. Or it could be—is even likely to be—some chain of events we are at present incapable of imagining.

After September 11, people rightly said that the world had changed forever. Before that event, who could have predicted the galloping transformation of the politics of the United States and the world, the escalating regional crises, the vistas of perpetual war? Yet the use of just one nuclear weapon could exceed the damage of September 11 ten-thousandfold. Would the global economy plunge into outright depression? Would the people of the world flee their menaced cities? Would anyone know who the attacker was? Would someone retaliate—perhaps on a greater scale? Would the staggering shock bring the world to its senses? Would the world at that moment of unparalleled panic and horror react more wisely and constructively than it has been able to do in a time of peace, in comparative calm, or would it fall victim to an incalculable cycle of fear, confusion, hatred, hostility, and violence, both between nations and within them, as it did after 1914—but this time, in all likelihood, far more swiftly and with incomparably direr consequences? In the face of these questions, predictive powers dim. But attempts at prophecy are in any case the wrong response. Decisions are required.

13

The Logic of Peace

The escalation of violence around the world has been so rapid since September 11, 2001, that this day may appear already to have been the August 1914 of the twenty-first century. The parallels are striking. In 2001 as in 1914 a period of political liberalization, economic globalization, and peace (at least in the privileged zones of the planet) was summarily ended by a violent explosion. The fundamental decision now, as it was then, is between force and peaceful means as the path to safety, and the world has seemed to make a decision for force. Again, observers have been compelled, as Henry James was in 1914, to recognize that the immediate past has been a time of illusion—a time when the world was heading toward a precipice but did not know it, or did not care to know it. Again, an unpredictable chain of violent events has been set in motion—some today have even said that a "third world war" is upon us.

And yet, since history does not repeat itself, the analogy between 1914 and 2001, like all measurements of the present with yardsticks from the past, is useful only for querying events, not for predicting them. There are equally important differences between the two moments, some of them obvious, others less so. In 1914, the great powers' preparations for war were complete. The arms were piled high, the troops massed, the war plans mapped out in detail, the mobilization schedules fixed, the treaties of alliance signed and sealed. Even before the first shot was fired, the whole of the long war to come lay waiting in the file cabinets of the chanceries of Europe, needing only the right incident to spring to life. And when that incident came and the armies were hurled across the borders, no power on earth, including the governments involved, could call them back until the war had run its full bloody course. Our moment, by contrast, is one of exceptional unpredictability and fluidity. No inexorable timetables or web of alliances among great powers threaten to drag everyone together into a new abyss. The unexpected—new crises, abrupt developments, sudden opportunities—is the order of the day. The strength of the forces that attacked on September 11 is unclear, and appears likely to wax or wane in response to events. The Bush administration has announced a series of wars that it may decide to fight, but there will be points of decision at every step along the way. Developments in the field can quickly alter political opinion at home. The proliferation of weapons of mass destruction can inhibit as well as provoke war. Elections can bring new people to power. Other countries are watching and waiting, uncertain where and how to bring the weight of their influence to bear. The effect of a series of wars, if such occur, on global economic integration is unknown, and huge uncertainties shadow the economic scene.

As shocking as September 11 was, it was not a decisive catastrophe, but rather a warning. No irrevocable decision has in fact been made. The scope for choice remains unusually large, and the new cycle of violence can still be broken or reversed, and new policies adopted. Seen narrowly, September 11 posed the specific question of how the United States and the civilized world should deal with a global terrorist network ready to commit any crime within its power. That question requires all the urgent attention and action that it is receiving. A the same time, I submit, we should be asking what the larger and more fundamental decisions for policy may be. If we take this broader approach, the profound changes that have occurred in the character of violence, politics, and power over the last century will command our attention. In 1918 and 1945, a decision in favor of coercive power clearly meant in practice choosing the old war system, and a decision in favor of cooperative power meant choosing to create ex nihilo a Wilsonian system of global collective security based on international law. Today, neither of these alternatives is open to us. Others are on the table. Let us consider each of the two paths, beginning with the choice of coercive power, then turning to the choice of cooperative power.

Violence as the Solution to Violence: The End of Balance

Now as in 1918 and 1945, organized violence plays a double role in the decision, for violence is both the problem to be solved and one of the solutions on offer—a solution to itself. This remedy is of course as old as history. When, as we have noted, Clemenceau rejected Wilson's vision in favor of an old system in which he still had "faith," he was referring to definite plans for defending his country within the framework of the global war system. And when the diplomat Harold Nicolson began to lose confidence in Wilsonism and repaired to that old system because the value of "armaments, strategic frontiers, alliances" was already proven, he was reverting to the same faith. Both held to the idea, codified in the realist school of political thought, of creating a balance of power, which had always been the main hope for peace of those who planned to deploy the instruments of violence to prevent violence. When nuclear weapons were invented, war among the great powers became unworkable, yet the idea of balance survived, in the new form of the balance of terror. Some have continued to call the balance of terror a balance of power, but a better term might be a balance of powerlessness, inasmuch as its stability rests on the willingness of the parties to enlist in a community of total jeopardy.

The balance of powerlessness may have been more effective than the balance of power exactly because the penalty for failure, nuclear annihilation, was so much greater. It cannot, of course, be demonstrated conclusively that nuclear terror prevented a third world war. Too many ifs of history are involved to make a firm judgment. (Since we cannot in the present predict what history *will* do, what makes us think that we can say what history *would have done* if such and such an imaginary event had occurred?) For example, we would have to determine that a third world war had been straining to occur—only to be checked by fear of the bomb. We would also have to show that the presence of nuclear weapons did more to prevent world war than to cause it. After all, the most acute crisis of the Cold War, the Cuban missile crisis, was brought about by the deployment of nuclear weapons. If nuclear strategic thinking had anything to do with resolving that crisis (something that is in itself difficult to demonstrate), it was only after causing the crisis in the first place.

Nevertheless, it is as possible as it is necessary, even without resolving these unanswerable questions, to acknowledge that the presence of the bomb weighed heavily in the calculations of the statesmen of the Cold War, inclining them against major war each time a crisis occurred. Their increasing recognition that, as President Ronald Reagan put it, "nuclear war cannot be won and must never be fought" was a central fact, in theory and in practice, of the Cold War.

With these developments, nuclear strategy acquired a Wilsonian dimension. It had evolved into a war stopper. The importance of the role of the balance of terror as a peacekeeper becomes clearer if we consider the varying fates of the century's two major organizations for peacekeeping, the League of Nations and the

United Nations. The League was discredited by a series of aggressions and conflicts it was unable to prevent or halt, then swept aside by the Second World War. The Cold War played a similar role in sidelining the United Nations.

President Franklin Roosevelt and Winston Churchill, who first called for such an organization in the Atlantic Charter in 1941, had sought to draw lessons from the fate of the League. Instead of assigning the peacekeeping function to a large council, as the League did, they vested it in an alliance of the prospective victors of the Second World War—the United States, the Soviet Union, China, England, and France—each of whom was given a permanent seat on the Security Council and a veto over its decisions. The hope was that this small, tight-knit group of great powers could guarantee the peace more effectively than the multitude of nations charged with that responsibility under the provisions of the League. But almost immediately after the organization's foundation in 1946, this arrangement was for all intents and purposes nullified by the advent of the Cold War. In 1950, the Korean War, sanctioned by the Security Council after the Soviet Union walked out of its proceedings, confirmed that the breakdown in relations between the United States and the Soviet Union was irreparable.

If this geopolitical split had been the only reason for the U.N.'s failure to perform its central role, the story would be a familiar one, well-known to analysts of the League's collapse: collective security fails to get off the ground because the powers that are supposed to enforce it fall out with one another. The designated peacemakers become the peace-breakers, and no one else is strong enough to bring them into line. In fact, however, the U.N.'s marginalization occurred for another reason as well—the onset of the nuclear age. By an accident of historical timing, the bomb was first tested and dropped in the hiatus between the designing of the United Nations and its founding.

In April of 1945, in San Francisco, the Conference on International Organization formally agreed on the outlines of the U.N.

Charter. On October 24, the U.N. came into existence. On August 6, however, the destruction of Hiroshima radically transformed the nature of the main problem, great-power war, that the new organization had been fashioned to solve. Conceived in one age, the U.N. was born in another. Having been designed to cope with a world dominated by the global war system, it came into existence after that system's death knell had been sounded. The central purpose of the U.N. was to prevent a third world war—to, in the words of the Preamble to its Charter, "save succeeding generations from the scourge of war, which twice in our lifetime has brought untold sorrow to mankind." But as the years passed it was not to the U.N., disabled by the Cold War, that the great powers turned to save them from a third world war but to nuclear arsenals. Even as the Cold War was wrecking the U.N. as an instrument for keeping the peace, nuclear deterrence was coopting it. Thus the U.N. was not swept away, as the League had been by approaching world war; it was permitted to live on to perform important, if secondary services—supplying humanitarian relief in disasters of every description, sending peacekeeping forces to calm local conflicts, providing a forum for the expression of international opinion.

With the end of the bipolar Cold War order, and the acceleration of nuclear proliferation, however, the new, nuclearized form the balance is crumbling. For reasons both political and technical, nuclear terror is rapidly shedding its "Wilsonian" role as a preserver of stability and peace.

Some, it is true, have argued to the contrary that the balance of nuclear terror can actually be extended and strengthened by proliferation. Just as nuclear weapons stopped the two superpowers of the Cold War from fighting a hot war, so, it is suggested, they can immobilize ten or twenty or thirty nuclear powers, in a grand peace based on universal terror. The political scientist Kenneth Waltz, for example, has suggested that "the gradual spread of nuclear weapons is more to be welcomed than feared." He hopes that the Soviet-American stalemate enforced by deterrence during the Cold War might be enlarged to include many more nations. What has not been explained, however, is how a steadily growing number of nuclear powers, each capable of annihilating some or all of the others, can balance their forces in a way that would leave any of them feeling safe. Mutual assured destruction is a policy whose logic fits a bipolar relationship. It defies adjustment to a multi-nuclear-power world.

Proliferation, indeed, undermines stability in every sense of that word. In the first place, it destroys strategic stability. Strategic balance during the Cold War was supposed to depend on the attempt to maintain a rough equality between the forces of the two sides; but in a world of many nuclear powers this goal would be unreachable. If Country A and Country B were to painstakingly craft a stable nuclear balance (something, incidentally, that the Soviet Union and the United States failed to do for as long as the Cold War continued), it could be overthrown instantly by any nuclear-armed Country C that suddenly allied itself with one or the other. The necessary changes in targeting could be accomplished in just a few hours or days. Even in today's world of eight nuclear powers (or perhaps nine, if North Korea's claim to possess nuclear weapons is true), some of the imbalances inherent in nuclear multipolarity are evident. There is little hope of balance, for example, in the quadrilateral relationship of the United States, China, India, and Pakistan. India has stated that it became a nuclear power to balance nuclear-armed China, by whom it was defeated in a conventional border war in 1962. Pakistan became a nuclear power to balance India. If India seeks again to balance China, however, will Pakistan seek to keep up? China, moreover, has supplied nuclear technology to Pakistan. And Pakistan has supplied some to North Korea, receiving missile technology in return. Will India therefore feel compelled to build a nuclear arsenal that equals both China's and Pakistan's? The United States meanwhile has decided to build national missile defenses, which, if they turn out to work, will erode or nullify China's capacity to strike the United States. China has already said that it will respond by building up its still modest nuclear forces. That will put additional pressure on India. Nor can we forget that Russia may, at any point, step into the picture with its still-huge arsenal. The spread of ballistic- and cruise-missile technology, whose proliferation is as predictable as that of nuclear technology, compounds the problem geometrically.

In the second place, proliferation is bound to undermine the foundations of technical stability. During the Cold War, the United States and the Soviet Union sought a kind of safety in the policy of mutual assured destruction. In practice, however, they found that their nuclear command-and-control systems were so vulnerable to a first strike that the retaliation required by the doctrine could not in fact be assured. To cure the problem, the two governments resorted to policies of "launch on warning"—that is, each planned to launch its retaliatory strike after receiving a warning that the other side had launched its first strike but before the missiles had arrived. This system placed severe time pressure on any decision to launch in retaliation, increasing the risks of accidental war. The presidents of the two nations were—and still are—required to make these decisions within five minutes of receiving warning of an incoming strike. The pressures on Russia, which now faces a technically superior American force, have grown especially severe.

If the United States and Russia, with all their resources and an ocean between them, cannot guarantee the survival of their command-and-control systems, is it reasonable to expect that smaller, poorer nations, facing many potential adversaries, with little or no warning time, will accomplish this? The warning time between India and Pakistan, for instance, is effectively zero. For them, not even launch on warning is possible. The requirements for nuclear stability under the doctrine of deterrence are thus altogether lacking.

In the third place, what the experts call arms-control stability—meaning conditions favorable to negotiated limits on or reductions of nuclear arsenals—would be destroyed. During the Cold War, the United States and the Soviet Union, unable to agree on numerical offensive limits, built up their collective arsenals to the preposterous collective level of some seventy-five thousand nuclear warheads. In a multipolar nuclear world, arms-control agreements would become exponentially harder to achieve. How could twenty or thirty nations, few of whom trusted the others or were sure what they were doing, be able to adjust the scores of nuclear balances among them? Containing proliferation (if someone should wish to return to that policy somewhere down the road) would be a pipe dream. How would, say, the twentieth nuclear power persuade the twenty-first that building nuclear weapons is a bad idea?

In the fourth place, multiplying nuclear arsenals would increase the danger of nuclear terrorism. A world of proliferation would be a world awash in nuclear materials. Terrorists who acquired them would be indifferent to nuclear threats from others. The balance of terror depends on fear of retaliatory annihilation, but many terrorists have no country of whose annihilation they are afraid. They are unafraid to lose even their own lives, and blow themselves up with the bombs they aim at others. The terrorist bent on self-immolation with a weapon of mass destruction is the nemesis of balance. Deterrence has no purchase on the dead.

Violence as the Solution to Violence: Empire

If the balance of power and the balance of terror are no longer available, does the storehouse of systems of coercive power still offer any resource for keeping peace in the world? One option remains to be considered: universal empire, substantially achieved only once in the history of the Western world, by the Romans. (Even they were unable to conquer certain outlying territories.) The nation now aspiring to a global imperial role is, of course, the United States. Its military dominance is one more reason that a balance of power has become impracticable. Obviously, there can be no balance when one power is mightier than all the others put together. Not a balance of power but a monopoly of power—or, at any rate, of force—is the present American ambition. The new state of affairs is sometimes referred to as "unipolarity," but the term is an oxymoron within a single word, for by definition "polarity" requires two poles. (The Bush administration's official statement of its global policy, the "National Security Strategy," falls into a similar confusion when it speaks of a "balance of power in favor of freedom." A balance that is "in favor of" one side is again by definition not a balance.)

Although both the balance-of-power system and the balance of terror were primarily based on coercion, both contained significant admixtures of cooperation. Both depended on a sort of brute equity among two or more powers. If the balance was to be maintained, neither could claim a right to attack the other: they must coexist. Under the balance of terror, the element of cooperation was even stronger. The two sides were bonded in the common project of avoiding the war that would annihilate both. They were paradoxical partners in survival. A global hegemonic peace, on the other hand, would mark the triumph of coercion. Its foundation would be not equality of any kind but the absolute and unchallengeable superiority of one power and the vassalage of others—not mutual nonaggression but preemption, not coexistence but the right of one, and only one, to execute "regime change."

The idea of American global hegemony thus carries the rule of force to an extreme. And yet, fantastic and unreal as the ambition may be, there is a logic underlying it. Means, this logic runs, must be adequate to ends. Since proliferation is in its nature global so must American domination. The United States will employ its overwhelming military superiority to stop proliferation all around the world. It applies to the world the reasoning that Bodin applied to the state four hundred years ago: the world is now a community; a community needs order; to provide order there must be a sovereign; the sovereign can be none other than the master of the sword; the United States alone can lay a claim to mastering the sword; therefore the United States must be the global sovereign. And so on behalf of its own and the world's safety, the United States will fight a series of what can be called disarmament wars. Under this plan the United States would, indeed, become a "disarmament empire," dedicated to preserving the world from nuclear destruction. (Of course, all empires are in a sense disarmament empires: they rule by defeating—by destroying or disarming—every foe and rival.) It is not going too far to say that *if* the solutions to the danger of nuclear proliferation were restricted to coercive systems, then some form of imperial domination would be the form it would have to take.

To acknowledge the existence of this logic, which lends the American bid for hegemony whatever legitimacy it has, is not to overlook the more mundane and sordid aspects of American imperial ambition. Every empire in history has concealed coarse self-interest behind a veil of noble ideals, and there is no reason to believe that American imperialism would be an exception. The most obvious and the rawest of these motivations is the wish to take control of the oil reserves of Central Asia, the Middle East, and elsewhere. Far more sweeping is the assertion in the "National Security Strategy" that in all the world there is now "a single sustainable model for national success": the American one of "freedom, democracy, and free enterprise." It is a formulation that, when wedded to the assertion of unchallengeable American military superiority and the right to intervene militarily anywhere on earth, plainly sets the stage for attempts to impose America's will on nations in almost any area of their collective existence.

A plan for global hegemony, however, has not suddenly become feasible simply because the balance of power and the balance of terror no longer work. Even if we supposed that the United States were to complete the transition from republic to empire, there are powerful reasons to believe that it would fail to realize its global ambitions, whether idealistic or self-interested. Any imperial plan in the twenty-first century tilts against what have so far proved to be the two most powerful forces of the modern age: the spread of scientific knowledge and the resolve of peoples to reject foreign rule and take charge of their own destinies. If the history of the past two centuries is a guide, neither can be bombed out of existence.

The most persuasive rationale for empire is its promise of deliverance from the threat of weapons of mass destruction. The views of most countries on this subject, however, are far different from those of the United States. The Bush administration looks out upon the world and sees "evildoers" trying to procure terrible weapons; the world looks back and sees a hypocritical power seeking to deny to others what it possesses in abundance and even plans to use preemptively. Most countries fear those who already have nuclear weapons at least as much as they fear those who are merely trying to get them. In their view, stopping proliferation deals at best with a secondary aspect of the nuclear problem. They still see what has perhaps become invisible to American eyes—that the United States and Russia have thousands of nuclear weapons pointed at one another and at others and have refused to surrender these arsenals. They also see that the club of possessors has grown to include South Asia, where the danger of nuclear war has become acute, and they note that no plan is on the drawing board to denuclearize these powers, either. On the contrary, nuclearization has been a ticket into the good graces of the United States for both countries. Finally, they observe that the Nuclear Nonproliferation Treaty, under which a hundred and eighty-two countries have agreed to forgo nuclear arms, is in jeopardy of breaking down because the five nations that possess nuclear arsenals under the terms of the treaty show no sign of fulfilling their pledge under its Article 6 to eliminate them. (Three other nuclear powers— India, Pakistan, and Israel—are nonmembers of the treaty, and the fourth, North Korea, has announced its intention of withdrawing.) It was in defiance of this nuclear double standard that India set off its nuclear tests in 1998, prompting Pakistan's responding tests. Was "regime change" an option in these cases? Is it in North Korea? Will it be if Iran, Egypt, Syria, or, for that matter, Japan or Germany builds a nuclear arsenal? Does the United States propose to overthrow the government of every country that, rebelling against the attempt to institutionalize the double standard, seeks to acquire weapons of mass destruction? The attempt indeed appears more likely to provoke than prevent proliferation, as has already happened in North Korea. Nations threatened with that nightmare of the ages, a great power seeking global domination, will go to desperate lengths to redress the balance. Weapons of mass destruction are an obvious means.

What is true for proliferation of nuclear weapons is also likely to be true for their use. Force, history teaches, summons counter-force. What goes around comes around. The United States is the only nation on earth that has used these weapons of mass destruction. An American attempt to dominate world affairs is a recipe for provoking their use again, very possibly on American soil.

It's unlikely that the passion for self-determination will be any easier to suppress than the spread of destructive technology. Empire, the supreme embodiment of force, is the antithesis of self-determination. It violates equity on a global scale. No lover of freedom can give it support. It is especially contrary to the founding principles of the United States, whose domestic institutions are incompatible with the maintenance of empire. Historically, imperial rule has rested on three kinds of supremacy—military, economic, and political. The United States enjoys unequivocal superiority in only one of these domains—the military, and here only in the conventional sphere. (Any attempt at regime change in a country equipped with even a modest deliverable nuclear arsenal is out of the question even for the United States.) American economic power is impressive, yet in this domain it has several equals or near equals, including the European Union and Japan, who are not likely to bend easily to American will. In the political arena the United States is weak. "Covenants, without the sword, are but words," Hobbes said in the late seventeenth century. Since then, the world has learned that swords without covenants are but empty bloodshed. In the political arena, the lesson of the world revolt—that winning military victories may sometimes be easy but building political institutions in foreign lands is hard, often impossible—still obtains. The nation so keenly interested in regime change has small interest in nation-building and less capacity to carry it out. The United States, indeed, is especially mistrusted, often hated, around the world. If it embarks on a plan of imperial supremacy, it will be hated still more. Can cruise missiles build nations? Does power still flow from the barrel of a gun—or from a Predator Drone? Can the world in the twenty-first century really be ruled from thirty-five thousand feet? Modern peoples have the will to resist and the means to do so. Imperialism without politics is a naive imperialism. In our time, force can win a battle or two, but politics is destiny.

Can a nation that began its life in rebellion against the most powerful empire of its time end by trying to become a still more powerful empire? It perhaps can, but not if it wishes to remain a republic. Secretary of State John Quincy Adams defined the choice with precision in 1821. After giving his country the well-known advice that the United States should not go abroad "in search of monsters to destroy" but be "the well-wisher to the freedom and independence of all . . . the champion and vindicator only of her own," he added that if the United States embarked on the path of dominating others, the "fundamental maxims of her policy would insensibly change from liberty to force. . . . She might become the dictatress of the world. She would no longer be the ruler of her own spirit."

A country's violence, Hannah Arendt said, can destroy its power. The United States is moving quickly down this path. Do American leaders imagine that the people of the world, having overthrown the territorial empires of the nineteenth and twentieth centuries, are ready to bend the knee to an American overlord in the twenty-first? Do they imagine that allies are willing to become subordinates? Have they forgotten that people hate to be dominated by force? History is packed with surprises. The leaders of the totalitarian Soviet empire miraculously had the good sense to yield up their power without unleashing the tremendous violence that was at their fingertips. Could it be the destiny of the American republic, unable to resist the allure of an imperial delusion, to flare out in a blaze of pointless mass destruction?

The Cooperative Path

In sum, the days when humanity can hope to save itself from force with force are over. None of the structures of violence—not the balance of power, not the balance of terror, not empire—can any longer rescue the world from the use of violence, now grown apocalyptic. Force can lead only to more force, not to peace. Only a turn to structures of cooperative power can offer hope. To choose that path, the United States would, as a first order of business, have to choose the American republic over the American empire, and then, on the basis of the principles that underlie the republic, join with other nations to build cooperative structures as a basis for peace.

For Americans, the choice is at once between two Americas, and between two futures for the international order. In an imperial America, power would be concentrated in the hands of the president, and checks and balances would be at an end; civil liberties would be weakened or lost; military spending would crowd out social spending; the gap between rich and poor would be likely to increase; electoral politics, to the extent that they still mattered, would be increasingly dominated by money, above all corporate money, whose influence would trump the people's interests; the social, economic, and ecological agenda of the country and the world would be increasingly neglected. On the other hand, in a republican America dedicated to the creation of a cooperative world, the immense concentration of power in the executive would be broken up; power would be divided again among the three branches, which would resume their responsibility of checking and balancing one another as the Constitution provides; civil liberties would remain intact or be strengthened; money would be driven out of politics, and the will of the people would be heard again; politics, and with it the power of the people, would revive; the social, economic, and ecological agendas of the country and the world would become the chief concern of the government.

Which path the United States will choose is likely to be decided in a protracted, arduous political struggle in the years ahead. Its outcome cannot be predicted. For the time being, the United States has chosen the coercive, imperial path, but that decision can be reversed. Of course, no American decision alone can secure peace in the world. It is the essence of the task that many nations must cooperate in it. If they do, however, they will find that twentieth-century history has presented them, together with all its violence, an abundance of materials to work with. There are grounds for optimism in the restricted but real sense that if the will to turn away from force and toward cooperation were to develop, history has provided more extensive and solid foundations for accomplishment than have ever existed before. For the anatomy of cooperative power has been transformed by the events of the past century as fully as that of coercive power.

Much that Woodrow Wilson hoped for has in fact come to pass. He wanted a world of popular self-determination. His vision is our reality (to a fault, as the tangled wars of self-determination of recent years demonstrate). He dreamed that the world would be made safe for democracy. We can begin to imagine, in the wake of the liberal democratic revival and the Western liberal settlement, that spreading democracy will help to make the world safe. He hated the territorial empires of his time. Today, they are on history's scrap heap.

Hopeful developments that Wilson could not have foreseen have also occurred. The Wilsonian peace was destroyed in good measure by the rise of totalitarianism. Now totalitarianism, too, lies in the dust. In Wilson's day, revolution was widely thought to be in its nature violent. We have witnessed the power of nonviolent revolution, which was responsible for the downfall of the greatest empires of the previous two centuries, the British and the Soviet. In his day, the global adapt-or-die war system was at the apex of its power. In ours, it is disabled. Each of the aforementioned developments indeed curtailed that system in a different way. The military power deployed at the top of the system ran into the buzz saw of even greater power based on popular will at the bottom. As in Alice in Wonderland's croquet game, in which the mallets were flamingos and the balls were hedgehogs, the pawns in the imperial game, mistaken for inanimate objects by the imperialists, came alive in their hands and began, universally and unstoppably, to pursue their own plans and ambitions. In this new dispensation, which can guarantee against global domination far more reliably than the balance of power ever could, the wills of innumerable local peoples play the role previously played by the resolve of major powers to go to war to stop a global conqueror.

While the self-determination movement was encasing the giant's feet in cement, nuclear weapons were immobilizing his head and limbs. What need was there to obey the dictates of the war system's global logic of force when at the end of every military path was neither victory nor defeat but a common annihilation? Coexistence had always been a wise policy; now it became a necessity. It remains so—American conventional military superiority notwithstanding—for all nuclear-capable powers. Even tiny, impoverished North Korea can deter the United States and all its might if it possesses half a dozen nuclear weapons and the means to deliver them. Of course, it is still quite possible to stumble across the dread threshold, committing genocide and suicide in a single act, but the option is hardly tempting.

Even as self-determination movements and nuclear arsenals were, in their different ways, paralyzing force as the final arbiter in global affairs, nonviolent revolution in the Soviet bloc and elsewhere was proving the existence of a force that now *could* arbitrate. Gyorgy Konrád was right, far-fetched as it may have seemed at the time, to suggest that his "antipolitics" pointed a way out of the Cold War and the nuclear stalemate, and so was Adam Michnik when he said that he and his colleagues had discovered a political equivalent of the atomic bomb. Has the effectiveness of what William James called the moral equivalent of war ever been more effectually demonstrated?

At the same time, the revival of liberal democracy was creating a growing, informal bloc of nations whose members enjoyed peaceful relations not because they bristled with arms or had established a cumbersome structure of collective security but merely because they lacked any reason or inclination for war and possessed cooperative means for resolving such disagreements as did arise.

The success of the self-determination movement, the rise of nuclear capacity, the success of nonviolent revolutions, and the liberal democratic revival are deep-rooted historical realities. Even as (with the exception of nonviolent revolution) they have created new dangers, they have laid down new foundations for a world that can move away from violence as the principle arbiter of its political affairs.

Shall we, then, return to the fray with a third round of Wilsonism? Shall we attempt once more to write a constitution for the whole world? We must answer in the negative. It would not make sense to apply twice-failed solution to problems that no longer exist. The entrenched war system defeated Wilson, and it is perhaps the most important of our inestimable advantages that we do not face this monster. Its fall has opened up new avenues for action. No longer is it necessary, as it was in his time, to put in place a global system of law as a *precondition* for dismantling the structures of force. The two tasks can proceed along separate tracks, each at its own pace. No longer do we face the impossible task of uprooting the war system in its entirety or leaving it in place. The all-or-nothing dilemma has dissolved. Seeing, just as Wilson did, that by continuing to rely on systems of violence we condemn ourselves to catastrophe and horror, we can adopt his radical goal of creating a peaceful world while remaining at liberty to carry it out step by step. We can borrow a leaf from the Eastern Europeans. Rejecting a choice between accommodation and violent, all-or-nothing revolution, they decided upon the incremental pursuit of revolutionary ends by peaceful, reformist means. Acting on the basis of common principles yet without any blueprint—"in cooperation without unification," in the phrase of the French sociologist Pierre Bourdieu—they pooled the variegated forces of society to achieve a radical renewal of their lives that in the end accomplished everything that was necessary. A revolution against violence in the world at large today would, in imitation of this process, not be the realization of any single plan drawn up by any one person or council but would develop, like open software, as the common creation of any and all comers, acting at every political level, within as well as outside government, on the basis of common principles.

One day, humankind may organize itself into a true body politic. Perhaps this will be some remote variation on the United Nations, whose hand now lies so lightly on the world; perhaps it will be some new organizational form. That day had not come in Wilson's time. It has not come in ours. Even as an ideal, the structure of a global body politic remains uninvented. Such a novel object is unlikely to take a familiar form. The need for global political structures to deal with the globalized economy and the swiftly deteriorating global environment is manifest. Yet it would be premature, for instance, to suppose that they should constitute a "world government" or a "world state." The words "state" and "government" carry too much unwanted baggage from the past. Why should an organization whose purpose and surrounding context would be so different from those of national governments repeat their structures? (The federal tradition is the most promising one perhaps, but no existing federation provides a model.) Nation-states, for example, have been in a condition of unceasing rivalry and conflict with one another and this condition has shaped basic elements of their anatomies. A global body politic, by contrast, would exist alone on earth—a circumstance that must have the profoundest consequences for its character, if only because of the blood-chilling possibility that, if it were endowed with anything like the powers to which existing states are accustomed, it might become repressive, leaving no corner of the earth free. There is a raw freedom in the plurality of states that the world should not surrender easily, or without the firmest confidence that a more civilized freedom can be defended and maintained.

In our new circumstances, the starting point of a world politics based in cooperative power would be not a blueprint for an ideal system of law but the reality that has already emerged on the ground. It is a reality for which there is as yet no adequate name. The word, when it appears, will refer to the power of action without violence, whether in revolution, the civil state, or the international order. I have followed convention in referring to this thing as nonviolence, but the word is highly imperfect for its purpose. "Nonviolence" is a word of negative construction, as if the most important thing that could be said about nonviolent action was that it was *not* something else. Yet that which it negates—violence—is already negative, a subtractor from life. A double negative, in mathematics, gives a positive result. And in fact the thing itself—nonviolence—is entirely positive, as Gandhi said. Yet in English there is no positive word for it. It's as if we were obliged to refer to action as "non-inaction," to hope as "non-hopelessness," or to faith as "non-unbelief." It was in search of a solution to this problem that Gandhi coined his untranslatable "satyagraha." Havel spoke, only somewhat less mysteriously, of "living in truth." Arendt sought to wrest the word "power" from its normal usage and turn it to this end. John Adams and Thomas Jefferson—who differed about many things—spoke of the power of citizens that flowed from the disposition of their hearts and minds, and recognized that such action was the foundation of all systems of political freedom. I have resorted in these pages to the plain phrase "cooperative power," as distinct from "coercive power."

The agenda of a program to build a cooperative world would be to choose and foster cooperative means at every level of political life. At the street level, this would mean choosing satyagraha over violent insurrection—the sit-down or general strike or "social work" over the suicide bombing or the attack on the local broadcasting station. At the level of the state it would mean choosing democracy over authoritarianism or totalitarianism (although some, such as Jefferson, Arendt, and Gandhi, have hoped for the invention of a political system that would provide more participation for citizens than representative democracy does); at the level of international affairs, it would mean choosing negotiation, treaties, and other agreements and institutions over war and, in general, choosing a cooperative, multilateral international system over an imperial one; at the level of biological survival, it would mean choosing nuclear disarmament over the balance of nuclear terror and proliferation. There is no reason to restrict the idea of cooperative power to individuals acting together. We can, to paraphrase Burke, just as well say, "freedom, when nations act in concert, is power." The choice at each level is never merely the rejection of violence; it is always at the same time the embrace of its cooperative equivalent.

Such a program of action, though lacking the explicit, technical coherence of a blueprint, would possess the inherent moral and practical coherence of any set of actions taken on the basis of common principles. History shows that violence incites more violence, without respect for national borders or the boundaries that supposedly divide foreign from domestic affairs. All forms of terror, from the suicide bombing in the pizza parlor to the torture in the basement to the globe-spanning balance of terror, foster one another. Nonviolence is likewise synergistic and contagious. For just as there is a logic of force, there is a logic of peace—a "cycle of nonviolence." Just as violent revolution creates the conditions for dictatorship, nonviolent revolution paves the way for democracy. Just as dictatorships incline toward war, democracies, if they can resist imperial temptations, incline toward peace with one another. Just as war is the natural environment for repression and dominance by the privileged few, peace is the natural environment for human rights and justice for the poor. Consider, for example, the ramifications of the peaceful rebellion against Soviet rule. It was met, as a violent revolution surely would not have been, with Gorbachev's nonviolent, reformist response, which led, however unintentionally, to the end of the Soviet regime, which in turn created the conditions for peace between the Cold War powers. And recall, by contrast, the outbreak of the First World War. It led to the rise of totalitarianism, which led to the Second World War, which led in turn to the advent of the Cold War and the species-threatening nuclear balance of terror. No one planned or could have foreseen these chains of consequences but they were as sure and real as anything anyone did plan.

A revolution against violence—loosely coordinated, multiform, flexible, based on common principles and a common goal rather than on a common blueprint—would encompass a multitude of specific plans, including ones for disarmament, conventional as well as nuclear; democratization and human rights; advancement of international law; reform of the United Nations; local and regional peacekeeping and peacemaking; and social and ecological programs that form the indispensable content of a program of nonviolent change. To neglect the last of these would be to neglect the lesson that campaigns of noncooperation are empty without constructive programs. Justice for the poor (victims of "structural violence") and rescue of the abused environment of the earth (victim of human violence done to other living creatures) are indispensable goals. They are already served by a rich new array of nongovernmental organizations and movements, constituting the beginnings of an international civil society. They range from local protest and rebellion by the poor against their exploitation, through movements of protest in rich countries against undemocratic and anti-environmental trade agreements, through nongovernmental organizations, and philanthropic organizations, both secular and religious, dedicated to human rights, the alleviation of poverty, and other causes, to former statesmen still eager to be of public service in the cause of peace (the former Soviet president Mikhail Gorbachev, the former American president Jimmy Carter, and the former president of Costa Rica, Oscar Arias, are notable examples).

Of equal or greater importance is the feminist revolution, itself a part of the much broader democratic revolution of modern times. The public world has hitherto been run by males, and it is clear that, whatever their virtues and vices, their way of doing things has reached an impasse. Experts can dispute whether the unmistakable male proclivity for war is innate or learned, the product of nature or nurture, but one thing we cannot doubt is that historically organized violence has been bound up with the male way of being human—with men's needs, men's desires, and men's interests. It is no less clear that historically the pursuits of women have been more peaceful. Could it be that nature in her wisdom created two genders in order to have a "second sex" in reserve, so to speak, for just such an emergency as the one we now face? There may be a less violent way of doing things that is rooted in female tradition and now will move to the fore, together with the gender that created it.

Peace begins, someone has said, when the hungry are fed. It is equally true that feeding the hungry begins when peace comes. Global warming cannot be stopped by B-52s any more than nuclear proliferation can; only cooperation in the form of binding treaties can accomplish either task. Peace, social justice, and defense of the environment are a cooperative triad to pit against the coercive, imperial triad of war, economic exploitation, and environmental degradation. Lovers of freedom, lovers of social justice, disarmers, peacekeepers, civil disobeyers, democrats, civil-rights activists, and defenders of the environment are legions in a single multiform cause, and they will gain strength by knowing it, taking encouragement from it, and, when appropriate and opportune, pooling their efforts.

Among the innumerable possible specific plans that such a program could entail, I have picked four to discuss here—not because they are in any way comprehensive, or even, in every case, necessarily the most important ones that can be imagined, but because they all bear directly on the choice between cooperation and coercion, and seem to me to be timely, realistic, and illustrative of the unity in diversity that a broad choice in favor of cooperation would manifest. They are a worldwide treaty to abolish nuclear arms and other weapons of mass destruction; a program of international intervention to ameliorate, contain, or end wars of self-determination on the basis of a reformed conception of national sovereignty; enforcement of a prohibition against crimes against humanity; and the foundation of a democratic league to lend support to democracy worldwide as an underpinning of peace and to restrain existing democracies from betraying their principles in their foreign policies.

A Decision to Exist

In Wilson's day, rejecting violence meant rejecting war—above all, world war. In our time, we must secure not only peace but survival. The menace of annihilation—of cities, of nations, of the species—arguably suppressed the menace of world war, and now we must suppress the menace of annihilation. A decision for non-violence, in our time, is a decision to exist.

An agreement to abolish nuclear arms and all other weapons of mass destruction is the sine qua non of any sane or workable international system in the twenty-first century. Any other attempted settlement of the issue of weapons of mass destruction will clash with other efforts to bring peace, with common sense, and with elementary decency. No tolerable policy can be founded upon the permanent institutionalization of a capacity and intention to kill millions of innocent people. No humane international order can depend upon a threat to extinguish humanity. Abolition alone provides a sound basis for the continued deepening and spread of liberal democracy, whose founding principles are violated and affronted by the maintenance of nuclear terror: "a democracy based on terror" is, in the long run, a contradiction in terms. And abolition alone can, by ending the nuclear double standard, stop proliferation and make effective the existing bans on other weapons of mass destruction. The logic of abolition is the real alternative to the logic of empire.

In practice, abolition means that the eight or nine nations that now possess nuclear weapons must join the hundred and eighty-two that have renounced them under the terms of the Nuclear Nonproliferation Treaty. (The four nations—Israel, India, Pakistan, and Cuba—that have declined to join the treaty must do so.) The signatories may also wish to convert the treaty into a Nuclear Weapons Convention, which would take its place alongside the existing conventions banning biological weapons and chemical weapons. At that point, the signatories might wish to merge these three conventions into one, banning all weapons of mass destruction, including any that might be invented in the future. The step would be logical and practical, inasmuch as the means of inspection and enforcement would overlap considerably and would gain strength through coordination.

But won't the abolition of nuclear weapons undo one of the very building blocks of peace that I have named? If the ever-present danger of nuclear annihilation has paralyzed great-power war, won't great-power war spring to life once nuclear weapons are removed from the picture? The answer to the question lies at the root of the nuclear predicament. It is a profound misunderstanding of the nuclear age to suppose that its basic features emanate from nuclear hardware. They do not. They emanate, as we have seen, from the knowledge that underlies the hardware. The number of nuclear warheads in the world can fall and the number of fingers on the nuclear button can decrease, even to zero, without subtracting a single digit from the physical equations on which the bomb is based.

It is the spread of this knowledge throughout the world that guarantees that the war system can never operate on a global basis as it did before. The persistence of the knowledge—the inherent capacity to rebuild nuclear arsenals, or to produce other weapons of mass destruction—will stand in the way. Let us imagine that nuclear weapons have been abolished by treaty, and that a nation then violates it by, secretly or openly, building a nuclear arsenal and threatening to use it to bully the world. As soon as the threat has been made, scores of other nations, all nuclear-capable, would be free to build and threaten to use their own nuclear arsenals in response, in effect deterring the violator. Not global hot war but a reflation of cold war would be the result. A crude system of mutual assured destruction would be reestablished, and wider war would be deterred, just as it is in our world of large nuclear arsenals. The important point, as always in matters of deterrence, is not that this would necessarily be done (although the scenario has a credibility that many existing ones lack) but that any government would know in advance that such a response was available, and would have every reason to desist from reckless schemes in the first place. The threat would not constitute nuclear deterrence in the classic sense of threatening instant nuclear retaliation; yet it would still be a kind of deterrence.

Abolition, when seen in this cold light, cannot mean a return to the pre-nuclear age, whether one might wish for such a development or not, nor can it rule out once and for all a resurgence of nuclear armaments in some future dark age, whose coming no one can preclude. It does, however, mean that a return to the global adapt-or-die war system is impossible. Abolition, in view of these circumstances, which as far as we know are unchangeable, would be nothing more—or less—than an indispensable though insufficient recognition by the human species of the terrible, mortal predicament it has got itself into, and a concrete expression of its resolve to find a solution. Abolition should not be undersold but it should not be oversold either.

There is thus more continuity between a policy of nuclear abolition and nuclear deterrence than at first meets the eye. It is as if we were saying, Let us take the deterrence theorists at their word that the goal of deterrence has been to prevent war. Unfortunately, we have to note an obvious fact: if you seek to avoid doing something by threatening to do that same thing, you have, at least to some extent, undermined your own purpose. So let us begin to move to a policy in which the "not using"—called by some "the tradition of nonuse"—gradually predominates, and the "threatening to use" fades away. Abolition then would fulfill the promise that deterrence now makes but cannot keep.

If this happened, the deterrence policy of the Cold War years might appear in history in a more favorable light than is now likely. It might then be seen as a system that in effect *extracted* the violence of the war system of the twentieth century, compacted it into a single world-destroying device, and *shelved* it—declaring to all: "If you want to use violence, then you must use *all* of it, so be wise and use none of it. And, just to make sure that you take us seriously, we are actually going to build and deploy tens of thousands of thermonuclear warheads and place them on rockets on hair-trigger alert." If followed by abolition, this act of extraction and consolidation would be revealed in retrospect as having been a halfway house to the full transformation of the war system into a peace system.

In this sequence, nuclear deterrence replaces the war system with a threat-of-annihilation system; abolition then replaces the threat-of-annihilation system with a peace system—or, at least, with the necessary foundation for a peace system. For abolition would not in itself constitute anything like a full peace system; it would only mark the world's commitment to creating one. The alternative is that Cold War deterrence will prove to have been the training ground for the full nuclearization of international affairs—that is, for nuclear anarchy.

Even after abolition, a critical decision remains to be made: whether or not to continue to rely as a matter of policy on nuclear rearmament in the event that the abolition treaty is violated. The nuts and bolts of any abolition agreement would be highly detailed arrangements for suppressing certain technologies—all, of course, inspected to the hilt. The agreement would specify exactly which nuclear-bomb materials are permitted, in what quantities, and where. There will assuredly be an enforcement provision in any such treaty, specifying what it is that the menaced nations of the world are entitled or obliged to do in the event of the treaty's violation. If nuclear rearmament is specified as a response, and technical arrangements suitable for it are provided, then, to an extent, the world would still be relying on nuclear terror to counter nuclear terror. Such provisions would embody what I have called "weaponless deterrence" and the scholar Michael Mazarr has called "virtual nuclear arsenals." If, on the other hand, the treaty bans nuclear arms absolutely, and forbids nuclear rearmament even in the face of its violation, whose remedy is to be sought by other means, then the world would formally and finally have renounced all dependence on nuclear terror for its safety.

The distinction between abolition, which is achievable, and a return to the pre-nuclear age, which is not, is necessary at the very least in order to understand and appreciate the radical difference between Wilsonism, which proposed to replace war with law, and abolition, which more modestly proposes merely to ratify the abolition of great-power war already imposed by the nuclear age, and to improve on this situation by retiring nuclear terror, which never can be utterly purged from human life, as deep into the background as is humanly possible. In practice, it may well be that if abolition of the hardware takes place, this will be such a momentous event morally, politically, and legally that, once some time has passed, and the world has gained confidence in its new arrangement, the deeper renunciation of nuclear terror will not be a difficult step. It would be deceptive, however, to suggest that a world without nuclear arms would be a world without danger, or even without nuclear danger. The risks, including the risk of nuclear rearmament, would be real. It is, rather, by comparison with the nuclear anarchy or the vain attempts at imperial domination that will otherwise probably be our future that the goal is attractive.

The dangers of abolition stem from potential violators of an abolition agreement. Two concerns have been uppermost—that the agreement could not be adequately inspected and that it could not be adequately enforced. I will confine myself here to a comment on each.

If historical experience is the test, possession of a nuclear monopoly (which a nation would have if it violated an abolition agreement) is much less valuable than nuclear theory predicts. At first glance, it appears that a country possessing a nuclear monopoly would possess an insuperable advantage over any adversary; nuclear-deterrence theory, which teaches that nuclear arsenals can be offset only by other nuclear arsenals, takes this for granted. The matter has already been put to the test several times in the history of the nuclear age, however, and in no case has possession of a nuclear monopoly translated into the foreseen military or political advantage—or, for that matter, into any detectable advantage at all. Nuclear powers have repeatedly fought, and even lost, conventional wars against small, nonnuclear forces, without being able to extract any benefit from their "ultimate" weapons. In the Suez crisis of 1956, nuclear-armed Britain, allied with France and Israel, failed to attain any of its aims against nonnuclear Egypt. France likewise found no utility in its nuclear monopoly in its war against the independence movement in Algeria. Neither did the Americans in Vietnam, or the Soviet Union in its war in Afghanistan, or Israel in its wars in Lebanon and in the West Bank, or China in the border war it fought and lost with Vietnam in 1979. If the only examples were the English, French, American, and Israeli ones, we might wonder whether democracies are constrained from using nuclear bombs by scruples absent in totalitarian regimes. The presence of the Soviet Union and China on the list, however, suggests that other factors are at work. (It's also worth recalling in this connection that the only country ever to use nuclear weapons was a democracy, the United States.)

The question of just why none of these powers used nuclear weapons in these losing wars is not easy to answer. Nevertheless, I would like to suggest a possible reason. Isn't it conceivable that heads of state are reluctant to use nuclear weapons simply because they don't want to kill millions of innocent people in cold blood at a single stroke? This "self-deterrence" may be a more powerful force than theorists have allowed. The moments in which the use of nuclear arms has in fact been seriously threatened have mostly been times when, as in the Cuban missile crisis, two nuclear-armed adversaries were in collision. One-sided threats of use—after the actual use on Hiroshima and Nagasaki—are conspicuous by their rarity. If these reflections have any foundation, then theory has libeled history, and the one clean secret of the nuclear age may be a hidden minimal sanity or humanity in the heads of state who have presided over nuclear arsenals.

However that may be, the relevance to the abolition question of this history is that if six powers, both democratic and totalitarian, in possession of nuclear monopolies, lost six conventional or guerrilla wars against small forces without nuclear arms, then we can hardly suppose that the entire family of nations, having recently staked its security on a nuclear abolition treaty, would stand helpless before a single miscreant regime that, having manufactured a concealed arsenal, stepped forward to give orders to the world. Since a prospective cheater would know that other nations would be fully capable of nuclear rearmament, violation of an abolition agreement could never be a rational plan. Indeed, a policy of one nation bellowing nuclear destruction to the whole world would be plain insanity. To this we can add that if it were done anyway, the world would possess more than adequate means to respond. It is unimaginable that a cowering world would knuckle under to the demands of the cheater. Far more likely, it would react with determination to quell the threat or, at the least, quickly reestablish a balance of terror.

The effectiveness of enforcement is linked to the effectiveness of verification. Verification would include the right of peremptory, unannounced inspection of all suspect facilities. One widely accepted conclusion among experts is that although the discovery of secret facilities for the construction of new nuclear arsenals, which are necessarily extensive, would be comparatively easy under a maximal regime of inspection, the discovery of caches of weapons hidden away before the agreement came into effect—of "bombs in the basement"—would be difficult. Some experts have even suggested that this problem is the fatal flaw in any plan of nuclear abolition. A nontechnical consideration, however, offers reassurance. Any nuclear arsenal, even a hidden one, must not only be maintained and guarded by a large cadre but also supervised by a military and political chain of command leading from the lowest technician up to the head of state. The United States' expenditure of four and a half billion dollars a year on "stockpile stewardship" shows that maintenance of a nuclear arsenal is highly complicated, requiring many hands and minds. There must also be delivery vehicles, plans for mating the warheads to the delivery vehicles, strategies, military and political, for using the weapons, and strategists to draw up the plans. Moreover, changes of regime, whether by violent or peaceful means, will multiply at a stroke the numbers of people privy to the secret. Many of those leaving office, often unwillingly, may be ill-disposed toward those replacing them and inclined to tell what they know; or else the newcomers may disagree with their predecessors' secret treaty violation and fear the wrath of the world. Few undertakings have ever been more secret than the Manhattan Project, yet some of its most highly classified information leaked in profusion to Stalin's spies.

In sum, it is in the nature of things that, over time, a growing body of people will share the secret of a hidden arsenal, and any one of them can reveal its existence to the world. With every year that passes, this body will grow. As in proliferation, the irresistible tendency of knowledge to spread shows itself—in this case to the advantage of disarmament. Time is the friend of inspection and thus of an abolition agreement. In the long run, the secret of a hidden arsenal would be as hard to keep as the secret of the bomb itself.

Like a nuclear monopoly, the bomb in the basement looks much more dangerous in theory than in the context of politics and history. In both circumstances, the natural repugnance that human beings have for nuclear weapons may have real-world consequences unforeseen in the denatured calculations of nuclear strategists—in the first case, inspiring among statesmen who wield monopolies an unexpected reluctance even to consider using their supposed advantage, in the second inspiring whistle-blowers to reveal activities that, under the terms of an abolition agreement, would be named and understood by all to be crimes against humanity.

All-or-Nothing Again?

Haven't I, though, simply reintroduced the fatal, all-or-nothing Wilsonian dilemma by insisting on the abolition of nuclear weapons rather than, say, their reduction to lower levels, or their reconfiguration in a more stable mode? Could it be that, by demanding abolition, we would be condemning ourselves to the same collapse of an overambitious plan that Wilson suffered? Admittedly, the proposal is ambitious. Yet nuclear abolitionism differs from Wilsonism in critical respects. The war system of Wilson's time was a workable and working machine, tightly integrated into the decision making of global politics, and so able to serve as the "pursuit of politics by other means." This cannot be said of the system of nuclear deterrence that supplanted it. After Nagasaki, no one has figured out how to gain political advantage from using, or even from possessing, nuclear weapons. The nuclear system is far more dangerous and far less useful than the war system was. As such, it should be much easier to clear out of the way.

Another difference is that nuclear arsenals, unlike the old war system, can be eliminated step by step. The first steps have in fact already been taken through arms control agreements. It is the unequivocal commitment to the goal, accompanied by unmistakable steps to achieve it, and not the rapidity of its achievement, that is most important. To be more precise, the period of implementation must be short enough to persuade potential nuclear proliferators that to build a new arsenal would be a worthless and dangerous expense, while being long enough to inspire confidence among the nuclear powers that inspection and enforcement are adequate.

Notwithstanding the absolutist ring of the word, abolition is not "all," even in the context of the nuclear predicament. Thanks to the indelible character of nuclear scientific know-how, the "all" in this matter, however ardently we might desire it, has been moved beyond our reach forever. All we can do in the circumstance is set ourselves against the evil day with the full force of our concerted political will.

It's in the context of a cooperative approach to nuclear nonproliferation that the logic of a cooperative approach to terrorism, nuclear or otherwise, is best understood. Like war, terrorism must now be divided into two categories. Just as we distinguish between conventional war and unconventional war (meaning war with weapons of mass destruction), so we must distinguish between conventional terrorism, using ordinary explosives, and unconventional terrorism, using weapons of mass destruction. Unconventional terrorism—the problem of the small group that wields immense destructive power because it has got hold of one of these weapons—can be addressed only by gaining control over the technology involved. After all, not even the most successful war on terrorism imaginable can reduce the population of terrorists to zero. The rigorous global inspection system of an abolition agreement would be the ideal instrument to choke at its source the danger that terrorists will acquire weapons of mass destruction. Even if such a system were in place, it must be admitted, the problem would not be completely solved. It might still be possible for a group to clandestinely create the needed technology. But the problem might be 98 percent solved, which is perhaps the most that can be hoped for. At each step along the path, the danger of diversion or construction of weapons of mass destruction would decline.

The hope of combating stateless global terrorism of the kind represented by the Al Qaeda network (which must be distinguished from the innumerable local varieties of terrorism around the world) likewise appears destined for disappointment without the creation of cooperative international structures involving the great majority of nations. A global threat requires a global response, and a global response will be possible only if governments work together rather than against one another. Historically, the greatest successes in reducing terrorism have been accomplished by a combination of police action and political attention to underlying causes. There is no reason to suppose that a global version of these largely national efforts would be different.

It is difficult to imagine the United States, acting alone or together with just a few nations, will be able to coerce or overthrow every regime that "supports" terrorism or, for that matter, defeat or destroy every proliferator of weapons of mass destruction. The cooperation of governments, not their antagonism, is the indispensable precondition for a successful policy of opposing and reducing global terrorism of any kind. A cooperative policy alone likewise avoids the danger, posed by the imperial approach, that hostile action, in the Middle East or elsewhere, will widen the pool of recruits for terrorist groups. At the same time, it is the likeliest basis for the political efforts that, over the long run, are the only lasting solution to terrorist threats.

Delaminating Sovereignty

Sovereignty, the conceptual crystallization of the all-or-nothing trap, is, as its first intellectual exegete Jean Bodin knew so well, a bundle of powers forced together under the pressure of military necessity or ambition. That was why at the birth of the concept of sovereignty its two inseparable defining principles were complete reliance upon the sword and indivisibility. That, too, was why, in the later, popular incarnations of sovereignty, the people, their territory, and the land had to be congruent, excluding all overlaps, mixed national populations, collective rights, or divided authorities. Yet long experience with popular government, in the United States and elsewhere, has revealed that when power is cooperative rather than coercive—based on action willingly concerted rather than compelled—then, in the domestic sphere, at least, it does not have to be indivisible. It can be federated; it can be divided among branches of government and localities; it can be delaminated.

It was not clear, on the other hand, whether such division could occur in the international sphere. Certainly, division was out of the question as long as the global adapt-or-die war machine subjected nations to its crushing pressure. However, now that that machine has been paralyzed and the pressure lifted, we can ask the question again. And in fact there are already signs of change. In regions in which coercive power, sovereign and indivisible, has yielded, structures of cooperative power, limited and divisible, have flourished. The most striking example is the European Union. Let us recall that sovereignty was first asserted in Europe by absolutist kings as a scythe to cut down the tangled thickets of medieval political institutions, with their dense, overlapping webs of ecclesiastical as well as secular rights, privileges, and duties. Although sovereignty is now defended as the guarantor of the plurality of states, originally it was diversity's enemy. It was the instrument of a radical simplification of politics, reducing the array of political actors to subjects on the one side and a sovereign on the other. The development of the European Union, however, shows that democratic states at peace with one another are now free to create a rich variety of hybrid arrangements, most of them unimaginable under the terms of the choice between a Wilsonian global constitution and the old war system. The E.U., as the former chancellor of Germany Helmut Schmidt has commented, "marks the first time in the history of mankind that nation-states that differ so much from each other nevertheless . . . have *voluntarily* decided to throw in their lot together." The result has not been a simplification of politics. The union's economic and political institutions, which inch forward year by year, are already characterized by a complexity not far from the medieval. They defy analysis on the basis of such simple, clear principles of the recent past as sovereignty, whether of the people, the state, or anyone else.

Formulas for shared or limited sovereignty are also a necessary part of any solution to most wars of national self-determination, in so many of which the requirement of one state for one people on one territory has proved to be a recipe for nightmare. The most ingenious and promising solution is the on-and-off Good Friday accord of 1998, which may one day lead to a resolution of the conflict in Northern Ireland. In the European Union, the absence of conflict made structures of divided power possible; in Ireland, divided structures of power are being used to try to end a conflict—a more difficult challenge.

The Irish conflict, although possessing many singular local and historical features, nevertheless arose out of a dilemma of a kind shared by many other wars of national self-determination. Two neighboring peoples (in this case, the Irish and the English) have a long history of conflict (in this case going back at least four centuries). Between them is a disputed territory, on which their peoples are intermixed. (Northern Ireland, which remained under British rule after Irish independence in 1922, contains a narrow Protestant majority dedicated to preserving the union with Britian and a large Catholic minority of "nationalists" eager to join the Irish Free State.) Similar elements can be found in lands as diverse as Sri Lanka, Kashmir, Crete, Rwanda, several of the former Soviet republics, almost all the former Yugoslavian nations, and Palestine.

The two communities in Northern Ireland appeal to common principles—the right of self-determination and majority rule. The problem is that each has drawn the boundaries of the "self" that is to be "determined" differently. The Protestant unionists draw a line that encompasses Great Britain, then crosses the Irish Sea and runs around the borders of Northern Ireland. Within that circle, which describes an existing institutional reality, the majority is British and Protestant. The Catholic nationalists wish to draw a line that simply circumscribes the Irish island (including, of course, Northern Ireland). Within that circle, representing the dream of a unified Ireland, the majority would be Irish and Catholic. The two circles overlap in Northern Ireland. If the first circle is accepted as "the nation," then majority rule for now dictates that Northern

Ireland will remain part of Great Britain; if the second circle is accepted, then Northern Ireland would join Ireland. The problem is the one that lies at the heart of the separation question: Which groups have the right to form themselves into a body politic, in which a vote of the majority binds the minority? This is the question to which liberal democratic thought, from the time of the American Revolution down to our day, has been unable to offer any answer. Indeed, two of its elementary principles, self-determination and majority rule, seem to be part of the problem. An answer can be found only by dividing the supposedly indivisible—by disaggregating the powers fused in national sovereignty. That is what the Good Friday accord does.

The immediate problem was the savage internecine warfare that broke out between nationalist and unionist extremists in Northern Ireland. The path to a solution could not be found in Northern Ireland alone. It lay, as John Hume, the leader of the nationalist Social Democratic and Labour Party, came to understand, also in London, Dublin, Brussels (home of the European Parliament), and even in Washington, where President Bill Clinton played a mediating role. First, the two outside state parties, the United Kingdom and the Irish Republic, had to surrender any claim to a right of sovereignty over Northern Ireland. The Irish Republic did so by amending its constitution, which had claimed sovereignty over the whole island. Great Britain, to which Northern Ireland now belonged, renounced any "selfish, economic" interest in the territory. That is, if Northern Ireland itself wanted to leave the United Kingdom, Great Britain would let it.

The remaining question was how, if the two outside claimants were ready to surrender their claim, the future national status of Northern Ireland was to be determined. The accord's answer was "the principle of consent": the people of Northern Ireland would decide their own future by democratic procedures. In the language of the accord, "It is hereby declared that Northern Ireland in its entirety remains part of the United Kingdom," unless, "voting in a poll," it decides to "form part of a united Ireland."

These provisions ended the tug-of-war between the United Kingdom and the Republic of Ireland for control over Northern Ireland but left intact the tug-of-war—the sanguinary terrorist conflict—between extremists in the two local communities, each longing for union with a different country. The Protestants, still in the majority (though a dwindling one, as the Catholic population is growing faster than the Protestant), would opt for continued union with the United Kingdom, and also might continue to use their majority power to abuse and repress the Catholic minority. Inasmuch as such repression had been a primary cause of the conflict in the first place, it could hardly be taken lightly.

The accord addressed that problem with several further provisions, among them a plan to include a due proportion of nationalists in the Northern Ireland police force and a plan for political power sharing between the two communities. One important feature of the latter was an agreement to apportion ministers of the government of Northern Ireland in accord with party strength in the assembly, rather than adopting a winner-take-all arrangement. This provision was a dramatic grant of exactly the sort of collective minority rights that classical liberal democratic theory was unable to approve. It ordained something that has always been a bête noire of classical liberalism—"concurrent majorities," in which overlapping communities each vote separately for their representatives, who then must share power. In the first government under the accord, half of the ministries went to the minority nationalists.

Still another provision established a North/South Ministerial Council to make decisions on matters of mutual concern, such as agriculture, inland waterways, trade, and tourism. Created by legislation passed both in the British Parliament and in the Irish Republic's Oireachtas, the council includes the Irish Taoiseach and First Minister of Northern Ireland as well as other ministers, and is to arrive at decisions "by agreement of the two sides." A Council of the Isles was also created to deal with matters involving all of Ireland and Britain.

The parties to the Good Friday accord did not set out to dismantle sovereignty, yet that is what the accord does. We will look in vain in this agreement for power that can be called sovereign. The people of Northern Ireland remain citizens of the United Kingdom, yet they have been granted a constitutional right that the citizens of few, if any, other nation-states enjoy—the right to remove themselves and their land and goods to another country upon a majority vote. (It is a right that the Muslims of Kashmir, the Tamils of Sri Lanka, and the Tibetans in China, to give three of many possible examples, would love to acquire.) They have a clear *right* to remain British but no *obligation* to do so. Such a right is, indeed, perhaps the most elementary collective right a people can possess, the right of self-determination, which is the essence of national sovereignty. And yet in Northern Ireland this right, which is in truth a power, is obviously conditioned and limited. It was created by decisions in the United Kingdom, and can be suspended by the United Kingdom, which can restore direct rule over Northern Ireland, as it has done several times in the past three decades. (However, if the people of Northern Ireland once were to exercise their right to join the Irish Republic, England's power to suspend the government would be at an end.) And although it permits the people of Ulster to define themselves politically by a vote, their options are limited. They are not permitted, for example, to establish themselves as an independent state.

As for the Irish Republic, it explicitly renounced its demand for sovereignty over Northern Ireland, yet thereby gained, through the Ministerial Council, more actual influence over the North than ever before. This arrangement has left traditional notions of sovereignty in the dust, clearing the path, as the peoples involved may decide, for all kinds of incremental, mixed institutions and arrangements for shared power that would be far richer and more nuanced than the bare choice between union with Great Britain and union with the Irish Republic. All the while, the Irish Republic can expect a day when Northern Ireland may of its own volition switch allegiance from the United Kingdom to Ireland by a mere majority vote.

At the same time that the United Kingdom was entering into this agreement, it was devolving new powers upon Scotland and Wales, in the most radical constitutional reforms in Britain of the twentieth century. When we consider that both innovations were occurring within the context of the steadily evolving constitutional arrangements of the European Union, we arrive at a picture of fundamental political transformation at every level of European politics, and grasp that national sovereignty is now in the process of giving way to new forms in the very Europe in which the concept was born.

The influence of the Good Friday accord, if it succeeds, may extend far beyond Europe. It would be the first peaceful settlement since the end of the Cold War of a war of national self-determination—the first squaring of the circle. The Irish protagonists admittedly enjoy advantages that the parties in other wars of national self-determination lack. Probably the most important is that all the governments involved—the Irish Republic's, the British, and Northern Ireland's—operate according to democratic principles. Alternatives to the gun—elections, parliamentary debates, free discussion—have always been available for use and have been used. For example, a gradual shift of the Irish Republican Army from violent struggle to electoral struggle has been one of the keys to progress brought by the agreement. In addition, the two governments in the dispute were willing to renounce their claims in favor of a decision by the people of the territory.

Such a combination of advantages is unavailable in almost any of the world's other many wars of national self-determination, in most of which either one or both of the warring parties is authoritarian or is unyielding in its territorial claim. (For example, India, though a democracy, has never been willing to let the people of Kashmir decide their future in a vote.) Nor would a success in Ireland have much value as a model in the lands of failed states, where the problems are more likely to be extreme poverty, lack of civil institutions, and underdevelopment than to be the excessive, murderous strength of political factions. There are parts of the world where neither violent nor nonviolent solutions offer ready answers, where patience is the better part of wisdom, and amelioration of the worst evils, such as famines, or merely heading off further catastrophic deterioration of a situation, may be the best that outside intervention can provide for the calculable future.

Nevertheless, the value of a successful Good Friday accord as a precedent for resolving wars of self-determination could be real, and the idea of delaminating sovereignty has already been proposed as a component of the settlement of other conflicts. In Sri Lanka, any solution to the conflict between the Tamil Tigers, who have been seeking an independent state in the north of the island, and the government that represents the Sinhalese majority will undoubtedly require some kind of power sharing. Some analysts have proposed that if the Israelis and the Palestinians ever return to a peace process, they may want to provide for dual sovereignty over the holy sites of Jerusalem, where not only national populations but religious buildings of high symbolic importance to several faiths are under contention. The Wailing Wall forms one side of a hill on which the Temple, the Jews' most holy site, once stood but on which the Al Aksa mosque, Islam's second-most holy site, now stands. One might suspect that a mischievous God, by permitting this interpenetration of holy objects, had decided to create, in the medium of architecture, a tangible symbol of the riddle of wars of national self-determination. The question He thus put before us was: How, when you cannot physically separate peoples (or their sacred buildings), can you organize the political world so that each people can be true to its deepest beliefs while living in peace with others? The tangible quandary of the holy sites poses an intangible riddle, which, in the words of the Israeli writer Avishai Margolit, is "How does one divide a symbol?" Precisely because a clash of faiths is involved in Jerusalem, which is a holy land for three religions, a settlement there one day would transcend the Good Friday accord in symbolic meaning.

Delaminating Self-Determination

The possibility of addressing wars of self-determination by delaminating sovereignty could open wider horizons of international reform. The scholar of international law Gidon Gottlieb, for example, has outlined a provocative legal program of surgery upon sovereignty. It would be foolish, he recognizes, to suppose that theoretical breakthroughs can solve real conflicts with long histories. "How 'relevant' are mere ideas and concepts," Gottlieb asks, "when much blood has been shed and where enemies are locked in mortal combat? . . . The setting for peacemaking in ethnic wars is both grim and discouraging. Political efforts are invariably situated in the context of long and complex local histories of strife, of grievances, and of crimes well remembered. Layers upon layers of promises ignored, broken pledges, and treaties violated form the usual background to new promises, new pledges, and new treaties offered."

Yet new ideas have a role to play when they are based on new realities in the situations in question. Gottlieb proposes that the two basic components of sovereignty, the nation and the state, might in some circumstances be separated. The problem of mixed populations, he has suggested, might be easier to solve if the international community created, alongside states but separate from them, a juridical status for nations. The individual person would then have available two internationally recognized statuses—one as a citizen of a state, the other as a member of a nation. In this "deconstruction" of sovereignty, the old unity of state, people, and territory would be dissolved. Each of the two statuses would confer rights and privileges but not the same ones. State rights, for instance, might include all the classical rights of individual liberty, while national rights might include such collective rights as the right to speak one's own language, to control local schools, or to practice one's faith. Special passports to travel between the states that are hosts to one nation might be granted. One nation then could overlap many states, and vice versa.

Among other examples, Gottlieb cites the dilemma of the Kurdish people, now living under the sovereignty of Turkey, Iraq, Iran, and Syria, in all of which they are more or less embattled. The classic solution to the dilemma, establishment of a sovereign Kurdish state according to the traditional rules of self-determination, would solve the problem for the Kurds but at the certain cost of bloody upheaval in four states and the possible creation of the reverse problem of repression of Turks, Iraqis, Iranians, and Syrians within newly drawn Kurdish borders. Instead of heading down this road, something that seems exceedingly unlikely to happen in any case, Gottlieb proposes conferring his formal national status upon the Kurds, guaranteeing them certain cultural and other rights and privileges within the framework of each of the four states. He proposes similar solutions for the struggles of national self-determination in Cyprus, in Canada (over the status of Quebec), and in Armenia and Azerbaijan (over the contested Nagorno-Karabak and Nakhichevan enclaves).

Delaminating sovereignty entails delaminating self-determination, at least as this has traditionally been conceived. Self-determination, one might say, must yield to self-*determinations* and *selves*-determination—that is, to permission for more than one nation to find expression within the border of a single state and to permission for individuals and groups to claim multiple identities—for example, Kurdish and Turkish. As the story of American independence demonstrates, the connection between the concepts of sovereignty and self-determination, otherwise called independence, has been close. Reasoning about the nature of sovereignty compelled the colonists to conclude that the choice they faced belonged in the all-or-nothing category—either full independence or full subordination to Britain. It could not be otherwise in an age when sovereignty was regarded as the prime attribute of a body politic.

Yet even during the age of the colonial empires, some of the best minds cast sidelong glances at middle courses between empire and independence. We have already mentioned the plan that called for replacement of the British Empire by "an association of states endowed with British liberties, and owing allegiance directly to the sovereign head." Similar in character was the "Galloway plan," for a "colonial union under British Authority which included a legislative council made up of representatives from the colonial assemblies and a president general to be appointed by the king." For such plans to have succeeded, either the empire would have had to transform itself into a body based on consent, which is to say into a true federation, or the colony would have had to bow to force. Burke, one of the few Englishmen of his time ready to apply English principles of liberty and consent to the empire as a whole, was also one of the first to glimpse the full difficulty of the task, even in purely intellectual terms. "There is not a more difficult subject for the understanding of men," he commented in words that have held true down to this day, "than to govern a large Empire upon a plan of Freedom."

The difficult subject would arise many more times in the history of modern empires. The French-Algerian crisis of the 1960s inspired the novelist and thinker Albert Camus to tackle another incarnation of it. France had settled a large colony of its citizens—the *pieds-noirs*—in Algeria, whose native population began, in the 1950s, to agitate for independence. Camus, himself a *pied-noir,* devised a confederal plan, in which the fundamental character of the French state would change to incorporate Algeria. An Algerian regional assembly representing Algerian citizens and dealing with Algerian problems would be established under a unicameral federal Senate, which would preside over a Commonwealth consisting of France and Algeria, and elect a confederal government. It would mean, Camus explained, the end of the single nation-state born in 1789, and "the birth of a French federal structure" that would create a "true French Commonwealth." Camus understood, as Burke did, what a profound reconception of the state, called *une et indivisible* in the French Declaration of the Rights of Man and the Citizen, would be entailed in such a plan for a multi-national state. "Contrary above all to the deep-rooted prejudices of the French Revolution, we should thus have sanctioned within the Republic two equal but distinct categories of citizens," Camus wrote. "From one point of view, this would mark a sort of revolution against the regime of centralization and abstract individualism resulting from 1789, which, in so many ways, now deserves to be called the *Ancien Régime*." Of particular note in our context is Camus's hope that the new structure might show the way for "the European institutions of the future."

As Jeffrey C. Isaac, a scholar of Camus and of Hannah Arendt, has pointed out, Arendt had been prompted to think along similar lines in the late 1940s in regard to the establishment of Israel. The problem, once again, was two nations—Palestinian and Jewish—on one soil. She, too, believed that the only peaceful solution to dilemmas of this kind was a confederal one. The alternative was imposition of Israeli rule on Arabs and Arab territory by force. "The 'victorious' Jews," she wrote, "would live surrounded by an entirely Arab population, secluded inside ever-threatened borders, absorbed with physical defense to a degree that would submerge all other interests and activities." The accuracy of this prediction does not mean that Arendt's solutions were feasible. (The fact that one solution fails doesn't mean the alternative would have worked.)

What is certain is that the hour of the consensual multinational state had no more come in the Middle East in the late 1940s than it had come in England in the 1770s or France in the 1960s. Indivisible national sovereignty remained the rule, and force remained its guiding principle. Not until our day has that hopeful hour perhaps arrived for one or two regions of the world.

Enforcement

In a program whose overall object is to wean politics from its reliance on force, the question of *enforcement* is obviously vexatious. It's clear, however, that if the international community should ever embark on such a program, enforcement will be a necessary element. The question is what its scope, provenance, and limitations should be. At one extreme is the American imperial plan, which is almost all enforcement—the unilateral right of a single power to attack and overthrow other governments at will. At the other extreme is no enforcement. Somewhere in between is a vision of an international community that fundamentally relies on consent and the cooperative power consent creates, but nevertheless reserves the right to resort to force in certain well-defined, limited circumstances. A nuclear-abolition agreement, for example, would require enforcement in the event of a violation, as would a coordinated international effort to combat global terrorism. Ideally, force would play the restricted policing role it does in a democratic state. I say "ideally," because if an international police force is to be legitimate there must exist an international order whose legitimacy is generally recognized, and this is just what is largely missing in the world today.

In these circumstances—which not even the implementation of every proposal in this book would fundamentally alter, since they do not envision a world state, legitimate or otherwise—there could hardly be a police force acting in the name of such a body to enforce its laws. Yet, as we tackle this question, the advantage of our circumstances over Wilson's are again evident. Because of the war system's demise, we are not in any way required to establish an overwhelming international military force that could impose its will on all miscreants. For excellent reasons, this idea no longer even crosses most people's minds; the only plan remotely like it is the current fantasy of hegemony that tempts American policy makers. And so we are free in the area of enforcement, too, to proceed incrementally. To whatever extent the international community decides to exist—and no further—it can seek to enforce a few selected internationally agreed-upon principles. Such an approach, it is true, would not end war at one stroke, as the League of Nations was supposed to do, but it would close the all-too-familiar demoralizing gap between grandiose rhetoric and trifling deeds—a perennial consequence of the bad faith of good intentions that was the curse of attempts at international peacemaking in the twentieth century.

The immediate need is for a principle defining a task that is achievable, or may soon be achievable, by the international community. One such principle has already been identified: the obligation to prevent and punish crimes against humanity. The concept of crimes against humanity first gained currency at the trials at Nuremberg in 1945, in which the victors of the Second World War held Nazi leaders accountable for the atrocities of their regime. Recently, it has been applied again in legal proceedings in special international tribunals against the former president of Yugoslavia Slobodan Milosevic and against the perpetrators of genocide against the Tutsis in Rwanda. The newly constituted International Criminal Court (I.C.C.), making use of the language of the Nuremberg Charter, has defined crimes against humanity as acts, including murder, torture, rape, forced disappearance, and persecution, when committed "as part of a widespread or systematic attack directed against any civilian population . . ." The key distinction therefore is between abuses of individuals, which are not crimes against humanity per se, and abuses that occur as part of an assault against a defined group, whether ethnic, religious, racial, or national.

The most historically important of the crimes against humanity—specifically outlawed by the Convention on the Prevention and Punishment of the Crime of Genocide, of 1948—is genocide, which may be roughly defined as an assault upon the life of one of the earth's peoples. There has been debate over whether the definition should include only ethnic, national, and racial groups or social classes and political groups, too. If the more expansive definition is accepted, then the definition of genocide will be hard to distinguish from the I.C.C.'s definition of crimes against humanity, and the two concepts would merge.

Why groups, however? Why should the international community concern itself especially with collectivities rather than individuals as such? An obvious pragmatic reason is that if the international community accepted responsibility for enforcing individual human rights, it would in effect have to constitute itself as a world state. The justifications for collective international intervention would be unlimited, since there is no country on earth in which some human-rights abuses do not occur. There is also a legal reason. All positive law is the law of a community. Whereas each national community is a community of individuals, the international community has, so far, been mainly a community of states, whose sovereignty has been guaranteed by international law (including the U.N. Charter). It therefore makes sense that international law would be especially concerned with states and peoples. When one person kills another, the order of the national community is violated. When a state kills a people, the order of the international community is violated.

Laws mandating international action to set aside sovereignty in the name of stopping crimes against humanity would revise this understanding without throwing it out. The *state* would still be recognized as the prime international actor, but it would no longer necessarily be recognized in every case as the *nation's* legitimate representative. The international community (although not any single power) would assert a sharply limited and exceptional right to judge the fitness of a state to represent its people. Such a recognition would form a natural complement to the revisions of sovereignty needed to settle the wars of national self-determination. In most cases the claims of states, even of repressive states, to represent a nation would be recognized. But when a state perpetrated crimes against humanity upon its own population, it would forfeit its claim to represent them and open itself to international intervention. The right of states to rule in their own territories would cease to be absolute; rather, it would be like a license, valid in almost all circumstances but revocable in limited and extreme cases, to be defined by stringent and well-known principles.

In this shift, the rights of states would not be eliminated in favor of the rights of individuals, thereby opening the floodgates of unlimited intervention; rather, the rights of states would partially yield to the rights of nations—that is, of peoples—whose right of self-determination would remain untouched, and might at times be supported by intervention from without. When Slobodan Milosevic sought to forestall intervention against his genocidal campaign in Kosovo, he invoked sovereignty. In response, the international community could only argue circuitously that his crimes within his own borders were a "threat to peace." A simpler and stronger answer would have been, "In what sense can you call yourself the sovereign representative of a people that you are seeking to destroy? Your genocide nullifies your sovereignty."

Stopping crimes against humanity would be a new vocation for the international community, which has generally looked the other way when such crimes have occurred. Not until very recent times has the concept of collective rights made headway. An enforced prohibition of genocide, based on the conviction that the international community can no more tolerate the murder of one of its peoples than national communities can tolerate the murder of a person, would meet this welcome trend coming the other way. It would be a sheet anchor for the collective rights of peoples. (It is obvious, however, that enforcement even of this limited principle faces large obstacles. It is one thing, for example, to bring the former leader of a small, weak state, such as Serbia, to book for his crimes. It would be quite another to do the same to the leader of a large powerful state, such as Russia or the United States.)

Once established, collective rights might, over the long run, take their place as elements of a grand bargain, a new settlement of the rights, powers, and obligations of the individual, states, nations, and the international community. In such a settlement, the rights of peoples would be increasingly protected by a coherent body of law. Most important, peoples would possess the negative right not to be extinguished. They would possess in addition the positive right to self-determination. This right, while recognized in law, would be guaranteed chiefly by each people's own powers of resistance—powers whose effectiveness were put on such stunning display in the anti-imperial independence movements of the twentieth century—and only secondarily by limited collective assistance from the international community. The right would be understood as belonging, in the last analysis, to nations rather than to their governments. On the other hand, even when thus properly located, it would not be absolute—not be, that is, sovereign.

A commitment to stop crimes against humanity is a natural corollary to a program that demands nuclear abolition, fosters democracy, and delaminates sovereignty. The required shift in principle would look beyond states to peoples, in whom the roots of political legitimacy would be acknowledged. The principle would also apply to the nuclear threat, whereby not only every people but the human species as a whole has been placed at risk of extinction. The doctrine of deterrence, which "assures" the safety of one people from nuclear attack at the hands of another by menacing both with annihilation, is—described without hyperbole—a policy of retaliatory genocide. Adoption of this policy was the destination to which the great powers, once they had failed to agree on the abolition of nuclear weapons in 1946, were to a certain extent helplessly driven by the logic of the war system in which they were entangled. Nevertheless, it is inescapable that carrying out genocide in the event of nuclear attack is the heart of the policy. One of the deepest and most important consequences of a prohibition of genocide would be a prohibition of the policy of nuclear deterrence.

A Democratic League

Even as the main structures of coercive power are gradually being retired from use, structures of cooperative power must gradually be built up. One of these would be the foundation of a democratic league, designed to foster and build upon the peaceful proclivities already found in the core of the democratic process. It is true that the power of democratic states to promote democracy outside their own borders is, by the nature of democracy, limited. States cannot create democracies; only peoples can, through their actions and consent. (On the other hand, states are perfectly capable of creating dictatorships, which rule by force over unconsenting peoples.) Nevertheless, democratic states can give assistance to one another or to peoples already seeking to found or preserve democracy. Such assistance would be strengthened by the foundation of an alliance made up of the democratic countries of the world.

The idea first appears in history in the fourth century B.C., when the Athenian statesman Arata, facing a threat to Greece from Philip of Macedon, who was making common cause with autocratic Greek city-states, founded an alliance of the democratic city-states. Whereas Arata's ultimate objective was to win a war, the purpose today would be to preserve and strengthen democracy where it exists, to give it support where it is struggling to come into existence, and, most important, to jointly curb and correct the warlike and imperial tendencies that historically have accompanied the rise of this form of government and forestalled its potential contributions to peace. Such was precisely the purpose of Kant's proposal of a "peaceful union" of republics, which would "gradually spread further and further by a series of alliances."

The main alliances in which the democracies now are involved present an anomalous picture. They are founded on every possible principle but democracy itself. The Clinton administration participated in the establishment of a Community of Democracies devoted to some of these purposes, but, though it now counts 110 nations among its members, it has yet to become a major forum for foreign policy decisions or international policy. NATO is an alliance made up entirely of democracies, but its purpose is strictly military. The central obligation of the treaty—to come to the defense of any member who is attacked—depends in no way on the character of the regimes involved. In the absence of the Soviet Union, whose advance into the center of Europe at the end of the Second World War prompted the alliance's creation, the need even for this pledge of mutual assistance is unclear. The only war in NATO's history—the campaign to drive Serbian forces out of Kosovo—did not involve an attack on a member.

The European Union is another alliance made up of democracies. (It was not until 2001 that the Organization of American States adopted a "democratic charter.") Founded originally to foreclose a military danger—recurrence of war among the nations of Europe—it has evolved over the decades into an organization in which economic concerns predominate. Recently, the European nations have been asking themselves what political and military functions the union might also assume. Although the union has led to many remarkable and hopeful political innovations, including the European Parliament, the European Commission, and the European Court of Human Rights, its boldest initiatives, culminating in the launch of the euro, have so far been commercial. In consequence, when the time came for the West to embrace the newborn democracies in Eastern Europe in the wake of the Soviet collapse, the chief consideration was not the strength of their commitment to democracy but the weakness of their economies. Blocked by this economic hurdle from "joining Europe"—a phrase often used in the broad sense of joining the now-democratic system of the West through joining the E.U.—Poland, Hungary, and the Czech Republic took the easier step of joining NATO. Had a democratic league existed at the time, it would have provided all the Eastern European countries with a way to "join Europe" that was appropriate to the new situation (the end of Soviet rule and the foundation of democracy); that was possible (no economic hurdle would have stood in the way); and that was inoffensive to Russia. Not until 2002 was the decision to invite these countries into the E.U. finally made. A democratic league would also serve to bind the Atlantic community by a tie that really should continue to bind it; namely, a commitment to freedom. The military glue that binds NATO is weakening in the absence of an enemy; and the economic glue of the E.U., although strong, tends in many areas to divide the Europeans from other democracies in the world. A democratic league, on the other hand, would possess a clear, positive, common purpose that NATO lacks—adherence, irrespective of wealth or geographic boundaries, to democracy.

The qualifications for joining the league would of course be observance of exacting standards of democratic governance and human rights. No state that failed to meet the standards could join; any state that departed from them would be subject to sanctions or expulsion. The league's requirements would give expression to the strong interest that every democratic country has in the preservation of democracy elsewhere in the world. The democratic character of all the states involved would also make supranational institutions among them far easier to establish than they are at the United Nations, where dictatorships have equal voice with democracies in votes on human rights. Juridical and legislative institutions of restricted scope could be added to executive ones. The European Convention on Human Rights, which established the European Court of Human Rights, and gives that court jurisdiction over human-rights violations within member states, could be a model—as could the European Parliament, whose members are directly elected, giving limited expression to an all-European public opinion.

The simplest and most obvious direct contribution that such a league could make to international peace would be to pledge to resolve disputes among its members without recourse to war, thus formalizing the historically demonstrated inclination of democracies to remain at peace among themselves. A vow by democratic Finland not to attack democratic India and vice versa would perhaps not be the end of history, yet the creation of a large body of nations in all parts of the earth that, both formally and actually, had renounced war in their mutual relations would provide a powerful example and, over time, perhaps a direction for the world as a whole.

Natural corollaries would be a commitment by the league to support the elimination of weapons of mass destruction, to steadily reduce the sale of conventional arms to other countries, and to devote its resources to restraining or ending wars of self-determination wherever it could.

Far more important and difficult would be a commitment to checking the aggressive tendencies that, in modern as in ancient times, have constituted the brutal, exploitive side of many democracies' relations with the rest of the world. The most serious and lasting contribution of a democratic league would be to choose democracy over imperialism once and for all. In order to be worthy of the name, a democratic league must be an anti-imperial league. Member nations would jointly resolve not to create or support repressive regimes, not to use armed force merely to advance commercial or other national interests, and in general to address international problems on a cooperative basis. A democratic league that sought to keep the peace among its own members even as it fostered aggressive ambitions in the world would destroy its own purpose.

Merely to state such goals, however, is once again to throw into distressing relief the policies of the one democracy in the world that today threatens to make the fearful transition from republic to empire, the United States. It is hard to know which is the greater tragedy—that, as the twenty-first century begins, the United States approaches the world with a drawn imperial sword, or that it discredits and disables its rich and in many ways unique republican traditions, which, especially in their treatment of sovereignty, offer many useful starting points for the new forms of international cooperation, peacemaking, and peacekeeping that the world so badly needs.

The Unconquerable World

Fifty-eight years after Hiroshima, the world has to decide whether to continue on the path of cataclysmic violence charted in the twentieth century and now resumed in the twenty-first or whether to embark on a new, cooperative political path. It is a decision composed of innumerable smaller decisions guided by a common theme, which is weaning politics off violence. Some of the needful decisions are already clear; others will present themselves along the way. The steps just outlined are among the most obvious.

I have chosen them not merely because their enactment would be desirable. They represent an attempt to respond to the perils and dangers of this era as it really is, by building on foundations that already exist. For even as nuclear arms and the other weapons of mass destruction have already produced the bankruptcy of violence in its own house, political events both earthshaking and minute have revealed the existence of a force that can substitute for violence throughout the political realm. The cooperative power of nonviolent action is new, yet its roots go deep into history, and it is now tightly woven, as I hope I have shown in these pages, into the life of the world. It has already altered basic realities that everyone must work with, including the nature of sovereignty, force, and political power. In the century ahead it can be our bulwark and shield against the still unmastered peril of total violence.

In our age of sustained democratic revolution, the power that governments inspire through fear remains under constant challenge by the power that flows from people's freedom to act in behalf of their interests and beliefs. Whether one calls this power cooperative power or something else, it has, with the steady widening and deepening of the democratic spirit, over and over bent great powers to its will. Its point of origin is the heart and mind of each ordinary person. It can flare up suddenly and mightily but gutter out with equal speed, unless it is channeled and controlled by acts of restraint. It is generated by social work as well as political activity. In the absence of popular participation, it simply disappears. Its chief instrument is direct action, both noncooperative and constructive, but it is also the wellspring of the people's will in democratic nations. It is not an all-purpose "means" with which any "end" can be pursued. It cannot be "projected," for its strength declines in proportion to its distance from its source; it is a local plant, rooted in home soil. It is therefore mighty on the defensive, feeble on the offensive, and toxic to territorial empires, all of which, in our time, have died. It stands in the way of any future imperial scheme, American or other. This power can be spiritual in inspiration but doesn't have to be. Its watchwords are love and freedom, yet it is not just an ideal but a real force in the world. In revolution it is decisive. Allied with violence, it may accomplish immense things but then overthrow itself; tempered by restraint it can burn indefinitely, like a lamp whose wick is trimmed, with a steady flame. Under the name of the will of the people it has dissolved the foundations first of monarchy and aristocracy and then of totalitarianism; as opinion, it has stood in judgment over democratically elected governments; as rebellious hearts and minds, it has broken the strength of powers engaged in a superannuated imperialism; as love of country, it has fueled the universally successful movement for self-determination but, gone awry, has fueled ethnic and national war and totalitarian rule, which soon suffocate it, though only temporarily. It now must be brought to bear on the choice between survival and annihilation. It is powerful because it sets people in motion, and fixes before their eyes what they are ready to live and die for. It is dangerous for the same reason. Whether combined with violence, as in people's war, sustained by a constitution, as in democracy, or standing alone, as in satyagraha or living in truth, it is becoming the final arbiter of the public affairs of our time and the political bedrock of our unconquerable world.

Notes

"cannot be considered to": Clausewitz, *On War*, p. 90.

19 *"Rain can prevent a":* Ibid., p. 120.

"a force appeared that": Ibid., p. 591.

"slowly, like a faint": Ibid., p. 589.

20 *"tendency toward the extreme":* Ibid., p. 589.

"the great democratic revolution": Alexis de Tocqueville, *Democracy in America*, ed. and trans. Henry Reeve (New York: Schocken Books, 1961), p. lxviii.

"one fact [of] the": José Ortega y Gasset, *The Revolt of the Masses* (New York: W. W. Norton, 1932), p. 11.

21 *"The various occurrences of":* Tocqueville, *Democracy in America*, p. lxxi.

"From this moment on": Simon Schama, *Citizens* (New York: Knopf, 1989), p. 762.

22 *"War, untrammeled by":* Clausewitz, *On War*, p. 592.

Clausewitz has often been: For example, the British military historian B. H. Liddell Hart charged in 1931 that Clausewitz "had proclaimed the sovereign virtues of the will to conquer, the unique value of the offensive school carried out with unlimited violence by a nation in arms and the power of military action to override everything."

23 *"It is, of course":* Clausewitz, *On War*, p. 605.

24 *"Is war not just":* Ibid., p. 605.

"all proportion between": Ibid., p. 585.

"Were [war] a complete": Ibid., p. 87.

"the terrible battle-sword": Ibid., p. 606.

26 *"The natural solution soon":* Ibid., p. 604.

"no conflict need arise": Ibid., p. 607.

29 *"The Great Powers were":* A. J. P. Taylor, *The Struggle for the Mastery of Europe* (New York: Oxford University Press, 1954), p. xxiv.

30 *"She [Russia] was beaten":* Bruce D. Porter, *War and the Rise of the State* (New York: Free Press, 1994), p. 227.

32 *Charles Tilly, "War made":* Ibid., p. xix.

"must increase in size": Ibid., p. 59.

"The benefits of [scientific]": Francis Bacon, *Novum Organum* (New York: Modern Library, 1930), p. 85.

33   *On the bridge of:* Lewis Mumford, *The Pentagon of Power* (New York: Harcourt, Brace, Jovanovich, 1964), p. 119.

Tocqueville's word, "irresistible": Tocqueville's claim that the democratic revolution is "the most permanent tendency to be found in history" closely parallels Bacon's claim that scientific findings benefit "the whole race of men . . . through all time." When Tocqueville called the democratic revolution a "providential" fact, he was not making a theological point. He was reaching for the strongest possible metaphor to express the inexorability of the social phenomena he wished to describe. (His advice was that since you couldn't stop democracy, the wisest course was to guide and direct it as well as you could.)

34   *Brissot, who proclaimed:* Albert Mathiez, *The French Revolution* (New York: Knopf, 1928), p. 285.

"Tacticians could never": Jules Michelet, *The French Revolution,* trans. Charles Cooks (Chicago: University of Chicago Press, 1967), p. 328.

35   *"had no place for":* E. J. Hobsbawm, *Nations and Nationalism since 1780* (Cambridge: Cambridge University Press, 1990), p. 26.

36   *"I see in the":* Richard Cobden, *The Liberal Tradition,* eds. Alan Bullock and Maurice Shock (New York: Oxford University Press, 1956), p. 53.

Emerson declared that "trade": Liah Greenfeld, *Nationalism* (Cambridge, Mass.: Harvard University Press, 1992), p. 448.

37   *Between 1870 and 1900:* Walter La Feber, *The American Search for Opportunity 1865–1913* (Cambridge: Cambridge University Press, 1993), p. 85.

As late as 1890: Ronald Robinson and John Gallagher, *Africa and the Victorians* (New York: Anchor, 1968), p. 78.

38   *Lord Curzon spoke for:* Kenneth Rose, *Superior Person* (New York: Weybright & Talley, 1969), p. 229.

Lord Haldane, describing his: Barbara Tuchman, *The Guns of August* (New York: Dell, 1963), p. 72.

39   *An expedition of:* David Levering Lewis, *The Race to Fashoda* (New York: Weidenfeld & Nicolson, 1987), p. 3.

40   *Queen Victoria, ordinarily:* Thomas Pakenham, *The Scramble for Africa* (New York: Avon, 1991), p. 552.

France, lacking comparable naval: Ibid., p. 549.

41 *In a state paper:* George F. Kennan, *The Fateful Alliance* (New York: Pantheon, 1984), p. 268.
Therefore, once war had: Ibid., p. 264.
War against "all neighbors": Ibid., p. 265.

42 *The Russian foreign minister:* Ibid., p. 105.
And when General: Ibid., p. 95.
The war that now: Ibid., p. 253.

43 *"The war's political objects":* John Keegan, *A History of Warfare* (New York: Knopf, 1993), p. 21.
"of forgetting that force": Kennan, *Fateful Alliance,* p. 254.

45 *"Through a blur of":* J. B. S. Haldane, as quoted in Freeman Dyson, *Weapons and Hope* (New York: Harper & Row, 1984), p. 122.

2. "NUCLEAR WAR"

47 *As early as 1952:* McGeorge Bundy, *Danger and Survival* (New York: Random House, 1988), p. 235.
At the height of: Michael Beschloss, *The Crisis Years* (New York: HarperCollins, 1991), p. 87.

51 *He wrote, "Thus far":* Jonathan Schell, *The Abolition* (New York: Knopf, 1984), p. 42.

52 *"The decision by arms":* Carl von Clausewitz, *On War,* eds. Michael Howard and Peter Paret (Princeton, N.J.: Princeton University Press, 1976), p. 97.

53 *"The essence of the":* Lawrence Freedman, *The Evolution of Nuclear Strategy* (London: Macmillan, 1981), pp. 397–99.

54 *stated, "We will not":* Aleksandr Fursenko and Timothy Naftali, *One Hell of a Gamble* (New York: W. W. Norton, 1997), p. 246.
In 1960, for example: Beschloss, *Crisis Years,* p. 65.

55 *In August of 1961:* Fursenko and Naftali, *Hell of a Gamble,* p. 138.
On one occasion: Beschloss, *Crisis Years,* p. 244.
In a speech delivered: Ibid., p. 330.

56 *He was led to:* Ibid., p. 523.

57 *Acheson counseled that:* Bundy, *Danger and Survival,* p. 375.
"The most ardent and": Ibid., p. 376.

58 *But, Kennedy explained:* Ibid., p. 452.

59 *We may suspect that:* Beschloss, *Crisis Years,* p. 446.

60 *When the Soviet ambassador:* Ibid., p. 547.

61 *McNamara answered, "I am":* Bundy, *Danger and Survival,* p. 448.

3. PEOPLE'S WAR

66 *Their philosophy in the:* John A. Hobson, *Imperialism* (Ann Arbor: University of Michigan Press, Ann Arbor Paperbacks, 1971), p. 123.
Or, as Kipling: Richard Koebner and Helmut Dan Schmidt, *Imperialism* (Cambridge and London: Cambridge University Press, 1964), p. 216.

69 *The rebellion blazed most:* J. Christopher Herold, *The Age of Napoleon* (Boston: Houghton Mifflin, 1963), p. 217.
"No supreme command had": Ibid., p. 218.
"Clearly, the tremendous": Carl von Clausewitz, *On War,* eds. Michael Howard and Peter Paret (Princeton, N.J.: Princeton University Press, 1976), p. 609.

70 *"The military art on":* Ibid., p. 610.
"It follows that the": Ibid.

71 *The renowned military writer:* Walter Laqueur, *Guerrilla* (New York: Little, Brown, 1976), p. 109.
The experience left Jomini: Ibid., p. 109.
"All action is undertaken": Clausewitz, *On War,* p. 97.
Yet a French captain: Robert B. Asprey, *War in the Shadows* (New York: William Morrow, 1994), p. 97.

72 *"a book of wisdom":* Ibid., p. 87.
The Spanish guerrilla leader: Laqueur, *Guerrilla,* p. 40.
And a Prussian officer: Ibid., p. 40.
The superior importance: Harry B. Summers, *On Strategy* (San Francisco, Calif.: Presidio Press, 1982), p. 89.

73 *"the days of guerrilla wars":* Laqueur, *Guerrilla,* p. 98.

74 *"in no other period":* Leonard Woolf, *Imperialism and Civilization* (New York: Garland Publishing, 1971), p. 12.

76 *"Suddenly the whole black":* Winston Churchill, *The River War* (London: New English Library, 1973), pp. 249–50.
"about twenty shells": Ibid., p. 263.
"The range was short": Ibid., p. 268.

77 *"They fired steadily and":* Ibid., p. 264.

When it was over: Karl de Schweinitz, Jr., *The Rise and Fall of British India* (London: Methuen, 1983), p. 242.

"extraordinary miscalculation of": Churchill, *The River War*, p. 264.

"For I hope": Winston S. Churchill, *The River War: An Historical Account of the Reconquest of Soudan* (London: Longmans, Green & Co., 1899), p. 162.

78   *In the battle of:* C. E. Carrington, *The British Overseas* (Cambridge: Cambridge University Press, 1968), p. 319.

     At the battle: Ibid., p. 165.

     In 1865, in Tashkent: V. G. Kiernan, *From Conquest to Collapse* (New York: Pantheon, 1982), p. 63.

     "a Royal Niger Co.": Daniel R. Headrick, *The Tools of Empire* (Oxford: Oxford University Press, 1981), p. 8.

     "The remnant simply turned": Kiernan, *Conquest to Collapse*, p. 71.

79   *"We are still":* Mao Zedong, *Selected Works*, 2 vols. (London: Lawrence & Wishart, 1954), 2: 168.

     "a powerful imperialist country": Ibid., 2: 167.

80   *Mao never tired of:* Asprey, *War in the Shadows*, p. 255.

     And the most famous: Ibid.

82   *"the more enduring the":* Mao, *Selected Works*, 2: 177.

     "the whole party must": Ibid., 2: 270.

     "It can therefore": Ibid., 2: 20.

83   *"China's weapons are":* Ibid., 2: 159.

84   *Mao rejected the idea:* Asprey, *War in the Shadows*, p. 254.

86   *"Politics forms the":* quoted in Jonathan Schell, *The Real War* (New York: Pantheon, 1988), p. 16.

     "Our political struggle": quoted in Douglas Pike, *Viet Cong* (Cambridge, Mass.: M.I.T. Press, 1966), p. 106.

87   *"The purpose of this":* Pike, *Viet Cong*, p. 111.

     "in the effective control": Bernard Fall, *The Two Vietnams* (New York: Praeger, 1967), p. 133.

     "the existence of guerrilla": Ibid.

88   *"the 'kill' aspect":* Bernard Fall, *Last Reflections on a War* (New York: Doubleday, 1967), p. 210.

"This is where": Ibid., p. 221.

89   *De Gaulle remarked that:* Laqueur, *Guerrilla,* p. 294.

90   *In the words of:* Neil Sheehan, *A Bright and Shining Lie* (New York: Random House, 1988), p. 631.

91   *"Their missile power":* quoted in Lawrence Freedman, *The Evolution of Nuclear Strategy* (London: Macmillan, 1981), p. 230.

92   *It would lead to:* A. J. Langguth, *Our Vietnam* (New York: Simon & Schuster, 2000), p. 371.

96   *When Richard Nixon:* Ibid., p. 514.

   After Tet, in the: Schell, *The Real War,* p. 30.

4. Satyagraha

104   *They believed, with Max:* Gene Sharp, *Gandhi as a Political Strategist* (Boston: Porter-Sargeant Publishers, Extending Horizons Books, 1979), p. 240.

   "force without right": John Locke, *The Second Treatise on Government* (New York: Macmillan, 1952), p. 13.

   "in all states and": Ibid., p. 88.

   "becomes a case of": Edmund Burke, *Reflections on the Revolution in France* (New York: Anchor, 1973), p. 42.

   At the beginning of: J. Christopher Herold, *The Age of Napoleon* (Boston: Houghton Mifflin, 1963), p. 37.

   "Violence is the midwife": Karl Marx, *Capital* (New York: Modern Library, 1959), p. 824.

105   *The leader of the:* Merle Fainsod, *How Russia Is Ruled* (Cambridge, Mass.: Harvard University Press, 1963), p. 135.

   In a still broader: Adam Ulam, *The Bolsheviks* (New York: Macmillan, 1992), p. 455.

   Lenin sneered at: Martin Green, *The Challenge of the Mahatmas* (New York: Basic Books, 1978), p. 85.

   And Max Weber: Bruce D. Porter, *War and the Rise of the State* (New York: Free Press, 1994), p. 303.

   "All greatness, all power": quoted in Isaiah Berlin, *The Crooked Timber of Humanity* (New York: Knopf, 1991), p. 117.

107   *On a train from:* Stanley Wolpert, *Gandhi's Passion* (New York: Oxford University Press, 2001), p. 35.

His colleagues at dinner: Mohandas K. Gandhi, *Essential Writings,* ed. V. V. Ramana Murti (New Delhi: Gandhi Peace Foundation, 1970), p. 39.

108   *"I arose with the":* quoted in Joan Bondurant, *The Conquest of Violence* (Princeton, N.J.: Princeton University Press, 1958), p. 155.

109   *"I clearly saw that":* Mohandas K. Gandhi, *The Selected Works of Mahatma Gandhi,* ed. Shriman Narayan, 6 vols. (Ahmedabad, India: Navajivan Publishing House, 1968), 3: 135.

In 1858, Queen Victoria: Mohandas K. Gandhi, *The Moral and Political Writings of Mahatma Gandhi,* ed. Raghavan Iyer, 3 vols. (Oxford: Clarendon Press, 1986–87), 3: 278.

"The Empire has been": Mohandas Karamchand Gandhi, *The Collected Works of Mahatma Gandhi,* 100 vols. (New Delhi: Publications Division, Ministry of Information and Broadcasting. Government of India, 1999), 4: 302. The edition of the Collected Works cited here may also be found on the CD "Mahatma Gandhi" produced by the Publications Division, Patiala House, Tilak Marg, New Delhi.

110   *"By her large heart":* Ibid., 4: 293.

"We are all fired": Ibid., 2: 325.

an "empty boast": Gandhi, *Moral and Political Writings,* 1: 291.

He denounced "the invention": Ibid., 1: 288.

111   *"The English honor only":* Gandhi, *Collected Works,* 5: 384.

112   *"No one ever imagined":* Ibid., 4: 312.

"When Japan's brave": Ibid., 8: 405.

"unity, patriotism and": Ibid., 4: 313.

"overwhelmed" by it: Gandhi, *Essential Writings,* p. 55.

"to conquer that hatred": Gandhi, *Collected Works,* 2: 433.

113   *"fearless girls, actuated":* Ibid., 5: 327.

"This time they have": Ibid., 5: 8.

114   *"could not live both":* Ibid., 44: 326.

"How was one to": Ibid., 44: 287.

115   *"Like Arjun, they":* Ibid.

Of his pursuit of: Judith M. Brown, *Gandhi* (New Haven: Yale University Press, 1989), p. 83.

"For God appears": Erik H. Erikson, *Dimensions of a New Identity* (New York: Norton, 1974), p. 44.

116 *As he began a:* Sharp, *Gandhi as a Political Strategist,* p. 49.

118 *"would spell absolute ruin":* Gandhi, *Selected Works,* 3: 135.
"I could read in": Ibid., 3: 140.
"a man who lightly": Ibid., 3: 144.

119 *"that some new principle":* Gandhi, *Collected Works,* 1: xi.
"The foundation of the": Gandhi, *Essential Writings,* p. 440.

120 *"dictate to the colonies":* quoted in Gandhi, *Collected Works,* 4: 208.
"I have now got": Gandhi, *Collected Works,* 10: 184.

121 *The nineteenth-century British:* J. F. C. Fuller, *Military History of the Western World,* 3 vols. (New York: Da Capo Press, 1955), 2: 240.
Chen Duxiu, a moderate: Jonathan Spence, *The Search for Modern China* (New York: W. W. Norton, 1990), p. 315.

122 *"different sections of ONE":* Gandhi, *Collected Works,* 4: 313.
"This civilization is": Gandhi, *Moral and Political Writings,* 1: 214.

123 *"The condition of England":* Ibid., 1: 209.
"bad men [to] fulfil": Ibid., 1: 220.
"neither real honesty nor": Ibid., 1: 211.
was "a prostitute": Gandhi, *Collected Works,* 10: 256.
"nine-days' wonder": Ibid., 10: 58.
"The tendency of the": Gandhi, *Moral and Political Writings,* 1: 233.
"It is . . . fitting that": Vivekananda, *The Yogas and Other Works,* ed. Swami Nikhilananda (New York: Ramakrishna-Vivekananda Center, 1953), p. 698.

124 *"My countrymen . . . believe":* Gandhi, *Essential Writings,* p. 440.
In the words of: Erik H. Erikson, *Gandhi's Truth* (New York: W. W. Norton, 1969), p. 265.

125 *"East and West are":* Gandhi, *Collected Works,* 8: 211.
"Suppose Indians wish": Gandhi, *Essential Writings,* p. 8.
"The Whites were fully": Ibid., p. 49.

126 *"You [British] have great":* Mahatma Gandhi, *Hind Swaraj and Other Writings,* ed. Anthony Parel (Cambridge: Cambridge University Press, 1997), p. 114.

127   *"They came to our"*: Gandhi, *Collected Works,* 10: 256.
      "It is because the": Gandhi, *Essential Writings,* p. 179.

128   *For instance, the:* Peter Duvall Ackerman, *A Force More Power-ful* (New York: St. Martin's Press, 2000), p. 11.
      "The sultan of Egypt": quoted in Maurizio Passerin d'Entreves, *The Notion of the State* (Oxford: Clarendon Press, 1967), p. 196.
      "All governments rest": James Madison, Alexander Hamilton, and John Jay, *The Federalist Papers,* No. 49 (London: Penguin Classics, 1987), p. 314.

129   *"I believe and everybody"*: quoted in Sharp, *Gandhi as a Political Strategist,* p. 11.
      "The causes that gave": Gandhi, *Moral and Political Writings,* 1: 216.
      it was "by the": Philip Curtin, *Imperialism* (New York: Harper & Row, 1971), p. 293.

130   *"it is an intensely"*: Gandhi, *Essential Writings,* p. 99.
      "It is better to": quoted in Bondurant, *Conquest of Violence,* p. 28.
      "I am not built": Raghavan Iyer, *The Moral and Political Thought of Mahatma Gandhi* (New York: Oxford University Press, 1973), p. 10.
      "Never has anything": Mohandas K. Gandhi, *Non-violent Resistance* (New York: Schocken, 1951), p. 110.
      "There is no love": quoted in Ved Mehta, *Gandhi and His Disciples* (New York: Viking Press, 1976), p. 183.

131   *"Another remedy [to injustice]"*: Gandhi, *Essential Writings,* p. 99.
      "A new order of": quoted in Erikson, *Gandhi's Truth,* p. 338.

132   *"Nonviolence is without"*: Gandhi, *Essential Writings,* p. 136.
      "The practice of ahimsa*"*: Ibid., p. 137.

133   *"To be incapable of"*: Friedrich Nietzsche, *On the Genealogy of Morals,* trans. Walter Kaufmann and R. J. Hollinsdale (New York: Vintage, 1967), p. 39.

134   *That, at least, was:* Martin Green, *The Origins of Nonviolence* (State College, Penn.: Pennsylvania State University Press, 1976), p. 35.
      "Through deliverance of India": Gandhi, *Essential Writings,* p. 226.

135   *"A series of passive"*: quoted in Wolpert, *Gandhi's Passion,* p. 96.

"the search for a": Brown, *Gandhi,* p. 121.

"I can as well": quoted in Brown, *Gandhi,* p. 122.

136   *"the greatest battle of":* quoted in Wolpert, *Gandhi's Passion,* p. 99.

"In the place I": quoted in Brown, *Gandhi,* p. 132.

"All of us should": quoted in Wolpert, *Gandhi's Passion,* p. 114.

137   *In a campaign of:* Wolpert, *Gandhi's Passion,* p. 151.

On the other hand: Brown, *Gandhi,* p. 359.

139   *"Satyagraha is not":* quoted in Bondurant, *Conquest of Violence,* p. v.

"To me," the reader: Gandhi, *Essential Writings,* p. 259.

140   *"Constructive effort is the":* Ibid.

"One must forget the": Ibid., p. 274.

"Where do congratulations come": quoted in Green, *Challenge of the Mahatma,* p. 29.

141   *"exact proportion" to success:* Iyer, *Moral and Political Writings,* 1: 306.

"When a body of": Gandhi, *Essential Writings,* p. 33.

"English rule without": Gandhi, *Hind Swaraj,* p. 205.

England as "pitiable": Ibid., p. 237.

"Not only could swaraj": quoted in Brown, *Gandhi,* p. 67.

"Do men conceive": Gandhi, *Essential Writings,* p. 254.

5. NONVIOLENT REVOLUTION, NONVIOLENT RULE

144   *"If one thousand":* Henry David Thoreau, *The Annotated Walden; Or Life in the Woods,* ed. Philip Van Dorenstern (New York: Clarkson N. Potter, 1970), p. 465.

146   *"It was true that":* Thomas Babington Macaulay, *The History of England* (London: Penguin Classics, 1986), p. 272.

"That prompt obedience": Ibid.

"The material strength of": Thomas Babington Macaulay, *The History of England,* 2 vols. (New York: Dutton, 1966), 2: 267.

Unfortunately for James: Ibid., 2: 263.

147   *"That great force":* Ibid., 2: 384.

"No encounter of the": George Macaulay Trevelyan, *The English Revolution, 1688–89* (New York: Oxford University Press, 1938), p. 117.

"William of Orange": J. G. A. Pocock, "The Revolution of 1688–89: Changing Perspectives," in *The Varieties of British Political Thought*, ed. Lois G. Showerer (Cambridge: Cambridge University Press, 1993), p. 55.

148 *"The King . . . had greatly"*: Macaulay, *History of England*, 1: 578.

149 *"Sir, if your Majesty"*: Ibid., 1: 126.
"The minister who had": Ibid., 1: 209.
"Actuated by these": Ibid., 1: 238.

150 *"His only chance of"*: Ibid., 2: 284.

151 *"No jurist, no divine"*: Ibid., 2: 319.
"For call himself what": Ibid., 2: 320.

152 *"To him she was"*: Ibid., 2: 16.
"power enough to bring": Stephen B. Baxter, *William III, and the Defense of European Liberty* (New York: Harcourt, Brace, 1966), p. 234.

153 *"The Revolution gave"*: Trevelyan, *The English Revolution*, p. 240.

154 *"There is no way"*: Pocock, "The Revolution of 1688–89," p. 61.
"For twenty years": quoted in Trevelyan, *The English Revolution*, p. 105.
"What happened was": Trevelyan, *The English Revolution*, p. 106.

155 *"In 1689, both"*: Pocock, "The Revolution of 1688–89," p. 202.
As the conservative Burke: Ibid.
"Never, within the memory": Macaulay, *History of England*, p. 279.

156 *"The appeal to heaven"*: Pocock, "The Revolution of 1688–89," p. 61.
George Washington hinted at: Page Smith, *A New Age Now Begins*, 2 vols. (New York: McGraw Hill, 1976), 2: 1,664.

157 *"We may be beaten"*: quoted in ibid., 2: 1,826.

158 *" 'Tis not in numbers"*: quoted in John Keane, *Tom Paine* (Boston: Little, Brown, 1995), p. 121.
"In the unlikely": Ibid., p. 146.
"Rulers can rule": Ibid., p. 121.
As the British general: Conor Cruise O'Brien, *The Great Melody* (Chicago: University of Chicago Press, 1992), p. 155.

"If nothing but force": quoted in ibid., p. 159.

159   "Do you imagine": Edmund Burke, Selected Writings (New York: Random House, 1960), p. 175.

160   "confine himself to military": John Adams, The Works of John Adams, vol. 10 (Boston: Little, Brown, 1956), p. 85.
      "A history of the": Ibid., p. 180.
      "General Wilkinson may": Ibid.
      "As to the history": Ibid., p. 172.

161   "The cool, calm": Ibid., p. 197.
      "It will be": Ibid., p. 253.
      "the real American revolution": Ibid., p. 283.
      "What an engine!": Ibid., p. 197.

162   "Let me ask you": Ibid., p. 159.
      "The royal governors stood": Gordon S. Wood, The Creation of the American Republic (New York: W. W. Norton, 1972), p. 314.
      "For if, as Jefferson": Ibid., p. 132.

163   "The Union is much": quoted in Mario M. Cuomo, Lincoln on Democracy (New York: HarperCollins, 1990), p. 204.
      "Heaven decided in our": Adams, Works, p. 159.

6. The Mass Minority in Action: France and Russia

165   "French soldiers are not": quoted in Simon Schama, Citizens (New York: Vintage, 1990), p. 371.
      The King's cavalry: Ibid., p. 380.
      "The bastille was not": Jules Michelet, The French Revolution (Chicago: University of Chicago Press, 1967), p. 176.

166   "Shame for such cowardly": Ibid., p. 177.
      "Good is grapeshot": Thomas Carlyle, The French Revolution (New York: Oxford University Press, 1989), p. 179.
      "The French revolution": quoted in Carl Becker, The Declaration of Independence (New York: Vintage, 1942), p. 30.

169   When it was suggested: Richard Pipes, The Russian Revolution (New York: Vintage, 1991), p. 472.
      "In times of revolution": quoted in ibid., p. 358.

170   "No matter how important": quoted in Isaac Deutscher, The Prophet Armed (New York: Oxford University Press, 1954), p. 156.

"a sort of fabulous": N. N. Sukhanov, *The Russian Revolution, 1917* (New York: Oxford University Press, 1955), p. 74.

"A whole world of": quoted in Pipes, *Russian Revolution*, p. 336.

171 *"the decisive revolutionary"*: Martin Malia, *The Soviet Tragedy* (New York: Free Press, 1994), p. 90.

172 *"After the February"*: Leon Trotsky, *The History of the Russian Revolution* (Ann Arbor, Mich.: University of Michigan Press, 1957), p. 131.

"We can (if we": quoted in Pipes, *Russian Revolution*, p. 472.

173 *The Bolsheviks had "no"*: Trotsky, *Russian Revolution*, p. 154.

The Party, they observed: Ibid., p. 159.

"eliminate the mass": quoted in Deutscher, *The Prophet Armed*, p. 334.

174 *So important did Trotsky:* Pipes, *Russian Revolution*, p. 479.

"full support in all": Ibid., p. 487.

"On October 21": Sukhanov, *Russian Revolution*, p. 583.

175 *"War had been declared"*: Ibid., p. 592.

"three hundred volunteers": Ibid., p. 589.

"This, to put it": Ibid., p. 592.

176 *"He, Trotsky," would:* Ibid., p. 596.

"declaration of October 23": Trotsky, *Russian Revolution*, p. 118.

"We don't know of": Sukhanov, *Russian Revolution*, p. 627.

"The unique thing about": Trotsky, *Russian Revolution*, pp. 181–82.

177 *"This does not mean"*: Ibid., p. 181.

"Only an armed": Ibid., p. 87.

178 *"The final act of"*: Ibid., p. 232.

In despair at what: Pipes, *Russian Revolution*, p. 490.

179 *"And now we are"*: quoted in Sukhanov, *Russian Revolution*, p. 639.

180 *"had been their own"*: Sukhanov, *Russian Revolution*, p. 529.

181 *"lavish with promises"*: Ibid.

"The October revolution": quoted in Trotsky, *Russian Revolution*, p. 232.

"At the end of": Trotsky, *Russian Revolution*, p. 294.

"As a matter of": Ibid., p. 232.

The Social Revolutionary Party: Pipes, *Russian Revolution,* p. 543.

184 *"the least bloody revolution":* quoted in Joachim Fest, *Hitler* (New York: Harcourt, Brace & Jovanovich, 1973), p. 447.

7. LIVING IN TRUTH

187 *"A wall is a":* quoted in Michael Beschloss, *The Crisis Years* (New York: HarperCollins, 1991), p. 278.

"Never will we consent": Adam B. Ulam, *The Communists* (New York: Scribners, 1992), p. 309.

188 *"There was a special":* Nadezhda Mandelstam, *Hope Against Hope* (New York: Athenaeum, 1970), p. 48.

"The terrifying thing": quoted in Jeffrey C. Isaac, *Arendt, Camus, and Modern Rebellion* (New Haven, Conn.: Yale University Press, 1992), p. 43.

190 *"hotbed out of which":* George Kennan, *Memoirs* (New York: Pantheon, 1967), p. 534.

"Successful revolts on": Ibid., p. 533.

191 *"To believe in":* Adam Michnik, *Letters from Prison* (Berkeley: University of California Press, 1985), p. 142.

192 *"the Soviet military":* Ibid., p. 14.

"It is impossible to": George Konrád, *Anti-Politics* (New York: Harcourt Brace Jovanovich, 1984), p. 70.

"The morality of Yalta": Ibid., p. 2.

"In the stalemated world": Václav Havel, *Living in Truth,* ed. Jan Vladislav (London: Faber & Faber, 1986), p. 37.

193 *"If we consider how":* Ibid., p. 111.

"Defending the aims": Ibid., p. 89.

194 *"Society is produced by":* Thomas Paine, *Common Sense* (New York: Peter Eckler, 1998), p. 1.

"I believe that what": Michnik, *Letters from Prison,* p. 144.

195 *"Why post-totalitarian?":* Adam Michnik, *Letters from Freedom* (Berkeley: University of California Press, 1998), p. 59.

196 *"We introduced a new":* Václav Havel, *Disturbing the Peace* (New York: Knopf, 1990), p. 83.

Havel says, "individuals": Timothy Garton Ash, *The Uses of Adversity* (New York: Random House, 1989), p. 192.

"Individuals can be": Havel, *Living in Truth*, p. 57.

197 *"it must be declared"*: Mohandas K. Gandhi, *Essential Writings*, ed. V. V. Ramana Murti (New Delhi: Gandhi Peace Foundation, 1970), p. 225.

"People who so define": Havel, *Living in Truth*, p. 76.

"Under the orderly": Ibid., p. 57.

198 *In his scheme*: Konrád, *Anti-Politics*, p. 73.

"iceberg of power": Ibid., p. 145.

"Proletarian revolution didn't": Ibid., p. 73.

199 *"We were scared"*: quoted in Ulam, *The Communists*, p. 104.

"Everything suddenly appears": Havel, *Living in Truth*, p. 59.

200 *The step beyond that*: Ash, *Uses of Adversity*, p. 195.

202 *"The struggle for state"*: Michnik, *Letters from Prison*, p. 89.

"People who claim": Ibid., p. 86.

203 *"Before the violence"*: Ibid., p. 87.

"My reflections on violence": Ibid., p. 106.

"a profound belief that": Havel, *Living in Truth*, p. 93.

"The political leadership": Konrád, *Anti-Politics*, p. 91.

205 *"which would be different"*: Gandhi, *Essential Writings*, p. 49.

206 *"The world rests upon"*: Mohandas K. Gandhi, *The Selected Works of Mahatma Gandhi*, ed. Shriman Narayan, 6 vols. (Ahmedabad, India: Navajivan Publishing House, 1968), 2: 389.

"At the basis of": Havel, *Living in Truth*, pp. 137–38.

209 *"By the mid-1980s"*: Mikhail Gorbachev, *Memoirs* (New York: Doubleday, 1996), p. 349.

211 *"Necessity of the principle"*: quoted in Archie Brown, *The Gorbachev Factor* (New York: Oxford University Press, 1996), p. 225.

213 *He declared, "Today"*: John Morrison, *Boris Yeltsin, from Bolshevik to Democrat* (New York: Dutton, 1991), p. 222.

214 *"It was clear"*: quoted in ibid., p. 143.

8. Cooperative Power

216 *"nauseating and humiliating"*: Martin Green, *Challenge of the Mahatmas* (New York: Basic Books, 1978), p. 122.

Upon hearing of the: Ibid.

218 *"violence and power are"*: Hannah Arendt, *Violence* (New York: Harcourt Brace Jovanovic), p. 56.

"Power and violence are": Ibid.

"the rule of men": quoted in ibid., p. 35.

"Power corresponds to": Ibid., p. 44.

"solemnly and mutually": Ibid., p. 172.

219 *"Democracy does not"*: Alexis de Tocqueville, *Democracy in America* (New York: Schocken, 1961), p. 295.

220 *"Where power is not"*: Hannah Arendt, *The Human Condition* (Chicago: University of Chicago Press, 1958), p. 200.

"To command and": Hannah Arendt, *On Violence* (New York: Harvest, 1970), p. 37.

"Power means every": Max Weber.

221 *"never the property of"*: Arendt, *On Violence*, p. 44.

"In a head-on": Ibid., p. 37.

"While violence can": Arendt, *The Human Condition*, p. 202.

"Nowhere is the": Arendt, *On Violence*, pp. 54–55.

222 *"The climax of terror"*: Ibid., p. 55.

"the head-on clash": Ibid., p. 53.

"general "reversal in the": Ibid., p. 11.

223 *"the situation changes"*: Ibid., pp. 48–49.

"Power is actualized": Arendt, *The Human Condition*, p. 200.

224 *"Gandhi's enormously powerful"*: Arendt, *On Violence*, p. 53.

"Popular revolt against": Arendt, *The Human Condition*, p. 200.

225 *"taken as the spring"*: Arendt, *On Revolution*, p. 89.

"Only in His strength": Mohandas Karamchand Gandhi, *Non-violent Resistance*, ed. Bharatan Kumarappa (New York: Schocken, 1951), p. 364.

226 *"One is obtained by"*: Raghavan N. Iyer, *The Moral and Political Thought of Mahatma Gandhi* (New York: Oxford University Press, 1986), p. 53.

228 *"What has made so"*: Alexis de Tocqueville, *The Old Regime and the French Revolution* (New York: Anchor, 1969), p. 168.

"If God who is": quoted in Judith M. Brown, *Gandhi* (New Haven, Conn.: Yale University Press, 1989), p. 199.

"love and not fear": quoted in Gordon S. Wood, *The Creation of the American Republic* (New York: W. W. Norton, 1972), p. 67.

"love of the laws": Montesquieu, *The Spirit of the Laws* (Berkeley and Los Angeles: University of California Press, 1977), p. 130.

229   *"Men love at their"*: Niccolò Machiavelli, *The Prince* (New York: Random House, Modern Library, 1950), p. 63.

"What is meant": John Stuart Mill, "Considerations on Representative Government," in *Utilitarianism*, ed. H. B. Acton (London: J. M. Dent & Sons, 1972), pp. 196–97.

230   *"a more powerful social"*: Ibid., p. 197.

Power, according to: A more recent exposition of the power of opinion is the concept of "soft power," introduced by Joseph Nye, Dean of the Kennedy School of Government at Harvard. According to Nye, a nation's soft power, which he distinguishes from its "hard power" (which corresponds to coercive power), is the attractive pull of its best qualities—its culture, its ideology, its prosperity. "This aspect of power—getting others to want what you want—I call soft power," he writes. "It co-opts people rather than coerces them" (from Joseph Nye, *The Paradox of American Power* [New York: Oxford, 2002], p. 9). A difference between soft power and cooperative power is that whereas the first is generated by a single actor (whether a saint or a country) and belongs to that actor, the second, being a product of action in concert, in its nature can belong only to a group. However, the two are related. Cooperation depends on agreement, and agreement depends on the discovery of common ground. For example, the admiration that one country inspires in another—or that both feel for a common goal or principle—is the sine qua non of common ground. Thus does the "soft power" that countries exert upon one another lay a basis for action in concert, which is the foundation of cooperative power. It follows that it is just as important—though less remarked on—for the United States to find things to admire in other countries as for other countries to admire the United States. Mutual respect creates the opportunity for joint action—for cooperative power.

9. THE LIBERAL DEMOCRATIC REVIVAL

236   *He advocated a "civic"*: Immanuel Kant, *On History*, ed. Lewis White Beck (Indianapolis, Ind.: Bobbs-Merrill, 1963), pp. 16–17.

237   *"The latent causes of"*: James Madison, Alexander Hamilton, and

John Jay, *The Federalist Papers* (New York: Penguin, 1987), p. 124.

"If any two men": Thomas Hobbes, *Leviathan* (Cambridge: Cambridge University Press, 1996), p. 87.

"They are free": quoted in Orlando Patterson, *Freedom,* vol. 1 (New York: Basic Books, 1991), p. 93.

"He obeys the laws": Cicero, *On the Commonwealth,* trans. George Holland Sabine and Stanley Barney Smith (Columbus, Ohio: Bobbs-Merrill, Library of Liberal Arts, 1960), p. 55.

238   *"Liberty, or freedom":* Hobbes, *Leviathan,* p. 145.

239   *"No society can":* Raghavan N. Iyer, *The Moral and Political Thought of Mahatma Gandhi,* (New York: Oxford University Press, 1986) p. 351.

240   *"so foolish that they":* John Locke, *The Second Treatise on Government* (Indianapolis, Ind.: Hackett Publishing, 1980), p. 53.

243   *"They'll shoot us":* quoted in Taylor Branch, *Pillar of Fire* (New York: Simon & Schuster, 1999), p. 331.

244   *"Unearned suffering is":* quoted in Diane McWhorter, *Carry Me Home* (New York: Simon & Schuster, 2001), p. 154.

"the freest man on": quoted in ibid., p. 61.

"They can't enjoin": Ibid., p. 109.

245   *"I think we just":* quoted in Branch, *Pillar of Fire,* p. 94.

But because the deepest: King's radicalism emerged clearly in his opposition to the Vietnam War. Not content to rest on his laurels as an elder statesman of the highly successful civil-rights movement, he felt compelled in the late 1960s to apply his nonviolence in this new area against the very president—Lyndon B. Johnson—who had brought the civil-rights movement to legislative fruition.

246   *"We mean to kill":* quoted in McWhorter, *Carry Me Home,* p. 22.

"You know my friends": quoted in Taylor Branch, *Parting the Waters* (New York: Simon & Schuster, 1998), p. 140.

"If we are wrong": quoted in ibid.

247   *"Standing beside love":* Ibid.

Later he said: Ibid., p. 166.

When an officer: McWhorter, *Carry Me Home,* p. 228.

250　*In 1958, Prime Minister:* Bruce Ackerman and Jack Duvall, *A Force More Powerful* (New York: Palgrave, 2000), p. 357.

251　*the organization's black:* Anthony Sampson, *Mandela* (New York: Vintage, 1999), p. 89.
　　"The attacks of the": quoted in ibid., p. 149.
　　"I saw nonviolence": Ibid., p. 68.

252　*"Luthuli, Mandela and":* Ibid., p. 259.
　　These, he said, would: Ackerman and Duvall, *Force More Powerful,* p. 345.
　　Only then could they: Ibid., p. 347.

253　*The first to meet with:* Allister Sparks, *Tomorrow Is Another Country* (Chicago: University of Chicago Press, 1995), p. 24.
　　"Mandela had become": Sampson, *Mandela,* p. 512.

254　*Mandela's friend Fatima:* Ibid., p. 68.
　　"I'm just a sinner": quoted in ibid., p. 415.
　　"the unselfconscious manifestation": Ibid., p. 546.
　　"When one is faced": Ibid., p. 242.
　　"Bitterness would be": Ibid., p. 406.
　　"Courageous people do not": Ibid., p. 515.

255　*"the most predicted":* Ibid., p. 484.

259　*"If it is true":* Hannah Arendt, *The Origins of Totalitarianism* (New York: Harvest/Harcourt Brace Jovanovic, 1973), p. 460.
　　"Our British colonizers": Arundhati Roy, *The Nation,* February 18, 2002.

261　*"Whoever wants to deprive":* Jean-Jacques Rousseau, *Political Writings* (Madison, Wisc.: Wisconsin University Press, 1986), p. 242.
　　"If a democratical": Montesquieu, *The Spirit of the Laws* (Berkeley and Los Angeles: University of California Press, 1977), p. 193.
　　"Imperialism and popular": John A. Hobson, *Imperialism* (Ann Arbor: University of Michigan Press, Ann Arbor Paperbacks, 1965), p. 150.
　　"European civilization, with": Leonard Woolf, *Imperialism and Civilization* (New York: Garland Publishing, 1971), p. 34.

262　*"The two ideas of":* quoted in Philip D. Curtin, *Imperialism* (New York: Walker, 1971), p. 292.
　　"a sea of vague": Hobson, *Imperialism,* p. 206.

263 *The decisive advantage:* Victor Davis Hanson, *Carnage and Culture* (New York: Doubleday, 2001), p. 48.

264 *"an exclusive Western monopoly":* Ibid., p. 252.
rise to "universal dominion": Polybius, *The Rise of the Roman Empire,* ed. F. W. Walbank (London: Penguin, 1979), p. 42.
"The veteran legions of": Madison, Hamilton, and Jay, *The Federalist Papers,* Article 1, Section 8, Clause 12, p. 268.

10. LIBERAL INTERNATIONALISM

266 *"busy with a scheme":* G. J. Renier, *William of Orange* (New York: D. Appleton, 1933), p. 84.

267 *When Jeremy Bentham:* Carlton J. Hayes, *The Historical Evolution of Modern Nationalism* (New York: Richard R. Smith, 1931), p. 131.
Wasn't it "monstrous": Alan Bullock and Maurice Shock, *The Liberal Tradition* (Oxford: Oxford University Press, 1956), p. 158.

268 *"the passing of good":* quoted in ibid., pp. 177–76.
To the intense indignation: Philip Magnus, *Gladstone* (New York: E. P. Dutton, 1964), p. 240.
"What our duty is": quoted in ibid., p. 241.
"There is not": Ibid., p. 242.

269 *"Fortresses may be":* quoted in Bullock and Shock, *Liberal Tradition,* p. xxxix.
He proposed a strengthened: Ibid., p. 163.
"Certain it is": quoted in Henry Kissinger, *Diplomacy* (New York: Simon & Schuster, 1994), p. 161.

270 *"Would the President propose":* Ibid., p. 223.

271 *Wilson intended to:* August Heckscher, *Woodrow Wilson* (New York: Macmillan, 1991), p. 508.
"The question upon which": quoted in Kissinger, *Diplomacy,* p. 51.
"the destruction of every": Ibid., p. 52.

272 *"All the great wrongs":* quoted in Robert Tucker, *The New Republic,* February 24, 1992, p. 30.
The second of his: Arthur Walworth, *Woodrow Wilson, World Prophet,* vol. 2 (New York: Longmans & Green, 1958), p. 156.

"He has saved his": quoted in Ferdinand Czernin, *Versailles, 1919* (New York: G. P. Putnam & Sons, 1964), p. 430.

274 *"War had lain at"*: Ibid., p. 398.

"constitution for the whole": quoted in Heckscher, *Woodrow Wilson*, p. 520.

"Instinctively, and rightly": Harold Nicolson, *Peacemaking, 1919* (New York: Harcourt, Brace & World, 1965), p. 70.

276 *Clemenceau spoke in:* Heckscher, *Woodrow Wilson*, p. 510.

277 *"The defensive value of"*: Nicolson, *Peacemaking, 1919*, p. 192.

"In spite of bitter": Ibid., p. 36.

278 *"the unquestioned opportunity"*: Ibid., p. 191.

11. SOVEREIGNTY

280 *"Guarantees must be fulfilled"*: quoted in Ferdinand Czernin, *Versailles, 1919* (New York: G. P. Putnam & Sons, 1964), p. 112.

282 *"In matters of state"*: Jean Bodin, *On Sovereignty*, ed. Julian H. Franklin (Cambridge: Cambridge University Press, 1992), p. 108.

"An absolute sovereign": Jean Bodin, *Six Books of the Commonwealth*, trans. M. J. Tooly (Oxford: Basil Blackwell, 1967), p. 36.

"holds of another": Ibid.

"an analytic truth": Julian H. Franklin, *Jean Bodin, and the Rise of Absolutist Theory* (Cambridge: Cambridge University Press, 1973), p. 23.

"the principle mark of": Bodin, *Six Books*, p. 32.

"If the prince can": Ibid., p. 43.

283 *"Just as God"*: Bodin, *On Sovereignty*, p. 50.

"Reason and common sense": Bodin, *Six Books*, p. 19.

284 *"Man's salvation occurs"*: quoted in Liah Greenfeld, *Nationalism* (Cambridge, Mass.: Harvard University Press, 1992), p. 115.

"Sovereignty is one": www.Britannica.com.

"one people, one body": John Locke, *The Second Treatise on Government* (Indianapolis, Ind.: Hackett Publishing, 1980), pp. 47–48.

"an absolute despotic power": quoted in Hannah Arendt, *On Revolution* (New York: Compass, 1967), p. 160.

"The power and jurisdiction": quoted in R. R. Palmer, *The Age of*

Democratic Revolution, vol. 1 (Princeton, N.J.: Princeton University Press, 1959), p. 142.

285 *"What is a nation?":* C. A. Macartney, *National States and National Minorities* (London: Oxford University Press, 1934), p. 46.

"is the soul that": Locke, *The Second Treatise,* p. 108.

286 *Macartney quotes Acton:* Macartney, *National States and National Minorities,* p. 17.

"aspires to political expression": Ibid., p. 16.

287 *"is usually nationally identical":* Ibid., p. 18.

292 *The Virginia Resolves, authored:* Frank Friedel, Richard N. Current, and T. Harry Williams, *A History of the United States,* vol. 1 (New York: Knopf, 1961), p. 120.

"it was as if": Gordon S. Wood, *The Creation of the American Republic* (New York: W. W. Norton, 1972), p. 285.

293 *"Every town government":* quoted in ibid., pp. 186–87.

"miniature constitutions that": Wood, *American Republic,* p. 288.

294 *"union of the society":* Locke, *The Second Treatise,* p. 119.

"the greatest question ever": quoted in ibid., p. 345.

295 *"The doctrine of sovereignty":* Wood, *American Republic,* p. 345.

some suggested that America: John Keane, *Tom Paine* (Boston: Little, Brown, 1995), p. 100. Cartright's famous letters in favor of American independence were called *American Independence, the Interest and Glory of Great Britain.* They demanded, Keane writes, "the replacement of the British Empire by a free association of states endowed with British liberties and all of them recognizing the king as their sovereign head."

was "imperium in imperio": Wood, *American Republic,* p. 351.

described by Adams as: Ibid.

Benjamin Franklin—who had: Ibid.

296 *"If, intemperately, unwisely":* quoted in Conor Cruise O'Brien, *The Great Melody* (Chicago: University of Chicago Press, 1992), p. 143.

297 *For example, Samuel Adams:* Wood, *American Republic,* p. 528.

James Madison now found: Ibid., p. 559.

"an assemblage of societies": James Madison, Alexander Hamilton,

and John Jay, *The Federalist Papers* (London: Penguin, 1987), p. 122.

299 *The "true distinction" of:* Alexander Hamilton, James Madison, and John Jay, *Federalist Papers,* ed. Clinton Rossiter (New York: Penguin, 1961), p. 355.

12. NIAGARA

305 *"Black and hideous to":* Henry James and Leon Edel, eds., *Henry James Letters* (Cambridge, Mass.: Harvard University Press, 1984), p. 713.

314 *"The position of the":* Leo Szilard and Nina Byers, "Physicists and the Decision to Drop the Bomb," *CERN Courier,* November 2002, p. 270.

317 *"As this enormous":* Bill Joy, "Why the Future Doesn't Need Us," *Wired,* April 2000.
Its logical end point: Francis Fukuyama made use of these terms of Nietzsche's in his book *The End of History and the Last Man.* With all respect to Fukuyama and Nietzsche, my use of the terms seems to me more fitting than theirs. Their first man was an energetic savage, and I follow them in this. Their last man, however, was an enervated, hypercivilized person, who, all savage energy spent, was incapable of almost any feat. It's hard to see how he would be the "last" of anything, unless he expired out of sheer boredom. My last man, on the other hand, would literally and truly be the last, since he would destroy everybody, himself included. It has always struck me likewise that *The End of History* was a perverse term to use in the nuclear age to refer to anything but human extinction by nuclear arms.

319 *"an atavism, a holdover":* Francis Fukuyama, *The End of History and the Last Man* (New York: The Free Press, 1992), p. 265.

321 *"absolute monarchs will often":* *The Federalist Papers,* p. 14.

322 *"What's the point":* Bill Keller, "The World According to Powell," *New York Times,* November 25, 2001.

328 *"If Pakistan doesn't change":* quoted in Rajiv Chandrasekaran, "Terrorism Casts Shadow Over India's Campaign," *Washington Post,* January 27, 2002.

"the perpetrator of that": quoted in Celia Dugger, "Indian General Talks Bluntly of War and a Nuclear Threat," *New York Times,* January 12, 2002.

"as a last resort": quoted in Rory McCarthy and John Hooper, "Musharraf Ready to Use Bomb," *The Guardian,* April 6, 2002.

13. THE LOGIC OF PEACE

336 *"the gradual spread of":* Scott Sagan and Kenneth Waltz, *The Spread of Nuclear Weapons* (New York: W. W. Norton, 1997), p. 44.

344 *"fundamental maxims of her":* quoted in James Chace, "Imperial America," *World Policy Journal* (spring 2002).

358 *For abolition would not:* This understanding of abolition as shifting the source of deterrence from hardware to software leaves open an important question. If deterrence survives beyond abolition, aren't we still snared in the riddles and corruption of threatening annihilation to avoid annihilation? Formally speaking, the objection is valid. Abolition so conceived does not purge the "sin" mentioned by Robert Oppenheimer, the scientific leader of the Manhattan Project, in his remark, "In some irredeemable way, the physicists have known sin." What it does do is to back the world across a critical symbolic threshold in the moral and psychological realm (psychology being the whole essence of deterrence in the first place).

359 *The dangers of abolition:* For a fuller treatment of my views on these matters, see my books *The Abolition* (New York: Knopf, 1984) and *The Gift of Time* (New York: Metropolitan Books, 1998).

367 *If the first circle:* This state of affairs may be changing, for a surprising reason. To the great dismay of the Ulster Protestants, the people of Britain, according to recent polls, are not eager to hold on to the Ulster counties, and would not mind seeing them join the Irish Republic.

373 *"How 'relevant' are mere":* Gidon Gottlieb, *Nation Against State* (New York: Council on Foreign Relations, 1993), p. 50.

375 *"There is not a":* quoted in Conor Cruise O'Brien, *The Great Melody* (Chicago: University of Chicago Press, 1992), p. 113.

376 *"The 'victorious' Jews":* quoted in Jeffrey C. Isaac, *Arendt, Camus, and Modern Rebellion* (New Haven, Conn.: Yale University Press, 1992), p. 214.

383 *"gradually spread further":* Immanuel Kant, "Perpetual Peace," in *Political Writings,* ed. Hans Reiss (Cambridge: Cambridge University Press, 1970), p. 105.

Acknowledgments

This book was long in the making, and the list of those to whom I am indebted is long. I want to thank the John D. and Katharine T. MacArthur Foundation's Program on Global Security and Sustainability, the John Simon Guggenheim Foundation, the W. Alton Jones Foundation, and the Samuel Rubin Foundation for their support. The welcome stipend from the Lannan Literary Award for Nonfiction in 1999 was extremely helpful.

Since 1998, I have been the Harold Willens Peace Fellow at the Nation Institute, my indispensable professional home. I want especially to thank Hamilton Fish, the president of the Institute, who has been ingeniously and tirelessly resourceful in making it possible to work on the book and other projects having to do with nuclear disarmament, and Taya Grobow, who with infallible good cheer has kept my working life functional in this period. Elizabeth Macklin's editorial assistance was indispensable. I also wish to thank Matthew Maddy, Kabir Dandona, Jenny Stepp, and Marisa Katz for their long hours of careful research and fact-checking.

I am grateful to Strobe Talbott for holding a seminar at the Brookings Institution, which provided invaluable commentary on the manuscript, and to Paul Kahn who both read the manuscript and organized an equally helpful study session on it at the Yale Law School. I also wish to thank the Joan Shorenstein Center for the Press, Politics, and Public Policy and its wonderful staff, at the John F. Kennedy School of Government at Harvard University, where I was a fellow in the fall of 2002. A number of seminars, at the Center and elsewhere at the University, were sources of very helpful reactions and advice.

With superabundant generosity my friend Wallace Shawn provided detailed comments that became a turning point in the evolution of the book. Robert Del Tredici made wise and useful observations on a late draft. Jerome Kohn and Fred Leventhal made helpful suggestions regarding individual chapters. In the early years of writing the book, my conversations with Niccolo Tucci were an inspiration, and his memory shines as a model of what the writing life should be.

My agent, Lynn Nesbit, guided the book expertly through innumerable tangles over many years. Sara Bershtel, of Metropolitan Books, has been steadfast in her support, in the face of unmerciful delays. Shara Kay skillfully and tactfully saw me and the book through the ins and outs of the publishing process.

My editor Tom Englehardt has become that rarest of treasures for a writer, a person whose opinions and reactions are as necessary as—going far beyond the call of duty—they are available.

I owe more than I can express to my wife, Elspeth, and my children, Matthew, Phoebe, and Thomas.

Index

About the Author

The author of several works, including *The Time of Illusion, The Fate of the Earth,* and *The Village of Ben Suc,* Jonathan Schell has been a contributor to *The Nation, The New Yorker, Harper's, The Atlantic,* and *Foreign Affairs,* and has taught at Wesleyan, Princeton, and Emory, among other universities. Currently a visiting professor at Yale and the Harold Willens Peace Fellow at the Nation Institute, he lives in New York City.